JOHN ADAMS

ARCHITECTS OF FREEDOM SERIES

JOHN ADAMS

by

Anne Husted Burleigh

ARLINGTON HOUSE   NEW ROCHELLE, N.Y.

The author extends thanks to the Belknap Press of Harvard University Press for permission to quote from the *Diary and Autobiography of John Adams,* four volumes, edited by Lyman H. Butterfield and others, copyrighted in 1961 by the Massachusetts Historical Society; *Adams Family Correspondence,* two volumes, edited by Butterfield and others, copyrighted in 1963 by the Massachusetts Historical Society; and the *Legal Papers of John Adams,* three volumes, edited by Lawrence K. Roth and Hiller B. Zobel, copyrighted in 1965 by the president and fellows of Harvard College. The University of North Carolina Press was kind enough to grant permission to quote from Lester J. Cappon's edition of *The Adams-Jefferson Letters,* published for the Institute of Early American History and Culture at Williamsburg.

Gratitude also goes to the American Antiquarian Society for permission to quote from Stewart Mitchell's *New Letters of Abigail Adams;* to Princeton University Press for permission to quote both from *The Papers of Thomas Jefferson,* edited by Julian P. Boyd and copyrighted in 1952, and from the *Letters of Benjamin Rush,* edited by Lyman H. Butterfield and copyrighted in 1951 by the American Philosophical Society; to Columbia University Press for permission to quote from *The Papers of Alexander Hamilton,* edited by Harold C. Syrett and Jacob E. Cooke, published in 1961; to the Massachusetts Historical Society for permission to quote from the *Warren-Adams Letters;* to George W. Corner of the American Philosophical Society for permission to quote from *The Autobiography of Benjamin Rush;* to Harper and Row Publishers for permission to quote from *The Spirit of 'Seventy-Six,* edited by Henry Steele Commager and Richard B. Morris; to Albert and Charles Boni, Inc., for permission to quote from *The Journal of William Maclay;* to Random House, Inc., for permission to quote from *Edmund Burke, Selected Works,* edited by W. J. Bate; and to Huntington Library Publications for permission to quote from *The Spur of Fame,* edited by John A. Schutz and Douglass Adair.

SECOND PRINTING, JANUARY 1970

SBN 87000-052-7

Library of Congress Catalog Card Number: 69-16950

MANUFACTURED IN THE UNITED STATES OF AMERICA

To Ralph W. Husted

A LAWYER WHOM JOHN ADAMS

WOULD HAVE ADMIRED

Contents

Introduction

THE rare man who can sift the unchanging out of our constantly changing world is a man for the ages, a man who spans more than his own generation. John Adams, philosopher of the Revolution and early America, participant in many of the major events of that period, strove to perceive the patterns of constancy that lend a universal character to the lives of all men. His life and ideas are as pertinent to our time as they were to his own—for we, too, are still pondering the nature of the unbreakable bond between liberty and law; we, as well as Adams, question how to relate man, whose goal is freedom, to the authority necessarily present in political society. If we observe Adams' life and thought, we find that he, too, spoke of equal laws equally applied; that he struggled with the problem of pressure groups; that he sought, as some men do today, to refute the theory of man as perfectible or determinable; that he tried to define the base of power in society. Achieving a fine balance between liberty and law troubled Adams as much as it disturbs us.

The way in which Adams viewed man, as a being of liberty but subject to God's law, determined the answer he gave to the fundamental problem of how to reconcile liberty and law. The solution that Adams offered to the world was not original; it was a classic answer, rooted in the thought of the classical Greek, Roman and English political philosophers and lawyers. Moreover, it was the answer of a lawyer who, by his very profession, could not escape viewing man as an historical being whose accumulated experience in history tells us more about human nature than anything else. Hence, Adams approached these problems of man and liberty and law not as a systematic theorist but in the manner of a lawyer compiling a brief. Because the principles of politics and human nature that he delineated are still relevant, Adams correctly shares a place as one of America's outstanding political thinkers; he is a man for our time.

Continuing publication of *The Adams Papers*, sponsored by the Massachusetts Historical Society and financed by Time Inc., on behalf of Life, increasingly facilitates research on the Adams family. The Adamses themselves, as remarkable and public-spirited today as in their first generations, made publication of the papers possible by deeding to the Society the Adams Manuscript Trust, the accumulation of personal and public papers of three centuries of the Adams family in Massachusetts.

The author wishes in particular to thank for inspiration John Quincy Adams of Dover, Massachusetts; Mrs. Abigail Adams Homans of Boston;

the staff of the Adams National Historic Site at Quincy; and Professor H. Trevor Colbourn of the University of New Hampshire, formerly of the Indiana University faculty. She is grateful to her husband, William Robert Burleigh, for advice in editing, to Joseph A. Ream for typographical assistance; and to Raymond W. Pence, Emeritus Professor of English at De-Pauw University, for lessons not forgotten.

CHAPTER I

JOHN ADAMS
Man of Braintree

THE boy was young but his roots ran old and tough as the granite outcroppings that stabbed the thin New England earth here on Penn's Hill. Though he was but a youth in his teens he belonged through ancient bonds to these rocks and this hill, for they had known his father, and his father's father, and his great-grandfather. Ruddy and strong, the boy felt his mind swell on this gusty October day, with poetry and the joyful ache of exuberant young manhood. Yet adolescent though he was, he had not the disordered look of a forlorn, gangling chap in temporary trousers. He had grown, in fact, into a small New England boulder himself—short, square, permanent, with muscles made hard behind a plow. Here, atop this hill, amidst these rocks, his substantial frame belonged to the landscape, combat-ready, indomitable. And just as the Massachusetts earth could wield only tenuous restraint over its granite core that ever sought to thrust through the surface, so did the boy struggle to keep a decent veil draped over his acutely sensitive soul which always threatened to expose him.

Standing at this tall vantage point, the boy scanned the scene that had been etched upon the hearts of his ancestors and himself. To the southwest the upper reaches of the Appalachians formed the haze-enshrouded slopes of the Blue Hills. Moving eastward, the land flattened into a pastoral idyl splashed with crimson and gold, dotted here and there with the farmhouses of Braintree. To the south lay Weymouth; in the distance to the north lay Dorchester Heights. Northeast of his hill the boy saw Colonel John Quincy's Mount Wollaston Farm on Quincy Bay; he could view the land jut northward along the bay toward Squantum and south to Hough's Neck and Germantown. Two miles or so out in the bay, out of sight, lay Hangman's Island, where screaming gulls strutted their white plumage upon pale legs, where fork-tailed terns soared in lilting flight only to plunge headfirst into the sea. Surveying the Braintree countryside from his chilly Penn's Hill overlook, the boy, John Adams, observed autumn cloak the land, watching the timeless, familiar trees and fields shifting hourly, minutely, into new seasonal nuances. The forms persisted, yet their colors and shadows ceaselessly emerged and receded in graceful, delicate harmony.

Adams men for more than one hundred years had marveled at this phenomenon of constancy in change that kept their land and their lives in equilibrium. They had watched their land of Braintree in an unfailing eternal pattern of change from seedtime and growth to harvest to hibernation to rebirth. They had seen their sons and daughters born, grow, learn, marry, and bear children of their own, and they had seen their loved ones die. They had studied human nature as they had the land: they expected their wives to cry sometimes; they knew when to let a son storm out his anger in private or when to leave a daughter alone with her young man. The Adamses had been in Massachusetts nearly as long as the first white man, long enough to lay down soul and stake in the flinty soil, a fact that marked a peculiar stamp upon them. For a century they had worked and died on their Braintree acres. And in their husbandry of the land and in their human affairs they had been as successful as any man. Young John Adams anticipated living just such a life in Braintree.

For him and for the people of Braintree the sea was their life-focus. Fishing was but one occupation—and one not followed in John's family. Nevertheless, to every Boston and Braintree man the white-capped sea, whether fierce or tender, meant both livelihood and luxury. To the farmer it meant salt marsh and fertilizer; to the distiller it meant West Indian molasses; to the shipwright it meant boats; to the merchant it meant British goods; to the colonial dames it meant silk and lace for special occasions, chocolate and tea. More than that, for these New Englanders and for John's family in particular the sea meant roots as deep as those they had implanted in Braintree. For across that sea lay England, whence they had all come more than a century before.

They were Englishmen, bearing English names, living under an English king. The first of the clan, Henry Adams, farmer and maltster, was an Elizabethan born in 1583, five years before the defeat of the Spanish Armada. Sometime before 1640 he left Somersetshire with his wife, Edith Squire, and eight sons. Upon his grant of forty acres at Mount Wollaston, then a part of the north precinct of Braintree, Henry Adams established a farm and malthouse.

The Adamses were English colonials who had come to Massachusetts Bay with all the principles of Magna Carta and the Petition of Right and later had adopted the Bill of Rights of 1689. It was their right and privilege to live under an English king (though not, they were eventually to decide, under an English parliament). They lived proudly under English law, the fundamental law of the land protecting the immemorial rights of Englishmen that Sir Edward Coke had so comprehendingly described. Trembling in fear of absolute monarchies and Frenchmen with "Jesuitical faces," these English settlers were totally loyal to their king, to English customs and English goods and, above all, to the common law that embodied all the rights they had possessed since ancient times. These were no Americans; these were Englishmen protecting the colony of Massachusetts Bay for their king.

In addition to the fact that they were men of both Massachusetts and England, two other factors shaped the background of John Adams and his Braintree neighbors. In the first place, they lived lives as free as any men have in history. Far across an ocean, they received less bothersome attention than their brethren in the Isles, for the British government before the 1760's followed a live-and-let-live policy toward the Colonies. Surely, too, they were freer than some of the succeeding generations of the nation John Adams was to help found. Here, in their little Braintree corner of the world, they lived in peace; they thought it was God's country.

Finally, John and his people were Puritans. True, they no longer believed in the strenuous old Covenant theology, nor did they live under a seventeenth-century theocracy. Yet, the cultural and moral tradition of Puritanism remained in their hearts. These eighteenth-century Puritans might not believe in a body of visible saints, but they squinted askance at those who failed to behave with sobriety, thrift, simplicity and diligence. John Adams might lean toward Arminianism if he wished; however, his upbringing in the Puritan tradition taught him a poignant awareness of the precarious circumstances of man. He knew that man is responsible for his every action, not only to his fellows but to God Himself. Yet man is a frail character, capable of good actions but so pitifully weak that he ever teeters on the dangerous brink of sin. Perhaps others might flirt with that favorite eighteenth-century doctrine of human perfectibility; John Adams would never be so foolish. He could study, right in Braintree, how countless neighbors skidded over the precipice of disaster. He knew his own flaws painfully enough; whenever he viewed his neighbors suffering their penalties he prayed thanks that he had received grace to escape a similar strait. Because the Puritan tradition always haunted his mind, John knew that man bears the mark of original sin; that he is ultimately alone in the world; that, in the end, his is a personal confrontation with God, when he must answer for his actions. Such a stark picture of man alone with God Almighty dictated that man should do God's will. The fact that man must follow God's will stirred in John an intense consciousness of his own personal history. We are not here to drift and amble, he knew. Rather, we always must be performing God's purpose for our lives and, in doing so, His purpose for all of history. Consequently, John Adams believed that he lived at a crucial point in history. And so he recorded everything, always writing, hurrying to get it all down, laying bare his hurts and triumphs, preserving both good and bad to be put before human and divine judgment.

John Adams' father, Deacon John Adams, farmer and cord-wainer, worked so diligently to provide for his wife and three sons, John, Peter Boylston and Elihu, that, as John later wrote, he "soon became a person of more property and consideration in the town than his patron had been."[1] There was scarcely a job in town he could not manage—selectman, tithingman, constable, militia officer, church deacon. He held them all, the last for fourteen years. John attested to his father's solidity and merit when in later years he wrote: "He was the honestest man I ever knew. In wisdom, piety, benevolence and charity in proportion to his education and sphere of life, I have never seen his superior."[2]

While Deacon John's family tree was thoroughly upstanding, worthy of all his pride, his wife's was a trifle fancier. Susanna Boylston came from the Boylstons of Muddy River or Brookline; her father was Peter Boylston; her grandfather, Thomas Boylston, a surgeon and apothecary. Uncle Zabdiel Boylston, a physician, had introduced into the Colonies inoculations for smallpox.

At the foot of Penn's Hill, fronting on the old Coast Road that ran from Boston to Plymouth, Deacon John owned a number of acres and a stout homestead.[3] Probably painted red, the house was a traditional New England saltbox with hand-hewn clapboard siding, a full two stories in front with a slope-roofed "leanter" attached in back. A triangular pediment above the front door with fluted pilasters, no doubt put on at least by mid-eighteenth century, lent the house a stately, classic air. The windows were neat rectangular wooden frames filled with small square panes. Neither rains nor earthquakes disturbed the house, as sturdy as its foundation of granite stones and its great center chimney. Altogether, to the travelers riding the Coast Road, the house must have looked cheerfully substantial behind its low fence of piled stones. Certainly it was one of the better dwellings of Braintree, built to endure for generations.

After buying his homestead in 1720, Deacon John saved his money until he was able to purchase from the Billings brothers in 1744 nine and one-half acres of the old Belcher property that lay

directly south, adjacent to his own land. On this property was a
house less than shouting distance from Deacon John's own cottage,
a dwelling that almost matched his own. It was this house, with
origins even older than Deacon John's, that John Adams would
inherit from his father and to which he would bring his bride Abigail.

Deacon John managed the two pieces of property as one, calling
them the Penn's Hill Farm. It was in the northern house, Deacon
John's cottage, where, in the southeast bedroom next to the road,
John Adams was born on October 19, 1735.[4] Deacon John recorded the event upon the flyleaf of his heavy, sober-looking Wil-
lard's *Body of Divinity*, the depository of family records.

Only through his *Autobiography* is much known of John Adams'
childhood—how he played, what he thought. It is certain, though,
by what he related, that this man to whom books would mean such
delight and consolation learned at an early age how to read. His
parents, who both enjoyed books, taught him at home. When he
reached school age he improved his reading efficiency at the school
that Dame Belcher operated in her home across the road from the
Penn's Hill Farm. His Latin school career began in the school kept
by Joseph Cleverly. But it proved to be such an agonizing period
of frustration for John that it nearly thwarted any bookish inclination. For while Cleverly was a "tolerable scholar and a gentleman"[5]
in John's opinion, he was still one of the laziest men in town. After
an evening of chat with Cleverly some years later, John was to
remark, "Mr. Cleverly was cheerful, alert, sociable and complai-
sant. So much good sense, and knowledge, so much good humor
and contentment, and so much poverty, are not to be found in any
other house, I believe, in this province. I am amazed that a man of
his ingenuity and sprightliness can be so shiftless."[6] In fact, Cleverly cared so little to exert himself to inspire his pupils that John
developed a hearty disgust for school, spending his time "as idle
children do, in making and sailing boats and ships upon the ponds
and brooks, in making and flying kites, in driving hoops, playing
marbles, playing quoits, wrestling, swimming, skating and, above
all, in shooting, to which diversion I was addicted to a degree of

ardor which I know not that I ever felt for any other business, study or amusement."[7] John's zest for shooting prompted him to take his gun to school, secreting it in the entry so that the moment school let out he might dash off to the fields after crows and squirrels. Cleverly's scolding did not daunt him; he simply began to leave his gun at the home of an old woman who lived close by. For nothing appealed to John more than lying in a cold, marshy blind waiting for wild game to fly overhead.[8]

Deacon John, however, did not intend that his oldest son, for whom he had planned a "liberal education," should continue in so unstudious a bent. When John protested to his father that he thought so little of books that he hoped his father would give up these notions of sending him to college, the Deacon asked, "What would you do, child?" John replied that he wanted to be a farmer.

"A farmer? Well, I will show you what it is to be a farmer. You shall go with me to Penny Ferry tomorrow morning and help me get thatch."[9] Next day Deacon John, with "great good humor," fulfilled his promise. When they had returned home that evening he asked, "Well, John, are you satisfied with being a farmer?" John, muddy and bone-tired, mustered a reply, "I like it very well, sir."

"Aye, but I don't like it so well," the Deacon retorted; "so you shall go to school. . . ."[10]

And so John went back to school, but not cheerfully. Because it angered him that Cleverly delayed putting him into arithmetic, he obtained his own copy of *Cocker's Decimal Arithmetick* and studied by himself at home until he had passed the whole class. But at length, when he was fourteen or so, John again went to his father, asking most seriously this time that he be allowed to quit school and go to work on the farm. Exasperated, his father questioned, "You know . . . I have set my heart upon your education at college and why will you not comply with my desire?"

"Sir," John explained, "I don't like my schoolmaster. He is so negligent and so cross that I never can learn anything under him. If you will be so good as to persuade Mr. Marsh to take me, I will apply myself to my studies as closely as my nature will admit and go to college as soon as I can be prepared."[11] Deacon John agreed.

Joseph Marsh, who ran a boarding school in Braintree, took in boys only from out of town, but the Deacon persuaded him to take John.

Under Marsh's kind tutelage John advanced with a great gust of progress. There was no doubt that he possessed a good mind, that he required only the proper inspiration and discipline. In little more than a year Marsh thought him ready for Harvard, already a venerable institution dating from 1636. Although William and Mary, Yale, Princeton and Pennsylvania existed, John considered only Harvard. Distances being too great, few Massachusetts men went to college elsewhere in the Colonies.

College entrance in those days was an informal matter. If an applicant showed that he had knowledge of the classics he was most certainly admitted. Nevertheless, entering college, in its sudden pitching of a fellow to the rigors of independence for the first time in his life, is a disconcerting event for any young man, particularly when, as John was, he is only sixteen. On the morning that John was to take his examination for Harvard he rode his horse up the road to call upon Mr. Marsh, who was to accompany him the eleven miles to Cambridge. But because the weather was gloomy and he felt poorly, Marsh declared that he would have to stay at home. John was beside himself: "Thunderstruck at this unforeseen disappointment and terrified at the thought of introducing myself to such great men as the president and fellows of a college, I at first resolved to return home; but foreseeing the grief of my father and apprehending he would not only be offended with me, but my master, too, whom I sincerely loved, I aroused myself and collected resolution enough to proceed."[12] Assured by Marsh that the tutors were expecting him and that he was ready for the examination, John departed, nonetheless feeling dismally unhinged.

Once at Cambridge, he presented himself to an awesome group of men: President Edward Holyoke and the tutors, Henry Flynt, Belcher Hancock, Joseph Mayhew and Thomas Marsh, who examined him. Then Mayhew handed him an English passage to translate into Latin. Glancing over it, John could see immediately that he did not know the Latin vocabulary for all the words in the passage.

"Thinking that I must translate it without a dictionary," he wrote, "I was in a great fright and expected to be turned by, an event that I dreaded above all things."[13] But Mayhew noted John's consternation and led him into an adjoining study. " 'There, child,' said he, 'is a dictionary, there a grammar, and there paper, pen and ink, and you may take your own time.' "[14] Relieved, John attacked his work. He was admitted and given a theme to write during vacation. Jubilant in his conquest, he returned home to receive the congratulations of his family and to recuperate from his ordeal by spending his vacation "not very profitably, chiefly in reading magazines and a British Apollo."[15]

When John entered Harvard he began a tradition of Adamses at Harvard that exists to this day. What is more, he was one of a surprisingly large number of pre-Revolutionary colonials who obtained a college education; those men who attended college were to be some of the significant political figures of the latter half of the eighteenth century.

When John Adams went to Harvard the college claimed a student body of hardly more than 100 students. Its buildings numbered only two or three, its library collection but a few thousand books. During a day that lasted from sunup to sundown the students heard lectures, recited, read, attended compulsory prayers and ate unimaginative meals in the refectory. Being boys, they conjured up games and pranks to break the monotony. Each tutor took one class through an entire four years. For that reason, with the exception of the scientific subjects taught by John Winthrop, IV, who had gained a solid reputation for his work, John took all his courses under his tutor, Joseph Mayhew.

John Adams at Harvard underwent a transformation. It is a common thing for a boy with a mind already enlarged with wonder at the fascinations of the outdoor world to be so annoyed with the confining details of elementary knowledge that during his early years he resists school altogether. However, toward the end of his public school education, suffering pangs of remorse that he has so squandered his time as perhaps to have cost himself college entrance, he makes a last-gasp effort to recover lost ground. Heaven smiles benignly on this late bloomer, and so his contrition is rewarded: he is admitted to college, where he is treated as if he had the mind of an adult, with capacity to reason and analyze—that power in which young minds revel because only so recently opened to use. Almost miraculously the boy within a few months attains intellectual manhood. His mind surges as he discovers the thrill of subjects that he always hated. He taps the mystery of words, their sound and their logic. He realizes the implications of learning in order to find the truth. In awe of minds greater than his own, he attaches himself to one or two professors whom he views with profound reverence. He discusses with friends and pronounces with finality to anyone whom he can corner.

Such was the case with John Adams: "I soon perceived a growing curiosity, a love of books and a fondness for study, which dissipated all my inclination for sports and even for the society of the ladies. I read forever, but without much method and with very little choice. I got my lessons regularly and performed my recitations without censure."[16] Mathematics and natural philosophy, that is, science, took up most of his time, which he later regretted "because I was destined to a course of life in which these sciences have been of little use, and the classics would have been of great importance. I owe to this, however, perhaps some degree of patience of investigation, which I might not otherwise have obtained." He added: "Another advantage ought not to be omitted. It is too near my heart. My smattering of mathematics enabled me afterwards at Auteuil in France to go, with my eldest son [John Quincy], through a course of geometry, algebra and several branches of the sciences with a degree of pleasure that amply rewarded me for all my time and pains."[17]

John collected a fine array of Harvard friends. Several, he frankly admitted, were "better scholars than myself, particularly Locke, Hemmenway and Tisdale." William Tisdale left college after a year. Reverend Moses Hemmenway later became minister at Wells, Maine, and Reverend Samuel Locke became president of Harvard, "a station for which no man was better qualified."[18] John enjoyed vying with these new friends in science and literature, claiming that "in the sciences, especially mathematics, I soon surpassed them, mainly because, intending to go into the pulpit, they thought divinity and the classics of more importance to them." Nevertheless, he granted that "in literature I never overtook them."[19] He himself was considering the ministry, but as yet was uncertain of his future career.

He made other close friends, too—John Wentworth, later New Hampshire's last royal governor; William Browne of Salem, who became justice of the Superior Court of Judicature and a loyalist; Philip Livingston, a bright youth who died very early; David Sewall of York, Maine, afterward a judge; and Tristram Dalton of Newburyport, later a United States senator. In the class ahead of John were his friends Daniel Treadwell, who became a professor at King's College but "whose early death . . . American science has still reason to deplore";[20] Samuel West, one day to be minister at New Bedford; and Samuel Quincy, son of Colonel Josiah Quincy of Braintree, later a lawyer and a loyalist, "the easy, social and benevolent companion, not without genius, elegance and taste."[21]

There were no fraternities in colonial days, but there were literary clubs. John was invited to join a group whose "plan was to spend their evenings together in reading any new publications, or any poetry or dramatic compositions that might fall in their way. I was as often requested to read as any other, especially tragedies, and it was whispered to me and circulated among others that I had some faculty for public speaking and that I should make a better lawyer than divine."[22]

John himself had serious doubts about entering the ministry. The fact that Deacon John had always anticipated a clerical career for his oldest son did not prevent John from considering other professions, for he knew his father "to be a man of so thoughtful and considerate a turn of mind, to be possessed of so much candor and moderation, that it would not be difficult to remove any objections he might make to my pursuit of physic or law or any other reasonable course."[23] Nor would his mother be dismayed at his choice of a career other than the ministry. To be sure, she was a pious woman, but not especially partial to the life of a divine. In the end it was

John's own confusion regarding his theological opinions that moved him to reject the ministry as a profession.

While John was at Harvard, New England struggled in the throes of the Great Awakening. As religious and philosophical movements generally wane in fervor the further they are removed in time from their origin, New England Puritanism had grown slack in the ardor of its theology until, by the first half of the eighteenth century, it retained only the force of its cultural and moral tradition. In the 1740's and 1750's, however, the Great Awakening that occurred in churches throughout the Colonies shot new life into New England theology, particularly into the Calvinist strain of Puritanism. Jonathan Edwards, a powerful, magnetic preacher from Northampton, Massachusetts, who taught a rejuvenated Calvinism, became a famous name in New England. Emphasizing the omnipotence of God and the depravity of man, he at the same time preached the necessity of a personal religious experience in which man expresses utter devotion to God. Moreover, Edwards reaffirmed the doctrines, first, of denial of human free will because free will would infringe upon the power of God, and, second, of unconditional election, the doctrine that God has arbitrarily marked some people for salvation and others for damnation. Edwards exercised so wide an influence that he recharged the Calvinist spirit of New England, leaving, after his death in 1758, a number of disciples to carry on his work.

In the meantime, between 1751 and 1755, while John was at Harvard, the Calvinist revival of the Great Awakening came into question in Braintree itself. Lemuel Briant, minister of Braintree's First Parish Church, became a figure of high controversy, on the one hand because of his "Arminian" leanings and on the other because of marital difficulties, in which his wife left him due either to her possible derangement or to his neglect. The word Arminian was an all-inclusive term in colonial days, a kind of cuss word aimed at unorthodox religion: whether it meant the doctrine of free will which Methodism adopted in the eighteenth century or whether it meant Unitarianism or something else was sometimes hard to tell. In any case it involved an acceptance of man's free will: although God knows ahead of time which choice of action man will make,

He does not predestine man to that choice; man is completely free. Thus the ageless free-will debate of the Middle Ages and Renaissance had arrived in Braintree.

John found himself puzzled by the whole doings concerning Briant: "Ecclesiastical councils were called and sat at my father's house. Parties and their acrimonies arose in the church and congregation, and controversies from the press between Mr. Briant, Mr. Niles, Mr. Porter, Mr. Bass, concerning the five points [of Calvinism].[24] I read all these pamphlets and many other writings on the same subject and found myself involved in difficulties beyond my powers of decision. At the same time, I saw such a spirit of dogmatism and bigotry in clergy and laity that if I should be a priest I must take my side and pronounce as positively as any of them, or never get a parish, or getting it must soon leave it. Very strong doubts arose in my mind whether I was made for a pulpit in such times, and I began to think of other professions. I perceived very clearly, as I thought, that the study of theology and the pursuit of it as a profession would involve me in endless altercations and make my life miserable, without any prospect of doing any good to my fellow men."[25]

The fact was that John probably agreed with Briant. As he grew older he would move further away from Calvinist thought. There is no doubt that he believed in free will. Moreover, as he matured he began to embrace Unitarianism, as did so many of his fellow Massachusetts Congregationalists. Though he always thought of himself as a Christian, he considered the term Christian to include all those who believed in Christian morality—and he did, most heartily. In his disregard for creeds, in his concern more for Christian *life* rather than *thought*, he bore a touch of the pietistic. Nonetheless, as an eighteenth-century man he was concerned with reason, as well, and his reason made him doubt that a being so mighty as God would ever become a lowly man. On the other hand, John would never become a deist, thinking that God had created the universe only to leave it to operate by itself. The fact was that John embraced a religion far more viable than either a mere set of ethics or a system of cold rational thought. Because of his Puritan background he had faith in Providence. He knew that God acted in his life and that of every man. He knew that his task was to do the will of God.

Bewildered by the Lemuel Briant controversy, John neared graduation unconvinced that he should pursue a divinity career. He was drawn toward both law and medicine. However, since his father had done as much for him as John's conscience and the Deacon's circumstances would permit, John had first to earn some money. For that reason he put out the news that he would like to teach school. Reverend Thaddeus Maccarty of Worcester, who happened to be present at the Harvard commencement in search of a Latin master for the Worcester grammar school, heard about John. He hired him that day.

And so, John wrote, "About three weeks after commencement in 1755, when I was not yet twenty years of age, a horse was sent me from Worcester and a man to attend me. We made the journey, about sixty miles, in one day, and I entered on my office."[26]

CHAPTER II

THE LAWYER

THE young schoolteacher at Worcester was a vigorous, positive fellow. He was as emphatic as he looked—of stocky but muscular build, ruddy complexion, red-gold hair, direct blue eyes.

In the first place, although he was a sensitive, disputatious youth who wore his feelings and his opinions on his sleeve, he was also a young man who delighted in the company of other people. This young John Adams was an enthusiastic observer of humanity. Despite his distress that he would never acquire the subtleties of affability, he was a thoroughly social being who thrived upon chat and camaraderie. To him the study of human nature was the most fascinating, all-absorbing occupation that he could imagine, one that caused his books to lie unopened and his paper to remain blank. He talked, he watched, and he recorded in his diary hilarious, touching and often severe observations of what he had seen. On the one hand he could speak fondly of his "dear friend Cranch" (later his brother-in-law) whom he had visited "in the usual social, friendly strain."[1] On the other hand he could, in one devastating passage, sear Parson Wibird of Braintree with the description that he "is crooked, his head bends forwards, his shoulders are round and his body is writhed and bended. . . . His nose is a large Roman nose with a prodigious bunch protuberance upon the upper part of it. His mouth is large and irregular, his teeth black and foul and craggy."[2]

The poet Alexander Pope, author of the dictum that the proper study of mankind is man, would have approved John's constant scrutiny of the human spirit.

"Let me search for the clue," John wrote, "which led great Shakespeare into the labyrinth of mental nature! Let me examine how men think."[3] To a remarkable degree John was successful in his pursuit. He was successful even though he himself would never be a popular man with the crowd. Probably no one other than his wife, family and a few close friends would ever love him. Regardless of his own capacities to love, he displayed to those not intimately close to him an awkward coldness and stiffness that belied the passionate, affectionate nature beneath. Yet it is often the very man who appears to have little knowledge of how to charm the multitude who in fact knows best how others are prone to act and think. Such was the case with John Adams.

He was not only a perceptive judge of other men but an astute critic of himself as well. So sensitive was the mechanism of his soul that he put up his every action, his every thought, for review by his second self, so to speak, which pronounced judgment harsher than any that he might meet in the world. Due to a Puritan upbringing that taught self-judgment and a temperament that so inclined, John himself was his sternest, most unrelenting critic. Hence he knew that his worst fault was vanity: "Vanity, I am sensible, is my cardinal vice and cardinal folly."[4] He wanted fame and distinction, complaining in loud and hurt tones when his achievements were not recognized. Nothing ruffled his feelings more than for someone to show him up in company or to take credit for one of his ideas. Yet at the same time he subjected these sins of vanity to his own unmitigating judgment; then in his painful sensitivity he realized his wrongs, sometimes with a touch of self-pity, setting to work to justify them to himself—quite often in writing:

> . . . Others have as good a right to think for themselves and to speak their own opinions as I have . . . another man's making a silly

speech does not warrant my ill nature and pride in grasping the opportunity to ridicule him and show my wit. . . . When in company with persons much superior to myself in years and place, I have talked to show my learning, I have been too bold with great men, which boldness will no doubt be called self-conceit. I have made ill-natured remarks upon the intellectuals, manners, practice, etc., of other people. I have foolishly aimed at wit and spirit, at making a shining figure in gay company, but instead of shining brighter I only clouded the few rays that before rendered me visible.[5]

But if John knew in his shrewdness that his gravest fault was vanity, then perhaps he knew that in his unflinching, granite character there was uncommon integrity. Some men might waver between following their own conscience and the way of the world. But with John there appeared never to be a question at all. He followed his conscience and that was that. Of course, in his ever-present pride, he loved to point out how he *had* acted by his conscience against all odds—and, like a little boy, was delighted when people praised him for that, angry when they did not. Yet he did possess a facility for making his principles and his actions coincide. He was honest enough to insist that the same principles should motivate his politics, his religion, his family life, his social life, his ideas on culture.

Furthermore, the young teacher was eternally, irritatingly opinionated. Perhaps because he was so cocksure that he was right, he rarely resisted the chance to tell what he thought. Never, from cradle to grave, did he learn the art of keeping his mouth shut, a trait that would embroil him in many an embarrassing situation. It is certain that he followed his own advice when he remarked, "Honesty, sincerity and openness I esteem essential marks of a good mind. I am therefore of opinion that men ought (after they have examined with unbiased judgments every system of religion and chosen one system on their own authority for themselves) to avow their opinions and defend them with boldness."[6] His definiteness must have revealed the fact that even as a young man he was developing the crusty, feisty personality of an old curmudgeon. Being a natural-born fighter, he rather liked to be contrary. Seemingly, his dander was up as much as it was down.

Because John was so thoroughly human, he was doubtless a character both annoying and endearing to those around him. In some respects he was only an average man, but in the realm of the mind he was superior. Without a doubt he was evolving, even at his early age, one of the most brilliant minds of his time. He was to become a political theorist of the first order, bold and perceptive. Yet he could theorize on politics simply because he understood human nature so well. No ivory-tower intellectual, he was a scholar who gathered his facts not only from books, but also from farmers and merchants, from comrades in a tavern or neighbor's kitchen, from lawyers and servant girls. Moreover, he would become a good theorist because he did not assume that he could theorize everything—he did not glorify his own or anyone else's reason. He knew that there were limits beyond which the human mind could not go without risking the most monstrous folly. Although his own mind searched endlessly for truth, sought restlessly to uncover the mysteries of life, he knew quite well that much of his quest must be vain. He yearned to be like Milton, of whom he wrote: "That man's soul, it seems to me, was distended as wide as creation. His power over the human mind was absolute and unlimited. His genius was great beyond conception and his learning without bounds. I can only gaze at him with astonishment, without comprehending the vast compass of his capacity."[7] But even so, he did not expect his own mind to perform miracles. It was, after all, an altogether human mind, though an exceptional one.

Hence John Adams, Worcester schoolmaster, had grown up to be a highly complex, intense young man. Emotional, irascible, cantankerous, affectionate, opinionated, ambitious—he urgently longed, as only the young can, for an unnameable something, a knowledge, a sureness, a wisdom, a prudence, an experience that he could not yet have. He analyzed his own personality with marvelous exactitude: "I had an aching void within my breast this night. I feel anxious, eager, after something. What is it? I feel my own ignorance. I feel concern for knowledge and fame. I have a dread of contempt, a quick sense of neglect, a strong desire of distinction."[8]

What the pupils at the Center School thought of the young fellow behind the high schoolmaster's desk can only be conjectured. Surely they must have been relieved that his discipline was considerably more lenient than that of some others of his time. At any rate, that roomful of squirming childhood apparently responded favorably to their master, for he noted that he had found in his school "that human nature is more easily wrought upon and governed by promises and encouragement and praise than by punishment and threatening and blame." He hastened to add that "we must be cautious and sparing of our praise, lest it become too familiar and cheap and so contemptible." Nevertheless, "corporal as well as disgraceful punishments depress the spirits, but commendation enlivens and stimulates them to a noble ardor and emulation."[9]

Just as does every teacher, John sometimes must have had to dive behind his book, smothering a grin at some childish absurdity. With their variegated personalities, living in their tiny replica of an adult world, the children fascinated him:

I sometimes, in my sprightly moments, consider myself in my great chair at school as some dictator at the head of a commonwealth. In this little state I can discover all the great geniuses, all the surprising actions and revolutions of the great world in miniature. I have several renowned generals but three feet high and several deep-projecting politicians in petticoats. I have others, catching and dissecting flies, accumulating remarkable pebbles, cockle shells, etc., with as ardent curiosity as any virtuoso in the Royal Society. Some rattle and thunder out A, B, C with as much fire and impetuosity as Alexander fought and very often sit down and cry as heartily, upon being out-spelt, as Caesar did when at Alexander's sepulchre he recollected that the Macedonian hero had conquered the world before his age. At one table sits Mr. Insipid, foppling and fluttering, spinning his whirligig, or playing with his fingers as gaily and wittily as any frenchified coxcomb brandishes his cane or rattles his snuff box. At another sits the polemical divine, plodding and wrangling in his mind about Adam's fall in which we sinned all, as his primer has it. In short, my little school, like the great world, is made up of kings, politicians, divines . . . fops, buffoons, fiddlers, sycophants, fools, coxcombs, chimney sweepers, and every other character drawn in history or seen in the world.

To guide these small humans was a grave charge but, too, brought pleasurable rewards:

> Is it not, then, the highest pleasure . . . to preside in this little world, to bestow the proper applause upon virtuous and generous actions, to blame and punish every vicious and contracted trick, to wear out of the tender mind everything that is mean and little and fire the newborn soul with a noble ardor and emulation? The world affords no greater pleasure. Let others waste the bloom of life at the card or billiard table, among rakes and fools, and when their minds are sufficiently fretted with losses and inflamed by wine, ramble through the streets, assaulting innocent people, breaking windows or debauching young girls. I envy not their exalted happiness. I had rather sit in school and consider which of my pupils will turn out in his future life a hero, and which a rake, which a philosopher, and which a parasite, than change breasts with them, though possessed of twenty laced waistcoats and £1000 a year.[10]

All the same, for a young man as thirsty as John for the heady stimulant of intellectual conversation and of intimate contact with the hub of life, the schoolroom was a confining place. To be truly content, John required something larger than the grammar school to impel him to full stature. Fortunately for his intellectual well-being, James Putnam, a lawyer, and Major Gardiner Chandler, two of the best minds in Worcester, included him in their social circle. Particularly did Mr. Putnam indulge John's enthusiasm for discussion of every topic. He and John chatted about deism, about the proper end of man, and surely about the law.

At any rate, as the earth blossomed into spring John found himself distracted from the schoolroom by the fields "covered with a bright and lively verdure." The air was so "filled with a ravishing fragrance," so "soft and yielding," that John could do little else but ramble about, "gaping and gazing."[11] When court week opened in mid-May he became caught up in the thrill of brisk activity. He "was interrupted by company and the noisy bustle of the public occasion" so that he neither "read or wrote anything worth mentioning."[12]

By this time he must have been crystallizing in his mind just what he would take up as a profession. As summer approached, his admiration for Putnam and his fascination with the doings of the court must have swayed him. By August 22, 1756, he had clinched his decision and so was able to declare with triumphant relief that it was settled at last: "Yesterday I completed a contract with Mr. Putnam to study law under his inspection for two years." He would keep the school and move in with the Putnams, paying them for his board and then $100 when he could. True to character, he resolved what his duty to the Putnams ought to be: "To oblige and please him and his lady in a particular manner. I o ight to endeavor to oblige and please everybody, but them in particular." Besides that he had an obligation as a lawyer "never to commit any meanness or injustice in the practice of law." And as if to assure posterity that he did not relinquish ethical behavior when he chose law over the ministry, he stated that "the study and practice of law, I am sure, does not dissolve the obligations of morality or of religion."[13]

The method by which John Adams took his legal education was standard for a Massachusetts man and indeed for most young men of any colony.[14] It was the usual practice for prospective lawyers to serve a period of apprenticeship in the office of a reputable member of the bar. In continental Europe, where law was primarily a Roman product only flavored with native influences, the study of law had flourished since the Middle Ages in the great universities. But in England, on the other hand, where law was a system of custom and precedent only incidentally influenced by Roman administrative law, it had remained a study taught by lawyers themselves. Naturally, the same method was followed in the Colonies.

Although a few young men of Virginia and the southern Colonies sailed to the mother country to attend the Inns of Court, particularly the Middle Temple, most colonials and in fact all New Englanders after the 1730's preferred to serve as clerks in a lawyer's office. Consequently, the law that John learned was the law of the courtroom. He must have spent his time reading law, filing papers, talking over cases with Putnam, following up steps in litigation, and attending court. But that is not to say that the law he learned was unsophisticated or devoid of theory. He, as did the best of his contemporaries, delighted in pondering the philosophy behind the law, how law fits into history, politics, religion.

In John's particular situation it appeared that Putnam left his young clerk to wander about on his own through the maze of legal knowledge. But it seemed that Putnam had a larger library than most lawyers, even though it would be small by today's standards. Accordingly John had much to devour.

He began in Mr. Putnam's office a habit of such wide and deep reading that sooner or later he would cover almost all of the legal and political authorities known in the eighteenth century. Although John in other matters was a thrifty man, book-buying was his extravagance. As a result, through the years he acquired the "best library of law in the state."[15]

In the first place, he read the ancient feudal lawyers, Ranulph de Glanville and Henry de Bracton, who delineated the familiar feudal principle that the King was at once head of the state and a partner in the contractual relationship with his vassals. Glanville, justiciar of Henry II, wrote, probably in 1181, the most ancient treatise in English law, *A Treatise on the Laws and Customs of England.* He was the first to make the law of England a written law. Bracton, in the time of Henry III in the thirteenth century, wrote his treatise *Of the Laws and Customs of England,* from which come the famous passages declaring that the King ought not to be subject to any man but he is under God and the law. John read these treatises. He also read *Fleta,* an old treatise of the time of Edward I copied largely from Glanville and Bracton, so named because it had been written by a judge jailed in Fleet prison. He read Sir John Fortescue's fifteenth-century work, *In Praise of English Law,* contrasting English common law with Roman law.

Among the more modern exponents of the common law, John read first of all that grand practitioner of the fundamental law and stout opponent of royal prerogative, Sir Edward Coke. In the curriculum of any legal student of John's era, Coke claimed the chief place. Primary to the study of Coke was his familiar authority on real property—*Coke-Littleton,* a commentary on Sir Thomas Littleton's treatise on tenures, the first part of the *Institutes of the Laws of England.* The second of the four parts of the *Institutes* was an important treatise on Magna Carta and the old statutes of Edward I; the third was a commentary on pleas of the Crown; the fourth was a report of the jurisdiction of the different kinds of courts. John studied the *Institutes* as well as Coke's *Reports* and *Entries.*

In addition to Coke, there were other authorities with whom John was familiar: the *Reports* of Edmund Plowden, Lord Robert Raymond, William Salkeld, Saunders and Comyns; the *Entries* of Lilly and Rastell; the *Pleas of the Crown* of Matthew Hale and William Hawkins; the *History of the Common Law* by Hale; the *Digest* of Comyns; the *Abridgment* of Matthew Bacon; the treatises on tenures, exchequer and chancery of Geoffrey Gilbert; the treatise for young clerks, *Instructor Clericalis,* by Robert Gardiner; Saint German's *Doctor and Students;* and finally, *An Institute of the Common Law in Imitation of Justinian's Institutes.* Later in the century John would read William Blackstone's *Commentaries.* But all this was only a part of the works that he would read on the common law.

He prided himself on knowing something more than most of his fellows on the civil law, the law that had derived from the system of Roman jurisprudence. To learn the principles of civil law John went to the final authority, Justinian's *Institutes.* He also read Thomas Wood's *Institutes* on civil law.

Finally, throughout his life he would read the great writers on natural law and the law of nations—Grotius, Pufendorf, Barbeyrac, Burlamaqui, De Vattel. That law and government were within the pale of morality, that there was a substratum of truth, perceptible to right reason, upon which positive law must be based, had been tradition in both pagan and Christian thought. But in the early decades of the seventeenth century Hugo Grotius was the first to subject the natural law to the light of mathematical logic in order to devise a system of international law. For him the law of nature was separate from the law of nations; natural law derived from God and so was obligatory, while the law of nations took its authority from consent of the people of those nations. On the other hand, Samuel Pufendorf, who commented upon Grotius, did not see how the two laws could be separate. He insisted that they were one law, deriving from God, obligatory, hence incapable of being based upon consent. Barbeyrac, professor of law at Groningen, wrote notes for the works of both Grotius and Pufendorf. The venerable head of the Boston bar, Jeremiah Gridley, who much admired Barbeyrac, was to advise John that he thought him "a much more sensible and learned man than Pufendorf."[16]

John read the lawyers on common law, civil law, natural law. Yet he went further. So conscious was he of the intimate relationship of law with history and politics that he read all that he could upon those two subjects. Among the historians one of his favorites was the Roman Polybius. John liked his theory that all unmixed forms of government become inevitably corrupt and that a proper government possesses elements of the monarchic, aristocratic and democratic, each imposing checks and balances upon the others. Sharing the concern of his eighteenth-century contemporaries for balanced government, John for the same reason admired Montesquieu's theory of separation of powers in the *Spirit of the Laws*. Among other theorists John read Bolingbroke, once before 1758 and at least twice after that, but he confessed "without much good or harm. His ideas of the English constitution are correct and his political writings are worth something: but in a great part of them there is more of faction than of truth; his religion is a pompous folly; and his abuse of the Christian religion is as superficial as it is impious." However, he did admire Bolingbroke's style, which was "original and inimitable: it resembles more the oratory of the ancients than any writings or speeches I ever read in English."[17]

John could not have lived in the eighteenth century without reading that favorite, Algernon Sidney, a republican whose *Discourses on Government* was used in 1683 to implicate him in the Rye House Plot against Charles II. Sidney was found guilty and executed, insuring his immortality in the Isles and Colonies alike.

Yet surely no theorist influenced John so much as did James Harrington, who in the middle of the seventeenth century published his classic, *Commonwealth of Oceana*. John always wholeheartedly accepted Harrington's central doctrines—first, that that class of citizens which holds the balance of property in the state correspondingly holds the balance of power and, second, that government ought to be an empire of laws and not of men.

Young Adams, who had now spent two years studying with Mr. Putnam, was becoming a well-read man in the legal and political literature known in the eighteenth century. Even at this early date he was reading important writers, and in the years to come he would dip into scores more. With each writer whom he picked up, whether he accepted him or threw him aside, his mind became more fully formed. Though he did not simply sew together a string of philosophies of various writers, declaring them his own, he naturally was affected by what he read.

After his sojourn in Worcester he returned home to Braintree, where he intended to practice. Because there was no lawyer in Suffolk County outside Boston the field was open in his own town.[18]

The process of admission to the bar of a particular court involved minimal effort. There were no written bar examinations. In most cases a candidate might be admitted to a court simply upon the recommendation of a sponsor and the recitation of an oath. Moreover, there was no complicated division in the Colonies, as there was in England, between the ranks of barrister and attorney. All were admitted as attorneys, doing the work of both barrister and attorney. In Massachusetts, however, there was a slight change after 1762. Thomas Hutchinson, chief justice of the Superior Court, aiming to add more dignity to his bar, formally named all the members barristers. John was to be one of those thus entitled to wear the scarlet gown, cambric band and vast tie wig.[19] But so far as duties were concerned, there continued to be no distinction between the two ranks.

After his return to Braintree John faced the job of getting himself admitted to the bar of the Suffolk County Inferior Court. However, due to an oversight on the part of Putnam, John had not been sworn in before the Inferior Court in Worcester. Consequently he came home without a certificate of admission from the Worcester bar, which document would have been enough to insure his admission in Suffolk County.

One October morning in 1758 John rode to Boston, arriving about ten-thirty. He went to the Town House, where the courts then met, seating himself beside Robert Treat Paine at the lawyers' table. But he "felt shy, under awe and concern, for Mr. Gridley, Mr. Prat, Mr. Otis, Mr. Kent and Mr. Thacher," the greatest men of the Boston bar, "were all present and looked sour." He "had no acquaintance with anybody but Paine and [Samuel] Quincy and they took but little notice." Nevertheless, John attended court all day. In the evening he went with Quincy and Dr. Silvester Gardiner, a physician and druggist, to an elegant party.[20]

Next morning John went to the office of Jeremiah Gridley, head of the bar, whom he found alone. In answer to John's question as to how he should be introduced into law practice in Suffolk County, Gridley answered, "Get sworn." John replied that he had no patron in the county.

Then Gridley declared, "I will recommend you to the court. Mark the day the court adjourns to in order to make up judgments. Come to town that day, and in the meantime I will speak to the bar, for the bar must be consulted because the court always inquires if it be with consent of the bar."[21]

Gridley then inquired what books John had read.

"Many more, I fear, than have done me any good. I have read too fast, much faster than I understood or remembered as I ought," John answered, rattling off his list of titles. "The last book I read and with most pleasure, because I thought I understood it best, was Hawkins' *Pleas of the Crown*."[22]

When asked if he read Latin, John replied, "A little sometimes. . . . Cicero's orations and epistles, and the last Latin I read was Justinian's *Institutes* with Vinnius' Notes."

"Where did you find that work?" Gridley queried. "Mr. Putnam had it not, I believe, and I know of no other copy than my own in the country."

"I borrowed it, sir, from Harvard College Library by the aid of a friend."

" . . . Vinnius is a commentator more suitable for persons of more advanced age and longer research than yours," Gridley observed.

" . . . follow me and I will show you something." He led John "up a pair of stairs into a chamber in which he had a very handsome library of the civil and canon laws and writers in the law of nature and nations." Showing John an array of small manuals on the civil law, he put one of them into his hand, saying, " . . . put that in your pocket, and when you return that I will lend you any other you choose."

Finally, Gridley wanted to know what John had read "upon the law of nature and nations."

"Burlamaqui, sir, and Heineccius in Turnbull's translation, and Turnbull's *Moral Philosophy.*"

"These are good books," the older gentleman agreed. "Turnbull was a correct thinker but a bad writer. Have you read Grotius and Pufendorf?"[23]

"I cannot say I have, sir. Mr. Putnam read them when I was with him, and as his book lay on the desk in the office for the most part when he had it not in his hand, I had generally followed him in a cursory manner, so that I had some very imperfect idea of their contents: but it was my intention to read them both as soon as possible."

"You will do well to do so: they are great writers. Indeed, a lawyer through his whole life ought to have some book on ethics or the law of nations always on his table. They are all treatises of individual or national morality and ought to be the study of our whole lives."

After some pause Gridley eyed John with a fatherly air. " . . . Mr. Adams, permit me to give you a little advice. . . . In the first place pursue the law itself, rather than the gain of it. Attend enough to the profits to keep yourself out of the briars; but the law itself should be your great object. In the next place, I advise you not to marry early."

So unexpected was Gridley's comment that John, considering his fondness for the girls, could not conceal a smile. Perceiving it, Gridley asked, "Are you engaged?"

"I assure you, sir, I am at present perfectly disengaged; but I am afraid I cannot be answerable how long I shall remain so." Then

Gridley smiled in his turn, adding, " . . . an early marriage will probably put an end to your studies and will certainly involve you in expense. . . ."[24]

He added several more items of counsel. "Another thing is not to keep much company. For the application of a man who aims to be a lawyer must be incessant. His attention to his books must be constant, which is inconsistent with his keeping much company.

"In the study of law the common law, be sure, deserves your first and last attention, and he has conquered all the difficulties of this law who is master of the *Institutes*. You must conquer the *Institutes*. The road of science is much easier, now, than it was when I set out. I began with *Coke-Littleton* and broke through."[25]

He looked at his watch. "You have detained me here the whole forenoon, and I must go to court. The court will adjourn to the last Friday in this month [October]. Do you attend in the morning, and I will present you to the court to be sworn."

John took his leave, weighing Gridley's advice so soberly that "no lawyer in America ever did so much business as I did afterwards in the seventeen years that I passed in the practice at the bar for so little profit: and although my propensity to marriage was ardent enough, I determined I would not indulge it till I saw a clear prospect of business and profit enough to support a family without embarrassment."[26]

Pleased with his interview, John went on to seek the approbation of several other leading men of the bar. Oxenbridge Thacher that evening declined to quiz John extensively, instead sipping tea and chatting amiably upon metaphysics.

"We had Clark and Leibnitz, Descartes, Malebranche and Locke, Baxter, Bolingbroke and Berkeley, with many others on the carpet," John later recalled, "and fate, foreknowledge, eternity, immensity, infinity, matter and spirit, essence and attribute, vacuum and plenum, space and duration, subjects which neither of us understood and which I have long been convinced will never be intelligible to human understanding."[27]

Next morning John went to call upon Benjamin Prat, who received him in some ill humor:

He inquired if I had been sworn at Worcester. No. Have you a letter from Mr. Putnam to the court? No. It would have been most proper to have done one of them things first. When a young gentleman goes from me into another county, I always write in his favor to the court in that county, or if you had been sworn there you would have been entitled to be sworn here. But now, nobody in this county knows anything about you. So nobody can say anything in your favor but by hearsay. I believe you have made a proper proficiency in science and that you will do very well from what I have heard, but that is only hearsay.[28]

As a result, John went off as angry over his time spent with Prat as he had been pleased over the talk with Gridley. However, the last member of the bar whom he elected to see, the brilliant, flamboyant James Otis, talked "with great ease and familiarity" upon Homer and Horace, promising to join the bar in recommending John to the court.[29]

Then, relieved that his introductions were finished, marking time until the date of his swearing-in, John lapsed into "absolute idleness, or what is worse, gallanting the girls."[30]

On the appointed day in November he went to town, directly to Gridley's office, but Gridley had not come in from Brookline. John left, fidgeted, returned, but still Gridley had not arrived. Attending court until afternoon, John grew uneasy that Sam Quincy would be sworn but that he himself would have no patron. At last Gridley made his appearance, "and on sight of me whispered to Mr. Prat, [Richard] Dana, Kent, Thacher, etc., about me. Mr. Prat said nobody knew me. Yes, says Gridley, I have tried him; he is a very sensible fellow. . . ."

John related how Gridley proceeded to initiate the swearing-in process:

. . . He rose up and bowed to his right hand and said, "Mr. Quincy," when Quincy rose up, then bowed to me, "Mr. Adams," when I walked out. "May it please your honors, I have two young gentlemen, Mr. Quincy and Mr. Adams, to present for the oath of an attorney. Of Mr. Quincy it is sufficient for me to say he has lived three years with Mr. Prat. Of Mr. Adams, as he is unknown to your honors, it is necessary to say that he has lived between two and three years with Mr. Putnam of Worcester, has a good character from him and all others who know him, and that he was with me the other day several hours, and I take it he is qualified to study the law by his scholarship and that he has made a very considerable, a very great proficiency in the principles of the law, and therefore that the clients' interest may be safely entrusted in his hands. I therefore recommend him with the consent of the bar to your honors for the oath."[31]

After Prat had said a few words, the clerk was ordered to swear in the young men. Then Gridley shook John's hand, wishing him much joy, recommending him to the other men of the bar, who all congratulated him. Glowing in his success, John "invited them over to Stone's to drink some punch, where the most of us resorted and had a very cheerful [chat]."[32]

And so John was now a member of the bar of the Suffolk Inferior Court. He and Sam Quincy would be sworn in before the Superior Court some three years later, in 1761.[33]

That John was a lawyer in mid-eighteenth-century British America meant something highly significant for both his private future and the course of colonial history. Indeed, the fact that an astonishingly large number of young lawyers were about to gain prominence in the Colonies hardly seems an historical accident. For in any period of revolution and constitution-making, lawyers are bound to be among the leading actors on the stage. In addition, it was consequential for American history that these lawyers were all trained in the common law of England rather than in the administrative, magisterial law of the Continent.

When the colonists arrived in America they brought with them all their rights under common law. For that reason it was as important for a colonial lawyer to know Coke as it was for a lawyer in England. And Coke was the most authoritative, widely read source in the Colonies before Blackstone. Quite naturally, then, a young lawyer like John, who spent anguished hours probing the *Institutes* of such a hearty endorser of the common law as Coke, would come out of his study with thorough respect and admiration for that law. Moreover, though John read a wide variety of political philosophers, though he agreed with many of their ideas, in the end it was his education as a common law lawyer that marked the boldest stamp upon his mind. Had he been simply a politician with background only in the philosophers he would have cut himself off from a worldly context, but as it was he developed the realistic, practical mind of a courtroom lawyer. Not only was he well trained in the law but he acquired an immensely busy practice. Further, because certain office duties that lawyers have today, such as drafting wills and deeds, were then the job of scriveners, notaries, and so on, John spent most of his time trying cases.[34] He was a lawyer who not only studied but practiced.

From their study of common law John and his fellow lawyers had drawn several concepts that would determine their feelings about the political events that would take place in the latter half of the eighteenth century. First of all, they believed in a fundamental law of the land that could be applied by the courts in litigation according to common law. All government officials must act in harmony with this fundamental law. Second, they believed in the immemorial rights of Englishmen, whether in the mother country or the Colonies. Third, they approved the idea of these rights being set forth in charters and bills of rights, such as the Magna Carta, the Petition of Right, the Bill of Rights, and the colonial charters. Fourth, they believed in an independent judiciary as established by the Bill of Rights of 1688. Finally, they believed that the courts could disallow statutes contrary to the fundamental law. There were precedents for this idea of judicial review, including the right of the Privy Council to disallow colonial laws that violated colonial charters.[35]

John Adams was a young man of deep ties with England. By ancestry, education and profession he had every reason to have the most profound affection for and loyalty to England. Yet he would become one of the most vocal spokesmen of the American Revolution. How did he evolve in his political theory from a position of loyalty to King and Parliament to rejection, first, of Parliament, and then even of the King?

The answer must lie in the way in which he, as an English

colonial, justified the Revolution. He did not think of his progression toward advocacy of independence as a move toward revolution at all. Certainly it was not a reconstitution of society or of government that he wanted—which is what revolutionaries are generally conceded to favor. Rather, he believed that he and his fellow colonials were preservers of society—preservers of the tradition of English liberty that Parliament and the British ministry violated. It was the ministry who were revolutionaries, not Americans. Only when the ministry and Parliament refused to end violation of the rights of Americans as Englishmen did Adams view a reconciliation as hopeless and revolution as the only means to preserve these same rights. As his wife Abigail would later state the issue, if redress of grievances by law became impossible, then the alternative could only be redress by the sword. Adams became a revolutionary—that is, he evolved slowly toward support of independence.

Yet the American Revolution itself was scarcely a revolution as the world has known the violent social upheavals of its history. The key to that revolution and to Adams' view of it lies in the fact that in contrast to most revolutionaries, who have sought to overthrow the law, the American revolutionaries aimed to uphold and preserve the law that Parliament threatened. The rights of Englishmen about which Adams and his friends talked and wrote could be cited as established principles which the law was intended to protect. They were not theoretical abstractions produced from a philosopher's conscious efforts to build a system, but were specific principles that had grown up in the law and which Adams could apply through the courts. They found their embodiment in the great documents—Magna Carta, Petition of Right, the Bill of Rights, and so on—and in the hundreds of institutes, commentaries, reports and entries that made up the great body of common law.

There came a time when Adams and his colleagues began to suspect that since their protests of grievances were bringing no redress by Parliament, then they might be forced to proclaim independence in order to keep their liberties. When they had begun to reach that conclusion, they realized that they could not speak of their rights as specifically those of *Englishmen* and set forth in a *British* constitution. For that reason, they began to speak of rights inherent in a law of nature—rights belonging to a man simply because of his human nature. This was merely a superficial change in terminology, however, for the rights of Englishmen and natural rights were the same—still concrete liberties with historical precedents that could be protected through the courts.

Thus, when Adams became the theorist of the American Revolution and later of the independent nation, he began as a lawyer, thought as a lawyer, and proved his case as a lawyer. The protection by law of these same real, provable liberties was always his concern —whether as a young man in the infancy of his career, a case-maker for the Revolution, a constitution-maker for the new states, a defender of the United States Constitution, a President, or an old man reviewing the political scene. Liberty, Adams felt, could be an actual condition only in the presence of law.

CHAPTER III

ABIGAIL ADAMS

JOHN Adams was in love. To be sure, he had been in love before, recording in his diary impressions of the girls, including references to one girl he almost married. In fact, he was of so amorous a bent that in his later life he would think it necessary to declare to posterity that he had managed to remain sound of virtue, saying of his youthful flames: "They were all modest and virtuous girls and always maintained this character through life. No virgin or matron ever had cause to blush at the sight of me, or to regret her acquaintance with me. No father, brother, son or friend ever had cause of grief or resentment for any intercourse between me and any daughter, sister, mother, or any other relation of the female sex. My children may be assured that no illegitimate brother or sister exists or ever existed."[1]

Now, in 1762, John had the wherewithal to court a girl in earnest. His father had died the year before, leaving him a substantial inheritance—a cottage on the Coast Road, a barn and forty acres of land.[2] John had begun making trips with his friend Richard Cranch to Weymouth to the household of the Reverend William Smith, where there were three attractive young ladies, Mary, Abigail and Eliza. Cranch was in the midst of a courtship with Mary, oldest of the sisters. Meanwhile, John felt attracted to Abigail, or "Nabby," for whom he was developing an affection that in depth and maturity had little in common with his previous infatuations. Abigail was young, only seventeen, nine years younger than John, but she was an unusual girl for any era, particularly for her own time and place in the eighteenth century. In an age when girls learned little beyond the domestic skills and basic reading and writing, Abigail read passionately: politics, philosophy, literature—they all captivated her. Her keen, absorbing intellect assured that in the life of the mind and spirit—where man and woman make some of their most lasting bonds—she would prove a proper complement to John. Moreover, in many traits of personality Abigail and John were cut from the same cloth, she delightfully feminine, he robustly masculine. A bit shy though Abigail was, and diminutive in size, she spoke her mind with engaging wit and resolution. It is not difficult to imagine that her eyes, so crackling and direct in her portraits, would have disarmed an onlooker with their dancing energy. Surely John must have been intrigued that in this girlish but bright little creature there were firmness and fire enough to match his own vigor. Saucy, he liked to call her. Besides that, they both possessed, beneath their New England reserve, characters emotional, intense, sensitive, attuned to profound and lasting attachments. It is not surprising, then, that they fell in love. By October of 1762 John was writing to his "Miss Adorable,"

> By the same token that the bearer hereof *sat up* with you last night, I hereby order you to give him as many kisses and as many hours of your company after nine o'clock as he shall please to demand and charge them to my account. . . . I presume I have good right to draw upon you for the kisses, as I have given two or three millions at least, when one has been received, and of consequence the account between us is immensely in favor of yours,
>
> JOHN ADAMS.[3]

John married Abigail on October 25, 1764, avowing that she who had "always softened and warmed" his heart would "polish and refine" his "sentiments of life and manners," and "banish all the unsocial and ill-natured particles" of his being.[4]

To know much about any man it is important to observe his wife; but in the case of John Adams it is essential to know a great deal about Abigail. It was not that she dominated him or cajoled him into following her will—no one could bend intractable, single-minded John. It was simply that they were so much of the same mind, sharing the same general view of life, the same first principles. What is more, although Abigail was a positive soul she knew her wifely role. She devoted her considerable energies to supporting her husband throughout his life, approving both his actions and his ideas.

For fifty-four years the Adamses lived together, two strong people who were notably well matched in disposition, character, philosophy and depth of affection. That they were uncommonly devoted—indeed, that they were an altogether extraordinary couple with some claim even to having a romance that stands up well among historic romances—is not mere conjecture but an obvious conclusion from their reams of letters. As a lawyer traveling a circuit, as a Revolutionary politician in the Continental Congress, as a diplomat in France and Holland, as Vice President and as President, John was often separated from his wife, sometimes, as during his sojourn in Europe, for several years at a time. But it is a tribute to their fervor, to the substance of their bond and to their powers of communication that their love did not wither during these absences but progressed to new heights. Letters were not the same as being together, but they were better than nothing; consequently, John and Abigail strove to make them as complete a means of union as possible.

During those months and years of the painful sacrifice of separation, the letters of the Adamses were mirrors of their thoughts on every human experience. Birth, death, marriage, child-rearing, work, play, state-building, constitution-making—all marched through the pages of those lively, enthralling epistles. Perhaps, on the whole, Abigail's letters were better—more literary, more poetic, more sentimental. John's were generally written in a rush, complaining of too much work, often too brief. Nevertheless, he spoke his feelings, too—tough, blurted passages full of the hurt of being

isolated from those he loved, unable to furnish protection and aid
to his wife, fatherly counsel to his children.

In the first place, the Adams letters continually declared unabated love between the partners, despite all hardship and separation. Even in a distant place, John wrote to his wife that "my fancy
runs about you perpetually. It is continually with you and in the
neighborhood of you. . . ."[5] When Abigail told him to burn her
letters, he insisted that the very thought made his "heart throb
more than a cannonade would," that he "must forget you first."[6]

For the most part these Adams love letters were sober pieces
reflecting upon solemn matters. Both John and Abigail viewed life
as a panorama of high seriousness. Though they both possessed wit
and humor, scattering entertaining vignettes through their letters,
they nonetheless found it a full-time and weighty business to attempt to fathom the truth of life. And in order to withstand the
bitter, unnatural separation that was their lot, it was necessary for
them to find meaning for their circumstances. Difficult though it
may be to comprehend such powerful feelings of patriotism as both
the Adamses possessed, it was indeed patriotism that buoyed them
above the waves. Both of them believed that their first duty was to
their country, that unless they labored for liberty, happiness could
come neither to them nor to their children.

Abigail's role at home was just as taxing as her husband's on the
scene of political action. "How many are the solitary hours I
spend," wrote Abigail, "ruminating upon the past and anticipating
the future, whilst you, overwhelmed with the cares of state, have
but few moments you can devote to any individual. All domestic
pleasures and enjoyments are absorbed in the great and important
duty you owe your country, 'for our country is, as it were, a secondary God and the first and greatest parent. It is to be preferred to
parents, wives, children, friends and all things, the gods only ex-
cepted. For if our country perishes it is as impossible to save an
individual as to preserve one of the fingers of a mortified hand.'
Thus do I suppress every wish and silence every murmur, acquiesc-
ing in a painful separation from the companion of my youth and the
friend of my heart."[7]

To be so fully endorsed by his wife was indeed a gift, and John from his post at the Continental Congress offered thanks. Seated among forty of his colleagues, all talking and whispering, he took time to tell Abigail of his gratitude:

> It is a cruel reflection, which very often comes across me, that I should be separated so far from those babes whose education and welfare lies so near my heart. But greater misfortunes than these must not divert us from superior duties.
>
> Your sentiments of the duties we owe to our country are such as become the best of women and the best of men. Among all the disappointments and perplexities which have fallen to my share in life, nothing has contributed so much to support my mind as the choice blessing of a wife, whose capacity enabled her to comprehend and whose pure virtue obliged her to approve the views of her husband. This has been the cheering consolation of my heart in my most solitary, gloomy and disconsolate hours. In this remote situation, I am deprived in a great measure of this comfort. Yet I read, and read again, your charming letters, and they serve me, in some faint degree, as a substitute for the company and conversation of the writer.

By the time he was a delegate to Congress he had four children whom he longed to see—Nabby, the oldest, named for her mother; John Quincy, Charles and Thomas Boylston. (Susanna, "Suky," had died when she was only a little more than a year old.)

"I want to take a walk with you in the garden," he told Abigail, "to go over to the common—the plain—the meadow. I want to take Charles in one hand and Tom in the other and walk with you, Nabby on your right hand and John upon my left, to view the cornfields, the orchards, etc."[8] But his homesick dreams were no substitute for the original.

Through one time of stress after another the Adamses were apart, Abigail writing to ask for consolation, John replying in agonized tones that it was surely harder on him to be unable to help her in these afflictions than it was for her to bear them. So often were they separated that, for example, from the time of his election to Congress in 1774 until he sailed for Europe in 1778 as a joint commissioner to France, John was home only five times—and then only a

month or so each time. During his European sojourn he was away
from Abigail from February, 1778, until August, 1779, and then
again from November, 1779, until August, 1784. To sustain themselves in their separation and periods of distress, both called upon
their exemplary faith. Abigail was particularly vocal in her dependence upon Providence, pleading for strength to endure what she
could not change. When her mother died during a severe influenza
epidemic in the fall of 1775, Abigail wrote to John:

> Have pity upon me, have pity upon me, O! thou, my beloved, for
> the hand of God presseth me sore.
> Yet will I be dumb and silent and not open my mouth because
> thou, O Lord, hast done it.
> How can I tell you (O, my bursting heart) that my dear mother
> has left me; this day about five o'clock she left this world for an
> infinitely better.
> After sustaining sixteen days severe conflict, nature fainted and
> she fell asleep. Blessed Spirit, where art thou? At times I almost am
> ready to faint under this severe and heavy stroke, separated from
> *thee* who used to be a comforter towards me in affliction, but blessed
> be God; His ear is not heavy that he cannot hear, but He has bid us
> call upon him in time of trouble.[9]

Realizing that his family had all been in the throes of violent
illness but not yet knowing of the death of his mother-in-law, John
wrote to his wife a letter typical of both of their beliefs that men
must bow to the will of God.

". . . Our lives are not in our own power," he said. "It is our duty
to submit. 'The ways of heaven are dark and intricate.' Its designs
are often inscrutable but are always wise and just and good."[10]

He was absent again during another crucial time. When in 1777
he had to return from Braintree to Congress, parting seemed even
more difficult than usual. Abigail was in her sixth pregnancy. It
appeared to John that the time was far off when he would be able
to return to his family. With sad heart he wrote on his first day away
from home that Abigail should present his "affection in the tender-
est manner to my little deserving daughter and my amiable sons."
He spoke of the "cruel parting this morning," through which he had

disguised his pain enough to appear composed.

"May God Almighty's Providence protect you, my dear, and all our little ones. My good genius, my guardian angel, whispers me that we shall see happier days and that I shall live to enjoy the felicities of domestic life with her whom my heart esteems above all earthly blessings."[11]

As her time drew near Abigail became uneasy. She felt "cut off from the privilege which some of brute creation enjoy, that of having their mate sit by them with anxious care during all their solitary confinement."[12] She grew impatient, harboring dark thoughts that her separations from her husband were only a prelude to an even more strenuous test. Even the strongest love was merely human; it could be plagued with doubts.

> I have sometimes melancholy reflections and imagine these separations as preparatory to a still more painful one in which even hope, the anchor of the soul, is lost, but whilst that remains no temporary absence can ever wean or abate the ardor of my affection. Bound together by many tender ties, there scarcely wanted an addition; yet, I feel that there soon will be an additional one. Many, many are the tender sentiments I have felt for the parent on this occasion. I doubt not they are reciprocal, but I often feel the want of his presence and the soothing tenderness of his affection. Is this weakness or is it not?[13]

For his part, John, sweltering in the July heat of Philadelphia, lapsed into depression, knowing that he could not help his wife, who was due that very month. He could not know that the little girl they hoped for would be stillborn. Worn out with cares of war, overcome with thoughts that he was missing life's greatest joys, he wrote one of his strongest, most touching letters to his wife:

> This day completes six months since I left you. I am wasted and exhausted in mind and body, with incessant application to business, but if I can possibly endure it, will hold out the year. It is nonsense to dance backwards and forwards. After this year I shall take my leave.
>
> Our affairs are in a fine, prosperous train, and if they continue so, I can leave this station with honor.

Next month completes three years that I have been devoted to the servitude of liberty. A slavery it has been to me, whatever the world may think of it.

To a man whose attachments to his family are as strong as mine, absence alone from such a wife and such children would be a great sacrifice. But in addition to this separation, what have I not done? What have I not suffered? What have I not hazarded? These are questions that I may ask you, but I will ask such questions of none else. Let the cymbals of popularity tinkle still. Let the butterflies of fame glitter with their wings. I shall envy neither their music nor their colors.

The loss of property affects me little. All other hard things I despise, but the loss of your company and that of my dear babes for so long a time I consider as a loss of so much solid happiness.

The tender, social feelings of my heart, which have distressed me beyond all utterance in my most busy, active scenes, as well as in the numerous hours of melancholy solitude, are known only to God and my own soul.

How often have I seen my dearest Friend a widow and her charming prattlers orphans, exposed to all the insolence of unfeeling, impious tyrants! Yet, I can appeal to my final Judge, the horrid vision has never for one moment shaken the resolution of my heart.[14]

Abigail, too, could summarize the anguish of being wrenched from her partner. Musing upon the long-range view of their lives, she declared, "The unfeeling world may consider it in what light they please; I consider it as a sacrifice to my country and one of my greatest misfortunes [for my husband] to be separated from my children at a time of life when the joint instructions and admonition of parents sink deeper than in maturer years."[15] Nevertheless, on October 25, 1777, their thirteenth anniversary, she declared again what John would have seconded—willingness to sacrifice domestic happiness to the welfare of their country:

This day, dearest of Friends, completes thirteen years since we were solemnly united in wedlock; three years of the time we have been cruelly separated. I have patiently as I could endured it with the belief that you were serving your country and rendering your fellow creatures essential benefits. May future generations rise up and call you blessed, and the present behave worthy of the blessings you are laboring to secure to them, and I shall have less reason to regret the deprivation of my own particular felicity.[16]

Not only were the Adams letters proclamations of love, but they were declarations of concern for the children. Both John and Abigail felt, as they expressed over and over, the keen loss of a father to act as teacher, counselor, guardian and judge. Thus, John made every effort to direct Abigail how the children ought to be reared; moreover, he was diligent in writing to the children himself. When he spoke of them or wrote to them, his austerity melted.

"Remember my tender love to my little Nabby," he would tell Abigail. "Tell her she must write me a letter and enclose it in the next you send. I am charmed with your amusement with our little Johnny. Tell him I am glad to hear he is so good a boy as to read to his Mamma for her entertainment and to keep himself out of the company of rude children. Tell him I hope to hear a good account of his accidence and nomenclature when I return. Kiss my little Charley and Tommy for me. Tell them I shall be at home by November, but how much sooner I know not."[17]

He knew that in Abigail he had a trustworthy deputy as teacher. He knew that she was as intent about proper education of their children as she was about everything else—and more than equipped to teach them. But he feared that one day his children would grow to resent the time he had spent away from them, that they might believe he ought to have labored a little more for them rather than for his country. Nonetheless, he would not bear their reproaches. He would tell them that he had "studied and labored to procure a free constitution of government for them to solace themselves under, and if they do not prefer this to ample fortune, to ease and elegance," then they would not be his children, and he would "care not what becomes of them." John and Charles both had "genius." Abigail should "take care that they don't go astray." She should "cultivate their minds, inspire their little hearts, raise their wishes. Fix their attention upon great and glorious objects, root out every little thing, weed out every meanness, make them great and manly. Teach them to scorn injustice, ingratitude, cowardice, and falsehood. Let them revere nothing but religion, morality and liberty."

He did not forget Nabby and Tommy. Tommy was still young. Nabby should receive a girl's education, of which Abigail was the best judge.[18]

As John Quincy grew older, both parents were well aware of his enormous potential. His father was "under no apprehensions about his proficiency in learning," agreeing that "with his capacity and opportunities he cannot fail to acquire knowledge." But he added sharply, "Let him know that the moral sentiments of his heart are more important than the furniture of his head. Let him be sure that he possesses the great virtues of temperance, justice, magnanimity, honor and generosity, and with these added to his parts he cannot fail to become a wise and great man." He inquired of Abigail whether John Quincy read the newspapers. "The events of this war should not pass unobserved by him at his years." Further, as their son progressed in his study of history, Abigail should "ask him what events strike him most, what characters he esteems and admires, which he hates and abhors, which he despises."[19]

To the children themselves John wrote affectionately. He could tell his "dear little Nabby" that "I have received your pretty letter, and it has given me a great deal of pleasure, both as it is a token of your duty and affection to me and as it is a proof of your improvement in your handwriting and in the faculties of the mind." He instructed her and her brothers to "be good children and mind their books and listen to the advice of their excellent Mamma, whose instructions will do them good as long as they live and after they shall be no more in this world." They should strive to be useful, so that they "may be blessings to their parents and to mankind, as well as qualified to be blessings to those who shall come after them."[20]

John could exhibit equal warmth in apologizing to his youngest son, Tommy, for not having written to him when he wrote to the other children. He did indeed love him just as much as the others; however, he had not written because he did not think Tommy knew how to read. Hastening to repair what Abigail had reported were some grieved feelings, John reminded his little son:

The only reason why I omitted to write you when I wrote to your brothers was because I thought you were as yet too young to be able to read writing, not because I had less affection for you than for them: for you may rely upon it, you have as great a share in your father's esteem and affection as any of his children.

I hope you will be good and learn to read and write well, and then I shall take a pride and pleasure in your constant correspondence. Give my love to your Mamma, your worthy sister and brothers, and to all the rest of the family.

Pray, when you write me a letter, let me know how many calves are raising, how many ducks and geese, and how the garden looks. I long to take a walk with you to see them and the green meadows and pastures.[21]

He could write to John Quincy in April, 1776, exhorting him and his sister and brothers to grasp the historical impact of events around them, to "take proper notice of these great events and remember under whose wise and kind Providence they are all conducted. Not a sparrow falls, nor a hair is lost but by the direction of infinite wisdom. Much less are cities conquered and evacuated." He hoped that they would "all remember how many losses, dangers and inconveniences have been borne by your parents and the inhabitants of Boston, in general, for the sake of preserving freedom for you and yours. . . ." In addition, he hoped that "you will all follow the virtuous example if, in any future time, your country's liberties should be in danger, and suffer every human evil rather than give them up."[22]

Besides loving her husband, rearing four children and overseeing a farm and two houses (informing John that his fields wanted manure, that his asparagus did nicely, or that inflationary war prices would surely make paupers of them), Abigail managed to be an intellectual companion of the first order. While John relayed as much as he safely could of his political doings, Abigail told him of developments in Massachusetts. Such discussion of politics involved not merely specific events but the whole compass of political theory. Abigail was nearly as intrigued by politics as her husband, a fact that both delighted and sustained him.

He was proud that she, along with Mercy Otis Warren, was one of the most accomplished women in New England. Indeed, an English gentleman visiting Braintree pronounced her the most accomplished lady he had met since he left England. Relating the compliment to his wife, John teased that she ought not to grow proud over such flattery.[23]

He must have been pleased when, after writing to her that "human nature with all its infirmities and depravation is still capable of great things,"[24] Abigail replied that she was "more and more convinced that man is a dangerous creature, and that power, whether vested in many or a few, is ever grasping and, like the grave, cries, give, give. The great fish swallow up the small, and he who is most strenuous for the rights of the people, when vested with power, is as eager after the prerogatives of government. You tell me of degrees of perfection to which human nature is capable of arriving, and I believe it, but at the same time lament that our admiration should arise from scarcity of the instances."

The difficulties of establishing a government, should the Colonies separate from Britain, did not escape her. "How shall we be governed so as to retain our liberties? Can any government be free which is not administered by general, stated laws? Who shall frame these laws? Who will give them force and energy?" True, she said, the resolutions of the Congress had heretofore had the force of law, but would they continue to have? When she considered such problems and "the prejudices of people in favor of ancient customs and regulations," she felt "anxious for the fate of our monarchy or democracy or whatever is to take place." At any rate, she only hoped that "justice and righteousness" would prevail, that order would "arise out of confusion."[25]

She read abundantly—history, political tracts, sermons, poetry (which she often included in her letters), plays, newspapers. She was as eager to receive John's discourses upon the varieties of style, upon Pliny, Pope and Swift as upon the knotty problems of politics. As the colonists were laying siege to Boston, where they had encircled the British at the outset of the war, she could write from the outskirts of the action, while the roar of cannon shook the house, that she had read with much interest Thomas Paine's *Common*

Sense. She inquired how such sentiments were received in Congress. At the same time she could report where the militia had been ordered and who was in charge.[26] It was just such ability that made her John's favorite conversationalist and writer and his most trusted advisor.

She was a remarkable woman, this bustling little Abigail— soulmate and helpmate to her husband, place and permanence to her children, mentor to both, loyal patriot to her country. To the man she married, to the children she nurtured she was a rare blessing— and of that no one was more aware than her husband.

CHAPTER IV

PRELUDE TO REVOLUTION

THE scene in the council chamber of the Boston Town House on that February day in 1761 was set with proper English stateliness. Compared with a similar setting in the House of Commons in England or the Statehouse in Philadelphia, it would have made a respectable showing. Round a great fire sat five Superior Court judges, with Lieutenant Governor Thomas Hutchinson at their head as chief justice, all brilliantly decked in robes of scarlet English broadcloth with great cambric bands and all looking soberly from beneath oversized judicial wigs. At a long table, also arrayed in robes, bands and wigs, were all the barristers of Boston and Middlesex County. As John Adams was to describe them later, "They were not seated on ivory chairs, but their dress was more solemn and more pompous than that of the Roman Senate when the Gauls broke in upon them."[1] Full-length portraits of Charles II and James II hung gold-framed upon the walls, impressing upon the company the nobility of the royal features and the richness of the ermine robes.

Looking, in his own words, "like a short, thick Archbishop of Canterbury," John Adams, pen in hand, sat at the table with the lawyers of Boston, now and then taking copious notes, at other moments so enthralled that he wrote nothing at all. Though he was but twenty-six, the events of that February so engraved themselves upon his mind that some fifty-six years later he could re-create the entire episode.[2]

This was the occasion of the well-known writs of assistance case in which James Otis first distinguished himself as an oracle of English liberties. Young Adams, with his instinctive perception of historic moments, sat spellbound in the midst of the debate.

". . . Otis was a flame of fire!" Adams later reported.

> With a promptitude of classical allusions, a depth of research, a rapid summary of historical events and dates, a profusion of legal authorities, a prophetic glance of his eye into futurity, and a torrent of impetuous eloquence, he hurried away everything before him. American independence was then and there born; the seeds of patriots and heroes were then and there sown to defend the vigorous youth, the *non sine Diis animosus infans.* Every man of a crowded audience appeared to me to go away, as I did, ready to take arms against writs of assistance. Then and there was the first scene of the first act of opposition to the arbitrary claims of Great Britain. Then and there the child Independence was born. In fifteen years, namely in 1776, he grew up to manhood and declared himself free.[3]

Hindsight of fifty years doubtless caused Adams to attribute more significance to the case than it actually deserved; nonetheless, it was a forebearer of later constitutional arguments, worthy of close attention.

A writ of assistance had originally been a document granted to a litigant in a court of Exchequer or Chancery, allowing him to have the sheriff assist him to collect a debt or to obtain possession of property that was due him. But the writs sought by the Boston customs officials in 1761 were not writs specifically meant for one case; they were general standing warrants, valid from the time of issue until six months after the death of the issuing monarch. These general warrants permitted the holder to go in the daytime with a constable or other officer into any house where he suspected there might be contraband and to search for the smuggled goods. Holding such a writ, he needed no special permission from a court.[4]

When George II died in October, 1760, the groundwork was laid for the 1761 crisis. Because the writs would be valid for only six months after the death of the King, the customs commissioners had to apply to the Superior Court for new ones—a step that was opposed by Boston merchants, who questioned the authority of the Court to grant these general warrants. Upon the petitions of several customs commissioners and the merchants who opposed them, the Court scheduled argument of the case for its February term. Jeremiah Gridley spoke for the Crown, Oxenbridge Thacher and James Otis for the merchants.[5]

In arguing the nature of the writ, the lawyers referred to several Acts of Parliament and a provincial statute. But it was only James Otis who, in addition to arguing from the statutes, brought up a constitutional question. Adams' abstract, emphasizing by underlines and capitalization the speaker's important words, quotes Otis as asserting that only special writs were legal, saying that he would admit the legality only of *"special writs, directed to special officers* . . . to search *certain houses,* etc., *especially set forth in the writ* . . . granted by the Court of Exchequer at home, *upon oath made before* the Lord Treasurer by the person who asks *that he suspects such goods to be concealed in* THOSE VERY PLACES HE DESIRES TO SEARCH." Modern judges, he stated, had "adjudged *that special warrants only are legal.* In the same manner I rely on it that the writ prayed for in this petition, being general, is illegal. It is a power that places the liberty of every man in the hands of every petty officer."[6]

Moreover, Otis objected that this writ was universal, directed to all justices, sheriffs, constables, subjects and so on—in short "to every subject in the King's dominions." Everyone with this writ might, consequently, be a tyrant.

The fact was that the writ violated the ancient English right against unreasonable searches and seizures. "Now one of the most essential branches of English liberty," Otis insisted, "is the freedom of one's house."

A man's house is his castle; and while he is quiet, he is as well-guarded as a prince in his castle. This writ, if it should be declared legal, would totally annihilate this privilege. Custom house officers may enter our houses when they please—we are commanded to permit their entry—their menial servants may enter, may break locks, bars and everything in their way, and whether they break through malice or revenge, no man, no court can inquire—bare suspicion without oath is sufficient. . . . What a scene does this open! Every man prompted by revenge, ill humor or wantonness to inspect the inside of his neighbor's house may get a writ of assistance; others will ask it from self-defense; one arbitrary exertion will provoke another until society will be involved in tumult and in blood.[7]

Further, the fact that these writs were perpetual during the life of the sovereign and for six months after made them doubly dangerous. "Writs in their nature are temporary things; when the purposes for which they are issued are answered, they exist no more; but these monsters in the law live forever; no one can be called to account. Thus reason and the constitution are both against this writ."[8]

The only justifiable precedent for the writ, Otis went on, was an Act of Parliament of 1662 made, after all, during the reign of Charles II "in the zenith of arbitrary power . . . when Star Chamber powers were pushed in extremity by some ignorant clerk of the Exchequer."[9] Now Otis tackled the constitutional question. Even if this writ had been in any lawbook whatever, it would have been illegal, he argued, for it was against the principles of the law. He then uttered his famous argument from fundamental law. Taking as his authority Coke's maxim upon void Acts of Parliament in *Dr. Bonham's Case*, Otis asserted: "An Act against the constitution is void; an Act against natural equity is void; and if an Act of Parliament should be made in the very words of this petition, it would be void. The executive courts must pass such Acts into disuse."[10] Here he cited Coke, who in *Dr. Bonham's Case* reported, "and it appears in our books that in many cases the common law will control Acts of Parliament and sometimes adjudge them to be utterly void: for when an Act of Parliament is against common right and reason, or repugnant, or impossible to be performed, the common law will control it and adjudge such Act to be void. . . ."[11]

Otis' argument reaped no immediate practical benefits; eventually, in fact, the court ruled in favor of the writ. But the theoretical implications of Otis' efforts were more far-reaching. Adams in later life remarked that "Mr. Otis' oration against writs of assistance breathed into this nation the breath of life."[12] Even though that statement must be taken more figuratively than literally, there was an important sense in which Otis contributed to the mainstream of constitutional controversy that was to follow him. Otis did not, as Adams recalled he did, voice in the writs case every argument of the Revolution; nevertheless, he did become one of the best-read of Revolutionary pamphleteers, summarizing and elaborating upon the arguments he used in 1761. Moreover, despite the fact that his argument did not change the law, he did indeed bring to the foreground an idea old in English legal history—that laws contrary to the law of the land, to common right and reason, cannot be effective; in medieval legal theory they had been declared "impertinent to be observed." True, this was not the sophisticated notion of judicial review and separation of powers that matured during the Confederation and Constitution period. Even so, there had always been in English theory an idea of a law of the land that superseded the powers of any king or parliament. Neither Coke nor Otis manufactured the principle; but James Otis certainly did his part to summon forth for the patriot cause the precedents of this idea. And John Adams and his contemporaries, in attempting to base their grievances upon unquestionably legal grounds, gladly took up Otis' argument from fundamental law. In fact, as the home government during the next fifteen years passed measure after measure that the colonists believed were contrary to their rights as Englishmen, Adams and his fellow lawyers denied the authority of such laws on the very ground that they were contrary to their rights under the English constitution.

John Adams understood that human beings live in history. He appreciated the scope of a phenomenon so large as the American Revolution. As an old man he would repeat again and again his theories on the meaning of the Revolution; and because he had been both participant and observer his ideas were pertinent.

"The American Revolution was not a common event," he would

write in 1818. "Its effects and consequences have already been awful over a great part of the globe. And when and where are they to cease? But what do we mean by the American Revolution? Do we mean the American war? The Revolution was effected before the war commenced. The Revolution was in the minds and hearts of the people: a change in their religious sentiments of their duties and obligations."[13] There was no sudden violent usurpation by wild masses in Boston or Philadelphia or Charleston. There was no class war urged upon the downtrodden by political maneuverers. There was no seizure of power by greedy aristocrats or proletarians. The real Revolution was a quiet, subtle thing that had already been accomplished by 1775. The fact was, Adams declared, that so long as King and Parliament were believed by the colonists to govern "in justice and mercy, according to the laws and constitution derived to them from the God of nature and transmitted to them by their ancestors," Americans gave them their utmost allegiance. But when King and Parliament appeared to be renouncing all principles of authority, endangering the life, liberty and properties of their subjects, "willing, like Lady Macbeth, to 'dash their brains out,' " then Americans dropped all filial affection for Britain.

"This radical change in the principles, opinions, sentiments, and affections of the people," Adams insisted, "was the real American Revolution."[14] There was no great upheaval of conflicting social forces, no realignment of classes or growing spirit of nationalism. There was, in fact, as Adams pointed out with a clear memory of those painful years of the Continental Congress, no spirit of nationalism at all. The thirteen Colonies were "all distinct, unconnected and independent of each other." Adams himself never ceased to wonder at the remarkable manner in which these thirteen quarrelsome Colonies managed to come around to one mind. Perhaps he was minimizing their predominantly common English background, but nevertheless he observed:

> The Colonies had grown up under constitutions of government so different, there was so great a variety of religions, they were composed of so many different nations, their customs, manners, and

habits had so little resemblance, and their intercourse had been so rare, and their knowledge of each other so imperfect, that to unite them in the same principles in theory and the same system of action, was certainly a very difficult enterprise. The complete accomplishment of it, in so short a time and by such simple means, was perhaps a singular example in the history of mankind. Thirteen clocks were made to strike together—a perfection of mechanism which no artist had ever before effected.[15]

Rather than study the "gloriole of individual gentlemen and of separate states," it was more important, Adams believed, to observe the "means and measures" by which British and Americans acted and reacted down a path toward separation. Speaking as one who had participated in the Revolution in his own country and had, as well, been a first-hand observer of another across the sea, Adams hoped that a study of those means and measures "may teach mankind that revolutions are no trifles; that they ought never to be undertaken rashly; nor without deliberate consideration and sober reflection; nor without a solid, immutable, eternal foundation of justice and humanity; nor without a people possessed of intelligence, fortitude, and integrity sufficient to carry them with steadiness, patience, and perseverance through all the vicissitudes of fortune, the fiery trials and melancholy disasters they may have to encounter."[16]

Speaking here was no angry rabble-rouser, but one who knew the pain and high cost of the decision to withdraw allegiance from the only state he and his family and all of their ancestors had ever known. Adams and most of his contemporaries did not think of themselves as revolutionaries. And, indeed, they were not. They had never clamored for institutions that were radically new. Rather, they were merely trying to preserve the English rights and institutions they already had. They were Englishmen who wished to preserve all the benefits that were rightfully theirs under English law. Consequently, for all their pleas to the Crown there were historical precedents. The effort to retain old rights rather than to obtain new ones was a fundamental fact of the Revolution. Hence, in the sense that revolutionaries seek to annihilate history, to sweep away all that has gone before, to erect new institutions that have

little relationship to those of the past, Americans were not revolutionaries in the way that the French were.

The American Revolution was, as Adams said, an *evolution* that
took place over a span of fifteen years or so in the minds and hearts
of the people. American impatience over Parliamentary encroachments upon the liberties of subjects grew gradually into complete
abhorrence for what those subjects came to feel was an intolerable
situation. For fifteen years they had complained and protested to
the mother country. When they came to understand that their
protestations were to no avail, they saw no choice but to sever
allegiance. If King and Parliament would not observe the rights of
Englishmen, then the people had been literally abandoned by their
government and it was up to them to preserve the law by other
means. For Adams and most other Americans it was the King and
Parliament that were revolutionary.

The colonists believed on two counts—the abstract level of political ideas and the practical level of everyday politics—that King and
Parliament were treating them unjustly. Adams, being both a legal
philosopher and a politician, argued on both levels. In the matter
of practical politics, trouble between the Colonies and Britain
stemmed from British attempts to raise money, an issue that would
balloon into a crucial question of balance between imperial control
and colonial self-government. No mistake about it, the Seven
Years' War with France had been a costly one. By the time it was
over in 1763, the English had piled up a tremendous debt and were
searching for every possible means to relieve themselves of some
of their burden. Why, they concluded, should the American Colonies not provide some of their wealth for aid of the mother country?
And thus the Grenville ministry, which came into office in Britain
in 1763, adopted a policy that formed a watershed in British-
colonial relations.

Before 1763, and in fact since 1650, the Colonies had operated
under a policy of British imperial control known as the Old
Colonial System. A typically mercantilistic arrangement replete
with the idiosyncrasies that mercantilism entails, the Old Colonial
System had all the earmarks of what seventeenth- and early eight-

eenth-century minds considered to be sound money policy: militant economic nationalism; planned economy; determination to make the nation self-sufficient; effort to gain maximum profit for both the middle class—whose success was believed to mean success for the whole nation—and the Crown; effort to create a favorable balance of trade; to export more than import; to sell more than buy; to export manufactured goods and to import raw materials. Essential to this economic picture were colonies, which were founded upon mercantilistic motives of the Crown. Colonies existed for the benefit of the mother country: they were to be sources of raw materials and markets for manufactures. Specifically, the Old Colonial System found expression in several hundred acts of trade regulation. Although navigation laws had existed since the time of Richard II in the fourteenth century, the commercial policy of the Old Colonial System began to be better defined during the second half of the seventeenth century and particularly after the Restoration of 1660. There were three principles behind this commercial policy: ships engaged in trade between the Colonies and England had to be built in England or in the Colonies and had to be manned by English or colonial crews; second, certain enumerated goods shipped from the Colonies could be sent only to England or to another colony; third, when foreign merchandise was imported to the Colonies from Europe it had to go through an English port, subject to another duty. A Board of Trade and Plantations and a Secretary of the Southern Department administered the trade laws from England, while in the Colonies the laws were administered by customs commissioners and, after 1697, courts of vice admiralty. The latter, set up to try—without a jury—cases of infringement of the trade acts, caused much resentment among the colonists. Adams, a lawyer, was always incensed by these courts without juries.

When Adams stepped into the political scene in the 1760's the British ministry was altering its policy toward the Colonies. There is some disagreement as to whether the navigation laws before 1763 had been well enforced. Some, like Adams, have declared that even though there were trade laws on the books they were so poorly enforced as to be almost ineffective. Adams reported that these acts of trade "had lain a dead letter, unexecuted for half a century, and some of them, I believe, for nearly a whole one."[17] And though the trade laws seem to have been better enforced than Adams believed, the English did let slip many violations. But even when enforced the navigation laws had not imposed too great a burden upon the Colonies.

However, the difference between policies before and after the Seven Years' War did not hinge most significantly upon enforcement but rather upon the purpose of the legislation, which had always been to regulate colonial trade, to encourage trade with England, to stimulate production of certain commodities, rather than to raise revenue. The American Act of 1764 initiated a new scheme of trade policy: for the first time a law was designed to raise direct revenue from the Colonies. As Adams put it: "It was not until the annihilation of the French dominion in America that any British ministry had dared to gratify their own wishes and the desire of the nation by projecting a formal plan for raising a national revenue from America by Parliamentary taxation."[18]

For with the close of the war with France, Britain saw herself in a new role. Her trade policy heretofore had been distinctly commercial; now it was to be imperial, befitting a nation that had worldwide dominions. Henceforth her ministry would tighten its reign on the acts of trade; diligently it would pursue a policy of preventing violations. But not only that—henceforth it would impose duties on the Colonies not merely for trade regulation but with the avowed intent of raising revenue.

Throughout the seventeenth and eighteenth centuries, England had been maturing in the business of running an empire. But what she did not count on was the fact that during this same period the American Colonies had been developing their abilities of self-government at an even faster rate. Until 1763 England may have done an adequate job of controlling colonial trade; yet she had left to the Colonies the task of governing themselves. As a result, in their internal affairs the Colonies had acquired real home rule. It was only natural, when England started interfering with them on matters they had decided for themselves for 150 years, that they began to realize that perhaps they no longer owed allegiance to the mother country.

The grounds upon which they protested interference with their self-government were ancient and valid ones under English law. From feudal times Englishmen had been represented in the assembly that had taxed them. Magna Carta (1215), as interpreted in England as early as the seventeenth century, guaranteed that they should not be taxed without their own consent; that they could not be deprived of their property but by due process of law—and this in turn meant representation in the assembly that levied taxes upon them. The colonists elected representatives to their assemblies, but they sent no one to Parliament. Consequently, although the provincial assemblies could levy taxes upon the colonists, Parliament had no power to tax them. Parliament could levy neither internal nor external taxes—customs duties levied with a purpose of raising revenue were as objectionable as an internal tax, such as the stamp duty. Though Parliament had authority to regulate trade through moderate customs duties, the colonists came to believe that even this was a power that they themselves delegated to Parliament, that in matters of taxation and all other affairs their own provincial assemblies were supreme because only in their own assemblies were Americans represented. As Parliament continued to press its authority over the Colonies, Americans rejected Parliament altogether, declaring that they owed allegiance only to the person of the King. And then, as appeals to the King fell on deaf ears, the colonists would begin to think of independence.

Just as on the political level Americans came to the conclusion that Parliament had no control over them in any case whatsoever, so on the legal plane they reached the same end. Adams, like most other lawyers of his time, was active on both levels. Indeed, one of the most significant facts about the American Revolution was that the burden of its success was carried by lawyers. The thinkers of the Revolution were not philosophers, as was to be the case in France; instead, they were lawyers who read English law. Even more than Locke or Sidney, Coke was their mentor. They had been so steeped in the reports, entries and treatises of common law authorities that instinctively they understood and accepted the rule of law as the underpinning of security and stability in the state. No product of abstract theory, this comprehension had rather come to them through their grappling with concrete legal problems and from their study of institutes, commentaries and case reports. From their very business of earning a living they derived an appreciation for the distinctly legal relationship that from the twelfth century had existed between subject and sovereign and between subject and subject. Hence it was natural that these practitioners of law should be law-abiding. Only when Parliament began to act contrary to the law did Adams and his fellow lawyers voice complaint. Not they but Parliament, they felt, swerved from the law. Thus, not from the writings of philosophers did they read the Revolution, but right from their law books.

During the eighteenth century a variation had developed between the stream of English and colonial legal theory. This divergence became the fulcrum of the revolutionary debate. The Revolution of 1688 had marked a profound change in the English constitution—Parliamentary sovereignty after that date replaced royal sovereignty. Only a residue of royal prerogative remained. The eighteenth century, then, was a period in England of rapid expansion of Parliamentary sovereignty.

In the Colonies, meantime, developments had taken a parallel turn. The power of the assemblies throughout the colonial period —and quite swiftly in the eighteenth century—had been eroding the Crown prerogative of the governors. At the same time, however, the theory of Parliament's absolute power had never made its way into the thinking of colonial lawyers, who still took their theories from Coke's polity of the seventeenth century. Coke's *Second Institute*, the commentary on Magna Carta, fixed in the minds of colonial lawyers their views on the nature of English law. Due process of law, which was synonymous with the law of the land as Coke defined it, was no mere method of procedure; it constituted the principles of justice underlying the whole body of prescriptive rights. Law was reason, not of one man nor of a group of men living at one time, but of successions of men, the collective reason of generations of men in history. Hence in the law and customs of England, which embodied what men had assumed to be right and just since time immemorial, was to be found the perfection of reason. Law was right reason, correct reason. Or, to put it another way, the common law meant the common right of the subjects. The common law was "the best and most common birthright that the subject hath for the safeguard and defense, not only of his goods, lands, and revenues, but of his wife and children, his body, fame, and life also."[19] Common law meant right. Thus, for Coke, the law of the land meant what was both reasonable and right. It could be neither unreasonable nor immoral.

Specifically, the common law could be found in ancient statutes (the most important of which was Magna Carta), in original writs, in judicial records and in the yearbooks. Coke's commentary on Magna Carta set down the interpretation that centuries of lawyers would follow regarding ancient English rights. Particularly did Coke immortalize Chapters 39 and 40 of Magna Carta, according to which no man may be imprisoned, outlawed, banished, destroyed or condemned but by law of the land, and according to which no man may be sold, denied or delayed justice or right. Upon each of these points Coke commented, granting to them the widest interpretation of liberty, declaring liberty, in fact, to be of three types: the laws of the realm, the freedoms that English subjects have, and finally, the franchises and privileges granted by the King to his subjects or claimed by them by prescription. Magna Carta set forth the rights of Englishmen; Coke interpreted them for posterity in his *Second Institute*. This law of the land was also reemphasized, of course, in other famous statutes, such as the Confirmation of Charters of Edward I, the Petition of Right of 1627 and the Bill of Rights of 1688. In addition to these documents used so heavily by colonial lawyers before the Revolution, there were the reports containing hundreds of cases, including three famous ones—*Dr. Bonham's Case*, 1610; *Day* v. *Savadge*, 1615; and *City of London* v. *Wood*, 1701, in each of which an Act of Parliament was adjudged void because in contravention of the fundamental law of the land.

To be sure, then, Adams and his fellow lawyers justly inherited the idea of a law of the land. Here was not an abstract idea, but a body of concrete rights of Englishmen that could be protected through the courts. Moreover, these lawyers duly inherited the idea that law contrary to the law of the land is void. For that reason they had a legal and not merely philosophical basis for opposing the legislation that Parliament enacted after 1763. Thus it was logical that between law as interpreted by the British ministry and law as interpreted by Adams and the colonial lawyers there would be wide cleavage. The ministry insisted that since 1688 Parliament had been sovereign; but colonial lawyers trained in common law clung to the belief that Parliament was not sovereign, that it was subordinate to a fundamental law of the land, and that any contravening act of Parliament was null and void.

Furthermore, although the theory of natural rights of man was highly popular in both Europe and America in the eighteenth century, colonial lawyers did not rely upon it until the Revolution was upon them. Instead, they argued from the rights of Englishmen. They began to cite the rights of man as their authority only when they began to conclude that, unless they obtained redress of their grievances, they would have to defy the King as well as Parliament. But even so, it is important to note that the rights of Englishmen and the rights of man coincided. The colonial lawyers may have altered their terminology; yet there was always an historical foundation for the rights they declared. Adams, then, might argue from the rights of Englishmen in the Stamp Act debate, from natural rights in the *Novanglus* papers; nonetheless, the rights of which he spoke were in both cases the same ones that Englishmen had always proclaimed.

It is a necessary conclusion, first, that Adams and the colonial lawyers were not radical revolutionaries attempting to upset the social order; they were merely reading the law in the only way they knew. Second, when Adams argued on the active political level he would see the problem as one of imperial control balanced against colonial self-government. When he argued on the theoretical and legal level, he would see it as two opposing views of the nature of law and of the British constitution. What the problem did indeed amount to—as Adams expounded in *Novanglus*—was a severe disagreement on the nature of the British constitution and empire. Politically and legally he and his fellow colonists reached an identical position regarding their place in the empire: that Parliament had no authority to tax them, either internally or externally; and then, when Britain pushed them too far, that Parliament had no control over them in any case; and, finally, when the King—their last resource—failed to come to their aid, that they must declare their independence even of him.

The year 1765 bristled with excitement in Massachusetts and in the life of John Adams. For Adams it meant his election as surveyor of highways in Braintree; the birth of his first child, Nabby; publication of his longest political essay to date; and, of course, the Stamp Act. The year commenced quietly but auspiciously; when Adams arrived in Boston for the January term of court, Samuel Fitch approached him with the news that he and Jeremiah Gridley had something to communicate to him "in sacred confidence." Adams hastened to Gridley's office, "after many conjectures what the secret might be." There the old gentleman told him that he and Fitch had been thinking of forming a law club, "a private association for the study of law and oratory." Gridley was concerned for the honor and dignity of the bar after the older lights should die. To that end, "he was very desirous of forming a junto, a small sodality," of himself, Fitch, Adams and Joseph Dudley, "in order to read in concert the feudal law and Tully's orations."[20] Zestful debate being the delight of his life, Adams entered into the sodality with enthusiasm. When his turn came to entertain the group, he took them to Blodget's, where "we were never in better spirits or more social."[21] But despite the fact that the group planned, after they had finished the feudal law, to read *Coke-Littleton* and then the statutes of one particular reign, it seems that the sodality dissolved. After the first few months of 1765 Adams mentioned it no more. During the time that the sodality met, however, Adams had mulled over his thoughts and produced a *Dissertation on the Canon and Feudal Law*. The *Boston Gazette* published the essay in August.[22] Five years later Adams would be somewhat embarrassed by his youthful piece, all the more because some had thought it to be the work of Gridley. Indeed, it is easy to see why Adams in later years spoke a little apologetically of the work. To a modern reader the *Dissertation* appears naively brash, a headlong harangue full of some non-sensical history. After all, even the staunchest anti-papist of the eighteenth century—and all good New Englanders were anti-papist—would have been hard-pressed to prove that the alliance between the "Romish clergy" and the feudal lords, between ecclesiastical and civil tyranny, held people in ignorance and darkness until the Reformation broke the confederation. That is exactly what Adams in the *Dissertation* tried to do. But a fellow thirty years old is still deadly earnest, delighting to thrill the company with his thesis—and a definitive one at that—of history. And in the case of Adams it is possible to chuckle at his intemperate outbursts, realizing that he sometimes slipped in his most difficult task of keeping himself in tow, and to go on to appreciate his characteristic utterances on liberty and tyranny.

Already Adams was stating some favorite themes—that men are motivated by love of power, a trait that may be confined to useful purposes or allowed to go wildly astray; that men have rights "antecedent to all earthly government—*rights* that cannot be repealed or restrained by human laws—*rights* derived from the great Legislator of the universe." He was already elucidating the first principles of balanced government, that "popular powers must be placed as a guard, a control, a balance, to the powers of the monarch and the priest in every government." He was already setting forth his favorite ideas that knowledge of human nature derives from observation of history and personal experience; that knowledge dispels tyranny and preserves liberty; that people, because their Creator has given them reason and a desire to know, have a right "from the frame of their nature" to knowledge. Especially do they have a right to "that most dreaded and envied kind of knowledge . . . of the characters and conduct of their rulers." Rulers, after all, Adams wrote in a statement showing his debt to Locke, "are no more than attorneys, agents and trustees for the people; and if the cause, the interest and trust is insidiously betrayed or wantonly trifled away, the people have a right to revoke the authority that they themselves have deputed and to constitute abler and better agents, attorneys and trustees."

In addition to his theoretical exposition, Adams, no doubt motivated by the American Act and by the Stamp Act that had been passed in March, tackled some problems of practical politics. The true source of the sufferings of the colonists, he said, had been their timidity.

"We have been afraid to think. We have felt a reluctance to examine into the grounds of our privileges and the extent in which we have an indisputable right to demand them against all the power and authority on earth." Meanwhile, Crown officials had taken advantage of this disposition of the people, prevailing upon them "to consent to many things which were grossly injurious to us and to surrender many others, with voluntary tameness, to which we had the clearest right." Crown officials had managed to persuade Americans that the word *rights* was an offensive expression; that it was the filial duty of Americans to obey their mother, Britain. But, questioned Adams, must the children do nothing when the mother turns a deaf ear to their cries? Let Americans not assume that the mother had grown deaf; let them, instead, presume "what is in fact true, that the spirit of liberty is as ardent as ever among the body of the nation, though a few individuals may be corrupted."

And, at the same time, let Americans cherish the means of knowledge. Let them examine the roots of their liberties. "Let them all become attentive to the grounds and principles of government, ecclesiastical and civil. Let us study the law of nature; search into the spirit of the British constitution; read the histories of ancient ages; contemplate the great examples of Greece and Rome; set before us the conduct of our own British ancestors, who have defended for us the inherent rights of mankind against foreign and domestic tyrants and usurpers, against arbitrary kings and cruel priests, in short, against the gates of earth and hell."

The pulpit should resound with doctrines of religious liberty, with sentiments on the dangers of ignorance, extreme poverty and dependence. Further, it was the task of the bar to proclaim the laws, rights and plan of power delivered from antiquity. It was the task of the bar to declare "that British liberties are not the grants of princes or parliaments but original rights, conditions of original contracts, co-equal with prerogative and coeval with government; that many of our rights are inherent and essential, agreed on as maxims, and established as preliminaries even before a parliament existed." Demonstrating that by the law of nature he meant no unrelated scheme of abstract thought but the law of human nature, Adams held that the true foundation of British laws and government is in "the frame of human nature, in the constitution of the intellectual and moral world." Truth, liberty, justice and benevolence are present in human nature. Hence, government must coincide with these elements or "the superstructure is overthrown of course."

A formal design, Adams protested, seemed to be present in Britain to enslave America, the first step of which seemed to be the introduction of the canon and feudal law into America. The very Stamp Act itself aimed to reduce men to feudal dependence, to "strip us in a great measure of the means of knowledge by loading the press, the colleges, and even an almanac and newspaper with restraints and duties; and to introduce the inequalities and dependencies of the feudal system by taking from the poorer sort of people all their little subsistence and conferring it on a set of stamp officers, distributors and their deputies." At that point Adams ended his argument.

It may be that in some respects the *Dissertation* was a piece of awkward, ill-reasoned juvenilia. Yet it served as a groundbreaking for Adams' efforts in political thought, a jumping-off place for his pre-Revolutionary writings. And, moreover, in the *Dissertation* there was adequate evidence of a mind emerging powerful and perceptive, a mind that already had a python's grasp on principles, a mind that would evolve into middle and old age more convinced but little changed in its main outlines. Belief in a law of human nature derived from history and personal experience, concern for excellence and virtue, insistence on a check upon arbitrary power —they were all present in the *Dissertation* and would remain with Adams throughout life.

CHAPTER V

PREPARING THE CASE

By the summer of 1765 America had received news of the Stamp Act. Enraged over this measure that levied the first tax of any kind other than customs duties, the Colonies resisted with a unity of spirit they had never before displayed. The issue of taxation touched not only importers and merchants but every colonist, burdening him with a definitely heavy tax, payable only in sterling. The tax covered nearly every kind of paper—legal documents, licenses, diplomas, warrants, deeds, newspapers, playing cards, almanacs. What was more, every item covered under the act had to be printed on paper sold by official stamp distributors, embossed with their stamp, or taken to a stamp office to be stamped and the duty paid. The act was to go into effect on the first of November. Violators would be tried in the admiralty courts.

What occurred in Massachusetts was typical of the Colonies' reaction to the act. Bostonians had caught wind of a report that Andrew Oliver, secretary of the province, had been appointed stamp distributor. They formed a mob on August 14 and hanged him in effigy and moved on in the afternoon to Province House to shout at Governor Bernard and his council. Then they marched to the dock on Kilby Street where they burned Oliver's building, built a huge bonfire on Fort Hill from the remains of the building, and burned the effigy. In the evening they ransacked Oliver's elaborate town house and garden and tossed brickbats at Lieutenant Governor Hutchinson, who had come with a sheriff to stop the activity.

The following day Adams wrote in his diary of the severe dishonor the mob had done to Oliver. Nevertheless, he wrote, "Let us ask a few questions." Would it not be prudent on the part of Oliver, Hutchinson and their friends, consistent with their dignity and station, "to remove these jealousies from the minds of the people by giving an easy solution of these difficulties?"[1]

In September, impelled by the Stamp Act, Adams made his formal entry into political life. As a member of a town committee he drafted the *Braintree Instructions* to Ebenezer Thayer, representative of the town to the General Court.[2] The *Boston Gazette* printed the letter on October 14. The nut of Adams' argument was that the Stamp Act, because it violated the rights of Englishmen as revealed in the constitution and the common law, most particularly in Magna Carta, was contrary to the constitution and therefore void. Three grievances most affected the colonists.

First of all, even if it were properly based in authority, the tax was so high that it would be objectionable. But "considering the present scarcity of money, we have reason to think the execution of that act for a short space of time would drain the country of its cash, strip multitudes of all their property, and reduce them to absolute beggary."

In the second place, the tax was unconstitutional. It was a maxim of the law that no freeman "should be subject to any tax to which he has not given his own consent, in person or by proxy." For that reason, it was inconsistent with the spirit of the common law and the essential principles of the British constitution that the colonists should be taxed by Parliament. They were not represented; they could not be taxed. The argument that the Colonies were virtually represented in Parliament—that their interests were represented— could hardly be constitutionally sound.

"We take it clearly, therefore," Adams wrote, "to be inconsistent with the spirit of the common law and of the essential fundamental principles of the British constitution that we should be subject to any tax imposed by the British Parliament; because we are not represented in that assembly in any sense, unless it be by a fiction of law, as insensible in theory as it would be injurious in practice, if such a taxation should be grounded on it."

In the third place, as a lawyer, Adams was shocked by "the most grievous innovation of all . . . the alarming extension of the power of courts of admiralty." In those courts one judge presided alone; no jury had any concern there. "The law and the fact," Adams objected, "are both to be decided by the same single judge," who held his office during pleasure of the King rather than during good behavior. In addition, that judge took a commission on all appropriations of smuggled goods. This put him "under a pecuniary temptation always against the subject." The colonists had all along thought trial in admiralty courts for violations of acts of trade had been a grievance. Yet the Stamp Act had "opened a vast number of sources of new crimes," all of which were "to be tried by such a judge of such a court!" A weak or wicked man upon the bench could "render us the most sordid and forlorn of slaves . . . the slaves of a slave of the servants of a minister of state." Hence, the Stamp Act would make an essential change in the concept of the jury, causing it to be contrary to the Great Charter itself, "for by that charter 'no amercement shall be assessed, but by the oath of honest and lawful men of the vicinage' and 'no freeman shall be taken, or imprisoned, or disseized of his freehold, or liberties of free customs, nor passed upon, nor condemned, but by lawful judgment of his peers, or by the law of the land.' "

Such being the sentiments upon the Stamp Act of the people of Braintree, their representative to the General Court was enjoined "to comply with no measures or proposals for countenancing the same, or assisting in the execution of it, but by all lawful means consistent with our allegiance to the King and relation to Great Britain to oppose the execution of it till we can hear the success of the cries and petitions of America for relief." Already Adams was speaking of allegiance to the King apart from allegiance to Parliament.

The town further recommended "the most clear and explicit

assertion and vindication of our rights and liberties to be entered on the public records, that the world may know, in the present and all future generations, that we have a clear knowledge and a just sense of them, and, with submission to Divine Providence, that we never can be slaves."

Finally, the town could not "agree to any steps for the protection of stamped papers or stamp officers." There were already "good and wholesome laws" for the preservation of peace; the Braintree populace had an aversion to tumult and disorder; but efforts to protect the stamp officers would merely "exasperate the people and endanger the public tranquillity." The representative should remember that "the public money of this country is the toil and labor of the people, who are under many uncommon difficulties and distresses at this time, so that all reasonable frugality ought to be observed." To that end, the town would recommend particularly "the strictest care and the utmost firmness to prevent all unconstitutional draughts upon the public treasury."

Adams took time to ponder the meaning of the Stamp Act that had thrust him into political life and brought every colony to a resounding angry rejection of Parliament's right to tax Americans. One day during that troubled December of 1765, he meditated upon the point to which history had taken him and his fellows. What righteous furor had stirred the continent! The colonists had even sent delegates to a Stamp Act Congress that had met in October in New York. Why had he not kept a regular journal through the exciting months of this year, he asked himself.

"The year 1765 has been the most remarkable year of my life," he mused.[3] "That enormous engine, fabricated by the British Parliament for battering down all the rights and liberties of America, I mean the Stamp Act, has raised and spread through the whole continent a spirit that will be recorded to our honor with all future generations." In every colony the stamp distributors and inspectors had been forced to renounce their offices. "Such and so universal has been the resentment of the people that every man who has dared to speak in favor of the stamps," no matter how great his virtues or his fortune, "has been seen to sink into universal contempt and ignominy." Even to the lowest ranks the people had taken *liberties* as their watchword, "more inquisitive about them and more determined to defend them than they were ever before known or had occasion to be." In the course of the year, pamphleteers had gone to work, "our presses have groaned, our pulpits have thundered, our legislatures have resolved, our towns have voted. The Crown officers have everywhere trembled, and all their little tools and creatures been afraid to speak and ashamed to be seen." But, all the same, popular opposition had not been enough to persuade the timid men in authority to conduct public business without stamped paper. Business had slowed to a standstill; writs could not be issued, and the courts were closed. There was no reason, Adams felt, why the courts should be closed—after all, the act had not even been proclaimed nor anyone's commission delivered. Still, people in authority remained irresolute. "The executive courts," Adams said,

> have not yet dared to adjudge the Stamp Act void nor to proceed with business as usual, though it should seem that necessity alone would be sufficient to justify business at present, though the act should be allowed to be obligatory. The stamps are in the castle. Mr. Oliver has no commission. The Governor has no authority to distribute, or even to unpack the bales; the act has never been proclaimed nor read in the province; yet the probate office is shut, the Custom House is shut, the courts of justice are shut, and all business seems at a stand. Yesterday and the day before, the two last days of service for January term, only one man asked me for a writ, and he was soon determined to waive his request. I have not drawn a writ since first November.

The halt in business could not last much longer. This passive acceptance of the act seemed to Adams a silent assent to Parliament's authority to levy taxes:

> How long we are to remain in this languid condition, this passive obedience to the Stamp Act, is not certain. But such a pause cannot be lasting. Debtors grow insolent. Creditors grow angry. And it is to be expected that the public offices will very soon be forced open

unless such favorable accounts should be received from England as to draw away the fears of the great, or unless a greater dread of the multitude should drive away the fear of censure from Great Britain. It is my opinion that by this timorous inactivity we discover cowardice and too much respect and regard to the act. This rest appears to be by implication, at least, an acknowledgment of the authority of Parliament to tax us. And if this authority is once acknowledged and established, the ruin of America will become inevitable.

Meanwhile, the state of business struck a hard blow to Adams' pocketbook and career. "This long interval of indolence and idleness will make a large chasm in my affairs if it should not reduce me to distress and incapacitate me to answer the demands upon me." However, he would use the winter to good advantage in devoting his time to study. He could not understand what had come over the members of the bar; they seemed to be struck dumb:

The bar seems to me to behave like a flock of shot pigeons. They seem to be stopped; the net seems to be thrown over them, and they have scarcely courage left to flounce and to flutter. So sudden an interruption in my career is very unfortunate for me. I was but just getting into my gears, just getting under sail, and an embargo is laid upon the ship. Thirty years of my life are passed in preparation for business. I have had poverty to struggle with—envy and jealousy and malice of enemies to encounter—no friends, or but few to assist me, so that I have groped in dark obscurity till of late, and had but just become known and gained a small degree of reputation when this execrable project was set on foot for my ruin as well as that of America in general and of Great Britain.

Yet Adams need not have been so forlorn. Only the next day, December 19, a Mr. Clark, one of the constables of Boston, came with a letter from William Cooper, town clerk, informing Adams that the town of Boston had voted unanimously to name him, Gridley and Otis as counsel to appear before the governor and council with a memorial from the town pleading for reopening of the courts without stamped paper. His *Braintree Instructions* had apparently impressed the people of Boston with its patriotism and logic.

Now, Adams wrote, "I am . . . under all obligations of interest and ambition as well as honor, gratitude and duty, to exert the utmost of my abilities in this important cause. How shall it be conducted? Shall we contend that the Stamp Act is void? That the Parliament have no legal authority to impose internal taxes upon us? Because we are not represented in it? And therefore that the Stamp Act ought to be waived by the judges as against natural equity and the constitution? Shall we use these as arguments for opening the courts of law? Or shall we ground ourselves on necessity only?"[4]

When he went to Boston the next day he sat in the Town House until after the candles had been lit, discussing the issue with his cousin Sam Adams and other members of the committee chosen by the town to present the memorial. While the gentlemen sat talking, a message came from Governor Bernard, announcing that he and the council were ready to hear the case. Adams and the company went upstairs to the council chamber, where the governor instructed them that in order to avoid repetition, they should divide the topics of argument among them. Gridley answered that he would speak last. Otis said he would speak second. To his consternation, Adams was left to open the argument; it fell upon him "without one moment's opportunity to consult any authorities, to open an argument upon a question that was never made before, and I wish I could hope it never would be made again, that is, whether the courts of law should be open or not."[5] There was nothing to do but to begin, and so he grounded his argument on the invalidity of the Stamp Act because the colonists had never assented to it. To put additional weight into his position he argued, first, the necessity of preventing a failure of justice and, second, the impossibility of carrying the act into execution. Otis chose to speak upon the judges' oaths requiring them to administer justice. Gridley finished with an argument that the interruption of justice caused great inconvenience.

The governor gave them a vague and unsatisfactory answer. The question was a judicial one, he said, not to be decided by him and his council, for the judges, being independent of the Crown, would never receive directions from the Crown upon a point of law. But he hoped that the Inferior Court judges would decide the question as soon as possible.[6]

Bernard's answer distressed Adams. What were the consequences of the courts being shut? The whole situation meant a denial and delaying of justice, abrogation of Magna Carta itself. The King was the fountain of justice; and it was a maxim of the law that the King never dies. Justice could never cease. Moreover, were not protection by the King of his subjects and allegiance by them to him reciprocal? If subjects were no longer under the King's protection, were they not also released from obligations to obey him? Would not all the ligaments of government then be dissolved? Was it not an abdication by the King of his throne?

"In short," lamented Adams, "where will such an horrid doctrine terminate? It would run us into treason!"[7]

On Christmas he scarcely felt like celebrating. He spent the evening at home with Abigail, "thinking, reading, searching, concerning taxation without consent, concerning the great pause and rest in business." By the laws of England justice flowed in an uninterrupted stream. "In that music the law knows of neither rests nor pauses. Nothing but violence, invasion or rebellion can obstruct the river or untune the instrument."[8] Nonetheless, as the old year went out, he gathered optimism that Britain would relieve the Colonies of the injustices of the Stamp Act. The year 1765 had been "a year in which America has shown such magnanimity and spirit as never before appeared in any country. . . ." He only hoped that the new year would "procure us innumerable testimonies from Europe in our favor and applause, and which we all hope will produce the greatest and most extensive joy ever felt in America, on the repeal both of the Stamp Act and the Sugar Act, at least of the former."[9]

In mid-January, 1766, the Inferior Court bowed to popular pressures to open its doors—without stamped paper. Although the Superior Court later opened formally, it did little business until after repeal of the Stamp Act.

In January, as well, Adams put some more of his thoughts before the public when the *Boston Gazette* published three of his "Claren-

don" letters. The *Boston Evening Post* on November 25, 1765, had
reprinted an article signed "Pym" that had run in the *London
Evening Post,* declaring that the British Parliament had power even
to set aside colonial charters, should it desire to do so. "Pym" was
answered by James Otis in several articles signed "Hampden" and
by Adams in letters signed "Clarendon." Clarendon had been a
man who had tried to keep the Revolution of 1640 from running
rampant and who helped restore Charles II to the throne. Perhaps
Adams chose the title to demonstrate that he was not a radical. At
any rate, as Clarendon he declaimed upon the British constitution
some characteristically Adamsean phrases as natural to him at
thirty as they would be at forty.

Government was "a frame, a scheme, a system, a combination of
powers for a certain end, namely, the good of the whole community."[10] The public good, the *salus populi*, in the case of the
British constitution was none other than liberty. Here lay the difference between the British constitution and other forms of government; liberty was "its end, its use, its designation, drift, and scope,
as much as grinding corn is the use of a mill, the transportation of
burdens the end of a ship, the mensuration of time the scope of a
watch, or life and health the designation of the human body."
Moreover, because liberty was the public good, it was intended for
all; even the lowliest figure was entitled to liberty, as much liberty
as possible without endangering the liberty of another.

"All men are born equal; and the drift of the British constitution
is to preserve as much of this equality as is compatible with the
people's security against foreign invasions and domestic usurpation." Adams then defined the British constitution, which had as its
aim the preservation of liberty. In a statement that showed he had
read Harrington and other advocates of mixed government, he
described the constitution as a "limited monarchy," a mixture of
the three forms of monarchy, aristocracy and democracy, a mixture
retaining "as much of the monarchical splendor, the aristocratical
independency, and the democratical freedom as are necessary that
each of these powers may have a control, both in legislation and
execution, over the other two, for the preservation of the subject's
liberty."

Constitutional power was divided, then, into those of legislation and those of execution. (The judicial power that we think of today was then considered as part of the executive; it meant the execution of justice through the courts.) Essential parts of the legislative power were King, Lords, Commons and people. The people exercised legislative power through representation in Commons, a means by which they exerted a popular check upon King, Lords and Commons.

Under the executive power of the constitution, the King was supreme executor. Either he or his judges distributed justice to the people. But even here there was a popular check upon power. In the law courts, questions of law were decided by judges and questions of fact were decided by juries. The jurors provided a check upon the executive power. Hence, through voting for members of Commons and through trials by juries there were popular checks upon both legislative and executive power, checks fundamental to the preservation of a mixed and balanced government. Indeed, a mixed and balanced government was the keynote of Adams' theory of politics.

Rumors flew throughout January of 1766 that Stamp Act repeal was imminent. Grenville's ministry had fallen the previous July; because the act could never be enforced, the Marquess of Rockingham and his Old Whig ministry were known to favor repeal. On the evening of January 15 Adams was invited by the Sons of Liberty to spend the evening with them in their tiny room in Chase and Speakman's Distillery on Hanover Square, near the Liberty Tree. This tight little club of true radicals fascinated Adams. Of every middle-class occupation, these men came as close to being professional rabble-rousers as anyone in the Colonies. Adams made mental notes on John Avery, distiller and merchant, "of a liberal education"; on John Smith the brazier; Thomas Crafts the painter; Edes the printer; Stephen Cleverly the brazier; Chase the distiller; Joseph Field, master of a vessel; George Trott the jeweler, as they cordially served him punch, wine, pipes and tobacco, biscuits and cheese. Rather to his relief Adams "heard nothing but such conversation as passes at all clubs among gentlemen about the times. No plots, no machinations." The men simply chose a committee to make preparations for great hullabaloo and rejoicing when news of repeal should come. Illuminations, bonfires, pyramids, obelisks, exhibitions, fireworks—all were to herald the good news.

"I wish," said Adams, "they mayn't be disappointed."[11]

They were not. Dr. Cotton Tufts, Abigail's uncle, stopped by to lodge with the Adamses on Friday, March 28, bringing with him a newspaper full of William Pitt's speech to Commons urging repeal of the Stamp Act. Impolitic, arbitrary, oppressive, unconstitutional, Pitt had claimed. Taking up the American hue and cry, he denied that the Colonies were represented in Parliament and denied that they could be taxed.

"What shall we think of Mr. Pitt?" Adams wondered. "What shall we call him? The genius and guardian angel of Britain and British America? Or what?" Would it be possible for Grenville, offensive to his King and to the people, to prevail against the new ministry and Pitt?[12]

By the end of April the newspapers were full of reports that Parliament was repealing the Stamp Act, yet at the same time was passing several troubling resolves that would lead to the Declaratory Act. Joyful though he was over repeal of the Stamp Act, Adams could not share his neighbors' indifference to these disconcerting additional reminders of Parliamentary authority. Willing to give up the Stamp Act, Commons had strangely thought it necessary in these resolves to assert baldly that Parliament had power to legislate for the Colonies in any case whatsoever. So jubilant were they over repeal of the despised tax that Americans seemed willing enough to overlook the proclamations. Adams, on the other hand, saw pernicious handwriting in the resolves, the first of which maintained that King, Lords and Commons had an undoubted right to make laws for the Colonies in all cases.

"I am solicitous to know," Adams could but wonder, "whether they will lay a tax in consequence of that resolution, or what kind of law they will make." Would Parliament now impose a tax even more baleful than the stamp tax? Just what implication would be drawn from the statement that King, Lords and Commons "in Parliament assembled had, hath, and of right ought to have, full power and authority to make laws and statutes of sufficient force and validity to bind the Colonies and people of America, subjects of the Crown of Great Britain, in all cases whatever?" Adams was at a loss about the political future of the Colonies. If Pitt were in office he might predict more surely; but what the Rockingham ministry would do he had no idea.[13]

News that the Stamp Act had definitely been repealed arrived in Boston on May 19. With Abigail and Nabby ill with the whooping cough, Adams' plans to take his wife to Boston to view the celebrations were thwarted. But he at least saw the festivities at Hingham, where people rang bells, fired cannon, beat drums, and "Landlady Cushing . . . illuminated her house." In addition to repeal, Adams could take further satisfaction in considering that in the Stamp Act battle between the two political parties—one supporting Crown officials, the other opposing the action of Parliament—the patriot party in most counties had come out victorious. Plymouth County had made a "thorough purgation" of its pro-British representatives to the General Court—"what a change!"[14]

Once the Stamp Act had been repealed, however, the Colonies, despite the Declaratory Act, re-wrapped themselves in their cocoon and went cheerfully on about their business. They had been roused to fury, but so sluggish was their revolutionary spirit that when the immediate thorn was removed, they were satisfied, choosing even to overlook Parliament's brazen move to get the last word. Adams in November of 1766 noted a general quietude in his neighbors, who were "in a state of peace, order and tranquillity . . . as quiet and submissive to government as any people under the sun —as little inclined to tumults, riots, seditions, as they were ever known to be since the first foundation of the government." Repeal had "hushed into silence almost every popular clamor and composed every wave of popular disorder into a smooth and peaceful calm."[15] Americans had been made further content by the fact that when the Rockingham ministry had fallen in July, 1766, William Pitt, now Earl of Chatham, was the man whom George III had called to form a government. Colonial interests suffered a blow, however, in the illness of Pitt that shortly followed. At the end of 1767 the Duke of Grafton succeeded Pitt, proving himself a genial fellow but scarcely a leader. It was this unfortunate circumstance that enabled Charles Townshend, vain and pompous Chancellor of the Exchequer, to put through his hated Townshend Act in June of 1767.

The British ministry had misunderstood the American argument; it had been led to believe that Americans differentiated between external and internal taxes, that they would accept customs duties for several purposes but would tolerate no internal taxes such as the stamp tax. Yet Americans had asserted no such argument. True, in 1767 they still conceded to Parliament the right to regulate trade; to that end Parliament had authority to levy customs duties. Even so, when the purpose was to raise revenue, Americans objected just as strongly to external as to internal taxes. Trade regulation through the external tax of customs duties was one thing; but revenue collection through the external tax of higher customs duties was quite another. The fact was that Americans simply did not distinguish between external and internal taxes as the British supposed they did. Taxes were taxes, not to be levied without consent. Consequently the Townshend duties would not receive the tolerant reception in the Colonies that the British ministry anticipated. Paper, paint, glass, tea were among the English items to be subject to heavy duties when imported by the Colonies. However, that was not all.

The administrative overhauling that accompanied the Townshend duties was an even deeper source of grievance to Americans. An American Board of Customs Commissioners, whose headquarters would be at Boston, would invigorate the old customs system; these new customs commissioners would have full power to utilize writs of assistance and to enforce collection of duties. In addition, the Townshend Act bestowed more authority upon the juryless admiralty courts. Finally, part of the revenue raised from the Townshend duties would go into a fund to provide salaries for royal governors and judges, to be used in case colonial assemblies should cut back the royal salaries or refuse them altogether. Naturally, the issue of Crown-granted salaries would prove a serious matter of contention.

Charles Townshend died in September, 1767, and was succeeded as Chancellor of the Exchequer by Lord North, member of the "King's Friends" faction. But Townshend was remembered in infamy by Americans, who hated his name and his act, greeting his duties with boycotts and non-importation agreements.

At the beginning of the next year, Adams, convinced that he was leading "a rambling, roving, vagrant, vagabond life,"[16] moved with his family to a house in Brattle Square, Boston. They arrived amidst a flurry of opposition to the Townshend duties. Sam Adams and James Otis had put together a circular letter denouncing the Townshend Act as unconstitutional, which they persuaded the Massachusetts Assembly to adopt to be sent to all other colonial assemblies. The letter called for united and dutiful supplications to the King to undo the harm caused by the Townshend Act. Lord Hillsborough, colonial secretary, viewed the circular letter with some alarm, instructing the General Court to rescind the letter or be dissolved by Governor Bernard. By a vote of 92 to 17 the assembly refused to rescind and was accordingly dissolved by Bernard. The 92 were not forgotten, however, for Paul Revere dedicated to them a silver punch bowl placed in a position of honor in the Bunch of Grapes Tavern.

In the meantime, Bernard had requested aid and was answered by the expedition of His Majesty's frigate *Romney* from Halifax to Boston. There the ship lay in Boston Harbor, raising the dander of local inhabitants but boosting the morale of the customs commissioners, who now dared to demonstrate their weight. John Hancock, son of the Braintree minister and nephew of a wealthy Boston merchant, had coupled his inheritance from his uncle with a substantial merchant and shipping income of his own. No man in Boston had been of more financial assistance to the patriot cause. Now the customs commissioners, acting on a trumped-up charge that Hancock's sloop *Liberty* had landed smuggled Madeira wine, had the *Liberty* seized and placed under the guard of the *Romney*, charging Hancock with smuggling. Bostonians would hardly stand for such high-handed activity; they indulged in a little high-handedness of their own, rescuing Hancock and his sloop and sending the commissioners scurrying off to protection at Castle William in the harbor. Governor Bernard, beside himself, asked for troops from Halifax.

Bostonians gathered in Faneuil Hall for a town meeting, but unable to squeeze everyone inside the building, they moved to the Old South Meeting House. Warm with choler and the June heat, they elected Otis moderator. They would request Governor Bernard to reconvene the assembly. And they would instruct the newly elected representatives to the General Court as to their conduct during this crisis. The town named Adams to a committee to draft the instructions to the representatives. As so often had become the case, the instructions were in his words.

To the representatives—Otis, Thomas Cushing, Sam Adams and John Hancock—Adams' committee directed a statement declaring Parliamentary taxation of the Colonies unconstitutional, protesting seizure of the *Liberty*, and requesting that troops not be quartered in the town.[17] After the repeal of the Stamp Act, the town, Adams said, had been pleased over the prospect of a restoration of the unanimity and harmony that had characterized relations between Britain and the Colonies before the detestable act. But, most grievously, "the principle on which that act was founded continues in full force, and a revenue is still demanded from America."

The town of Boston had the mortification of observing that, one after another, acts of Parliament had been passed for the express purpose of raising a revenue from them; that their money was continually collected without their consent by an authority in which they had no share; that the little circulating cash remaining among them must be sent off periodically to a distant country or, what was worse, go to maintain "swarms of officers and pensioners in idleness and luxury, whose example has a tendency to corrupt our morals, and whose arbitrary dispositions will trample on our rights."

Again, however, the town reaffirmed its "loyalty and duty to our most gracious Sovereign" and "a reverence and due subordination to the British Parliament. . . ." It was characteristic of Adams' thinking on the British empire that he added here, "a reverence and due subordination to the British Parliament, *as the supreme legislative in all cases of necessity*, for the preservation of the whole

empire. . . ." He had come to believe that only in cases of necessity
—and by necessity he meant trade regulation—did Parliament have
power as supreme legislative. In other words, it had no authority
to raise revenue from customs duties or any other taxes.

Besides taxation for revenue, the town listed several more recent
grievances. One was the appearance in the harbor of the *Romney*,
whose presence the town felt was designed "to overawe and terrify
the inhabitants of the town into base compliances and unlimited
submission. . . ." Moreover, the *Romney* had taken violent and
illegal possession of "a vessel lying at a wharf . . . without any
probable cause of seizure that we know of. . . ."

In addition, the town was "continually alarmed with rumors and
reports of new revenue acts to be passed, new importations of
officers and pensioners to suck the life-blood of the body politic
while it is streaming from the veins. . . ."

Finally, the town urged its representatives to remember an act of
Parliament of the reign of Anne, forbidding impressment by any
ship-of-war of any mariner unless he had deserted from that ship.
The representatives should remember that impressment directly
violated an act of Parliament. They should also inquire exhaustively
into rumors that more war ships would soon arrive to restrict trade
further, that requisitions had been sent to New York, Halifax and
England for regiments to preserve peace. In that regard, the representatives were free to introduce resolutions that anyone promoting
importation of troops was "an enemy to his town and province and
a disturber of the peace and good order of both."

Adams went on circuit in the fall. He was not present for the
convention that met in Boston. When Governor Bernard had
refused to convene the General Court, the town of Boston had
called a convention of Massachusetts towns to meet in Faneuil Hall
in September. Truly this was an extra-legal convention, but even
then the revolutionary temper of Massachusetts did not run high
enough for the convention to make any treasonable proposals.
After a few days it simply adjourned.

When Adams returned to Boston he found the town swarming
with troops. Throughout the entire fall and winter a Major Small
drilled his regiment in Brattle Square directly in front of Adams'

house, startling the family from bed each dawn with thunderous drum and ear-piercing fife. Even the Sons of Liberty, serenading beneath the windows each evening, could not by their "sweet songs, violins and flutes" completely console the family. But the nightly serenade set Adams to thinking. This was merely one of the small votes of confidence that he had lately received from the people. They apparently regarded him as one of their friends. He determined that they should not be disappointed. And the constant appearance before his door of those soldiers caused him to reflect "that the determination in Great Britain to subjugate us was too deep and inveterate ever to be altered by us; for everything we could do was misrepresented, and nothing we could say was credited."[18]

On the other hand, Adams was no rabble-rouser. Though often solicited he could not bring himself "to go to the town meetings and harangue there." No, he would tell his friend Joseph Warren, "That way madness lies." And considering the derangement into which Otis sometimes sank, perhaps it was so.[19]

It was in Adams' nature, in his Puritan background, in his years of legal and historical study, that he should be equally suspicious of the popular temper as of government. Human nature was human nature, whether in a town meeting or in the House of Commons; it had always had flaws—it always would have. Adams had "read enough in history to be well aware of the errors to which the public opinions of the people were liable in times of great heat and danger, as well as of the extravagances of which the populace of cities were capable, when artfully excited to passion, and even when justly provoked by oppression." He had witnessed some severe legal wrangles in which he had learned enough to prove to himself, "in all their dismal colors, the deceptions to which the people in their passion are liable, and the total suppression of equity and humanity in the human breast when thoroughly heated and hardened by party spirit." In short, he faced a dilemma: how to balance the scales between men's love of power and their quest for liberty. But he could only answer it in one way.

". . . I very deliberately, and indeed very solemnly, determined at all events to adhere to my principles in favor of my native country, which indeed was all the country I knew, or which had been known by my father, grandfather or great-grandfather: but on the other hand I never would deceive the people, conceal from them any essential truth, nor especially make myself subservient to any of their crimes, follies, or eccentricities."[20]

Adams soon had opportunity to put his philosophy to use, for one evening after his return from circuit, Jonathan Sewall, his long-time friend and now attorney general, called upon him saying that he had come to dine.[21] Though the two men were at political antipodes, they had always remained warm friends. After dinner, when Sewall indicated that he wished to speak to Adams privately, Abigail rose and went upstairs. Sewall then announced that he had come with a message from Governor Bernard. The governor had asked Lieutenant Governor Hutchinson and others to name a man of talent, integrity, reputation and consequence at the bar. He had decided that the post of advocate general of the court of admiralty, about to be vacated by Sewall, should be given to Adams. Unexpected as the offer was, Adams was prepared to answer. The office paid well; it would mean more profitable business in the province; it was "a first step in the ladder of royal favor and promotion." Yet Adams for seven years had weighed the subject in his mind, since his friends had often urged him to apply for a commission as justice of the peace. Nevertheless, he had always rejected these proposals, "on account of the unsettled state of the country" and his scruples "about laying myself under any restraints or obligations of gratitude to the government for any of their favors." Furthermore, the Townshend Act had gone into effect, the consequences of which he "could see no end."

He promptly declined Sewall's offer. But why, Sewall asked: What was his objection? Adams answered that "he knew very well my political principles, the system I had adopted and the connections and friendships I had formed in consequence of them; he also knew that the British government, including the King, his ministers and Parliament, apparently supported by a great majority of the nation, were persevering in a system wholly inconsistent with all my ideas of right, justice and policy. . . ."

Adams could not place himself in a position where duty and

inclination "would be so much at variance." The governor was well aware of Adams' political sentiments, Sewall replied; he did not object. Adams would be at full liberty to entertain any opinions he pleased. The governor simply intended to give the office to the man best qualified.

Adams thanked the governor. Even so, he knew the office would put him "under restraints and obligations" to which he could not submit; thus, he "could not in honor or conscience accept it." Sewall paused. What was the matter with his stubborn friend, that he should so jeopardize his career and future advancement? "Why are you so quick and sudden in your determination? You had better take it into consideration and give me an answer at some future day." Again Adams refused. His "mind was clear," his "determination decided and unalterable." Mr. Fitch should be appointed to the office, he suggested, since his views would be agreeable. Well, Sewall declared, he would give Adams more time to think. Little need for that, Adams replied, insisting "that time would produce no change and he had better make his report immediately."

Sewall could not bear to see his friend throw away his opportunity. He was back three weeks later, requesting a change of answer. Adams again declined with equal firmness. His "judgment and inclination and determination were unalterably fixed." He had hoped that Fitch would have been appointed by this time.

During the winter of 1768-1769 Adams tried a case more politically important than any in which he had participated prior to the Boston Massacre Trials. Both politically and legally this was an accomplishment for him: it was his defense of Hancock against charges of smuggling in the *Liberty* episode. The case of *Advocate General Jonathan Sewall* v. *John Hancock* was tried in admiralty court before Judge Robert Auchmuty.[22] Adams spent a discouraging winter in "painful drudgery," going almost every day to court, where "it seemed as if the officers of the Crown were determined to examine the whole town as witnesses. Almost every day a fresh witness was to be examined upon interrogatories." One by one nearly all of Hancock's relatives and friends were brought in as witnesses; the court even contemplated summoning his aged aunt, widow of Thomas Hancock, from whom John Hancock had received his fortune. Adams grew "thoroughly weary and disgusted with the court, the officers of the Crown, the cause, and even with the tyrannical bell that dongled me out of my house every morning. . . ."[23] Nonetheless, he put together an excellent argument that won the case for him, calling upon Coke and Magna Carta to show the injustice of trying Hancock without his English right of jury trial.

Meanwhile, Bostonians continued to view the troops stationed in Boston since the previous autumn as a grim reminder that theirs was an occupied city. They were more than ever alarmed when the main guard was quartered in an unoccupied dwelling across the street from the Courthouse, their small artillery positioned in front of the doorway of the headquarters. Governor Bernard had at last convened the General Court in May, 1769, but what did this weaponry indicate—pointed at the building where the legislature was to sit? Were the representatives to be intimidated, now that they were able to exercise their privilege? At the Boston town meeting that met in May, Adams was named to a committee to draft resolutions upon the quartering of troops in the town and the extension of power of the admiralty courts. Again he wrote the instructions to representatives Otis, Cushing, Hancock and Sam Adams.[24]

First of all, Adams emphasized the privilege of assembly, free from the intimidating presence of nearby troops. The "delegates there must be free," he stated. For that reason, the Boston representatives to the General Court must exert themselves "to remove everything that may carry the least appearance of an attempt to awe or intimidate." Common decency, as well as the "honor and dignity of a free legislative," would "require a removal of those cannon and guards, as well as that clamorous parade which has been daily around the Courthouse since the arrival of His Majesty's troops." Furthermore, the representatives should inquire why troops had been quartered in Boston "in contradiction to the express words, and, as we conceive, the manifest intention of an act of Parliament"; why the officers of these troops had not been called to account; why the "repeated offenses and violences committed by the soldiery against the peace" had gone unnoticed by the courts. Moreover, should the expense of maintaining the troops be handed to the General Court, the town of Boston enjoined its representatives not to comply with any such imposition.

"If the General Court is a free assembly, no power upon earth has authority to compel it to pay this money. Should it ever be deprived of its freedom, it shall never, with our consent, be made an engine to drain us of the little money we have left."

In addition to this grievance of troops stationed in the town, there were several other complaints to be mentioned. First of all, there had recently been a "flagrant and formal attack upon the constitution itself—an attempt not only to deprive us of the liberties, privileges, and immunities of our charter, but the rights of British subjects." Copies had been obtained of Governor Bernard's letters to the home government suggesting changes to be made in colonial government. These letters had "already produced effects alarming to the Colonies. . . ." The representatives should make every effort to erase the ill effects of these letters "before the poison shall have wrought the ruin of the constitution."

Furthermore, it was unnecessary for the town to repeat its sentiments upon the revenue that was demanded from its citizens. These opinions were in no way changed. But next to the revenue, the greatest source of irritation was the late extension of admiralty jurisdiction. The antipathy that Adams felt for admiralty's disregard for the rights of subjects pierced deep into the marrow of his lawyer's bones. These admiralty courts seemed "to be forming by degrees into a system that is to overturn our constitution and to deprive us entirely of our best inheritance, the laws of the land." Adams here began nearly the identical argument that he had expounded in *Sewall* v. *Hancock* concerning a point that he considered a grave breach of American liberties. Whereas cases of forfeitures and penalties in England were tried in the common law courts, Adams pointed out, in the Colonies they were, by the American Act of 1764, prosecuted in the courts of admiralty.

"Thus," Adams declared, "these extraordinary penalties and forfeitures are to be heard and tried, not by a jury, nor by the law of the land, but by the civil law of a single judge! Unlike the ancient barons who answered with one voice, 'We will not that the laws of England be changed, which of old have been used and approved,' the barons of modern times seem to have answered that they are willing those laws should be changed with regard to America in the most tender point and fundamental principle."

There was indeed a contrast between the law as applied in England and America. Within this same American Act there was a distinction made between English and American subjects. On the one hand Parliament guarded the people of the realm in their right to trial by jury and the law of the land, but on the other hand deprived Americans of the same right. Was this distinction not "a brand of disgrace upon every American—a degradation below the rank of an Englishman?" Did it not deny the thirty-ninth chapter of Magna Carta, by which, as Adams translated it, "No freeman shall be taken or imprisoned or disseized of his freehold or liberties or free customs or outlawed or exiled or any otherwise destroyed, nor will we pass upon him nor condemn him, but by lawful judgment of his peers or the law of the land." Englishmen were irrevocably attached to the right expressed in this clause, "which for many centuries has been the noblest monument and firmest bulwark of their liberties."

Just as he had in *Sewall* v. *Hancock*, Adams quoted that "great sage of the law," Lord Coke, who had found a statute of Henry VII "against this ancient and fundamental law" because it had not provided for jury trials in cases of penalties and forfeitures. The statute had been wrong, Coke had said, in allowing that both justices of assize and justices of the peace "without any finding or presentment of twelve men, upon a bare information for the King before them made, should have full power and authority by their discretions to hear and try men for penalties and forfeitures." Coke had likewise condemned the infamous Empson and Dudley, Henry's justices of the peace and masters of forfeitures, who had extorted great sums under this act. Adams quoted Coke as saying: "The ill success of this statute and the fearful end of these two oppressors should deter others from committing the like and should admonish parliaments that instead of this ordinary and precious trial by the law of the land, they bring not in absolute and partial trials by discretion."

"Such," concluded Adams, "are the feelings and reflections of an Englishman upon a statute not unlike the statute now under consideration, and upon courts and judges not unlike the courts and judges of admiralty in America!"

Each group of instructions that came from Adams' pen increased his reputation among members of the patriot cause. People found it natural to rally round a figure who could so well crystallize their sentiments. The Sons of Liberty, 350 in all, invited him in August to attend one of their merrymakings. At Robinson's Tavern in Dorchester, which bore the sign of the Liberty Tree, the Sons celebrated the anniversary of their founding. Some three or four hundred plates were spread upon two tables laid in an open field by the barn, an awning of sailcloth overhead. Philemon Dickinson, brother of John Dickinson, who had written the much-talked-of "Letters of a Pennsylvania Farmer," and Joseph Reed, secretary of New Jersey, both honored the Sons with their presence. After dinner, amid much toasting, a Mr. Balch entertained the company with a mimic rendition of the "Lawyer's Head" and the "Hunting of a Bitch Fox." The company then burst into the Liberty Song, shouting loudly on the chorus.

"This is cultivating the sensations of freedom," Adams said approvingly. "There was a large collection of good company. Otis and [Sam] Adams are politic in promoting these festivals, for they tinge the minds of the people; they impregnate them with the sentiments of liberty. They render the people fond of their leaders in the cause and averse and bitter against all opposers."[25] It was especially "to the honor of the Sons," Adams further commented, that "I did not see one person intoxicated or near it." Quite an accomplishment of self-control, since the men had drunk fourteen toasts at the Boston Liberty Tree beforehand and forty-five at the dinner! The *Boston Gazette* enthusiastically published the details on August 21.[26]

Adams' proficiencies and good name as a lawyer increased together with his political reputation. During the next several years he would acquit himself successfully in several significant cases: *Rex* v. *Corbet*,[27] in 1769, in which he defended Michael Corbet and three other sailors in admiralty court for the murder of Lieutenant Henry Panton of the British Navy; *Otis* v. *Robinson*, 1769-1771, in which as co-counsel he represented James Otis in a suit against John Robinson, a customs commissioner who had injured Otis in a tavern brawl; and *Rex* v. *Nickerson*, 1772-1773,[28] in which he defended Ansell Nickerson in admiralty court against a mysterious murder charge. But, of course, none of these trials was so famous or so important as the Boston Massacre Trials.[29]

On the evening of March 5, 1770, Adams attended his political club at the home of Henderson Inches in South Boston. About nine o'clock the men were alarmed to hear a clamor of bells. Supposing the commotion to be signaling a fire, they grabbed hats and cloaks and rushed outside to assist in quenching the flames. Out in the street they heard shouted reports that British soldiers had fired on some Bostonians near the Town House, killing some and wounding others. Adams and his friends joined the throng running to the scene. But when they arrived they saw nothing but "some field pieces placed before the south door of the Town House and some engineers and grenadiers drawn up to protect them."[30] Adams thought immediately of his wife, in the midst of pregnancy, who was at home in Cole Lane (they had moved from Brattle Square) with only her maids and a boy. And so, seeing that all was quiet around the Town House, Adams turned down Boylston's Alley into Brattle Square. There a company or two of British soldiers were lined up in front of Dr. Samuel Cooper's Brattle Square Church, "muskets all shouldered and their bayonets all fixed." Adams had no way to go but along a narrow path left for foot passengers directly in front of the soldiers; he hastened past them, "without taking the least notice of them or they of me, any more than if they had been marble statues. . . ." Once at home in Cole Lane he found Abigail calm enough, once she had heard that the town was quiet. They could do little that evening in the suspenseful stillness but reflect on the possible conclusions of the skirmish. Adams had seen for many months that "endeavors had been systematically pursued

. . . by certain busy characters to excite quarrels, rencounters and combats, single or compound, in the night between the inhabitants of the lower class and the soldiers and at all risks to enkindle an immortal hatred between them." He suspected that the explosion in front of the Town House, which would become known as the Boston Massacre, "had been intentionally wrought up by designing men who knew what they were aiming at better than the instrument employed." Adams detested any attempt to dishonor the law. Sam Adams and his radical patriots had gone too far in whipping up the sentiments of the crowd—surely they were responsible for the whole sorry mess. The gang which had taunted the soldiers into firing were "poor tools" of the radicals who, if they should be found guilty, would have to be punished. If the soldiers had killed in self-defense, then they deserved to be acquitted. But "to keep the town boiling in a continual fermentation" was dangerous. Moreover, no one knew how the British government or the other Colonies would react to this latest furor in Boston. Perhaps the rest of the Colonies would not support Boston—perhaps not even the rest of New England or the province. All these things Adams meditated upon during the night of March 5.

The following morning, as he sat in his office near the Town House, he was interrupted by an Irish merchant named James Forrest, called by some the "Irish Infant."

Tears streaming down his face, Forrest burst out, "I am come with a very solemn message from a very unfortunate man, Captain Preston, in prison." Preston had been leader of the soldiers in the episode of the day before.

"He wishes for counsel," Forrest exclaimed, "and can get none. I have waited on Mr. [Josiah] Quincy, who says he will engage if you will give him your assistance; without it positively he will not. Even Mr. Auchmuty declines unless you will engage. . . ."

Adams without hesitation answered him "that counsel ought to be the very last thing that an accused person should want in a free country, that the bar ought in my opinion to be independent and impartial at all times and in every circumstance, and that persons whose lives were at stake ought to have the counsel they preferred. . . ."It was part of his notion of law that he owed Captain Preston his counsel; but he sensed the tremendous implications and burdens of what he was about to undertake. Gravely he told Forrest that he should understand that "this would be as important a cause as ever was tried in any court or country of the world. . . ." Because "every lawyer must hold himself responsible not only to his country but to the highest and most infallible of all tribunals"—that is, the divine court of justice—because of that, Forrest could expect from him "no art or address, no sophistry or prevarication in such a cause, nor anything more than fact, evidence and law would justify."

Captain Preston, Forrest replied, expected no more. The captain had heard from all parties "that he could cheerfully trust his life" with Adams "upon those principles." "And," Forrest went on, "as God Almighty is my judge, I believe him an innocent man."

"That must be ascertained by his trial," Adams corrected him, "and if he thinks he cannot have a fair trial of that issue without my assistance, without hesitation he shall have it." At that, Forrest offered Adams a single guinea as a retaining fee. Not making any sign that he might be surprised at such a slim token, Adams readily took it.

"From first to last I never said a word about fees in any of those cases," he wrote years later, "and I should have said nothing about them here, if calumnies and insinuations had not been propagated that I was tempted by great fees and enormous sums of money. Before or after the trial, Preston sent me ten guineas and at the trial of the soldiers afterwards, eight guineas more, which were all the fees I ever received or were offered to me, and I should not have said anything on the subject to my clients if they had never offered me anything. This was all the pecuniary reward I ever had for fourteen or fifteen days labor in the most exhausting and fatiguing causes I ever tried; for hazarding a popularity very general and very hardly earned; and for incurring a clamor and popular suspicions and prejudices which are not yet worn out and never will be forgotten as long as history of this period is read." Adams, in his characteristic fashion of believing that history had treated him harshly and that his country never recognized the labor he performed for its benefit, persisted in declaring that his defense of Preston and the soldiers was done at the highest expense of his public popularity. Experience, he would later write, had always proved to him "that the memory of malice is faithful and, more, it continually adds to its stock, while that of kindness and friendship is not only frail but treacherous. It was immediately bruited abroad that I had engaged for Preston and the soldiers and occasioned a great clamor which the friends of government delighted to hear and slyly and secretly fomented with all their art."

Yet Bostonians could not have thought too poorly of him, for when an election came up in June, 1770, for a Boston representative to the General Court to replace James Bowdoin, who had been chosen a member of the council, the town of Boston elected Adams by a large majority. But, all the same, Adams' decision to take the defense of Preston and the English soldiers could not have been an easy one. It was definitely the unpopular side in the case. In taking it, Adams made a public statement, so to speak, that he was before all else a lawyer, not subject to any flimsy popular attitudes, but determined to preserve at all cost the rights of subjects under the law of the land.

Just what happened in King Street on the evening of March 5 has been so long the theme of legend that it is difficult to extract more than a few facts. The British troops garrisoned in Boston since 1768 had always been an object of animosity of the people of Boston. The events of March 5 climaxed several incidents that had gone before. After a sentry at the Custom House on King Street that evening had braved a good amount of harassment by a cluster of hecklers, he called for help. Captain Thomas Preston, together with six soldiers and a corporal, arrived from the main guard. A riot resulted. The soldiers fired, killing three people instantly, one of whom was the Negro, Crispus Attucks. Two others died later.

Although Sam Adams, Joseph Warren and others strove to take advantage of the high temper of the town by attempting to have the case brought immediately to court, Thomas Hutchinson, now acting governor, succeeded in having the cases put off until autumn.

Hence the case of *Rex* v. *Preston*[31] was brought to trial in the Suffolk Superior Court on October 24, 1770, with Adams, Josiah Quincy and Robert Auchmuty for the defense and Robert Treat Paine and Samuel Quincy for the Crown. (The Quincys were brothers, sons of Colonel Josiah Quincy of Braintree.) The question, that of homicide in self-defense, was decided in favor of Preston. The case of the soldiers, *Rex.* v. *Wemms*,[32] came to trial in Suffolk Court on November 27. The jury acquitted all of the soldiers except Kilroy and Montgomery, whom they convicted of manslaughter. On December 14 these two were asked, as was usual, if they knew of any reason why they should not be sentenced to death for their capital offense. The defendants then pleaded benefit of clergy,* were, according to the ancient custom, branded on the thumb and released.

Adams was satisfied with the outcome of both cases. The authorities had been so clear and full, he said later in his *Autobiography*, "that no question of law was made. The juries in both cases, in my opinion, gave correct verdicts." He had industriously tried to lay before the jury "the law as it stood," hoping that they and the people of Boston "might be fully apprised of the dangers of various kinds which must arise from intemperate heats and irregular commotions. Although the clamor was very loud among some sorts of people, it has been a great consolation to me through life that I acted in this business with steady impartiality and conducted it to so happy an issue."[33]

Adams always protested—and in some measure he was correct —that his part in the Massacre trials subjected him to sarcasm, ridicule and criticism. Nevertheless he always took pride in the fact that he had defended a group of Englishmen in their historic right to a free and fair trial. Moreover, he had seen in the Boston Mas-

*Benefit of clergy was a holdover of English medieval law, a result of the struggle between royal and ecclesiastical jurisdictions. It had provided that no clergyman could be tried in a secular court but, if he could prove his status, he could be tried, instead, in an ecclesiastical court, where punishment was much less severe. In order to prove his clerical status, the clergyman, who in medieval times was almost the only man who was literate, had to read Psalm 51, verse I, the "neck verse."

sacre a threat of mob rule to which Americans must not succumb. Crowds, when whipped to high heat, could go dangerously beyond their own or anyone else's control. If liberty were to be a common possession of all, then law, not throngs, must prevail. Adams would express this view in a letter to Benjamin Hichborn in 1787: "I begin to suspect that some gentlemen who had more zeal than knowledge in the year 1770 will soon discover that I had good policy, as well as sound law, on my side when I ventured to lay open before our people the laws against riots, routs and unlawful assemblies. Mobs will never do to govern states or command armies. I was as sensible of it in 1770 as I am in 1787. To talk of liberty in such a state of things!"[34] Yet, at the same time, Adams further understood that the Massacre was a crucial political event. Were it not for the British government having stationed troops in the city, the episode would not have happened. Americans now refused to put it out of their minds. On the eve of Revolution, in 1774, Adams wrote to James Burgh: "The death of four or five persons, the most obscure and inconsiderable that could have been found upon the continent, on the 5th March, 1770, has never yet been forgiven by any part of America. What, then, would be the consequence of a battle in which many thousands must fall, of the best blood, the best families, fortunes, abilities, and moral characters in the country?"[35]

Adams' argument of the Massacre trials, as well as his session with the General Court, which had been removed to Cambridge upon orders of Hutchinson, had left him tired and unwell. When he had been elected to the General Court in June, 1770, he had taken his position in dismal humor. At the time he had more business at the bar than anyone in the province. He believed that in taking office he "was throwing away as bright prospects as any man ever had . . . ," devoting himself "to endless labor and anxiety, if not to infamy and to death. . . ." And for what? Nothing but a sense of duty. Even Abigail, "that excellent lady who had always encouraged me," could not exhibit her customary cheerfulness over his decision. She only distressed him further by bursting "into a flood of tears." But then she told him that although "she was very sensible of all the danger to her and to our children, as well as to me . . . she thought I had done as I ought; she was very willing to share in all that was to come and place her trust in Providence."[36] However, after a year of struggling through the controversy over removing the assembly to Cambridge and then arguing the Massacre trials, Adams could think only of Braintree. It irritated him to hear anecdotes associating his name with every political wrangle. In November, 1770, for instance, a dispute had come up between Hutchinson and the General Court regarding the words "In General Court assembled and by the authority of the same." This phrase had been used in acts of Parliament and in the provincial laws until the administration of Governor Shirley, when they were struck out. Old Governor Shirley, in retirement at his home in Roxbury, read in the papers that the phrase had been brought out again.

"Who has revived these old words?" he demanded. "They were expressed during my administration."

"The Boston seat," a gentleman answered.

"And who are the Boston seat?"

"Mr. Cushing, Mr. Hancock, Mr. Samuel Adams and Mr. John Adams."

"Mr. Cushing I know and Mr. Hancock I know," snorted the old man, "but where the devil this brace of Adamses came from, I know not."[37]

Adams was weary. He longed for the country—and so he left his place in the General Court and moved his family back home. Even though he still kept an office in Boston, he could enjoy "the air of my native spot . . . the fine breezes from the sea on one side and the rocky mountains of pine and savin on the other, together with daily rides on horseback and the amusements of agriculture. . . ."[38] Now there would be no more trips to Cambridge, no more General Court to attend. Drinking tea with Abigail on a Saturday late in April, 1771, he felt relieved that he could now divide his time "between Boston and Braintree, between law and husbandry."

"Farewell, politics," he resolved.[39]

His family and friends sent him to the fashionable mineral springs at Stafford, Connecticut. But on the way home, he fussed miserably.

"I begin to grow weary of this idle, romantic jaunt. . . . I shall not suddenly take such a ramble again, merely for my health. I want to see my wife, my children, my farm, my horses, oxen, cows, walls, fences, workmen, office, books, and clerks. I want to hear the news and politics of the day. But here I am, at Bissall's in Windsor, hearing my landlord read a chapter in the kitchen and go to prayers with his family, in the genuine tone of a Puritan."[40]

Adams found it expedient, however, to move back to Boston in 1772. He bought a brick house and lot in South Queen Street near his office, to which he moved his family in November. Nonetheless, he was still determined not to re-enter politics. He was now thirty-seven. More than half his life had been spent, he thought; his best years were behind him—yet he had done so little, made so small a mark in the world, accomplished so little for his wife and children.

"What an atom, an animalcule I am! The remainder of my days I shall rather decline in sense, spirit and activity. My season for acquiring knowledge is past. And yet I have my own and my children's fortunes to make. My boyish habits and airs are not yet worn off."[41]

When Samuel Adams and Samuel Pemberton invited him to give the oration for the anniversary of the Boston Massacre on the following March 5, he declined. Though he felt that there was no inconsistency between the theme of the oration and the verdicts of the juries in the Massacre trials, he knew that the world would not understand that there was no difference. By making the oration he would simply expose himself to needless tongue-lashings. Besides, he was "too old to make declamations."[42] Adams had chosen a propitious time to foreswear politics, for, since 1770 when all the Townshend duties but the tax on tea had been repealed, the Colonies had given up non-importation and the continent had been both remarkably prosperous and quiet.

However, events early in the year 1773, the result of circumstances that stemmed from the previous summer, forced Adams back into public life. Thomas Hutchinson, now governor, was a sincere, intelligent and honest man, but he had managed, through his removal of the General Court to Cambridge—in order to protect it from the Boston mob—and through several other moves, to seal the enmity of Bostonians against him. Now, on the sixth of January, 1773, he said in an ill-chosen speech to both houses of the legislature that Parliament was the sovereign legislature of the Colonies, that it had a right to make laws for them in all cases whatsoever, and that it might levy any kind of taxes it might wish. Naturally, the House exploded with fury, appointing Sam Adams, Major Joseph Hawley of Northampton, and others to a committee to answer the speech. The draft that the committee drew up was filled with the specious arguments upon the rights of man and "those democratical principles" that would become so popular among the radicals of the later Revolutionary and Constitution period. Hawley, however, was displeased with the draft. He insisted upon asking Adams for advice. Subsequently, Adams, though not a representative, took a large hand in the debate with Hutchinson. As tactfully as he could, he had the objectionable clauses expunged from the draft, replacing the airy statements with arguments from "the law authorities and . . . legal and constitutional reasonings."[43] To Adams, any argument not founded in legal and historical facts and precedents was as good as no argument at all.

In addition to this dispute, Adams was soon embroiled in a controversy whose subject was close to his heart. That subject was Crown-granted salaries of the Superior Court judges, which was part of the larger question of Crown-granted salaries of both governors and judges. In order that Crown officials might be free of fractious assemblies, the hated Townshend Acts had permitted customs revenue to go toward paying the salaries of governors and judges. Whereas the Townshend duties had been repealed in 1770, this provision for reorganization of administration had not. Thus, in the summer of 1772 Governor Hutchinson had received word from the ministry that he might collect his salary from the royal exchequer. Only too delightedly he had informed the assembly that he no longer needed or would accept a salary from them. Then, on October 30, word had come that the Superior Court judges should also receive their salaries not from the assembly but from the Crown.

Bostonians, who saw these moves for what they were—attempts

to render Crown officials independent of the assembly—had reacted with vigor. In the town meeting of November, 1772, Sam Adams had found them eagerly willing to set up a Committee of Correspondence that would communicate with other Colonies upon these and any following crises. But John Adams left these political machinations to his cousin Sam; he himself was more concerned with the constitutional questions. And perhaps even he would not have become publicly involved in the debate over the judges' salaries had he not been directly challenged by General William Brattle of Cambridge. In December, 1772, the town of Cambridge in its meeting had voted instructions condemning the measure to make Superior Court judges' salaries payable by the Crown rather than by the assembly. Brattle had opposed the instructions, going so far as to challenge Adams by name, among others, to a debate upon the subject. Brattle tried to show in his statement that the judges were appointed for life and so were independent. But Adams saw the heart of the issue: the colonists had never received the privilege that Englishmen of the realm had had all through the eighteenth century—that of seeing their judges truly independent because they were given tenure for good behavior. Tenure of judges in the Colonies was during the pleasure of the Crown; that fact in combination with the new order that they should receive Crown salaries would make them "entirely dependent on the Crown for bread as well as office."[44] The governor possessed an absolute veto on all acts of the General Court; with judges now reliant upon the Crown not only for their commissions but for their salary, there was no assurance that Massachusetts men would receive any kind of justice. Brattle's argument that the judges enjoyed life tenure and consequently would not sacrifice their independence by their Crown-granted salaries was absurd, Adams believed, mere "vain and frothy harangues and scribblings." He could not let such doctrine take root in the minds of the people. It seemed to him, in fact, that the events of the winter had been providential, a "period in which the seeds of great events have been ... plentifully sown. ..."[45] He now entered the lists against Brattle.

Poor Brattle must have been sorely remorseful that he had ever elected to tangle with such a doggedly relentless little scrapper as Adams. He dared to write a single rebuttal—a pathetic one, at that —but he was made mincemeat by seven devastating articles in which Adams rained a torrent of authorities upon him—not only common law authorities such as Coke, Bracton, Fortescue, Holt, Hawkins, Raymond and Blackstone, but historians Hume, Rapin, Rushworth and Stryk.[46] According to common law, Adams said, English judges had always held their commissions at the pleasure of the King. Not until this custom was changed by an act of Parliament of the reign of William III and again by the Act of Settlement of 1701 did judges in England hold their commissions during good behavior. However, in the meantime, judges in the Colonies had continued to be subject to dismissal at any time without cause. To be sure, there was a lamentable discrepancy between British and colonial practice.

Throughout the year 1773 Adams' fears increased that soon all royal officials would be tools of the governor.[47] His colleagues at the bar were equally worried, "but no man presumed to say what ought to be done, or what could be done." Word flew that no matter what, the judges could not be allowed to become puppets of the Crown. Such talk disturbed Adams, who suspected that if no action were taken, the Boston mob would do with the judges what they had done with Secretary Andrew Oliver—march them to the Liberty Tree and there force them to take an oath renouncing their salaries. Most of the judges were men of resolution; Chief Justice Peter Oliver, especially, had made such a show of his tough spine that Adams "shuddered at the expectation that the mob might put on him a coat of tar and feathers, if not put him to death." Furthermore, Adams respected the judges. Several—William Cushing and the scholarly Edmund Trowbridge, for example—were his friends. Oliver and Nathaniel Ropes "abstracted from their politics were amiable men, and all of them very respectable and virtuous characters." Adams despised the thought of violence to the judges; it would be violence to law, mob coercion of authorities. He "dreaded the effect upon the morals and temper of the people, which must be produced by any violence offered to the persons of those who wore the robes and bore the sacred characters of judges, and, more-over, I felt a strong aversion to such partial and irregular recur-rences to original power." It was a sad truism that "the poor people themselves, who by secret maneuvers are excited to insurrection, are seldom aware of the purposes for which they are set in motion or of the consequences which may happen to themselves, and when once heated and in full career, they can neither manage themselves nor be regulated by others."

One evening at dinner with Samuel Winthrop, clerk of the Su-perior Court; John Winthrop, the Harvard professor; Dr. Cooper and several other gentlemen, the conversation turned to the current topic—what was to be done about the judges? Crown-granted sala-ries, they all agreed, "was a fatal measure and would be the ruin of the liberties of the country: but what was the remedy? It seemed to be a measure that would execute itself. There was no imaginable way of resisting or eluding it." Amidst the gloomy speculation, Adams sat silent.

"Mr. Adams," Dr. Winthrop inquired, "we have not heard your sentiments on this subject; how do you consider it?" Adams an-swered that he agreed that "the measure had created a crisis, and if it could not be defeated, the liberties of the province would be lost. The stroke was leveled at the essence of the constitution, and nothing was too dear to be hazarded in warding it off. It leveled the axe at the root, and if not opposed the tree would be overthrown from the foundation."

"But," said Winthrop, "what can be done?"

Adams replied that he did not know whether anyone would approve of his opinion but he believed there might be an answer—a constitutional resource.

"A constitutional resource!" the company cried out. "What can it be?"

"Nothing more nor less than an impeachment of the judges by the House of Representatives before the council."

"An impeachment! Why, such a thing is without precedent." Adams "believed it was," in Massachusetts. "But there had been precedents enough and by much too many in England. It was a dangerous experiment at all times, but it was essential to the preservation of the constitution in some cases that could be reached by no other power but that of impeachment."

"But whence can we pretend to derive such a power?" they pressed him.

"From our charter, which gives us in words as express, as clear and as strong as the language affords, all the rights and privileges of Englishmen; and if the House of Commons in England is the grand inquest of the nation, the House of Representatives is the grand inquest of this province, and the council must have the powers of judicature of the House of Lords in Great Britain."

The men said this was a new doctrine, that they knew not whether it might be supported, but they intended to examine it. "After all," they asserted, "if it should be approved by the House, the council would not convict the judges."

That, Adams pointed out, was "an after-consideration; if the House was convinced that they had the power and that it was their duty to exercise it, they ought to do it and oblige the council to inquire into their rights and powers and duties. If the council would not hearken to law or evidence, they must be responsible for the consequences, and the guilt and blame must lie at their door."

When the group broke up, Adams knew that the governor and judges, indeed the entire legislature, shortly would have wind of the discussion. Only the next day Major Hawley hurried in. What strange doctrine was this that Adams had propounded? Hawley himself "hardly knew what an impeachment was; he had never read any . . . never had thought on the subject." Adams told him that he might read as many as he wished. "There stood the *State Trials* on the shelf, which were full of them, of all sorts good and bad." He gave his friend Selden's *Works*, in which there was a treatise on judicature in Parliament.

"That judicature in Parliament," Adams commented, is "as ancient as common law and as Parliament itself " and "without this high jurisdiction" it would be "impossible to defend the constitution against princes and nobles and great ministers who might commit high crimes and misdemeanors which no other authority would be powerful enough to prevent or punish." Furthermore, the Massachusetts charter was a miniature of the British constitution. The charter gave the people of Massachusetts "every power, jurisdiction and right within our limits which could be claimed by the people or government of England, with no other exceptions than those in the charter expressed." The two men even looked into the charter together, after which Hawley declared that "he knew not how to get rid of it."

Shortly after, another member of the bar came to Adams, explaining he had come to examine the same sources that Hawley had seen and to hear what Adams had to say. The issue was soon the topic of discussion of every lawyer in Boston.

In the meantime Hawley, a long-time friend of Judge Trowbridge and admirer of his legal knowledge, went to Cambridge for the judge's advice. Trowbridge, although by that time he had probably renounced his salary, could not feel very kindly toward the impeachment proposal. However, "he could not deny," he told Hawley, "that the constitution had given the power to the House of Representatives," that the charter was full and express. Even so, he insisted, even if they heard the impeachment trial the council would undoubtedly acquit the judges.

The next time that Trowbridge saw Adams he remarked, no doubt a little wearily, "I see, Mr. Adams, you are determined to explore the constitution and bring to life all its dormant and latent powers in defense of your liberties, as you understand them."

"I should be very happy if the constitution could carry us safely through all our difficulties without having recourse to higher powers not written," Adams replied.

In March, 1774, the members of the House, taking heart over Adams' proposal, appointed a committee to draw up impeachment proceedings against Chief Justice Oliver. Major Hawley, a member of the committee, brought the articles to Adams for his approval cf each paragraph. Each evening lawyers and representatives flocked to Adams' house to confer over the business, causing Benjamin Gridley, Jeremiah's nephew, to observe in his pompous style, "Brother Adams, you keep late hours at your house; as I passed it last night long after midnight, I saw your street door vomit forth a crowd of senators."

In the end only Chief Justice Oliver refused to renounce his salary. Accordingly, impeachment proceedings against him went from House to council, although there they died, as had been expected. Nonetheless, the people of Boston had the final say. When the Superior Court came to sit at its August term in Boston, a mob paraded up and down the streets outside. In the courtroom the grand jurors and petit jurors refused to take their oaths, saying to Oliver, "The Chief Justice of this Court stands impeached by the representatives of the people of high crimes and misdemeanors and of a conspiracy against the charter privileges of the people. I therefore cannot serve as a juror or take the oath."[48] In every county the scene was the same. The courts, in effect, were closed and would remain so.

Meanwhile, dramatic events had begun to crowd one upon another in Boston and, indeed, throughout the continent. Americans had been so incensed by retention of the tea duty that they refused to drink British tea, and used only smuggled foreign tea. Now irate over a late measure of Parliament that favored the British East India Company by allowing it to undersell smugglers of foreign tea and so give the colonists every incentive to drink British tea but still pay the tea duty, the Sons of Liberty, in December of 1773, had staged their own Tea Party, dumping several hundred chests of British tea into the Boston harbor.

"The die is cast," Adams wrote James Warren the next day. "The people have passed the river and cut away the bridge."[49] Perhaps somewhat surprisingly he called the Tea Party "the most magnificent movement of all." There was "a dignity, a majesty, a sublimity, in this last effort of the patriots" that he greatly admired. This move had been "so bold, so daring, so firm, intrepid and inflexible," that he felt it must surely have important consequences. But it was a destruction of property, he realized. No one recognized more than he the solemn implications of that sort of action: "Another similar exertion of popular power may produce the destruction of lives." Yet, he felt the question to be "whether the destruction of this tea was necessary." And he affirmed, "it was absolutely and indispensably so."[50]

Adams' approval of the Tea Party as an outright destruction of property may, at first glance, appear puzzling. For the first time he condoned the use of force by a mob. His position on the Tea Party is all the more intriguing since almost at the same time he was involved in the case of *King v. Stewart*, in which he sought to obtain a damage settlement for Richard King, whose home and property had been destroyed by a raging mob of patriots.[51]

". . . I know of nothing that happens in society which is such a nursery of scandal and calumny," Adams addressed the jury, "of obloquy and defamation as a mob."[52] Likewise, he wrote to Abigail, "these private mobs I do and will detest." Yet, all the same, he could justify the Tea Party on the ground that it had been done in defense of a constitutional principle. When the tea ships had landed, a meeting of Bostonians had demanded their return to England with cargoes intact. The owners could do nothing, however, because the governor and customs officers would not arrange for the tea to be sent back. Adams blamed the governor and his men for destruction of the tea, for "it was in their power to have saved it. . . ." Since the tea could not be returned, the only choice was to destroy it or let it be landed. To let it be landed, Adams felt, would be conceding that Parliament could tax the Colonies—a principle "against which the continent has struggled for ten years"; it would be dismissing ten years of labor "and subjecting ourselves and our posterity forever to Egyptian taskmasters—to burdens, indignities, to ignominy, reproach and contempt, to desolation and oppression, to poverty and servitude."[53] Adams, whose objection to "private mobs" was characteristic, concluded that in rare cases such as this they might be excused: "If popular commotions can be justified in opposition to attacks upon the constitution, it can be only when fundamentals are invaded, nor then unless for absolute necessity and with great caution."[54] Parliament, however, did not agree with Adams that the attack on tea had been necessary. Now it imposed the harshest measures of all—the Coercive or Intolerable Acts.

Adams was now to accept his greatest political responsibility to date, for in June, 1774, he was elected a Massachusetts delegate to the Continental Congress. Furthermore, he was about to contribute to the patriot cause the best political tract he had written thus far. In fact, that work, the *Novanglus* papers, was to be what many colonists considered their greatest apology, the sum of the constitutional argument since 1761.

CHAPTER VI

TRYING THE CASE—
The Verdict: Independence

ALL men now and then catch fleeting gimpses of themselves as figures in history. They are momentarily awed, thrilled,
mystified. Those few men whose places in history are more public
must experience an even more pronounced feeling of wonder, reverence and bewilderment in the face of something greater than their
comprehension. During the summer of 1774 the men who were to
attend the Continental Congress in Philadelphia that September
must have known that feeling. For over ten years they had battled
for their liberties and those of their fellow men, and now events had
come to a crucial pass for which they were greatly responsible.

It has sometimes been said that unlike any other revolution, the
American Revolution was both begun and concluded by the same
men. Those who waged revolution were not swept out by more
radical men, but once they had secured freedom they were able to
go on to the far more difficult task of imposing the law and order
necessary to retain it. These Americans were not revolutionaries in
the ordinary sense of the word; they did not intend to destroy but
to preserve. Liberty was a condition to which they had always been
accustomed—not a right they were trying to acquire. Their political
framework had given these Americans a tradition of liberty. For
that reason, not only from their reading, but in the largest measure

from their own political experience, these men knew that liberty presupposes that there can be liberty only in law.

The men who were to attend the Congress had no idea in June of 1774 how it would all turn out. Most of the delegates, whether in Virginia, in the Carolinas, in Rhode Island or Connecticut, felt much as John Adams did that summer. He was determined that the Colonies should not back down on the question of the authority of Parliament—which was the crucial constitutional issue at stake. But he was not in favor of independence, for he still hoped that petitions to the King would obtain redress of grievances. In fact, he shuddered at the thought of being cast outside the pale of the only nation he had ever known. He had little idea of life in any colony other than his own, or at most his own section of the country. Consequently, he had little notion of a union of colonies, other than such collaboration as was necessary to solve the difficulties with Britain. At the same time he felt himself about to become part of a significant historic drama. And how would he play his role? Sadly, he felt, for right now he could only cower with fright in the wings. He had forgotten his lines, his costume was shabby, his presence awkward. How could a plain country fellow walk upon the grandest stage in America in the finest city on the continent and expect to match prowess with the best actors in the Colonies? But for all his feelings of smallness he felt a surge of excitement that he was about to become part of the drama. The knowledge that this play would be larger in scope than anything he had ever seen only contributed to his tingling expectation.

Riding for the tenth and last time on the eastern circuit in Maine, John Adams, now almost thirty-nine, contemplated what autumn would bring. There was "a new and a grand scene" open before him, "a Congress . . . an assembly of the wisest men upon the continent, who are Americans in principle," not merely in blood, men who were "against the taxation of Americans by authority of Parliament."

"I feel myself unequal to this business," he worried. "A more extensive knowledge of the realm, the Colonies and of commerce, as well as of law and policy, is necessary than I am master of."

He wondered what the Congress would be able to do. "Will it be expedient to propose an annual congress of committees to petition —will it do to petition at all to the King, to the Lords, to the Commons?

"What will such consultations avail? Deliberations alone will not do." Must they "petition or recommend to the assemblies to petition," or what? Moreover, it was difficult to determine the opinions of the people of Massachusetts. Their ideas were "as various as their faces," one demanding no more petitions, that they would do no good, another talking for "spirited resolves," others calling for "bolder councils."[1]

After the Superior Court adjourned at Ipswich, Adams wandered on a long walk one June afternoon through the fine fields of corn, rye and grass.

"I muse, I mope, I ruminate," he wrote. "I am often in reveries and brown studies. The objects before me are too grand and multifarious for my comprehension. We have not men fit for the times. We are deficient in genius, in education, in travel, in fortune, in everything. I feel unutterable anxiety. God grant us wisdom and fortitude!"

If the Congress should fail he could not bear to think of the consequences. "Should the opposition be suppressed, should this country submit, what infamy and ruin! God forbid. Death in any form is less terrible."[2] The unalterable finality of the crisis impressed itself upon his mind even more when at Falmouth he parted regretfully from his old friend Jonathan Sewall. Atop Munjoy Hill, overlooking Casco Bay, the two friends talked a long time about the divergent politics to which each had committed himself. They did not see each other again until years later when the cause of their differences had been dissipated.

The Congress that had been called was a direct response to the passage in late spring, 1774, of the Coercive Acts. The Boston Port Act, first of the acts, completely shut up the port of Boston until the tea tossed overboard should be paid for. There was to be no shipping activity at Boston at all; customs machinery was moved up to Salem. The Massachusetts Government and Administration of Justice acts provided that the provincial council of Massachusetts, heretofore elected by the assembly, be appointed by the governor, as was the case in other royal colonies. The governor could now appoint all judges, sheriffs, justices of the peace, and so on. The powers of town meetings were strictly curtailed and the method of appointing juries was changed. Moreover, officials accused before local courts of capital offenses committed while carrying out their duties might, at the discretion of the governor, be tried in some other colony or in Britain. The Quartering Act allowed any royal governor, if need be, to order troops to be quartered in private homes. There was not much question that all these acts were devices of tyranny.

Finally, another act, though not really part of the Coercive Acts, was considered as such by the colonials. This was the Quebec Act, which, to remedy the lack of civil government in the northwest territories since the Proclamation of 1763, extended the boundary of the province of Quebec south to the Ohio River. In addition, this act recognized the heavy French Catholic population of Quebec by retaining French civil law and the legality of the Roman Catholic Church in the whole province. Actually, the Quebec Act was in part a wise acknowledgment that a colony might best be governed by allowing it to continue in its political and cultural tradition, but the Americans did not see it in that light. The boundary extension, they felt, was a tactic designed to cut them out of future expansion into lands already claimed by four colonies. Further, and far worse, it was a first step toward establishing a monstrous Catholic empire in America.

To enforce the Coercive Acts in Massachusetts, General Thomas Gage replaced Hutchinson as governor of the province. He vetoed John Adams and twelve others as members of the council and adjourned the legislature from Boston to Salem. Faster than he could move, however, the assembly voted to send five delegates—James Bowdoin, Thomas Cushing, Samuel Adams, Robert Treat Paine and John Adams—to the Continental Congress in Philadelphia on the first of September. Gage immediately dissolved the General Court, but the deed had already been done. Virginia, in the meantime, had leaped to the defense of Massachusetts, likewise making plans to send delegates.

August was searingly hot that summer, scarcely a fitting time for a long, tedious coach ride to Philadelphia. But the delegates—all but Bowdoin, who was ill—were in high spirits when they departed from Cushing's Boston house on August 10. They rode to Coolidge's in Watertown, where some fifty or sixty men from Boston had gathered to fete them with a going-away dinner, and then they were off.[3] Abigail fretted about her husband having to travel such dusty, hot roads; yet in her romantic style she longed to have him "upon the stage of action." She thought perhaps the first of September or the month of September would "be of as much importance to Great Britain as the Ides of March were to Caesar."[4]

Adams, for his part, bumped along in the stuffy coach day after day, studying first the cheerful, imperturbable face of his cousin Sam, then the irritable countenance of his long-time colleague, Bob Paine. These were dangerous times. He was anxious for his "perplexed, distressed province." However, resignation to whatever Providence would bring was the only proper attitude, he thought. "Prudence and caution" should be his watchwords.[5] After all, he would do well, he reminded himself, to profit by the words of that famous eccentric, Reverend Samuel Moody, who had advised his flock that whenever a man was in a difficult or dangerous state and knew not what to do, he must be careful not to do he knew not what.[6]

On Monday, August 29, the quartet of Massachusetts delegates arrived in Philadelphia where, dirty, dusty and tired as they were, they could not resist dropping by the famous City Tavern, on the west side of Second Street between Walnut and Chestnut, a handsome place decorated in the style of the best London taverns. From there they went across the street and took rooms at Mrs. Yard's stone house, which thereafter they inelegantly referred to as "headquarters."[7]

In the few days before Congress was to convene on September 5, Adams took the opportunity to cast his critical eye upon the company of men who were gathering in the city. There would be fifty-six eventually, but not all had arrived. Most of the group were lawyers, some were planters, a few were merchants. They were uniformly well educated, many having attended college. Though most of them were strangers to each other, they had more in common than they themselves perhaps realized. Though they knew little of colonies other than their own, their English heritage and similar education gave them a common ground of understanding more important than geographical boundaries.

There was Thomas Mifflin of Philadelphia, who so hospitably entertained the delegates in his spacious, elegant house. Charles Thomson, they all said, was the "life of the cause of liberty," a kind of "Sam Adams of Philadelphia." Thomson was about to marry a wealthy woman who was a relative of "Farmer" John Dickinson.[8] Although not yet a delegate, Dickinson, in a coach drawn by four beautiful horses, called upon the Massachusetts delegates, his first time out after a siege with the gout. The fellow was a "shadow," tall and "slender as a reed, pale as ashes." On first observing him, Adams thought that he could scarcely live a month—but on second inspection decided that he looked "as if the springs of life were strong enough to last many years."[9] Joseph Galloway of Pennsylvania was speaker of the house in his colony, a reserved man, as was James Duane of New York. Another delegate from the Middle Colonies, Caesar Rodney of Delaware, was "the oddest-looking man in the world," tall, thin, with a face "not bigger than a large apple. Yet there is sense and fire, spirit, wit and humor in his countenance."[10] William Livingston of New Jersey was a "plain man, tall, black," and wore his own hair—"nothing elegant or genteel about him." Although they said he was no public speaker, he was reputed to be "very sensible and learned and a ready writer."[11]

The gentlemen from South Carolina had arrived as early as the Massachusetts delegation. Henry Middleton was "silent and reserved"[12] and the elder Rutledge gave a not very promising appearance, there being "no keenness in his eye, no depth in his countenance."[13] But young Edward Rutledge seemed bright, even if a little too brash and not especially deep. He had an irritating way, however, of mumbling and speaking through his nose.[14] Christopher Gadsden was noted for his fervent support of the patriot cause. Particularly, though, did Adams like Thomas Lynch, "a solid, firm, judicious man." Over dinner with Lynch and his wife and daughter, Adams heard the report of Colonel George Washington's speech to the Virginia convention in which Washington had declared that he would raise a thousand men and subsist them at his own expense and himself march at their head for the relief of Boston.[15] (Despite the fact that it was a popular rumor, Washington never made the speech.)

The delegation that Adams most wished to meet, however, was the one from Virginia, which did not arrive until later. He wanted to lay eyes upon these men who had been as ardent in the resistance as those from Massachusetts. The reality did not disappoint him. Richard Henry Lee, tall and spare, was "a masterly man," Peyton Randolph, speaker of the Virginia House, "a large, well-looking man," Richard Bland, "a learned, bookish man," who said "he would have gone upon this occasion if it had been to Jericho." Colonel Benjamin Harrison insisted he would have come on foot if necessary.

"These gentlemen from Virginia," Adams declared approvingly, "appear to be the most spirited and consistent of any."[16] Apparently he had not yet met either Patrick Henry or George Washington, for he did not mention them.

Richard Henry Lee he classified as a deep, sensible thinker. Breakfasting with him at Dr. William Shippen's, he listened to the big Virginian assert that the end of the Congress ought to be repeal of every revenue law, of the Boston Port Act, the Massachusetts Governing Act and the Quebec Act, and removal of all troops. To accomplish this goal Congress should call for non-importation of dutied articles—rum, molasses, sugar, tea, wine, fruits and so on.

"He is absolutely certain," Adams reported, "that the same ship which carries home the resolution will bring back the redress."[17] Such optimism was the prevailing mood of most of the delegates as they prepared to convene.

On Monday morning of the fifth of September the delegates congregated at the City Tavern at ten o'clock; whence they walked to the brand-new Carpenter's Hall to take a look at the room in which they were to meet. They admired the fine library there, the long entry hall where they would be able to walk, and the convenient chamber opposite the library. Altogether an excellent room, the company agreed, voting it their meeting place.

Then, after nomination by Thomas Lynch of South Carolina, Peyton Randolph was elected chairman. Lynch proposed Charles Thomson of Pennsylvania for secretary; Thomson, although not a delegate, was elected.[18]

No sooner were these formalities out of the way than the oft-to-be-haggled question of voting arose. After considerable debate, in which it was variously suggested that voting be by each colony, by a poll of each delegation, by interest, by population and by wealth, the Congress agreed that the only feasible answer was for each colony to have one vote.

Adams was greatly impressed with the general character and intelligence of this body of congressmen. He was heartened by their genuine concern for liberty, their sturdy intent to alleviate the colonial situation.

"There is in the Congress a collection of the greatest men upon this continent," he enthusiastically informed Abigail, "in point of abilities, virtues and fortunes. . . . The addressers and the new councilors are held in universal contempt and abhorrence from one end of the continent to the other."[19]

"A Tory here," he reported, "is the most despicable animal in the creation." Adams was further gratified to realize that Massachusetts was venerated in Congress as "the saviors and defenders of American liberty."[20] Indeed, the Massachusetts delegation had been so taken into the bosom of Philadelphia society that life, he complained, threatened to be one long round of feasting—"everything which could delight the eye or allure the taste, curds and creams, jellies, sweetmeats of various sorts, twenty sorts of tarts, fools, trifles, floating islands, whipped syllabubs, and so forth, Parmesan cheese, punch, wine, porter, beer. . . ."[21]

Sympathy of the delegates for Massachusetts was enhanced by a frenzied report on September 6 that Boston had been bombarded.

It proved untrue; Gage's troops had simply seized the powder stored in a Charlestown magazine. That, of course, was bad enough, Adams agreed, but until the rumor was found to be false, "War! War! War!" had been the cry in Congress, "pronounced in a tone which would have done honor to the oratory of a Briton or a Roman. If it had proved true," he told his wife, "you would have heard the thunder of an American Congress."[22]

Suffolk County became a byword in Congress after Paul Revere arrived in Philadelphia on September 16 with news of the Suffolk Resolves. Drafted by Joseph Warren, the Resolves had been adopted by a Suffolk County convention held at Dedham and Milton from the sixth to the ninth of September. The Resolves demanded repeal of the Coercive Acts, calling for Massachusetts to form a new government until repeal should come and urging nonimportation of dutied goods. Adams beamed with pride that his province had acquitted itself with so much valor. It was "one of the happiest days" of his life; Congress was moved to "generous, noble sentiments and manly eloquence" in favor of the Resolves, convincing him "that America will support Massachusetts or perish with her."[23]

Meanwhile, Congress made faltering attempts to get down to other business. If Adams had been optimistic about the unanimity of the delegates, he soon lapsed into justifiable pessimism. There were factions already, a situation to be expected even among men of good will, but it was exasperating at best. He could see that while he on the liberal side had allies in such men as his cousin Sam, Patrick Henry, Richard Henry Lee, Christopher Gadsden, Roger Sherman, and Governor Stephen Hopkins of Rhode Island, there were a good number of conservatives—John Dickinson and Joseph Galloway of Pennsylvania, John Rutledge and Henry Middleton of South Carolina, John Jay and James Duane of New York. Most, however, like Washington, were moderates.

The business of Congress went tediously, "slow as snails," agony to Adams, the impatient soul who had "not been used to such ways." But he understood the reason: "fifty gentlemen meeting together, all strangers, are not acquainted with each other's language, ideas, views, designs. They are therefore jealous of each other—fearful, timid, skittish."[24] He summed up the general mood of the Congress, which though one of unwillingness to buckle to suppression was also a mood of yearning for reconciliation: "There is a great spirit in the Congress. But our people must be peaceable. Let them exercise every day in the week, if they will, the more the better. Let them furnish themselves with artillery, arms and ammunition. Let them follow the maxim. . . 'In times of peace, prepare for war.' But let them avoid war, *if possible, if possible,* I say."[25]

In this First Continental Congress none of the so-called radicals, except perhaps Sam Adams, desired independence from Britain. If the British ministry would but recognize the intractable spirit of liberty in the Colonies there was yet time to effect a reconciliation. As Abigail wrote to the British historian, Catharine Sawbridge Macaulay, ". . . connected as we were by blood, by commerce, by one common language, by one common religion as Protestants, and as good and loyal subjects of the same King, we earnestly wish that the three-fold cord of duty, interests and filial affection may not be snapped asunder. 'Tis like the Gordian knot. It never can be untied, but the sword may cut it, and America, if she falls, to use the words of the revered and ever-honored Mr. Pitt, will fall like a strong man, and will embrace the pillars of state and pull down the constitution along with her."[26] Patrick Henry was not the only one who would see the issue in terms of liberty or death. Abigail did, too; it was redress of grievances by law or redress by the sword—"The only alternative which every American thinks of is liberty or death."[27]

Joseph Galloway tried to solve the dilemma with a proposal for a British-American legislature. Each colony should take care of its own internal affairs, but matters of trade would be the consideration of the legislature, in which Britain and America would each have a veto over acts concerning America. Adams carefully minuted the September 28 debates on this plan of union. Although Duane, Jay and Edward Rutledge approved the plan, Adams and most of the delegates did not. Patrick Henry scoffed, "We shall liberate our constituents from a corrupt House of Commons but throw them into the arms of an American legislature that may be bribed by that nation which avows in the face of the world that bribery is a part of her system of government."[28] That evening Lee, Washington and Dr. Shippen came to consult with Adams and the men from Boston about the plan, which eventually was voted down.[29]

Nearly as soon as Congress had convened, Adams was appointed to its most important committee, one to state the rights of the Colonies, instances in which these rights had been violated and the means by which they might be restored. Sam Adams was the other Massachusetts delegate.

In their general and subcommittee debates and in their informal discussions with each other, the committee on rights and grievances displayed the marked character of eighteenth-century political philosophers. Orating upon the proper basis of colonial rights, these men showed themselves to be wholly of their century—that age when philosophical banter was a favorite parlor game. Further, they demonstrated in these debates that despite their geographical diffusion, they were remarkably close in political theory. They began from a common fund of understanding saturated with the ancients, with Coke and Blackstone, with Harrington, Sidney and Montesquieu. The question they asked themselves was whether they ought to have recourse to the law of nature as well as to the British constitution and colonial charters and grants. Most definitely they should, Adams believed, fearing that the law of nature might eventually be the only ground that would withstand assault, the final argument to which they might be forced to retreat.[30] Lee, Jay and William Livingston shared this opinion. Roger Sherman, as well, echoed Adams' theory that the Colonies had never adopted the eighteenth-century English doctrine of the supremacy of Parliament, commonplace in England after the accession of William and Mary, when he said, "The Colonies are not bound to the King or Crown by the Act of Settlement but by their consent to it.

"There is no other legislative over the Colonies but their respective assemblies.

"The Colonies adopt the common law, not as the common law, but as the highest reason."[31]

It was the same opinion that Adams would expound in his *Novan-*

glus papers. Galloway and Duane, on the other hand, thought natural law an insecure basis for colonial rights; they preferred arguing from the British constitution. The committee decided to use all these arguments, to found colonial rights upon the laws of nature, the principles of the English constitution and charters and compacts.[32] Significantly, the law of nature was listed first, an indication of a shift in strategy from speaking not so much of English rights as of natural rights. Nevertheless, regardless of what tag these rights carried, they were identical and had been proclaimed for centuries in English political tradition.

Adams was appointed a member of a committee to draw up a statement of rights and a member of another committee to prepare an address to the King. He spent an evening with fellow committeeman Patrick Henry discussing the petition to His Majesty, fascinated to hear that Henry had had no public education, that at fifteen he had read Virgil and Livy but that after his father left him at that age, he since had not looked into a Latin book.

"He has high notions," Adams observed. "Talks about exalted minds. . . . He has a horrid opinion of Galloway, Jay and the Rutledges. Their system, he says, would ruin the cause of America. He is very impatient to see such fellows and not be at liberty to describe them in their true colors."[33]

The result of the debates of the committees was the Declaration of Rights and Grievances, the most important document of the Revolution before the Declaration of Independence. The first declaration forecast the second. It is clear that Adams had a great deal to do with drafting the Declaration of Rights—though perhaps not quite so much as he recalled in later years.

Philosophize as the delegates might over the law of nature and the British constitution, they still did not agree upon the crucial issue: the authority of Parliament. What authority should they concede or deny—should they deny the authority of Parliament in all cases, or only in internal affairs? Should they allow Parliament any authority at all in trade regulations?

"Some," Adams later related, "were for a flat denial of all authority, others for denying the power of taxation only. Some for denying internal but admitting external taxation." He reported that after a long debate was waged and there was still no agreement, John Rutledge of South Carolina said to him, "Adams, we must agree upon something. You appear to be as familiar with the subject as any of us, and I like your expressions, *the necessity of the case* and *excluding all ideas of taxation external and internal.* . . .Come take the pen and see if you can't produce something that will unite us."[34]

Adams then drafted an article which, though not universally liked, was still approved. This critical Article Four was in part a resumé of Adams' arguments over the past ten years, declaring that representation of the people in their legislature was a fundamental English right, essential to free government; that because English colonists could not be and were not represented in Parliament, then that body had no control over them; that only by consent of the Colonies—which America cheerfully granted—did Parliament have a right to regulate trade, but regulation, of course, must not have as its purpose the raising of any kind of revenue.[35]

After toiling over the Declaration of Rights, Adams was tired and eager to bring things to a close. Congress was forever "nibbling and quibbling." There was "no greater mortification than to sit with half a dozen wits, deliberating upon a petition, address or memorial. These great wits, these subtle critics, these refined geniuses, these learned lawyers, these wise statesmen, are so fond of showing their parts and powers as to make their consultation very tedious."[36]

Congress adjourned on October 26. The delegates spent the evening together at the City Tavern, no doubt reflecting upon their work of the past two months. They had passed resolves (some of the resolves at Adams' behest) in favor of the resistance of Massachusetts; they had adopted a petition to the King stating their rights and entreating redress of grievances; they had adopted both non-importation and non-exportation resolutions. As of December 1, 1774, they would not import or consume British goods. For the benefit of the Southern Colonies, the non-exportation agreement would not go into effect until September 10, 1775; upon and after that date goods would no longer be exported to Britain or the West

Indies. In addition, Congress had voted that if grievances had not been redressed by the spring of 1775, they should hold another session at Philadelphia in May.

Adams must now have wondered what good the work of Congress would do. Sometime before adjournment he had talked with Patrick Henry upon the subject. All these "resolves, declarations of rights, enumeration of wrongs, petitions, remonstrances and addresses, associations and non-importation agreements" would cement the union of the Colonies, but, Adams feared, "would be but waste paper in England." Henry agreed; they might impress the people of England, yet he was sure they would be lost upon the government. Adams read aloud a letter he had received from Major Hawley.[37]

"We must fight," Hawley wrote, "if we cannot otherwise rid ourselves of British taxation, all revenues, and the constitution or form of government enacted for us by the British Parliament. It is evil against right—utterly intolerable to every man who has any idea or feeling of right or liberty."

While Adams read, Henry listened attentively. Again Adams read, "Fight we must finally, unless Britain retreats." At those words, Henry shouted, "By God, I am of that man's mind!" He took the letter and read the whole thing, assenting with vehemence.

Richard Henry Lee, on the other hand, was perfectly confident that colonial grievances would be redressed. Upon parting he told Adams cheerfully, "We shall infallibly carry all our points. You will be completely relieved; all the offensive acts will be repealed; the army and fleet will be recalled, and Britain will give up her foolish project."

"Washington only was in doubt," Adams recalled later. "He never spoke in public. In private he joined with those who advocated a non-exportation, as well as a non-importation agreement. With both [agreements], he thought we should prevail; without either, he thought it doubtful. Henry was clear in one opinion, Richard Henry Lee in an opposite opinion, and Washington doubted between the two. Henry, however, appeared in the end to be exactly in the right."[38] Adams himself looked bleakly upon the future of the resolves of Congress. He could not see any hope that the ministry would repeal the baneful acts. If it should, it would act fortunately contrary to its pattern of behavior thus far.

When Adams departed from "the happy, the peaceful, the elegant, the hospitable, and polite city of Philadelphia," he never expected to see that part of the world again.[39] But scarcely did he arrive home than he was elected to the provincial congress sitting at the Cambridge meeting house. In turn that body elected him to serve a second term as delegate to the Continental Congress that was to meet again in May. He was to return with Sam Adams, Thomas Cushing and Robert Treat Paine. John Hancock was elected to replace Bowdoin, who had never attended.

All through the winter of 1774-1775 Adams was busy. Of his activities he left little record—except for one great monument, his *Novanglus* papers. Though he had small hope that the British ministry would come round, he went to work to explain the colonial case. The product of his labor was a series of newspaper essays, a lawyer's brief, that presented the colonial case in such clarity that the American position could not possibly be misunderstood.

During the early part of 1775, a group of loyalist essays signed *Massachusettensis* appeared in the *Massachusetts Gazette and Boston Post Boy.* Adams, sure that they were the work of Jonathan Sewall (they were actually written by Daniel Leonard of Taunton), charged into the fray to produce the *Novanglus* essays, which were published in the *Boston Gazette* from the latter part of January until the historic skirmish at Lexington in April.

The theme of Adams' argument had to do with the nature of the British Empire. He held simply that the American Colonies were properly what today would be called dominions, self-governing entities within a commonwealth, united under one king for purposes of amity and commerce. Because the Colonies were not represented in Parliament, they could not be justly under its authority. But because the Colonies consented—and merely because they consented—Parliament did have the right to govern their commerce on the high seas.

In brief, Leonard's position was that the Whigs were wrong in their first principle that the constitutional authority of Parliament did extend to the Colonies.[40] He argued that the Colonies were part of the British empire, claiming that when a nation took possession of and settled a distant land, that colony, even though separated from the mother country, became part of the state. There could not possibly be two supreme authorities within the same state. Thus, if the Colonies were part of the British Empire then, although Parliament delegated to them legislative and executive powers to regulate their own internal police, they were subject to the supreme power of Parliament. Furthermore, if the Colonies denied the authority of Parliament, they were declaring themselves separate states from Britain. In doing so, they would deprive themselves of English liberties and the British constitution embodied in that happy mixture of monarchic, aristocratic and democratic elements found in King, Lords and Commons.

With his pointed style and rather pedantic display of learning, Adams unhesitatingly took on each of his opponent's points. That he won there is no doubt—and he was still going strong when the *Gazette,* thrown into some confusion by the outbreak at Lexington, suspended publication. Essentially, the *Novanglus* argument regarding the authority of Parliament remained the same as the one that Adams had time and again set forth in his previous essays: a Parliament that did not represent a people had no power over them. But this time the reasons which Adams outlined were somewhat different from the ones he had recited before. Formerly, he had argued from the English constitution: he had stressed *English* liberties, the *English* rights deriving from the common law. Now—though he continued to call for the identical rights as before, chief of which was the ancient right of the people to have their property represented in the legislature that taxed and governed them—now Adams took his own advice, which he had given at the Continental Congress, to recur to the law of nature, as well as to the British constitution and colonial charters, for the source of colonial liberties. Of course, these rights were English liberties—but they were the rights of all men, essential to the fact of their human nature.

(The law of nature for Adams meant the law of human nature.) From the very fact of their being men it followed that people were entitled to certain rights, which the British constitution fortunately guaranteed. English liberties were "but certain rights of nature, reserved to the citizen by the English constitution, which rights cleaved to our ancestors when they crossed the Atlantic, and would have inhered in them. . . although they had taken no patent or charter from the King at all."[41]

Adams used the argument from natural law because he realized that when the problem became one of colonization and the nature of the empire, the common law grew shaky as the basis of argument. The plain fact was that colonization was *"casus omissus* at common law"; there was "no such title known in that law." There was neither a provision in that law for governing colonies by the authority of Parliament nor any provision for the King to grant charters to subjects to settle abroad. The King did have the power to prohibit emigration, but if a subject left with permission of the King, "he carried with him, as a man, all the rights of nature." Yet, once he left the realm, he left the jurisdiction of the common law.

"How then, " Adams inquired, "do we New Englandmen derive our laws?" The answer was ". . . not from Parliament, not from common law, but from the law of nature, and the compact made with the King in our charters." Those men of the Massachusetts Bay Company who received a charter from the King were under the common law while they remained within the realm. But when they emigrated, they left the jurisdiction of the common law of England. These ancestors "were entitled to the common law of England when they emigrated, that is, to just so much of it as they pleased to adopt and no more."[42] Naturally, they did adopt it, for they had brought their charter along, and the charter declared that residents of that colony should have all the rights and liberties of Englishmen. Certainly they would want to carry on with the common law, that perfection and embodiment of right reason. However, the fact remained that they had every right to establish a British constitution, a democracy, an aristocracy, or whatever they might choose. The common law of England went into effect in America—not because it extended across the seas, but because the colonists assumed it.

This was the logic, then, behind Adams' principle that America merely consented—from expedience rather than from right—to Parliamentary authority over commerce on the seas. He expressed it as follows:

> The Whigs allow that from the necessity of a case not provided for by common law, and to supply a defect in the British dominions, which there undoubtedly is if they are to be governed only by that law, America has all along consented, still consents, and ever will consent, that Parliament, being the most powerful legislature in the dominions, should regulate the trade of the dominions. This is founding the authority of Parliament to regulate our trade upon *compact* and *consent* of the Colonies, not upon any principle of common or statute law; not upon any original principle of the English constitution; not upon the principle that Parliament is the supreme and sovereign legislature over them in all cases whatsoever. The question is not, therefore, whether the authority of Parliament extends to the Colonies in any case, for it is admitted by the Whigs that it does in that of commerce; but whether it extends in all cases.[43]

Leonard had declared that the Colonies were subject to Parliament because they were part of the British empire. Adams retorted, "We are not a part of the British empire because the British government is not an empire." The British government was rather a limited monarchy, he argued.

"If Aristotle, Livy, and Harrington knew what a republic was," Adams pointed out, "the British constitution is much more like a republic than an empire. They define a republic to be a *government of laws, and not of men.* If this definition be just, the British constitution is nothing more nor less than a republic, in which the King is first magistrate." The fact that the office was hereditary, that it possessed some great prerogatives, did not keep the government from being a republic, so long as it was "bound by fixed laws which the people have a voice in making and a right to defend." An empire, on the other hand, was a despotism and the emperor a despot, bound by nothing but his own will, "a stretch of tyranny beyond absolute monarchy." Even France and Spain were no empires; at least their edicts had to be registered by parliaments. Only the Holy Roman, the Russian, and the Ottoman empires then existed in Europe.[44]

In English law there was known only the kingdom of Great Britain. Hence, the question ought to be whether the Colonies were part of the British kingdom, the realm. The answer, of course, was that they were not.

Since they were not part of the realm, then they were not governed by Parliament. The constitution required "that every foot of land should be represented in the third estate, the democratical branch of the constitution."[45] Yet, no American land was represented in Parliament. To say, as *Massachusettensis* did, that the supreme power over the Colonies was vested in the estates of Parliament was "an affront to us; for there is not an acre of American land represented there; there are no American estates in Parliament."[46] If Parliament in such a case were accepted as supreme authority over the Colonies, then America would not be under the British constitution at all but under an oligarchy of a few grandees.

If Parliament were not supreme legislature over the Colonies, then that designation belonged to the provincial assemblies. Leonard had said that there could not be two supreme authorities in one state. Adams answered him, "I agree that 'two supreme and independent authorities cannot exist in the same state,' any more than two supreme beings in one universe; and, therefore, I contend that our provincial legislatures are the only supreme authorities in our Colonies. Parliament, notwithstanding this, may be allowed an authority supreme and sovereign over the ocean, which may be limited by the banks of the ocean, or the bounds of our charters; our charters give us no authority over the high seas. Parliament has our consent to assume a jurisdiction over them."[47]

And what of Leonard's claim that a denial of authority of Parliament over the Colonies meant, first, destruction of the idea that Americans were under the British constitution, and, second, that they were declaring themselves independent of Britain? In the first place, Americans would never lose title to English liberties, for they were the liberties of all men and their charters guaranteed them these liberties. Second, they would not deprive themselves of the benefits of the British constitution either; in the Colonies the British constitution existed in the provincial assemblies. Governor, council, and assembly corresponded identically to King, Lords, and Commons; as monarchic, aristocratic, and democratic elements resided in King, Lords and Commons, likewise they were in the colonial counterparts.[48]

Finally it was true, Adams agreed, that Britain and the Colonies were distinct states, but that was a harmless fact.

"Distinct states may be united under one King. And those states may be further cemented and united together by a treaty of commerce. This is the case." By their own express consent and by long years of usage, Americans had contracted to observe the navigation acts. Such acquiescence might be compared to a treaty of commerce.

The relationship of the Colonies to the King was a personal, rather than a political one. The second Massachusetts charter was granted by King William and Queen Mary; the oaths of allegiance were established by provincial law. Consequently, there was no act of Parliament but, instead, provincial laws and the provincial charter that insured allegiance to the King. The people of Massachusetts had made a specific, original contract with King William.[49]

Moreover, it was not possible to hold lands of a King in any other than a personal nature.

"Holding lands, in feudal language," Adams explained, "means no more than the relation between lord and tenant. The reciprocal duties of these are all personal. . . . No lands here, or in England, are held of the Crown, meaning by it the political capacity; they are all held of the royal person, the natural person of the King." Holding lands of the Crown meant holding lands of whoever wore the Crown.[50]

There were three ways in which it was possible for a country or person to be subject to a King: to his person, whether or not the King was in the realm; to his Crown, in which case allegiance was due to whoever wore that Crown, following it through all revolutions and so on; to his Crown and realm of state, in which case the King was united as a body with the kingdom, that is, with his Parliament. The Colonies, Adams believed, were subject to the King in the second sense. It was quite reasonable, he felt, that the Colonies should be subject to the Crown without at the same time being annexed to the realm or subject to Parliament.[51]

Adams faced squarely and candidly the accusation that the Whigs had resolved to become independent. They had never desired independence, he insisted, although they were "clear in theory that, by the common law and the English constitution, Parliament has no authority over them." But, he said, "none of the patriots of this province, of the present age, have ever denied that Parliament has a right, from our voluntary cession, to make laws which shall bind the Colonies, so far as their commerce extends." Contrary to what Leonard stated, there was indeed a possible medium between absolute independence and subjection to the authority of Parliament.

"An absolute independence on Parliament, in all internal concerns and cases of taxation, is very compatible with an absolute dependence on it, in all cases of external commerce."

And in a few sentences he set forth exactly the patriot temper, a summary of the colonial case for the past ten years, the final proof that he and his colleagues did not wish to be revolutionaries, that if war came, it would be through the fault of the British ministry, not the colonists:

> That there are any who pant after "independence" (meaning by this word a new plan of government over all America, unconnected with the Crown of England, or meaning by it an exemption from the power of Parliament to regulate trade) is as great a slander upon the province as ever was committed to writing. The patriots of this province desire nothing new; they wish only to keep their old privileges. They were, for one hundred and fifty years, allowed to tax themselves, and govern their internal concerns as they thought best. Parliament governed their trade as they thought fit. This plan they wish may continue forever. But it is honestly confessed, rather than become subject to the absolute authority of Parliament in all cases of taxation and internal polity, they will be driven to throw off that of regulating trade.[52]

It was the colonial case capsulized. It was Adams' ultimate testimony and a remarkable portrayal of continental feeling. In the dominion proposal there was a solution to the colonial-imperial power struggle, but if the British ministry did not accept that solution there was nothing more to do but to declare independence.

There was a small but brilliant and eloquent group of Englishmen who did seek to persuade the North ministry of the imprudence and injustice of their policy. Men like Chatham, Burke, Fox, Camden, Barré, Shelburne, Rockingham saw virtue in the American position, laboring diligently but to no avail for concessions to that position. Indeed, old Pitt, the Earl of Chatham, came out of retirement that January of 1775 to deliver his great oration to the House of Lords in support of his proposition to remove Gage's troops from Boston.

"This resistance to your arbitrary system of taxation might have been foreseen," the old man intoned:

> It was obvious from the nature of things and of mankind. . . . The spirit which now resists your taxation in America is the same . . . which established the great fundamental, essential maxim of your liberties—*that no subject of England shall be taxed but by his own consent.* . . . This distinction between external and internal control is sacred and insurmountable; it is involved in the abstract nature of things. Property is private, individual, absolute. . . .When you consider their decency, firmness and wisdom, you cannot but respect their cause. . . . For solidity of reasoning, force of sagacity, and wisdom of conclusion . . . no nation or body of men can stand in preference to the general Congress at Philadelphia. . . . We shall be forced ultimately to retract; let us retract while we can, not when we must.[53]

But the motion was lost, 68-18. A bill that Chatham a few days later introduced in Commons was also voted down, a measure calling for recognition of the Continental Congress; repeal of the Coercive Acts, the Quebec Act and the tea duty; removal of the troops from Boston; appointment of colonial judges during good behavior; and guarantee of colonial charters.

Nor could the profound and forcible Edmund Burke accomplish what Chatham had failed. A large collection of English merchants had gotten together a petition urging repeal of the Coercive Acts.

Yet despite the fact that Burke delivered to Commons the first of his famous speeches on conciliation with America, the House still refused to repeal the Coercive Acts.

To all this Lord North replied with an obnoxious "conciliatory resolve" that conceded nothing. He offered in March the last of a long train of intolerable measures. This was the New England Restraining Act, declaring that the four New England Colonies could no longer trade with anyone other than Great Britain and Ireland and refusing to allow their fishermen to work the coast of Newfoundland and Nova Scotia.

Burke implored Commons to realize that "the proposition is peace," that "peace implies reconciliation; and where there has been a material dispute, reconciliation does in a manner always imply concession on the one part or on the other. . . . The proposal ought to originate from us," he advised.[54] The House answered with a smashing 271-78 defeat.

CHAPTER VII

THE GREATEST QUESTION

WHEN the Second Continental Congress convened on May 10, there were some new, distinguished representatives— George Wythe and, later, Thomas Jefferson from Virginia, John Hancock from Massachusetts, Benjamin Franklin and James Wilson from Pennsylvania.

Adams himself made a distinguished impression upon the company. Benjamin Rush later recalled that the short, ruddy-faced man from Massachusetts had been "a most sensible and forcible speaker. . . . acknowledged . . . to be the first man in the House." In fact, one member of the Congress, said Rush, fancied that when Adams spoke "an angel was let down from heaven to illuminate the Congress." Adams "saw the whole of a subject at a single glance, and by a happy union of the powers of reasoning and persuasion often succeeded in carrying measures which were at first sight of an unpopular nature." What was more, he had wit, replying "to reflections upon himself or upon the New England states . . . with the most poignant humor or satire." He was "fearless of men and of the consequences of a bold assertion of his opinion in all his speeches. . . . He was a stranger to dissimulation and appeared to be more jealous of his reputation for integrity than for talents or knowledge. He was strictly moral and at all times respectful to religion. . . . He possessed more learning, probably, both ancient and modern, than any man who subscribed the Declaration of Independence. His reading was various. Even the old English poets were familiar to him. He once told me he had read all Bolingbroke's works with great attention. He admired nothing in them but the style, and to acquire it, he said he had when a young man transcribed his 'Idea of a Patriot King.' "[1] Rush was as keen an observer of men as the subject of his sketch.

By and large, the members of this Second Congress gathered in a more pessimistic frame of mind than they had brought to the First Congress. The Declaration of Rights had been to no avail; British troops imprisoned Boston; Massachusetts patriots had set up an extra-legal assembly beyond Gage's reach; news of the Battle of Lexington had run to every corner of the land; militiamen in every colony rallied their supplies and ammunition.

Adams himself listened to conversations and debates in meeting rooms, libraries, taverns, recording the tenor of opinion of this new Congress. He found, he wrote to Moses Gill, that the general intention was "to prepare for a vigorous defensive war, but at the same time to keep open the door of reconciliation; to hold the sword in one hand and the olive branch in the other; to proceed with warlike measures and conciliatory measures *pari passu.*" For himself, he yearned for reconciliation—"upon a constitutional basis"—as much as any man. But at the same time, considering the education of the King and the long-time propensity of Lords, Commons, electors, army, navy and officers of excise and customs for being easy bedfellows with corruption, he was sure that "we shall be convinced that the cancer is too deeply rooted and too far spread to be cured by anything short of cutting it out entire."

By the spring of 1775 Adams had come the entire road toward resolving that if Parliament rejected a reconciliation on American grounds—as it appeared would be the case—then a declaration of independence even of the King would be necessary to restore trampled American liberties. With *Novanglus* Adams had reached the ultimate in the search for an alternative to independence: he had described a commonwealth. Now, however, almost his last vain hope had flickered out; he was ready now to take up arms. If any faint chance for reconciliation still existed, it was only by showing the British through physical force that the Colonies were deadly serious in their demands.

But he was a full year ahead of most of his countrymen in his decision for independence. Most people did not want war; they did not want independence. Adams knew that, and he did not blame them, for he would not have it himself, if it were not the only means to liberty and happiness. The people had no enthusiasm for collecting powder; any petition or negotiation that held out wan hopes of reconciliation without bloodshed was "greedily grasped at and relied on . . . they could not be persuaded to think that it is so necessary to prepare for war as it really is."

Adams knew that he could not expect people to come round to his position so readily. It was a stand bitterly arrived at, after all—one not embraced without the severest soul-searching. He had been searching for years; he could not hope that others would catch up to his head start. Patience was an unnatural virtue to him—but he was being forced to learn it. These were human minds and souls whom he faced, each one tuned a little differently. He might hope, pray, anticipate, yet there was always the factor of a land full of free wills, all apt to act contrary to what was expected of them.

". . . this continent is a vast, unwieldy machine," he told Moses Gill. "We cannot force events. We must suffer people to take their own way in many cases when we think it leads wrong, hoping, however, and believing that our liberty and felicity will be preserved in the end, though not in the speediest and surest manner. In my opinion, powder and artillery are the most efficacious, sure, and infallible conciliatory measures we can adopt."[2]

With Boston in such pitiful straits, Adams knew that Congress could no longer afford to offer an olive branch in one hand without pointing a musket in the other. Abigail poured forth detailed descriptions of the scene around Braintree. Lately a small battle had taken place at Grape Island out in Hingham Harbor, prompting people and rumors to fly down from the Iron Works and up from Weymouth. Abigail opened her hospitable heart during every period of alarm, housing American soldiers and relatives for supper or tea or overnight. Sometimes she had "refugees from Boston, tired and fatigued," seeking "an asylum for a day or night, a week —you can hardly imagine how we live."[3]

Adams wrote back to her that Philadelphia turned out 2,000 military men every day. Every man in Congress, it seemed, was an officer—all but him, he might have added. Mr. Dickinson was a colonel, Mr. Read a lieutenant colonel, Mr. Mifflin a major, but the last "ought to have been a general for he has been the animating soul of the whole." Washington appeared at Congress in his uniform, helpful in his experience in military matters.

"Oh, that I was a soldier!" Adams exclaimed boyishly. "I will be. I am reading military books. Everybody must and will and shall be a soldier."[4]

Adams performed a far greater service than anything he could have done in the field. It was he who proposed Washington for the post of commander-in-chief of the American forces. The circumstances which surrounded Washington's appointment were contorted, involving, as Adams described, not only a party of patriots confronting a party of trimmers, but a Northern against a Southern faction. Southerners refused to accept a New England general. Moreover, the New England men themselves were uncertain on the subject of who should be head of the army. Hancock and Cushing hemmed and hawed (even though Adams was sure that Hancock wanted the job). Paine said nothing, and even Sam Adams seemed in a quandary. Though Adams had contemplated Hancock in the position, he dismissed the thought. Hancock's service in the patriot cause and in the militia had been outstanding, yet his want of robust health and lack of actual military experience ruled him out in Adams' mind. Washington appeared to be the best choice: militarily experienced, financially able, of impeccable character and strong, quiet judgment. But embarrassingly enough, he was not the unanimous choice of his own Virginia delegation. More than one Virginian was cool toward the idea of Washington being appointed, Adams had found in his sounding of their opinions.

One morning he walked with Sam Adams in the Statehouse yard, taking a little exercise and fresh air before Congress convened. What would they do, they questioned each other, about the distressing lack of agreement on a plan of action? Every day alarming news arrived from Boston; Congress could not sit idle. John told his cousin that he had taken great pains to persuade the delegates to agree on a plan acceptable to all; now he was "determined to take a step which should compel . . . all the other members of Congress to declare themselves for or against something."

"I am determined this morning," he said, "to make a direct motion that Congress should adopt the army before Boston and appoint Colonel Washington commander of it." Sam intently studied his cousin but did not reply. Then, after Congress had assembled, John Adams rose. In a short speech he covered the state of the Colonies, the uncertainty of the people, the critical shape of the army, the probability that the British would take advantage of delays, "march out of Boston and spread desolation as far as they could go." He ended with a motion that Congress adopt the army at Cambridge and appoint a general. Though he did not feel this was the time to nominate a general, he could say without hesitation that he had only one man in mind, "a gentleman from Virginia who was among us and very well-known to all of us, a gentleman whose skill and experience as an officer, whose independent fortune, great talents and excellent universal character would command the approbation of all America and unite the cordial exertions of all the Colonies better than any other person in the union." Hearing these words, the modest Washington darted from his seat by the door into the library. At the same time, Hancock, who in his chairman's seat was easily accessible to Adams' view, changed his expression from one of obvious pleasure at the speech on the state of the Colonies to one of "mortification and resentment" on hearing Washington's name. When Sam Adams seconded the motion, it "did not soften the president's physiognomy at all." In the debate that followed, Pendleton of Virginia and Sherman of Connecticut insisted that they had no personal objection to Washington; they feared, however, that because the army was all from New England and had a general it appeared to find satisfactory, and because it had been able to keep the British army in Boston, which was all that was expected at that time, it might not accept a Virginia general. Cushing and several others expressed their agreement. Paine expressed a loyalty to the present general, Artemas Ward. The subject was then postponed. And as the days went by, opposition to Washington dwindled. He was at length nominated by Thomas Johnson of Maryland and unanimously elected.

The problem of who should be second in command was equally touchy. General Charles Lee had rugged support, particularly from Thomas Mifflin, who felt that Washington was the only one under whom a man of Lee's rank and experience might be expected cheerfully to serve. Adams, in his turn, opposed Lee. It would be a great deal, he pointed out, to expect that General Ward ought to serve under anyone, but particularly he should not serve under a stranger. Although Adams had a high opinion of Lee, he said, it would be humiliating to Ward to ask him to serve under Lee. Congress then voted to make Ward second in command and Lee third.

Only one sorry conclusion came out of Adams' proposal of Washington for commander-in-chief. That was the resultant coolness of Hancock, which never abated entirely, even in later years —or so the ever sensitive Adams fancied. Furthermore, it was the beginning of a shift in alliance among the Massachusetts delegates, since thereafter Hancock drifted away from that bloc.[5]

"The modest and virtuous, the amiable, generous and brave George Washington, Esquire,"[6] as Adams described him, now set off for Boston, only to be met on the way with the news that General Joseph Warren had fallen at the Battle of Bunker Hill.

Congress proceeded to act a little more as if they were conducting a war, voting ten companies of riflemen to be sent from Pennsylvania, Maryland and Virginia to join the army at Boston.

"These are an excellent species of light infantry," Adams told his wife. The troops had given up muskets for a weapon called a rifle that had "circular . . . grooves within the barrel and carries a ball with great exactness to great distances. They are the most accurate marksmen in the world."[7]

Adams' head spun with plans of action that he thought Congress should take. The danger now was disunion and dissension among colonies and delegates. By this time, he felt, petitions and remonstrances would be fruitless, accomplishing only loss of precious time which the British could use to advantage in sowing seeds of discord. First of all, Congress ought to recommend to the people of every state "to seize on all the Crown officers and hold them with civility, humanity and generosity as hostages for the security of the people of Boston and to be exchanged for them as soon as the British army would release them." Congress should then recommend to each state that it form its own government under its own authority. It should declare the Colonies free, sovereign, independent states; it should inform Britain that America was willing to negotiate for redress of all grievances and restoration of harmony on a permanent basis. After that, Congress should negotiate for alliances with France, Spain and other European powers, telling Britain what America intended to do. Finally, Congress should assume responsibility for the pay, subsistence, and munitions of the troops it had adopted.[8]

But no such plans went forward just then, for the Pennsylvania Quaker, John Dickinson, pushed for a second petition to the King —a "measure of imbecility."[9]

With a long speech Dickinson introduced his motion for a second petition, suggesting that it be sent over with Richard Penn, who was about to sail for England. Then Adams rose to oppose the measure. To his delight, John Sullivan of New Hampshire eloquently supported him. Just then someone beckoned Adams to the Statehouse yard to discuss some business; taking his hat, he went outside, with an angry Dickinson upon his heels. In a manner extraordinarily abrupt for the soft-spoken Dickinson, "and with an air, countenance and gestures as rough and haughty as if I had been a school boy and he the master," the Pennsylvanian exclaimed: "What is the reason, Mr. Adams, that your New Englandmen oppose our measures of reconciliation? There now is Sullivan in a long harangue following you, in a determined opposition to our petition to the King. Look ye! If you don't concur with us in our pacific system,

I and a number of us will break off from you in New England, and we will carry on the opposition by ourselves in our own way."

Adams had been caught in a happy humor. He was able to muster the coolness to reply, "Mr. Dickinson, there are many things that I can very cheerfully sacrifice to harmony and even to unanimity; but I am not to be threatened into an express adoption or approbation of measures which my judgment reprobates. Congress must judge, and if they pronounce against me, I must submit, as if they determine against you, you ought to acquiesce."[10]

Unfortunately, however, he could not long maintain such uncharacteristic smoothness. Later mulling over the incident, he fumed over Dickinson's outburst. The fact that Congress approved the petition did not calm his ire. Taking pen in hand, he vented his anger in two letters, one to Abigail, the other to James Warren, both of which he gave to a young man from Boston, Benjamin Hichborn. The letter to Abigail complained of the "behavior of my compatriots—no mortal tale could equal it."

"The fidgets, the whims, the caprice, the vanity, the superstition, the irritability of some of us, is enough to—," he wrote angrily.[11]

To James Warren, then president of the Massachusetts provincial congress, he wrote more venomously, "A certain great fortune and piddling genius, whose fame has been trumpeted so loudly, has given a silly cast to our whole doings. We are between hawk and buzzard. We ought to have had in our hands a month ago the whole legislative, executive, and judicial of the whole continent, and have completely modeled a constitution; to have raised a naval power and opened all our ports wide; to have arrested every friend of government on the continent and held them as hostages for the poor victims in Boston; and then opened the door as wide as possible for peace and reconciliation. After this, they might have petitioned, negotiated, addressed, and so on, if they would."[12]

On his way to Boston bearing Adams' letters, Hichborn was captured near Newport, Rhode Island. He did not destroy the letters. The British gleefully swooped them up, printing them far and wide. Adams subsequently gained the reputation of a warmongering bogyman who pumped for independence, a constitution

and, most notoriously, a navy. The bad publicity pierced Adams'
thin skin, but he tried not to care; after all, he had made no secret
of his feelings that independence had become a necessity.

Despite opinions for and against, all the delegates, including
Adams, signed the Olive Branch Petition, this last plea to the King
himself to intervene to repeal the Coercive Acts and bring about a
reconciliation. Perhaps even Adams held a thin hope. But the King
saw no dramatic ultimatum in the petition; he saw no final appeal
for restoration of age-old filial ties. Instead he refused to accept a
petition from a rebel body.

Even so, it was another year before the delegates could bring
themselves to vote for independence. The terrifying question for all
the delegates—even those like Adams who favored independence
—was what would come after? Not a man among them failed to
recognize that for all its flaws, the British constitution was the best
that men had ever devised. Would they be substituting a far worse
government for what might yet be patched up? None of these men
was under any illusions as to the imperfectibility of men; they had
governed themselves far too long to gloss over the examples of
fallen nature they had observed in their own assemblies. The perils
of democratic government loomed great in their eyes. What was to
become of the rule of law after independence had been declared?
At home between sessions, Adams, upon one occasion in particular, was made to feel the intensity of the problem. He happened to
meet a man who had once been his client, a horse jockey who had
been in and out of the courts more times than he could count.

"Oh! Mr. Adams," the fellow saluted him. "What great things
have you and your colleagues done for us! We can never be grateful
enough to you. There are no courts of justice now in this province,
and I hope there never will be another!" Adams did not answer. In
other times he would have laughed; now he fell to wondering. "Is
this the object for which I have been contending?" he said to
himself. "Are these the sentiments of such people? And how many
of them are there in the country? Half the nation for what I know;
for half the nation are debtors, if not more, and these have been in
all countries the sentiments of debtors. If the power of the country

should get into such hands, and there is great danger that it will, to what purpose have we sacrificed our time, health, and everything else? Surely we must guard against this spirit and these principles or we shall repent of all our conduct." He grew melancholy, but then the thought of "the good sense and integrity of the majority of the great body of the people" consoled him.[13]

Yet if the prospect of what might come disconcerted him, he was equally distressed by the present lack of government. There was little government in the Colonies, and what existed was entirely extra-legal. It was a credit to Americans that they managed to live so quietly, bolstered only by the framework that their extra-legal assemblies had established. Congress could not permit such a precarious situation to continue. Months ago the states should have formed governments, but independence had not even been declared.

At last, however, in May of 1776, Adams was able to write Abigail, "Great Britain has at last driven America to the last step, a complete separation from her, a total absolute independence, not only of her Parliament but of her Crown, for such is the amount of the resolve of the fifteenth."[14] On May 10 Congress had voted a resolve recommending to the colonial assemblies and conventions that they adopt governments adjudged by representatives of the people to be conducive to the happiness of their constituents and of America. Adams introduced this resolution, after laboring a year to obtain it. He wrote the preamble, which was even stronger than the resolve itself. Much to the displeasure of James Duane, it was passed on the fifteenth. A "machine to fabricate independence," Duane scoffed. No, Adams said, it was independence itself.[15] Truly it was tantamount to a declaration of independence. Still, more formality was needed.

Richard Henry Lee took that initiative on June 7 when he moved for independence. With the New York, Pennsylvania, Delaware and South Carolina delegations uninstructed by their assemblies as to how to vote, the question was postponed. On June 11, however, Adams, Jefferson, Franklin, Roger Sherman and Robert R. Livingston were named to a committee to draw up a declaration.

Adams gave an offhand account of the proceedings of the committee, pointing out how Jefferson acquired the task of drafting the document. Jefferson had been in Congress a year but talked very little. In fact, during the whole time Adams had sat with him in Congress "he never heard him utter three sentences together." The largest speech Adams ever heard him deliver "was a gross insult on religion, in one or two sentences, for which I gave him immediately the reprehension which he richly merited." But Adams went on to explain: "Eloquence in public assemblies is not the surest road to fame and preferment. . . ." Jefferson "had the reputation of a masterly pen"; moreover, because Richard Henry Lee was not universally liked by his Virginia colleagues, "Jefferson was set up to rival and supplant him. This could be done only by the pen, for Mr. Jefferson could stand no competition with him or anyone else in elocution and public debate."

After the committee had decided what the articles should say, they appointed Jefferson and Adams to formulate them. Jefferson suggested that the older man write the draft, but Adams declined for several reasons: Jefferson, as a Southerner, would be more acceptable to the company; Adams "had been so obnoxious for my early and constant zeal in promoting the measure that any draft of mine would undergo a more severe scrutiny and criticism in Congress than one of his composition"; finally, and most important, "I had a great opinion of the elegance of his pen and none at all of my own." Accordingly, Jefferson went home to work up a draft. He reported to the committee, which in turn reported to Congress "where, after a severe criticism and striking out several of the most oratorical paragraphs, it was adopted on the fourth of July, 1776, and published to the world."[16]

Independence was voted on July 2; the Declaration, a denial at last of the King himself, was adopted on July 4. In the July 1 debate on independence, John Dickinson, as spokesman for the losing side, performed magnificently. Adams gave his opponent credit for an oration delivered "not only with great ingenuity and eloquence but with equal politeness and candor. . . ."

"No member rose to answer him," Adams recalled, "and after

waiting some time, in hopes that someone less obnoxious than myself, who had been all along for a year before and still was represented and believed to be the author of all the mischief, I determined to speak." Benjamin Rush, in later years, wrote that his friend had begun with an invocation to the god of eloquence.

"This is a misrepresentation," Adams objected. "Nothing so puerile as this fell from me. I began by saying that this was the first time of my life that I had ever wished for the talents and eloquence of the ancient orators of Greece and Rome, for I was very sure that none of them ever had before him a question of more importance to his country and to the world." He spoke without notes and with no preparation, but he must have spoken concisely and convincingly. He had recited the arguments for independence so often, he had examined them so closely that surely he had as great a command of them as anyone there. Certainly he had labored for independence as industriously as any delegate.

Just before the final question was put, the new delegation from New Jersey came in, "very respectable characters" who had been empowered to vote for independence—Richard Stockton, John Witherspoon and Francis Hopkinson. They requested to hear the arguments for independence. Silence fell on the group. Finally, Edward Rutledge laughed, turning to Adams, "Nobody will speak but you upon this subject. You have all the topics so ready that you must satisfy the gentlemen from New Jersey." Adams was embarrassed, but he laughed, too; he would feel like an actor or gladiator, he said, trying to entertain the audience. He "was ashamed to repeat what I had said twenty times before, and I thought nothing new could be advanced by me." Still the New Jersey men insisted on hearing a summary of the arguments, at least; with no one else willing to speak, Adams set forth the arguments as quickly as he could.[17]

Richard Henry Lee, as well, apparently spoke for independence that day. Then New Hampshire, Connecticut, Massachusetts, Rhode Island, New Jersey, Maryland, Virginia, North Carolina and Georgia proceeded to vote in favor of the Lee resolution for independence. South Carolina, oddly enough, and Pennsylvania voted against it. New York, protesting that it must receive new instructions from its constituents, abstained. Delaware was divided. That night, Caesar Rodney raced 80 miles through a thunderstorm from Dover to Philadelphia, arriving in time the next day to cast Delaware's vote for independence. South Carolina then switched its vote in favor. Dickinson and Robert Morris agreed to stay away and James Wilson voted in favor, allowing Pennsylvania to line up in favor of independence. New York again abstained, making the vote on July 2 unanimous.

With his capacity to be in the midst of happenings and yet perceive their relevance to the fabric of history, Adams was able, as few men have been, to look back and size up, to look forward and predict—all with uncanny accuracy. Some men, it seems, ride the surface of life; others, like Adams, swim deep in the current. These are the men who feel the majesty of the events in which they partake, who see the grand workings of history in every occasion, personal or public. That is why Adams was always taking stock. In the midst of his countless duties he always found it imperative to sit down, clear away the mist, and use that most painful but most helpful of all disciplines, writing, to clarify the meaning of what had come to pass.

And so it was that on July 3, the day after independence had been resolved, Adams delivered his commentary on the proceedings to the person in whom he always struck a sympathetic chord. To Abigail he wrote two letters that day, in which he said,

Yesterday the greatest question was decided, which ever was debated in America and a greater, perhaps, never was or will be decided among men. A resolution was passed without one dissenting colony "that these united Colonies are, and of right ought to be, free and independent states, and as such they have, and of right ought to have, full power to make war, conclude peace, establish commerce, and to do all the other acts and things which other states may rightfully do." You will see in a few days a Declaration setting forth the causes which have impell'd us to this mighty Revolution and the reasons which will justify it in the sight of God and man. A plan of confederation will be taken up in a few days.

When I look back to the year 1761 and recollect the argument concerning writs of assistance in the Superior Court, which I have hitherto considered as the commencement of the controversy between Great Britain and America, and run through the whole period from that time to this and recollect the series of political events, the chain of causes and effects, I am surprised at the suddenness, as well as the greatness of this Revolution. Britain has been fill'd with folly and America with wisdom, at least this is my judgment. Time must determine. It is the will of heaven that the two countries should be sundered forever. It may be the will of heaven that America shall suffer calamities still more wasting and distresses yet more dreadful. If this is to be the case, it will have this good effect, at least: it will inspire us with many virtues which we have not, and correct many errors, follies, and vices which threaten to disturb, dishonor and destroy us. The furnace of affliction produces refinement in states as well as individuals. And the new governments we are assuming in every part will require a purification from our vices and an augmentation of our virtues or they will be no blessings. The people will have unbounded power. And the people are extremely addicted to corruption and venality, as well as the great. I am not without apprehensions from this quarter. But I must submit all my hopes and fears to an overruling Providence, in which, unfashionable as the faith may be, I firmly believe.[18]

When she read that passage, Abigail must have thought how truly it expressed her husband's view of life. Adams went on:

The second day of July, 1776, will be the most memorable epocha in the history of America. I am apt to believe that it will be celebrated by succeeding generations as the great anniversary festival. It ought to be commemorated as the day of deliverance by solemn acts of devotion to God Almighty. It ought to be solemnized with pomp and parade, with shows, games, sports, guns, bells, bonfires and illuminations from one end of this continent to the other, from this time forward forevermore.

You will think me transported with enthusiasm but I am not. I am well aware of the toil and blood and treasure that it will cost us to maintain this Declaration and support and defend these states. Yet through all the gloom I can see the rays of ravishing light and glory. I can see that the end is more than worth all the means. And that posterity will triumph in that day's transaction, even although we should rue it, which I trust in God we shall not.[19]

CHAPTER VIII

THE PLAN OF GOVERNMENT

FROM July of the Olive Branch Petition, 1775, until July of the Declaration of Independence, 1776, Americans spent an agonizing year. King George rejected their final peace offering, scorning any proposed settlement from a "rebel" Congress. By early 1776 Americans heard that Parliament had subjected them to the further indignity of prohibiting all trade with the Colonies, warning that colonial ships were now legal booty and that their crews might be impressed into the English navy. Meanwhile, the Battle of Bunker Hill had clinched into certainty the fact that Americans faced out-and-out war. Attacked by a collection of minutemen, a provoked Captain Mowatt bombarded Falmouth, Maine, one of the towns that had been on John Adams' circuit. Retreating American forces burned Norfolk, Virginia. Militiamen ousted a force of loyalist Scotsmen at Moore's Creek Bridge near Wilmington, North Carolina. Commodore Ezek Hopkins captured Nassau, along with a great supply of ammunition. The Canadian expedition, led by General Montgomery and Benedict Arnold, fizzled, ending in the death of Montgomery at Quebec. Washington managed to occupy Dorchester Heights, a scene which Abigail could see from the excellent vantage of Penn's Hill. For several days the booming cannonade ceased for only a few hours at a time, shaking the house most of the night until the windows rattled, sending such shivers through Abigail that her "heart beat pace with them all night."[1]

This was war, independence declared in substance if not in form. Yet Americans dragged their heels the whole miserable way to the ultimate severance of filial ties. Because it charged their emotions so deeply, it was a private as much as a public decision, fraught with the same kind of racking implications for men as would face their luckless descendants in 1861. Americans in 1775-1776 fought, prayed, bickered, preached, read, agonized over their decision. They praised their leaders in one moment, deprecated them in another. The word went out in the Braintree neighborhood, for instance, that Adams, on his way to Congress, and Hancock had hopped aboard a British man-of-war at New York and sailed for England. Unfortunately, some of "the gaping vulgar swallowed the story," Abigail wrote angrily, causing such dispute in a local pub "that some men were collared and dragged out of the shop, with great threats for reporting such scandalous lies, and an uncle of ours offered his life as a forfeit for you if the report were true."[2]

From July to July was a hellish year for those who struggled to reach a moment of truth. In addition to the aspect of genuine sentimental attachment to England, beyond the perturbation that one felt when speculating upon the unknown of independence, there were moral questions that a man had to decide before he could bring himself to favor independence.

For John Adams the dark hours of decision had come a little earlier than for most. He had wrestled with his dragon for ten years, really, and by July, 1775, he had long since made up his mind. Throughout that year between midsummers he campaigned for independence, but much of his energy and deepest interest soared on to a new and, in the long run, more encompassing problem—that of government. Independence he continued to work for, yet he counted on it as being inevitable. It was even more important, he felt, to concentrate on a problem whose solution—good government—was not inevitable. The condition of non-government, or at best extra-legal government, in which the states existed was anathema to Adams' lawyer's soul. It was a hazardous tightrope to try to walk, a temptation to evil on the part of rebels, mobs and general malcontents. Moreover, without state governments Adams could hardly see how the Colonies might call themselves independent. Prodding the states to form governments and suggesting a form of government to them was a grave problem—and one which no one did more to solve than Adams. With his classical and legal background and the philosophical bent of his mind, he could tackle the problem with a skillful hand. Because he knew that it is necessary to reconcile the freedom with which man is born with the authority necessary to preserve order within society, Adams understood the difficulty that most fundamentally besets man in society. He could provide some answer to that dilemma because he also understood much of the essence of human nature that makes men of all epochs alike in aspirations, problems, needs and failings.

But, meanwhile, in the fall of 1775 Adams entered an activity that kindled his boyish soul with more jubilant enthusiasm than almost any other event of his life. This was his part in the founding of the American Navy. It took some impudence to propose setting up a naval force against the most powerful fleet in the world. John Adams and a few other New Englanders bred with the sea in their bones dared to try.

For years Adams had ridden the coast of Massachusetts, attending court at Plymouth, Barnstable, Martha's Vineyard. In the counties of Essex, York and Cumberland he had talked with cod fishermen and whalers. Hearing of the "activity, enterprise, patience, perseverance, and daring intrepidity of our seamen," he had decided that if they were given a free hand upon the ocean, they would be valuable assets in the war. A navy, Adams believed, was essential to the translation of independence from the realm of ideas to that of fact. Without a navy, America could never maintain the neutrality so indispensable to independence, he argued.

As he recorded everything, so did Adams write down the events of the exciting days of October and November, 1775, when the navy was born. The Rhode Island delegation, directed by their provincial assembly, initiated action on October 3 with a motion for setting up a continental navy. There was impassioned opposition to the idea of a fleet: it was a wild, visionary project, an infant taking a mad bull by the horns. Edward Rutledge expressed his alarm with so much eloquence that Adams suspected some Philadelphia merchants had instructed him out-of-doors. But the Adams naval faction responded to these attacks with equal ardor and sagacity.

On October 5 Congress discussed disturbing letters they had just received from London, informing them that two brigs carrying powder and munitions had sailed without convoy for Quebec. In a flurry of debate, Congress resolved to appoint a committee to prepare a plan for intercepting these vessels. The three members appointed were those who had most zealously greeted the motion for a navy—Adams, Silas Deane and John Langdon.

After deliberating only a few hours the committee hustled back in, laying before Congress a report that called for a letter to General Washington, directing him to apply to Massachusetts for its two armed vessels and to dispatch them to head off the English vessels and secure the valuable ammunition cargo. The vessels of Rhode Island and Connecticut should also be put into service, all to be under Continental pay.[3]

Debate on the question of setting up an American Navy continued on October 7. It was "the maddest idea in the world to think of building an American fleet," exclaimed Samuel Chase. "We should mortgage the whole continent."

"If the plans of some gentlemen are to take place," Rev. John Zubly said, "an American fleet must be a part of it—extravagant as it is."

"I wish it may be seriously debated," Deane commented. "I don't think it romantic at all."[4]

On October 13 Congress resolved to outfit two swift vessels for a three-month cruise to intercept the British ships. Seven men, including Adams, ultimately were named to a naval committee, agreeing to meet in a room in a local pub at six o'clock each evening.

Throughout November this committee brought in resolutions for drawing $100,000 upon the Continental treasury, for enlisting seamen and granting them prizes for interception, and for commissioning officers. Congress on November 25 adopted a recommendation to establish prize courts. There occurred on this day, according to Adams' later account, "the true origin and formation of the American Navy," an event that he "had at least as great a share in producing . . . as any man living or dead. . . ." His zeal and exertions in 1798, 1799 and 1800, he wrote a little pompously, "at every hazard and in opposition to a more powerful party than that against me in 1775 [were] but a perseverance in the same principles, systems and views of the public interest."

Congress on November 28 discussed and adopted a set of rules and orders for an American Navy, a significant paper drafted by Adams himself. It became known as *Rules for the Regulation of the Navy of the United Colonies of North-America.*

Adams had a particular fondness for his work on the naval committee. Indeed, it was "the pleasantest part of my labors for the four years I spent in Congress. . . ." He always found Richard Henry Lee and Christopher Gadsden sensible, cheerful men. Yet it was spry old Governor Hopkins, over seventy years old, who "kept us all alive." Upon the business at hand his experience and wisdom were indispensable. Then with the evening business concluded, Hopkins took his fortification of Jamaica rum and water, entertaining the men until almost midnight with his anecdotes and discourses upon history and poetry.

Purchasing and naming their five vessels, the committee must have been like a pack of gleeful boys glorying in visions of grandeur. The first ship, Adams wrote proudly, "we named Alfred in honor of the founder of the greatest navy that ever existed. The second Columbus after the discoverer of this quarter of the globe. The third Cabot for the discoverer of this northern part of the continent. The fourth Andrew Doria in memory of the great Genoese admiral, and the fifth Providence for the town where she was purchased, the residence of Governor Hopkins and his brother Ezek, whom we appointed first captain. We appointed all the officers of all the ships. At the solicitation of Mr. Deane we appointed his brother-in-law, Captain Saltonstall."[5]

Early in 1776 a standing marine committee replaced the naval committee as administrator of the Navy. Adams, who had gone home on leave at the end of 1775, was consequently not named to this second group. Nonetheless, he retained his affection for the Navy, ever delighting to recite his part in its founding.

Throughout the period of his work on the naval committee—indeed, throughout the entire year from Olive Branch to Declaration—Adams continued to exert him elf in the cause of urging the states to form governments. Now, in addition to working in the practical art of government, he applied himself to formal theory. He had read thoroughly the classical political thinkers; Harrington, Sidney, Hobbes, Nedham, Locke were all in his repertoire. But until now he had never had occasion to do much theorizing himself. Still, the background was there; now he began to turn over and over in his mind the principles of government. The core of the difficulty, he saw, was to balance human liberty against the equally human faculty for misusing the coercive power of government. He thrust into more concentrated research, beginning the labors which led finally to such important political works as *Thoughts on Government*, the Massachusetts Constitution of 1780, the *Defence of the Constitutions of the United States* and *Discourses on Davila*, works that he later believed to have influenced the New York constitution, the second constitutions of Pennsylvania and Georgia, the United States Constitution, and *The Federalist Papers*.[6] From his knowledge of political writers and from his experience with colonial government, he took material which he now applied to relief of the stricken states.

The confusion that gripped the states could not continue much longer. One by one, each colony now requested Congress to recommend a form of government that it might adopt. Massachusetts, torn asunder as it had been for months, was the first of the Colonies to cry for help in its predicament. In June of 1775, Congress took up a letter from the provincial convention of Massachusetts, explaining the difficulties of the colony in operating without a regular government. The colony requested advice from Congress on the government it should adopt, declaring that it was ready to follow Congressional directions.

Adams leaped at this opportunity to deliver a speech upon the question that was so close to his heart. Since he supposed that no man there had any idea of consolidating the continent under one national government of centralized power, he proposed that they follow the Greek, Swiss and Dutch plan of a confederacy of states, each with a separate government. These goverments should follow the principle of balance between legislative, executive and judicial powers. Their legislative power should be divided between a lower house, upper house and governor—a continuation of the English forms minus the aspect of inheritance or nobility. Adams hoped that the states would see fit to continue their English tradition of what he called republican or mixed government.

Nevertheless, this man, who strangely enough would one day have to defend himself against accusations of monarchism, stressed that it was up to the states to decide what kind of government they should adopt. Because he believed that government originates in the people, he was concerned with the method the states should use to decide upon a plan of government. Adams' suggestion was that they adopt government by means of the constitutional convention, an institution which he worked diligently to promote and which became one of his particular bequests to American political tradition. Putting to practice the theories of the wisest writers, Congress, Adams thought, should "invite the people to erect the whole building with their own hands upon the broadest foundation." This could be done "only by conventions of representatives chosen by the people in the several Colonies in the most exact proportions." In a state which existed for the benefit of the people, rather than the other way around, in a state where the equality of self-governing men under the rule of law was the first axiom of justice, there must be a reasonable, orderly provision for changing the system under which laws were made and administered. If government were to exist for the protection of the liberty and happiness of every man, then the foundation of government must be popular consent. If by popular consent the decision was that government no longer impartially protected liberty, then that government might be changed without bloodshed by a constitutional convention. The constitutional convention provided the answer to the problem of how to effect a peaceful revolution. Congress, Adams said, "ought now to recommend to the people of every colony to call such conventions and set up governments of their own, under their own authority." The people were ". . . the source of all authority and original of all power."

The ideas of new state governments, of a confederation, of constitutional conventions, were "new, strange and terrible doctrines to the greatest part of the members," Adams admitted, "but not a very small number heard them with apparent pleasure. . . ."[7]

The committee that had discussed the letter from the Massachusetts convention soon returned a report, recommending that the convention call for representatives to an assembly, which in turn should elect members of a council. Together the assembly and council should exercise the powers of government until one of King George's governors would consent to govern Massachusetts according to its charter.

Although this report, which was adopted, did not fully satisfy him, Adams felt encouraged. It could not be very long before other states would ask for advice, and now Congress at least had a precedent for recommending to the states that they form governments.

No doubt because of the diligence of John Sullivan, who took Adams' position, New Hampshire was the next colony to request from Congress advice upon a government. Hoping that this time he could coax Congress to recommend generally that all the Colonies call state conventions to erect regular governments, Adams bombarded the company with a list of plentiful arguments. He mentioned the danger to the people's morals "from the present loose state of things," the danger of insurrections throughout the country in favor of Britain, the inability of America to outlaw spying without assuming the powers of government, the picture of disunion that America presented both to allies and enemies, the absurdity of waging war against a King to whom countless subjects still paid allegiance, the refusal of Britain, France and Spain to take America seriously while she had no government; the poor hope of obtaining redress of grievances with so little display of independence and union, the incapacity of Congress, without state governments, to command the natural resources of the country—in short, to wage war.[8]

From Sullivan and John Rutledge, Adams received valued support on the floor of Congress. Sam Adams, too, agreed with his cousin upon the necessity of forming state governments, maneuvering the other delegates with the sort of tête-à-tête persuasion in which he excelled. Even so, Sam, the perpetual democrat with his inclinations toward one sovereign assembly, was not a sound political theorist in John's view. In the matter of what plan of government the states should adopt, neither could John Adams rely upon his Massachusetts colleagues Cushing and Paine. Cushing pushed for a unicameral assembly; Paine simply steered clear of the subject.[9]

Although in October, 1775, opposition to his proposal was still vehement, Adams was gratified to see that "many members of Congress began to hear me with more patience, and some began to ask me civil questions."

Once the constitutional convention had fabricated a government, his colleagues inquired, who knew whether the people would submit to it?

"If there is any doubt of that," Adams explained, "the convention may send out their project of a constitution to the people in their several towns, counties, or districts, and the people may make their acceptance of their own act." The people, he assured the men of Congress, knew more about government than they were given credit for. But what kind of government did Adams suggest, the congressmen asked.

"A plan as nearly resembling the governments under which we were born and have lived as the circumstances of the country will admit. Kings we never had among us, nobles we never had. Nothing hereditary ever existed in the country; nor will the country require or admit of any such thing; but governors and councils we have always had, as well as representatives. A legislature in three branches ought to be preserved, and independent judges."[10]

Congress gave to New Hampshire a more liberal direction than it had given to Massachusetts. This time a provincial convention was told to call together representatives who would establish whatever form of government they thought conducive to the happiness of the people and to good order.

South Carolina followed upon the heels of New Hampshire with a request for advice. On the South Carolina resolution Adams determined to strike out the word "colony" in favor of the word "state," to change "dispute" to "war" and "colonies" to "America" or "states."

"But the child was not yet weaned," he said, realizing that most members of Congress still harbored hopes of reconciliation. At this time he further sought to have the recommendation to South Carolina enlarged to include all the states, prompting his colleagues to ask once more what kind of government he thought the states should adopt. Adams knew that the natural thing to do then would have been to make a motion for Congress to appoint a committee to study a plan of government, which would be recommended to all the states. Yet he dared not try that.

"I knew that if such a plan was adopted, it would be, if not permanent, yet of long duration; and it would be extremely difficult to get rid of it. And I knew that every one of my friends, and all those who were the most zealous for assuming government, had at that time no idea of any other government but a contemptible legislature in one assembly, with committees for executive magistrates and judges." Consequently, he answered these questions "by sporting off hand" a number of short sketches of plans that the conventions might adopt. And since the questions came up nearly every day, Adams recalled later that he "had in my head and at my tongue's end as many projects of government as Mr. Burke says the Abbé Sieyès had in his pigeonholes. . . .I took care, however," he emphasized, "always to bear my testimony against every plan of unbalanced government."[11]

Exhausted by overwork and ill health, Adams hoped for respite when he took a leave of absence to Braintree in December, 1775, but that relief was all too short because he had to take his seat in the Massachusetts Council on the twenty-eighth. Even then he assumed more duties than were required. Anxious about the interim state of government in Massachusetts, he took time to draft a proclamation from the General Court to be read at the opening of the courts and town meetings.[12] This paper contained some of his characteristic thoughts on government.

In January Adams set out for Philadelphia for the fourth time, on this journey accompanied by Cushing's replacement, Elbridge Gerry. Adams was pleased with his new colleague, whose election would rid the Massachusetts delegation of internal bickering. On the way they dined with General Washington and his lady at Cambridge, the headquarters for the colonial troops who were sealing off Boston. It was a motley dinner group including six or seven Indian chiefs and warriors of the Caughnawaga tribe, who had arrived with some of their wives and children to offer their services to Washington.

"A savage feast they made of it," Adams wrote to his wife, "yet were very polite in the Indian style. One of these sachems is an Englishman, a native of this colony whose name was Williams, captivated in his infancy with his mother and adopted by some kind squaw—another, I think, is half French blood."

To the chiefs and warriors, Washington introduced Adams as a member of the grand council fire at Philadelphia, "which made them prick up their ears; they came and shook hands with me and made me low bows and scrapes, and so on. In short I was much pleased with this day's entertainment."

"Tomorrow," he said wistfully, "we mount for the grand council fire— where I shall think often of my little brood at the foot of Penn's Hill."[13]

As Adams again took up residence at Congress, he discovered that the infant nation had been hit by a "disastrous meteor," a phenomenon out of Philadelphia by the name of Thomas Paine. Paine was a mysterious fellow, of plain background and passionate nature, come rather recently from England, put onto the subject of independence by Dr. Rush, and a star overnight with his pamphlet *Common Sense.* By 1776 Americans were ready to be converted to independence; Paine, a sure calculator of the pulse of public opinion, was just the man to sway them.

"Sensible men think there are some whims, some sophisms, some artful addresses to superstitious notions, some keen attempts upon the passions in this pamphlet," Adams wrote to Abigail. "But all agree there is a great deal of good sense, delivered in a clear, simple, concise and nervous style." There was general approval of Paine's assessment of the difficulty of reconciling with Britain, Adams had found. But he himself thought little of Paine's ideas on government and even less as time went on. "His notions and plans of Continental government are not much applauded. Indeed this writer has a better hand at pulling down than building."

Somewhat to Adams' concern—for he had no wish to be associated with Paine's plan of government—*Common Sense* was thought by a good many people to have come from his pen. "But altho' I could not have written anything in so manly and striking a style," he told Abigail, "I flatter myself I should have made a more respectable figure as an architect if I had undertaken such a work. This writer seems to have very inadequate ideas of what is proper and necessary to be done in order to form constitutions for single colonies, as well as a great model of union for the whole."[14]

In answer, then, to Paine's advocacy in *Common Sense* of unmixed government, of government without balance of powers, Adams sometime late in March composed his own sketch of a plan of government. He wrote it upon the request of two North Carolina delegates, William Hooper and John Penn, who were about to return home for their state's constitutional convention. The original he gave to Hooper, a copy to Penn. George Wythe, glimpsing the paper, asked for a copy, which Adams supplied him after making a new one from memory. Jonathan Dickinson Sergeant of New Jersey chimed in with another request. When Richard Henry Lee came to ask for a copy, Adams was so tired of reworking the piece from memory that he borrowed Wythe's copy. Lee took it, publishing it as *Thoughts on Government, in a Letter from a Gentleman to his Friend.*[15]

Sometime after publication of the *Thoughts on Government,* Adams received a caller—Tom Paine. Paine's business, Adams recalled, "was to reprehend me for publishing my pamphlet. Said he was afraid it would do hurt, and that it was repugnant to the plan he had proposed in his *Common Sense.*" Of course it was repugnant, old warhorse Adams rejoined; that was the reason he had written it. He must have twinkled when he said that he was as much afraid of Paine's work as Paine was of his. Paine's plan "was so democratical, without any restraint or even an attempt at any equilibrium or counterpoise, that it must produce confusion and every evil work." And while he was at it, Adams "told him further that his reasoning from the Old Testament was ridiculous and I could hardly think him sincere." Much to Adams' surprise, Paine laughed. He had taken his ideas on the Old Testament from Milton, he said, "and then expressed a contempt of the Old Testament and indeed of the Bible at large. . . ." Seeing that Adams "did not relish this," he soon "checked himself with these words, 'However, I have some thoughts of publishing my thoughts on religion, but I believe it will be best to postpone it to the latter part of my life.' "

The whole conversation went in good humor, but Adams "perceived in him a conceit of himself and a daring impudence. . . ." There was certainly not much for Paine to be conceited about. After all, Adams felt, Paine's arguments for independence—the only decent ones of the pamphlet—were the very ones that he himself had been repeating time and again in Congress for the past nine months. "I am bold to say there is not a fact nor a reason stated in it, which had not been frequently urged in Congress." It was only that the popular temper was ready for Tom Paine, for his crowd-pleasing phrases such as "the royal brute of England," "the blood upon his soul," "and a few others of equal delicacy," as Adams put it, such as befitted the pen of "an emigrant from Newgate or one who had chiefly associated with such company."

Adams grumbled it was "a general opinion" that this pamphlet was "of great importance" in the Revolution, but he doubted it. Even so, "it probably converted some to the doctrine of independence and gave others an excuse for declaring in favor of it."[16]

It was characteristic of Adams that he composed the *Thoughts on Government* during the memorable year when he worked hardest for independence. Not many men are suited both to pulling down governments and constructing them, yet Adams worked on both problems at the same time, thus earning a position on both fronts unrivaled among his contemporaries.

Because it was a microcosm of what was to come, the *Thoughts*, brief as it was, occupied an important place in Adams' works on government. Written with clarity, it was a resumé of his plan of government, a definition of what a republic should be, a portrait of government by constitutional rule of law and not of men. What nature and experience dictated to Adams in the *Thoughts*, he elaborated upon but did not change in the Massachusetts Constitution, in the *Defence* and the *Discourses on Davila*. His *Thoughts* and additional political works were in the mainstream of Western political thought, derived from Aristotle, even more from Polybius and Cicero and, among the modern writers, especially from Harrington.

Adams composed his *Thoughts* upon two premises that were contrary to popular concepts of his day. In the first place, he thought men could never be perfect. Second, sovereignty in government should never reside exclusively in one body. Both human nature and the experience of history, he believed, supported him.

In his idea of human nature, Adams viewed humanity as he thought it was, not as he wished it might be. For that reason, he could be more than a mere closet philosopher. Always impatient with abstract theory, he could see little point in talking about what obviously did not conform to reality. All men contain the same essence, the same substance that makes them human. First, they have reason, the factor that renders them in a small way akin to God, and, hence, dignified and worthy of respect. But, second, all men in their fallen nature have enormous faults—due not so much to wickedness as to weakness. Consequently, it is necessary, on the one hand, to give reason its proper due, but, on the other, to allow for and protect against inevitable mistakes by reason and confusion by the passions. Human tendency to err is great, Adams felt, but fortunately men have a religious inclination that makes them seek moral action. Their conscience is their saving grace. Men, because of their moral and religious inclinations, seek the good, yet their vision is impaired and their wills are weak; their appetites interfere too often with their reason. Good government must recognize both facets of man's nature—his reason and appreciation of goodness, his tendency to go astray.

While there is unity in human nature resulting from common essence, there is diversity among individuals. United as men are in society, political creatures though they are, they are all different, all independent, all unequal. Because these distinctions among men are natural, any scheme that tries to erase differences is not consistent with human nature. No one can help the accidents of his appearance, parentage, mentality, place of birth, traits of personality, and so forth. These are natural distinctions, and they make people unequal. However, as Adams was to say later, men are equal morally and politically; that is, they are created equal. Thus, the only real and, consequently, natural equality is the one enjoined by the Golden Rule. "The precept . . . *do as you would be done by* implies an equality which is the real equality of nature and Christianity. . . ."[17]

Historical experience—particularly the history of the English and colonial forms that Adams proposed for the most part to continue—showed that government must conform to human nature. It must recognize both the similarities of men—that they are reasonable but weak and power-hungry—and their differences—that they are all free individuals. The problem of government, in other words, is to give the fullest possible reign to man's reason and free will, while at the same time restraining his inveterate disposition to succumb to his appetites.

A delicate balance of powers is the only solution to this problem. The simple structure of a unitary government in one body cannot harmonize the passions of man. It is rather necessary to play off the powers of government against one another, to pit legislative, executive and judicial powers against each other so that they meet in a fine mean. Hence acceptance of the complexities of imperfect man, first, and the need for a balance of power, second, were the two chief principles upon which Adams wrote his *Thoughts on Government.*

The blessings of society, Adams wrote in the *Thoughts,*[18] depend upon the constitution of government. It is an important task, then, to decide what kind of government is the best.

Since the happiness of the individual is the end of man, then, Adams said, the happiness—ease, comfort, security—of the greatest number of persons and in the greatest degree is also the end of government. Adams went on to add that happiness comes from virtue. "The happiness of man, as well as his dignity, consists in virtue." For that reason, government, in order to accomplish its end of promoting happiness, must have virtue as its principle and foundation. It may appear surprising that Adams declared virtue, rather than liberty, to be the principle of government. But the fact was that liberty could not exist without virtue. Always a key concept in Adams' thought, strictly moral action according to the noblest attributes of human nature. Virtue was attention to right, to law, to right reason; in order that law might rule as much as possible in society, virtue in government required impartial execution of the law. Only impartial rule of law could keep liberty alive.

Following the scheme of Montesquieu, Adams believed that the foundation of government is some principle in the minds of the people. He thought fear was the foundation of most governments, but he regarded it as so brutal a passion that it must not even be considered as a principle of governments. While honor as a principle is indeed sacred, it is nevertheless only a part of virtue. The noblest of principles, virtue, has then the best chance to support the noblest and most generous government.

As the best political writers had said for years past, Adams pointed out, the only good government is republican government, the model based on virtue, best of all governments because it is an empire of laws and not of men. Because there are various kinds of ways to combine the powers of society, there are countless varieties of republics. In this empire of laws, however, the form of government that secures the most impartial and exact execution of the laws will be best.

The crucial problem is, then, how the laws shall be made. In a large country all the people cannot possibly assemble to make the laws. In such a case, they must depute power to a few of the wise and the good.

The make-up of the representative assembly is a poser: "It should be in miniature an exact portrait of the people at large. It should think, feel, reason, and act like them." In order for it to be to the interest of the assembly to do strict justice at all times, "it should be an equal representation, or, in other words, equal interests among the people should have equal interests in it."

After the people have elected representatives to the assembly, Adams asked "whether all the powers of government, legislative, executive, and judicial, shall be left in this body?" Certainly not, he said, because "a people cannot be long free, nor ever happy, whose government is in one assembly." With terse pungency of phrase, Adams said the same thing even better a few months earlier in a letter to Richard Henry Lee: "A legislative, an executive, and a judicial power comprehend the whole of what is meant and understood by government. It is by balancing each of these powers against the other two that the efforts in human nature towards tyranny can alone be checked and restrained and any degree of freedom preserved in the constitution."[19]

There are three powers of government—legislative, executive, judicial, each derived from the sovereignty of the people. In order that laws may be made, administered and judged impartially, which is the hallmark of republican government, these powers must be independent of each other, so that each checks and balances the others. In addition to this separation of the broad powers of government, there is further separation within the legislative. Of the legislative power, Adams believed, there are three branches—lower house, upper house and executive—corresponding to the democratic, aristocratic, and monarchic elements of society. Adams thought that the democratic, aristocratic, and monarchic elements should balance, or mediate, between each other. In other words, the upper house or council should mediate between assembly and executive, and the executive should mediate between assembly and council. Although each branch acts integrally in the legislative power, each one is able to remain separate and independent because of its negative upon the others. No branch may tell another what to do; it has no power of coercion over the others. For that reason, a government with such separation of powers is able to avoid the pitfalls of simple government and to employ a mixture of the pure forms of monarchy, aristocracy and democracy. Founded upon the orders that exist naturally in society, such a government is in accord with human nature as it truly is; it cannot but succeed.

With his gift of applying theory to practical matters, Adams was able to specify how these concepts should be spelled out. The assembly will elect, from among themselves or their constituents, a council, or whatever this upper house shall be called. These same twenty or thirty men of the upper house will have free and independent exercise of judgment, "and consequently a negative voice in the legislature."

These two integral bodies of the legislature will by joint ballot elect a governor, "who, after being stripped of most of those badges of domination called prerogatives, should have a free and independent exercise of his judgment and be made also an integral part of the legislature." Realizing that this suggestion would meet with criticism, Adams conceded that "you may make him only president of the council, as in Connecticut," but he should still have a negative upon the other two bodies. Since he will be elected annually, he should have enough respect for the people and for their representatives and councilmen so that even though given independent judgment, he would not use it indiscriminately.

All the great offices of state—governor, lieutenant governor, secretary, treasurer, commissary, attorney general—should be annually elected, "there not being in the whole circle of the sciences a maxim more infallible than this, 'where annual elections end, there slavery begins.' " Men of state so elected would learn "the great political virtues of humility, patience, and moderation, without which every man in power becomes a ravenous beast of prey."

Adams added in a far-sighted note, however, that in quieter times the legislature may wish to make elections of the officials occupying the executive branch more popular, perhaps arranging for election by the people at large or for more extended terms of office.

In other provisions, a quorum of the legislative council could act as a privy council to advise the governor upon exercise of the executive power and in acts of state. The governor should command the militia and all armies. Governor and council should have the power of pardon.

Judges, justices and all civil and military officers should be nominated and appointed by the governor with advice and consent of the council, "unless you choose to have a government more popular." In the latter case, officers should be chosen by joint ballot of both houses.

There should be laws providing for the training and arming of a militia. Worthy of special note, in view of Adams' regard for education for virtue, there should be laws "for the liberal education of youth, especially of the lower class of people . . . ."

Adams devoted considerable time in his short essay to explaining the independence of judges, upon which "the dignity and stability of government in all its branches, the morals of the people, and every blessing of society depend so much . . . ." The judges "should be always men of learning and experience in the laws, of exemplary morals, great patience, calmness, coolness, and attention. Their minds should not be distracted by jarring interests; they should not be dependent upon any man, or body of men." For that reason, they should hold their offices for life, in other words, during good behavior. Their salaries should be fixed by law. If charged with misbehavior they should be tried by the house of representatives before the governor and council.

A constitution founded upon the principles Adams had enumerated:

> introduces knowledge among the people and inspires them with a conscious dignity becoming freemen; a general emulation takes place, which causes good humor, sociability, good manners, and good morals to be general. That elevation of sentiment inspired by such a government makes the common people brave and enterprising. That ambition which is inspired by it makes them sober, industrious, and frugal. You will find among them some elegance, perhaps, but more solidity; a little pleasure, but a great deal of business; some politeness, but more civility. If you compare such a country with the regions of domination, whether monarchical or aristocratical, you will fancy yourself in Arcadia or Elysium.

These were his *Thoughts on Government.* However, the separate states should adopt whatever forms they wished. If a Continental government were to be formed, "it should be a congress, containing a fair and adequate representation of the Colonies, and its authority should sacredly be confined to these cases, namely, war, trade, disputes between colony and colony, the post-office, and the unappropriated lands of the Crown, as they used to be called."

The Colonies "under such forms of government and in such a union would be unconquerable by all the monarchies of Europe."

And finally, at the conclusion of his piece, Adams described the thrill of living at such a rare time, when men were actually able to start fresh, to begin with a new constitution, when for once they did not have merely to make do.

"You and I, dear friend," he said, "have been sent into life at a time when the greatest lawgivers of antiquity would have wished to live. How few of the human race have ever enjoyed an opportunity of making an election of government, more than of air, soil, or climate, for themselves or their children! When, before the present epocha, had three millions of people full power and a fair opportunity to form and establish the wisest and happiest government that human wisdom can contrive?"

The fruits of Adams' labors on both theoretical and practical aspects of government came forth in the spring of 1776, in the May resolution of Congress recommending to all the states that they form governments. For Adams this resolution meant the beginning of a new era, independence itself, as he told James Duane.

Even more tedious labor lay ahead. His part in this work denoted a fork in the path of his career. Heretofore, with the exception of his work on the naval committee, his domain had been for the most part political—but now he was about to branch into military and diplomatic channels.

Four pivotal committees were named between the eleventh and the fifteenth of June, 1776. The first three of these committees were the famous triad on independence, confederation and negotiation, the three topics that Adams had always thought went hand-in-glove. Adams was a member of the first of these, the committee on drafting a Declaration of Independence. He was not a member of the second committee, one to prepare a plan of confederation among the Colonies. Together with Dickinson, Franklin, Benjamin Harrison and Robert Morris, he was named to the third committee, to prepare a plan of treaties to propose to foreign powers. In addition, he was chosen to a fourth and crucial committee, the Board of War and Ordnance, with Sherman, Harrison, James Wilson, Edward Rutledge as members and Richard Peterson as secretary. Adams was chairman or president, as they called him, the most choresome duty of his entire four years in Congress.

The powers of this Board of War were endless, involving the members in grinding, exasperating details. Adams' job amounted to his being secretary of war, keeping him in "continual employment, not to say drudgery, from this twelfth of June, 1776, til the eleventh of November, 1777, when I left Congress forever." Not only did he spend mornings and evenings in the business of the board, but he passed wearing hours "making, explaining and justifying our reports and proceedings" to Congress.

Some years later he wrote, "It is said there are lawyers in the United States who receive five thousand guineas a year and many are named who are said to receive to the amount of ten thousand dollars. However this may be, I don't believe there is one of them who goes through so much business for all his emoluments as I did for the year and a half, nearly, that I was loaded with that office." And his recompense was a pitiful sum.[20]

Although he recorded and participated in the debates on the Articles of Confederation, the fact that Adams was named to the committee on treaties rather than the one on confederation meant that he would not be connected so actively with the problem of government as he had been. Agreement on the Articles proceeded slowly.

"The great work of confederation drags heavily on," Adams wrote to Jefferson in May, 1777, "but I don't despair of it. The great and small states must be brought as near together as possible: and I am not without hopes that this may be done to the tolerable satisfaction of both."[21] The Articles were not accepted in final form until November, 1777; they were not ratified until March 1, 1781, when Adams was in Europe.

Adams was pleased with his appointment to the treaty committee. He had done considerable thinking about foreign alliances, had always included the question in agendas that he thought Congress should consider. Rodney, Duane and even Dickinson had already noted Adams' profundity on the subject, the former two remarking that Adams had considered the subject of foreign connections "more maturely" than anyone in America.[22]

Adams' policy was tough and unswerving—in fact, throughout his diplomatic career it never altered: "That we ought not to enter into any alliance with her [France] which should entangle us in any future wars in Europe, that we ought to lay it down as a first principle and a maxim never to be forgotten, to maintain an entire neutrality in all future European wars." It could never be to the advantage of America to unite with France "in the destruction of England or in any measures to break her spirit or reduce her to a situation in which she could not support her independence," nor to unite with Britain to unhorse France. Adams felt "that our real if not our nominal independence would consist in our neutrality." The answer, then, was treaties of commerce, not of military alliance.[23]

After the committee had deliberated for some months, Adams drafted a plan that was returned on July 18 and accepted with modification by Congress on September 17, 1776. This "Plan of 1776" became a model for treaties of amity and commerce, furnishing the framework for all but one of the diplomatic accords into which the young nation entered in the eighteenth century. The plan, in seeking to guarantee free trade for neutrals, charted the course of early American maritime policies. Furthermore, the committee drew up instructions to the first American commissioners who should be sent to France, directives pointing up the same strict principles of neutrality.

In line with his committee work, Adams received opportunity to engage in actual diplomacy.

Admiral Howe, head of British troops in America, had authority to act as a peace commissioner in the American difficulty. Hence, Congress on September 6 appointed a committee of Adams, Franklin and Edward Rutledge to journey to Staten Island for a talk with Howe. The three departed on September 9, disheartened at the straggling, undisciplined American soldiers they encountered along the way in the crowded taverns. When they arrived at New Brunswick, accommodations were so slim that Adams and Franklin had to share a tiny room with one bed, no chimney and only a small window, which was open. Adams, sufferer of minor aches and pains, ventured to shut the window.

"Oh!" Franklin urged, "don't shut the window. We shall be suffocated." When Adams replied that he was afraid of the evening air, the old gentlemen replied, "The air within this chamber will soon be and, indeed, is now worse than that without doors." Surely Adams had not heard his theory on colds. Opening the window and leaping into bed, Adams assured him he had heard only that Franklin thought nobody could take cold going into a cold church. The doctor then began a preachment upon cold air, perspiration and respiration, sending his companion off to sleep in amusement and soon lapsing off himself in the midst of his harangue.

Next morning the men continued their journey, arriving at Staten Island that day. Fiercely grimacing grenadiers with fixed bayonets surrounded the headquarters building, a filthy place that had housed military guards. Despite these liabilities, his lordship had made one large room handsome enough, spreading it with a carpet of moss and green sprigs from local shrubbery, creating an effect "not only wholesome but romantically elegant, and he entertained us with good claret, good bread, cold ham, tongues and mutton."

The mission, however, was a dismal failure. It seemed that the admiral had no more power than to grant pardons and to declare America to be in the King's peace. There was nothing for the commissioners to do but take leave.

Adams always enjoyed relating two anecdotes about the Staten Island mission. Lord Howe was particularly profuse in his thanks to Massachusetts for putting up in Westminster Abbey a monument to his brother, who had been killed in the French and Indian War. So grateful was he to America, he said, that he felt affection as a brother for that country; if America should fall, he would lament the loss as he would the loss of a brother.

"Dr. Franklin," Adams recalled, "with an easy air and a collected countenance, a bow, a smile and all that naivete which sometimes appeared in his conversation and is often observed in his writings, replied, 'My lord, we will do our utmost endeavors to save your lordship that mortification.' "

Then, when Howe made clear to the Americans that he could receive them only as private persons and British subjects, not as members of Congress, Adams hastened to tell him, "Your lordship may consider me in what light you please; and, indeed, I should be willing to consider myself, for a few moments, in any character which would be agreeable to your lordship, *except that of a British subject.*" Lord Howe then turned to Franklin and Rutledge, remarking solemnly, "Mr. Adams is a decided character." The double meaning was not lost.[24]

The war ground on. Washington managed to recover the Jerseys with his victories at Trenton and Princeton, but General Burgoyne, in his attempt to isolate New England, took Ticonderoga. Gates and Arnold, however, soon had Burgoyne in a tight position, bringing about the British disaster at Saratoga.

In the meantime, Howe had occupied Philadelphia, forcing Congress to retreat to York, Pennsylvania.

During this fall of 1777, Adams ached with homesickness and worry over his family and affairs. He was spending his fourth autumn in Congress, all to the ill fortune of his law practice and finances, not to mention his wife and children. He would return home to Braintree, he thought, letting another man take his place in Congress.

From General Daniel Roberdeau's home in York he wrote Abigail, "I long with the utmost impatience to come home—don't send a servant for me. The expense is so enormous that I cannot bear the thought of it. I will crawl home upon my little pony and wait upon myself as well as I can."[25] It was high time that he returned to his long-neglected duties as husband and father; it frightened him to realize that he had not been present to guide his children through nearly four crucial years of their growing up. Besides being all things to her children during her husband's absence, Abigail, he gratefully recognized, had performed financial miracles by getting along on their modest savings and small farming profits, for the tiny sum Adams had received for his services in Congress counted for nothing. Adams must go home, then, to resume his duties as head of his household and to resurrect from oblivion a once-promising legal practice. He departed for home on November 11.

But the longed-for joys of homecoming were to be only short-lived. While Adams was in Portsmouth in December defending Colonel Elisha Doane and the shipowner's son-in-law, Shearjashub Bourne, in the *Lusanna* case (probably the last case of his legal career), a fat packet of dispatches from Congress arrived for him at home. Abigail felt no compunction about opening her husband's mail and answering it, lest someone "should accuse him of neglect or inattention." Ripping open the packet, her heart sank at the stunning news. Congress, on November 28, had elected her husband to replace Silas Deane as one of the commissioners to France. Beside herself, Abigail wrote to James Lovell, member of the foreign affairs committee, "O, sir, you who are possessed of sensibility and a tender heart, how could you contrive to rob me of all my happiness?" She could forgive Elbridge Gerry, who had nominated Adams, "because he is a stranger to domestic felicity and knows no tenderer attachment than that which he feels for his country, tho' I think the stoicism which every bachelor discovers ought to be attributed to him as a fault." She would never wish for her husband to be less deserving, but she was "sometimes almost selfish enough to wish his abilities confined to private life, and the more so for that wish is according with his own inclinations." She had felt the want of his assistance in the years of his absence, "and that demand increases as our little ones grow up, three of whom are sons and at this time of life stand most in need of the joint force of his example and precepts."

"And can I, sir," she implored, "consent to be separted from him whom my heart esteems above all earthly things, and for an unlimited time? My life will be one continued scene of anxiety and apprehension, and must I cheerfully comply with the demand of my country?"

Nonetheless, there appeared to be no doubt in her mind as to the action her husband should and would take; she had used his absence "to bring my mind to bear the event with fortitude and resignation. . . ."[26] Nor was there much hesitation on Adams' part. Receiving the news at Portsmouth, he was astonished, since he had never solicited the appointment. He felt unprepared for the mission. His "dearly beloved wife and four young children excited sentiments of tenderness which a father and a lover only can conceive and which no language can express."[27] Yet he felt it his duty to serve.

The only question was whether Abigail and the children should accompany him. She was determined to go, but Adams thought the hazards of an ocean trip and the danger of capture by the British and ultimate imprisonment too great a risk. In the end it was only John Quincy, now ten years old, who was to go with his father.

Impatiently and apprehensively the Adamses waited until February 13, 1778, for the frigate *Boston* to arrive in Quincy Bay. On that day, after dinner at Uncle Norton Quincy's, John and John Quincy walked with Captain Samuel Tucker and Midshipman Griffin down to the barge anchored at Moon Head. Despite high winds and churning water, they managed to keep dry under heavy watch coats, arriving on board the frigate at five o'clock. They were disconcerted only by the ominous prophecy of a deranged old woman on Hough's Neck, where they had stopped on the way out to the ship.

"Mr. Adams," she had intoned, "you are going to embark under very threatening signs. The heavens frown, the clouds roll, the hollow winds howl, the waves of the sea roar upon the beach."

Adams, "not enough of a Roman to believe it an ill omen," still glumly reminded himself that his only sea experience had been a few hunting trips to Half Moon, a fishing trip to Cohasset rocks, and some forays to Rainsford Island and the lighthouse.

"It was only a prelude to a comedy," he thought—but a comedy was indeed what he feared all his voyages and negotiations would be.[28]

CHAPTER IX

WINNING THE PEACE

Ocean voyages in the eighteenth century tried the hardiest souls. Storms, disease, filth, cramped quarters, poor diet, marauding pirates, enemy sailors drove passengers and crewmen alike to disaster, if not to the grave. Both Adamses suffered with seasickness in a violent storm that sent furniture and casks reeling, soaking everything on board. Though John wished his son back in the security of Braintree, he confessed proudly that "Mr. Johnny's behavior gave me a satisfaction that I cannot express," that he bore the danger "with a manly patience."[1]

Adams' affection for the Navy set him to scrutinizing the ship with all her defects. She was over-metaled, had too many guns for her tonnage. She had no pistols, no good glasses. Her crew was undisciplined and unclean. Meals were irregular—"It ought to be penal for the cook to fail of having his victuals ready punctually." With his well-meaning, enthusiastic officiousness Adams was "constantly giving hints to the captain concerning order, economy and regularity. . . ." It produced results, apparently, for in answer to Adams' advice the captain went down into the cockpit and ordered everybody "from that sink of devastation and putrefaction."[2]

It was the first of April when the Adamses left the ship, and more than a week after that before they reached Paris. As Adams, with John Quincy beside him, clattered along in the coach toward the suburb of Passy, where Franklin had chosen lodgings for the American commissioners on the grounds of the Hôtel de Valentinois, he must have felt himself a plain New England codfish among superb French confectionery. Abrupt, tactless, opinionated, altogether undiplomatic, untutored by habit and unsuited by temperament to the graceful turn of parlor phrase, he must have felt uncomfortably raw as he was about to take his place beside the popular, urbane Franklin and the Virginia-bred Arthur Lee as a diplomat in a land where diplomacy was the rule of life. Here was a land where substance had ebbed away to such a degree that form had become the stuff of existence. In the French court manners proceeded according to prescription, all so perfectly studied that they seemed perfectly natural. A man's finesse was the criterion by which others judged him. Because he was an impatient creature who saw the heart of matters so keenly that he could not bear to squander time in veiling them with artifice, Adams by French standards was apt to be proclaimed a boor.

As his old friend Jonathan Sewall described him after their reunion in England following the war, "he is not qualified by nature or education to shine in courts—his abilities are, undoubtedly, quite equal to the mechanical parts of his business as ambassador; but this is not enough—he can't dance, drink, game, flatter, promise, dress, swear with the gentlemen, and talk small talk and flirt with the ladies—in short he has none of the essential *arts* or *ornaments* which constitute a courtier—there are thousands who, with a tenth part of his understanding and without a spark of his honesty, would distance him infinitely in any court in Europe."[3] Yet despite his blunt lack of grace, Adams possessed two characteristics that in the long run would serve him far better than any nicety of manner. First of all, he was fiercely independent, his own man from first to last. Second, he had extraordinary tenacity to hold out for a point, a factor that offset his impatience. He had come to France with long-held ideas that European powers should recognize American independence and that America should stay free of foreign entanglements where possible. Of the monarchs and foreign ministers who looked upon America as a supplicant, he asked a great deal. But he never relinquished those ideas.

With assiduous hospitality the French court welcomed Adams. He met Turgot, controller of finance and a noted *philosophe;* Vergennes, the crafty, knowledgeable secretary of foreign affairs; Maurepas, the prime minister; the Count de Noailles, a nobleman of a famous French house. He observed the ancient Voltaire applauded from his box at the theater; he heard D'Alembert at the Academy of Sciences. He attended the salons of Madame Helvétius, Madame Brillon, the Duchesse d'Ayen and the Duchesse D'Anville. He went with Franklin, Lee and Vergennes on a Friday in May to be presented to King Louis XVI. The stout young monarch greeted them in his bedchamber, where various officers decked him in his sword and coat.[4] Adams attended the peculiar ceremony of watching the King and Queen eating their supper, where, much to his mortification, he was made to sit amidst a dazzling flock of high-ranking ladies in gorgeous regalia who observed this alien bird as quizzically as he in Congress had gazed upon the Indian sachems who came to pay respects. Not yet knowing much of the French language, he found with relief that this was to be a silent affair where no one said a word; hence, he assumed a cheerful countenance and observed the entire scene "as coolly as an astronomer contemplates the stars."[5]

It disconcerted him somewhat to discover that everywhere he went, Frenchmen acclaimed him as "le fameux Adams" who had written the pamphlet *Common Sense.* Only with difficulty did he persuade them that he was not his cousin Sam, but he did not even attempt to convince them that Sam had not written *Common Sense.* Taken aback that he was not "le fameux Adams," the French decided that "the consequence was plain—he was some man that nobody had ever heard of before—and therefore a man of no consequence—a cipher." At least, Adams could chuckle to himself, "Nobody went so far . . . as to say I was the infamous Adams."[6]

With customary zeal Adams set out to acclimate himself to his new tasks. He studied French voraciously—reading Molière, Racine, Bossuet, even some law. With a diligent eye he studied French customs. But he could never bring himself to accept all of these modes. He was admittedly shocked by the casual attitude with which the French viewed marital fidelity. Almost every nobleman kept his wife and his mistress openly in the same household and neither woman appeared to mind. Adams, always severe on the point of private morality, lashed out in his writing: "From all that I had read of history and government, of human life and manners, I had drawn this conclusion, that the manners of women were the most infallible barometer to ascertain the degree of morality and virtue in a nation. . . . The manners of women are the surest criterion by which to determine whether a republican government is practicable in a nation or not. . . . The foundations of national morality must be laid in private families. In vain are schools, academies and universities instituted, if loose principles and licentious habits are impressed upon children in their earliest years. The mothers are the earliest and most important instructors of youth. . . ."[7]

Nonetheless, he resisted all impulses to lecture his French comrades, even accepting their foibles with levity and humor.

"Mr. Adams," a lovely young lady once startled him, "by your name I conclude you are descended from the first man and woman, and probably in your family may be preserved the tradition which may resolve a difficulty which I could never explain. I never could understand how the first couple found out the art of lying together."

Feeling himself blush, yet determined "to set a brazen face against a brazen face and answer a fool according to her folly," he replied jovially, "Madame, my family resembles the first couple both in the name and in their frailties so much that I have no doubt we are descended from that in Paradise. But the subject was perfectly understood by us, whether by tradition I could not tell; I rather thought it was by instinct, for there was a physical quality in us resembling the power of electricity or of the magnet, by which when a pair approached within a striking distance they flew together like the needle to the pole or like two objects in electric experiments."

"Well," his companion said, "I know not how it was, but this I know, it is a very happy shock."[8]

Scarcely had Adams arrived at Passy than he found himself enmeshed in the ugly dispute between Arthur Lee and the absent Silas Deane, whom he had come to replace. In the controversy boiling up around these two men, every member of Congress took a side, based not upon geography but upon theories of foreign policy. Those who supported Deane were pro-French and favored negotiating a peace with England along the realistic lines of a none-too-bright military situation; enthusiasts for the case of Lee, like Sam Adams, had suspicions of French good will toward the American cause and frankly wanted to expand their infant country at the peace table as much as they possibly could.

Franklin; Deane, a Connecticut merchant; and Lee of the Virginia family had been named in September, 1776, as the three commissioners to France. Both Franklin and Lee were former colonial agents in London, but in 1775 Franklin had returned to America to become a member of Congress. Lee remained in London. Deane, meanwhile, had been sent by Congress to Paris in the summer of 1776 as an agent to secure military supplies from France. Both Lee and Deane had dealings with the young, versatile Caron de Beaumarchais, who not only was to write *Le Barbier de Séville* and *Le Mariage de Figaro*, but had set up an imaginative banking house to sell supplies to America. Since Lee felt sure that the French court intended to give away the supplies that Deane agreed with Beaumarchais to buy, he set about accusing Deane of crooked dealings with the French. Lee, sour-tempered, envious, with more than his share of feelings of persecution, sent letters to Congress charging Deane with fraudulent activities. Some of the charges were tenable, others not. Lee succeeded in having Congress call Deane home for a report on his doings. Lee, however, hardly possessed an attractive personality; he, as well as Deane, had a strenuous body of opponents. Eventually he, too, would be recalled.

Throughout this nasty fight, Franklin remained placid and reticent, as was his way. He had nothing to gain by an airing of his collaboration with Deane in the Vandalia Company western land speculation. Hence he remained cheerfully neutral, if not leaning a trifle toward Deane's side, a stand that infuriated Lee, who was already jealous of Franklin.

When Adams arrived in France, he learned "with much grief and concern" of these disputes. They formed "a rope of sand. . . . What shall I say? What shall I think?" Deane seemed to have been involved in improper financial activities, but, on the other hand, Lee was said not to have the confidence of the French ministry— Americans in Paris thought him too friendly with the English, too ill-disposed to the French. With valiant determination Adams sought to stay out of the controversy; he was "sorry for these things, but it is no part of my business to quarrel with anybody without cause. It is no part of my duty to differ with one party or another or to give offense to anybody. But I must do my duty to the public, let it give offense to whom it will."[9]

Nevertheless, achieving impartiality was easier vowed than done. Though Deane, Adams conceded, had been "active, diligent, subtle, and successful," he had "lived expensively and seems not to have had much order in his business, public or private. . . ." In fact, to the frugal Adams it seemed incredible that the entire public business at Passy had "never been methodically conducted." No one had bothered to keep "a minute book, a letter book or an account book—and it is not possible to obtain a clear idea of our affairs."[10] With his tremendous energy Adams at least righted the latter situation, pouring all his efforts into bringing order to the business of the commission.

Nor was it possible for Adams to remain neutral in the face of the letter that Deane had published in the *Pennsylvania Packet* on the fifth of December, 1778. Unable to make himself properly heard among the congressional factions upon his return to America, Deane in desperation had gone over the heads of Congress, taking his case to the people. His newspaper letter not only defended his own actions but made severe countercharges against Arthur Lee and his brother William, alderman of London.

The Deane letter shocked and outraged Adams, who, "with great freedom and perhaps with too much warmth," told Franklin his opinion.

"I told him that it was one of the most wicked and abominable productions that ever sprung from an human heart. That there was no safety in integrity against such a man. That I should wait upon the Comte de Vergennes and the other ministers and see in what light they considered this conduct of Mr. Deane." To Dr. Edward Bancroft, a character who, unknown to the Americans, was a spy both against them and the British, Adams stormed "that such a contempt of Congress committed in the city where they sat, and the publication of such accusations in the face of the universe, so false and groundless as the most heinous of them appeared to me," were "evidence of such a complication of vile passions of vanity, arrogance and presumption, of malice, envy and revenge, and at the same time of such weakness, indiscretion and folly, as ought to unite every honest and wise man against him."[11] Adams admitted that he had declaimed too loudly, but he still did not change his mind about Deane.

In the meantime Adams felt increasing exasperation about his colleague, Franklin. Privately he came to feel that Franklin was a lazy, if talented, old gaffer who sacrificed the business of the commission for the company of pretty women. Furthermore, he thought Franklin infuriatingly silent and secretive, characteristcs so unlike Adams' own personality that he could not understand the old man. On the other hand, Lee had "such a bitter, such a sour in him, and so few of the nice feelings that God knows what will be the consequences to himself and to others." In addition, Lee had as much secrecy and cunning as Franklin. Altogether, Adams felt himself in an unenviable lot, remarking with a note of melodramatic self-pity, "The wisdom of Solomon, the meekness of Moses, and the patience of Job, all united in one character, would not be sufficient to qualify a man to act in the situation in which I am at present —and I have scarcely a spice of either of these virtues."[12]

Plainly he could see that since his "two colleagues would agree in nothing," it was up to him to take care of the business. With Franklin's life "a scene of continual dissipation," Adams could never get in to see his older colleague before breakfast, the most convenient time to discuss business. Franklin breakfasted late, then received the crowds who attended his levees—philosophers, academicians, economists, literary men, even women and children, "come to have the honor to see the great Franklin, and to have the pleasure of telling stories about his simplicity, his bald head and scattering straight hairs. . . ." No sooner had these visitors left than it was one or two o'clock, time to dress and leave for one of the countless dinner engagements. Adams, although he, too, received invitations, began to make considerable show of declining in order to study French and attend to business. When dinner was over, Franklin sometimes went to the theater but ordinarily had Madame Helvétius, Madame Brillon, Madame Chaumont, Madame Le Roy or some other elegant lady make tea for him, after which the ladies sang and accompanied themselves upon the pianoforte, offering to play chess or checkers with their guest.

Adams would not begrudge Franklin these amusements, he said, if he had simply been able to receive Franklin's attention and advice for a little while each day. However, Franklin seemed willing to spare only a few minutes, if that, often delaying several days before affixing his signature to papers that Adams and Lee had completed. Still the doctor rarely refused to sign, Adams granted.[13]

Though he undeniably procrastinated, though he dilatorily left to Adams the choresome duties of the commission, Franklin possessed, beneath his benign air of reserve and republican simplicity, a crafty intelligence, a combined quality of moderation and quickness that marked him as a far better diplomat than Adams cared to admit. Actually, Franklin maneuvered masterfully in the patient, endlessly detailed, artificial game of diplomacy. Adams, so hard put to restrain his opinions and emotions, found it a monumental, almost impossible task to check-rein his impatience and irritation with a game that refused to be played any faster. In short, he found it maximum labor to act in a style that to Franklin came naturally. The fact was that Adams, who so much sought the esteem of the world, harbored a streak of old-fashioned jealousy:

On Dr. F. the eyes of all Europe are fixed, as the most important character in American affairs in Europe. Neither L[ee] nor myself are looked upon of much consequence. The attention of the court seems most to F. and no wonder. His long and great reputation to which L.'s and mine are in their infancy are enough to account for this.[14]

Franklin himself eventually wearied of his eccentric colleague's suspicions, writing later in a moment of sarcasm, "I am persuaded that he means well for his country, is always an honest man, often a wise one, but sometimes, and in some things, absolutely out of his senses."[15] That particular remark probably did more to smudge Adams' name for future generations than any that was ever made about him.

Shortly after Adams arrived at Passy he perceived that one minister plenipotentiary in France was adequate but that three were a crowd. Franklin and Vergennes in February, 1778, had signed both a treaty of amity and commerce and a treaty of alliance. Hence, by the time Adams arrived in April, the major obstacle had been hurdled; one man could easily handle the ministry. Realizing that if a sole plenipotentiary were named, that man would surely be Franklin and that he himself would be left without a commission, he nonetheless wrote in May to Sam Adams in Congress that "one in the character of an envoy is enough."[16] Yet it was nearly a year later (February 12, 1779) before the commissioners received word that Dr. Franklin had been named sole plenipotentiary. To Adams, who was tired, homesick and distressed over Deane's letter in the *Pennsylvania Packet*, the news came as "the greatest relief."[17]

To his discomfiture, however, Congress sent him no definite recall or further instructions; it was left to his own judgment when to return home. Further, at the request of the "old conjurer" Franklin, he had to take a later passage, on the French frigate *La Sensible*, rather than the earlier one on the *Alliance* for which he had hoped.

Dismally he confided to his journal one of his most famous passages, words testifying that in spite of his external vanity and sometime pomposity, he inwardly felt quite humble:

> There is a feebleness and a languor in my nature. My mind and body both partake of this weakness. By my physical constitution, I am but an ordinary man. The times alone have destined me to fame

—and even these have not been able to give me much. When I look in the glass, my eye, my forehead, my brow, my cheeks, my lips, all betray this relaxation. Yet some great events, some cutting expressions, some mean [scandals] hypocrisies, have at times thrown this assemblage of sloth, sleep, and littleness into rage a little like a lion. Yet it is not like the lion—there is extravagance and distraction in it that still betrays the same weakness.[18]

Accompanying him on the voyage to America were the Chevalier de la Luzerne, replacing Conrad Alexandre Gérard as new French minister to America, and François Barbé-Marbois, a French diplomat who was to be secretary of legation. The Frenchmen must have considered it a windfall that they gained such perfect opportunity to observe at close range this hard-headed, touchy, vastly independent diplomat who already had not endeared himself to Vergennes and the French ministry.

Adams prided himself on the close check he kept on himself. "I have much satisfaction in reflecting that in all the conversations I have yet had with the chevalier, no unguarded word has escaped me. I have conversed with that frankness that makes a part of my character but have said nothing that I did not mean to say."[19] Yet he praised himself unduly. The chevalier, a suave, gentlemanly fellow of astute observation and a clever hand at flattery, cajoled more out of Adams than the New Englander realized. Injudicious remarks slipped from Adams regarding his differences with Franklin and his own attitudes on diplomacy. Crystallizing his impressions of Adams, the chevalier laid by a storehouse of ammunition that, once in Philadelphia, he would use to the American's disadvantage, for La Luzerne would contrive successfully to obtain an astonishing hold over Congress.

When Congress plunged the infant nation into the whirlpool of European diplomacy, neither its members nor the ministers it sent abroad, except Franklin, had any notion of the ground rules by which the Old World nations played the diplomatic game. The European nations for centuries had obeyed the ancient rule of the balance of power, struggling to keep each other's power in subtle equilibrium and to restrain any particular nation from becoming strong enough to dominate the others. To pursue the balance of power they went to every extreme of intrigue and Machiavellian treachery. With national interest the sole criterion, diplomacy was no game for those with faint hearts or weak stomachs.

Although America, in her isolated location as part of the British Empire, had never engaged on her own in international power politics, she had always been a mercantilistic object in the balance-of-power intrigues. When she rebelled, she so upset the European balance of power that she herself became a major contender in Old World politics. In order to benefit from England's distress with the Colonies, every monarch now tried to play the Revolution to his advantage. This fact could have boded disaster for the new American nation; instead, because of a group of quick-witted American peace commissioners, it worked to her good fortune. The commissioners refused to give in on the point of American independence; they refused to allow America to become a pawn in the power turmoil. They went into their missions unseasoned, unversed in the wiles of European courts; yet, greatly to their credit, they emerged as adept as any of their adversaries. Moreover, they concluded the peace to America's advantage. European nations gained very little; Americans gained a great deal.

CHAPTER X

THE TREATY

ROOTS of European diplomacy during the period of the American Revolution extended back to the Seven Years' War, the French and Indian War as Americans called its colonial counterpart. England, a proud power that had developed Europe's most muscular navy and most dazzling array of colonies, had come from that war a mighty, imperial nation. Much of Europe sought to punish her for this by isolating her diplomatically. Consequently, she had no allies in the American Revolution. She trusted no one, steadfastly refusing to allow any powers to mediate for her with her insurgent colonies and diligently trying to drive a wedge between America and her allies. That policy was a stroke of luck for the American peace commissioners who realized, as well, that it was not in their interest to allow mediators nor to allow their ally, France, too tight a control in the negotiations. England's diplomatic isolation, as well as her severe cabinet crises during the war, further aided the American cause. The fact that England went to war with three European powers made her eager, in the end, to conclude peace as swiftly as possible.

France came from the peace of 1763 a humiliated weakling, shorn of her New World possessions and her former prestige in Europe. Heretofore, she had followed a traditionally continental foreign policy, trying to prevent any concentration of power—German, Russian, Austrian—on her eastern flank. But in the Seven Years' War she had broken with that traditional policy; she had competed with England as an imperial power, allying herself with Austria, Russia, Poland and Saxony against England and Prussia. Since that action had proved such a disaster, France in the American Revolution resumed her continental role, content not to press claims for her lost New World possessions. She now concerned herself with reviving her old prestige and power at the expense of England. She saw the solution to that problem in encouraging the American Colonies in their rebellion, offering them secret aid and supplies and then outright help as an ally in the war. According to the Franco-American alliance, neither of the two parties could make a truce or peace with Britain until the other gave formal consent. Moreover, neither ally would lay down arms until American independence had been granted, either formally or tacitly, by a peace treaty. Yet securing American independence was not France's only concern. By the secret Treaty of Aranjuez, which tied her to Spain, France had agreed, first, not to make peace with England without Spain and, second, not to make peace until Spain had Gibraltar. Consequently, the Franco-Spanish alliance was at cross-purposes with the Franco-American alliance. Though they did not realize it, the Americans were obliged to remain at war to secure a prize for Spain, a nation with which they had never signed a treaty. The French played Spain and America against each other, a task that only the cunning Vergennes could handle.

Spain, too, played both ends against the middle. The world had come a long way since the naive days of the fifteenth century when the Pope, by a Line of Demarcation, had divided the New World between Spain and Portugal. Spain had long since seen her greatest glory in the days when she could threaten England as a naval power. No longer a prestigious mistress of colonies, she could only stand to lose by championing the cause of colonies whose rebellion she feared might spread to her own American possessions. The Revolution, moreover, stood as a threat to Spain's Mississippi territory. Thus, Charles III and his tough foreign minister, Floridablanca, followed a policy of procrastination. Though she nettled the other powers, Spain could profitably play only a waiting game. She was determined, however, to recover from England the fortress Gibraltar that guarded the Mediterranean. With this principal diplomatic aim in mind, she offered to mediate the peace for England —if England would give her Gibraltar. Both sides, Spain proposed, would end the war with a truce based on *uti possidetis*, that is, upon the ground each side held at the time the fighting stopped. England refused. But meanwhile Spain, always underhanded, had signed the Treaty of Aranjuez with France even before England had given an answer. By that treaty Spain went to war. Yet, although France tried to persuade her to recognize American independence, Spain still refused, for France had promised her Gibraltar, the guarantee she wanted.

The Netherlands, a neutral country, had always seen fit to ally with England to protect her borders from continental encroachments. In the end, however, Britain declared war on the Dutch to prevent them from joining the Neutral League as a protected neutral carrier of naval stores to France and Spain.

As for Austria, Russia and Prussia, they remained scrupulously out of the fray. None stood to gain by war; neither Russia nor Austria wanted anyone to notice its attempts to expand in its own corner of the globe. All the same, Joseph II of Austria and Catherine of Russia thought perhaps they might gain a slight advantage by offering to act as mediators in England's conflict. This they did with all cordiality—and were as cordially but firmly turned down.

Bearing diplomat Adams on his return from France, *La Sensible* dropped anchor in Boston Harbor on August 3, 1779. No sooner had he landed than Adams found himself again immersed in a diplomatic mission. Because of another big scrap between the Lee and Deane factions, he was unanimously elected (on a technicality) minister plenipotentiary to negotiate treaties of peace and of commerce with Britain. Congress at the same time appointed John Jay to the post of minister to the Spanish court.

Thus, in November, 1779—hardly two months after he had rejoined his Braintree family for the first time in a year and a half—

Adams boarded *La Sensible* for a return to France. Again he took with him John Quincy, now twelve, and this time Charles who was nine. Though the voyage proved less disagreeable than Adams' first, it ended on a sour note when the ship sprang a leak and had to anchor at Ferrol, Spain. Advised to journey to Paris by land, the Adamses spent weeks traveling along the muddy, rocky, mountainous roads of northern Spain. It was a grueling but eye-opening trip for these New Englanders who had never seen anything like the impoverished, devout peasants whose lives seemed to be spent for the Church.

Finally reaching Paris, the Adamses in February, 1780, took up residence at the Hôtel de Valois in the Rue de Richelieu.

For Adams, the fierce advocate of autonomy, who had often declaimed in Congress that he supported a treaty of commerce with France but not a treaty of alliance, his stay in Paris was to prove another frustrating trial. Vergennes returned Adams' distrust of him with an ardent dislike and annoyance that Franklin, instead, had not been chosen minister to treat for peace. The foreign minister had had his fill already of the outspoken, indelicate, lecturish New Englander, whose utter frankness and obstinacy he had found thoroughly disagreeable on Adams' first mission.

Adams began courteously enough, informing Vergennes that he had been elected "minister plenipotentiary to negotiate a peace with Great Britain and also to negotiate a treaty of commerce with that kingdom," fully empowered, whenever Britain should be so disposed, to join with the ministers of the other powers at war to conclude a peace treaty. In his impatience to get on with his mission, however, Adams then asked whether it might be "prudent" for him to acquaint the British ministry with his commission and his power to treat, whether it might be prudent for him to publish the nature of his mission, or whether he ought to remain "upon the reserve," as he had done until now.[1]

In return, Vergennes insulted him nastily. "I think," he wrote coldly, "that before I resolve the different points on which you consult me, it is convenient to wait for the arrival of Mr. Gérard [French minister to the U. S.], because he is probably the bearer of your *instructions* and he will certainly have it in his power to give me explanations concerning the nature and extent of your commission; but in the meantime, I am of opinion that it is the part of prudence to conceal your eventual character and above all to take the necessary precautions that the object of your commission remain unknown to the Court of London."[2] At this stinging rejection of his plenipotentiary powers, Adams—as might be expected—was much riled. The "instructions of a sovereign to his ambassador" were "a secret and a confidential communication between them: a sacred deposit," but the "Count de Vergennes had been so long in the habit of intrigues to obtain the instructions from foreign courts to their ambassadors, and probably paying for them very dear, that he had forgotten that the practice was not lawful."[3] Suspecting—and rightly so—that Vergennes hoped to push him to the limit of his instructions, to ease his claims regarding fisheries and boundaries, Adams saw that if he delivered his instructions to Vergennes, the foreign minister could put this information into the hands of the British, urging them to press their claims, once negotiations began.[4]

Though Adams would have preferred to have announced loudly to the British ministry his role in Europe, he showed the good sense simply to send Vergennes copies of his commissions, agreeing to keep quiet for the moment.

When Vergennes replied, he acted more civilly, saying that Adams' powers were "perfectly conformable to the account which Mr. Gérard had written me of them, and they leave us nothing to desire, either in their form or substance." Yet, although he now agreed that it would be proper to inform the public of Adams' powers as peacemaker, he still thought it best to maintain silence upon his powers to negotiate a treaty of commerce.[5] This further admonishment not to divulge his authority to negotiate a commerce treaty was viewed by Adams with alarmed suspicion. Why he should be made to conceal this half of his commission he could not understand. Later he surmised that Vergennes already hoped to get Congress to revoke Adams' instructions to negotiate a commerce treaty, intending "to keep us embroiled with England as much and as long as possible, even after a peace. It had that effect for eleven years," an obstacle to understanding with England never to be overcome until the Jay Treaty of Washington's administration.[6]

Hence, put off by Vergennes until the end of March from announcing even his power to treat for peace, Adams drowned his resentment and frustration in a barrage of hard work. Every tidbit of information from all over Europe he conveyed immediately to Congress, bombarding them with unceasing dispatches. He wrote propaganda literature, as well, supplying Edmé Genet with material for the *Mercure de France.* One such article, detailing a currency redemption action of Congress, dropped like a bomb upon Vergennes, who by this time could not tolerate this obtrusive, energetic busybody. The Frenchman began an open quarrel. Franklin, taking the quiet way out, did not help much to smooth the waters. Rather than drawing in his horns, Adams now once again applied to Vergennes for permission to convey his full powers to Lord George Germain of the British ministry.[7]

Vergennes answered him harshly; the time to tell Germain had "not yet come. . . ." Indeed, he went so far as to "require" Adams "in the name of the King" to inform Congress of Vergennes' disapproval of the American's suggestion, "and to suspend, until you shall receive orders from them, all steps relating to the English ministry." Furthermore, Vergennes wrote pointedly, he intended to send his observations on the matter to La Luzerne, "in order that M. de la Luzerne may make the members of Congress possessed of them. . . ."[8] The foreign minister even said that Franklin was "the sole person who has letters of credence to the King from the United States. . . ." Moreover, the King, he emphasized, "did not stand in need" of Adams' "solicitations to direct his attention to the interests of the United States."[9]

Adams writhed under this excoriation. Disgusted, inflamed with bitter disappointment, disillusioned with French concern for American interests, he marched off in an impulsive huff to Holland, determined to seek help there so that he might make America less dependent upon France. He was to accomplish some of his most important diplomatic work in Holland, but in the meantime Vergennes baited the trap to have Congress relieve Adams of his commission.

Franklin disapproved of Adams' departure to Amsterdam; Vergennes, alarmed that Adams would succeed in making America less dependent upon France, tried in vain to dissuade the intransigent Adams. If Adams should obtain Dutch recognition of the United States, then England would declare war on the Netherlands. And the Netherlands was more valuable to France as a neutral carrier of contraband than as an ally. Although Adams did not then realize that Vergennes hoped to find a way to negotiate a peace without consulting with him first, that Vergennes hoped, in fact, to control American foreign policy, Adams intensely suspected the foreign minister's clear motives. He was not to be put off in his plan to seek help in Amsterdam.

The Netherlands, a neutral nation, was not, however, a member of the League of Armed Neutrality formed by Catherine of Russia earlier in the year 1780. The league included Russia, Denmark, Sweden, later Prussia, Austria and Portugal. If enforced, its demands would have proved a threat to Britain. Actually, the League, in Catherine's own words, proved to be an "armed nullity." Adams expected naively, as did Congress, that the Netherlands and these neutral nations would recognize American independence. He soon learned that he had expected such good fortune too soon.

Whereas Adams by the nature of his personality never hit his stride with the French, finding them refined to the point of softness, he felt a real kinship with the Dutch. His solidity and candor, his high intelligence and common sense, his diligence and practicality, his learning in the law and constitutions struck an admiring chord in the republican-minded Hollanders. Adams for his part felt at home in the Netherlands. Though he criticized Amsterdam for being consumed in the business of making money, he made contacts there that resulted in several lifelong friendships. Indeed, he got along so well with the Dutch that in Holland he made one of the most significant diplomatic contributions of the Revolution.

Ever since the Union of Utrecht in 1579, the seven provinces of the Netherlands—Holland, Zeeland, Utrecht, Guelderland, Overyssel, Groningen and Friesland—had been united in a confederation not unlike the American Confederation. Their High Mightinesses of the States-General formed the central governing body, of imposing title but effectually weak because unanimity was required on any important question. The executive Stadholder, always a member of the House of Orange, was Willem V. Although his office was hereditary, the Stadholder fell under the thumb of the States-General, which could override him. In turn, the States-General owed homage to the provincial assemblies and municipal councils that sent delegates to it. In effect, the great municipalities of Amsterdam, The Hague, Rotterdam, Dordrecht and Haarlem wielded enormous power. The Stadholder, nevertheless, could usually control one of the rural provinces, consequently preventing the States-General from reaching unanimity.

A battle raged between the two political parties of the Netherlands—between the rural pro-English Orangeists who supported the Stadholder, and the anti-British, pro-French Patriots, a party which, though at this time it was not clearly divided, included both aristocrats and political liberals. The Patriots held forth in the banking and trading cities, particularly Amsterdam. Although these liberals showed some sympathy for the French Enlightenment, they knew little of American theories of government.

Neither Orangeists nor Patriots wanted open war with England. Not only was the Dutch navy inadequate and the Stadholder devoted to his ancestral English land, but the bourgeois Patriots feared to lose the profitable smuggling trade with America through the Dutch West Indies island of St. Eustatius.

Consequently, Adams shouldered two enormous tasks. He had, first, to impart an impression of the American cause favorable enough to incline the Dutch toward recognition of American independence; second, he hoped to secure a loan in Amsterdam, the European banking capital. Having gone to Amsterdam as a private citizen, he learned after his arrival that Congress had given him an official character by designating him to attempt a loan. He was to replace Henry Laurens, who was originally appointed for the mission. After being delayed in his departure, Laurens had been captured en route by a British ship and imprisoned in the Tower of London—a sad fate for Laurens but, in fact, a lucky stroke for Adams. Forthright, clear-headed, a fluent writer, Adams possessed a gift for proselytizing. With his didactic instincts, his zeal for penetrating political debate, he began his work of conversion of the Dutch. He contacted the Patriot brothers Nicolaas and Jacob van Staphorst; Jan de Neufville; Fizeaux and Grand; John Hodshon; Jan Gabriel Tegelaar; and Daniel Commelin—all bankers. Jean Luzac, a Leyden lawyer, editor and professor at the University of Leyden, published in the *Gazette de Leyde* the Massachusetts Constitution written by Adams. Luzac became Adams' fast friend and collaborator. Hendrik Calkoen, venerable lion of the law in Amsterdam, so admired Adams' thought that, unable to speak English, he requested Adams to write down the answers to his questions on the Revolution and American foreign policy. Adams complied in a series of twenty-six letters.[10] He received advice and friendship from Joan Derk, Baron van der Capellen tot den Pol, philosophical leader of the Patriot party. He met François Adriaan van der Kemp, a follower of Van der Capellen and Mennonite clergyman who later lived in the United States. Above all, Adams received untiring aid from an unsung champion of the American cause, Charles William Frederic Dumas, a paid American agent who had served at The Hague since the beginning of the Revolution. Adams convinced all these men and others of the gravity of the American cause, of the determination of his people to carry it through, even without a much-needed loan.

Nevertheless, Adams progressed with discouraging slowness through his program to win Dutch hearts. Assenting silently was one thing for the Dutch; assisting overtly was quite another. For too long the Netherlands had fretted over her neutral stance to be shaken into an about-face that might prove fatal. As Adams wrote to Congress in November, 1780, "This nation has been so long in the habit of admiring the English and disliking the French, so familiarized to call England the natural ally and France the natural enemy of the republic that it must be the work of time to eradicate these prejudices, although the circumstances are greatly altered."[11]

In vain did Adams strive to obtain a loan. With Congress making bank drafts upon him without his permission, his plight was growing desperate. The provinces argued over whether to join the Armed Neutrality. What was more, the entire nation suffered from the embarrassment caused by the seizure and publication of Laurens' papers by the British. Among them was a draft of an old unofficial Dutch treaty with America that the British now used to force the Netherlands out of neutrality.

Protest as the Dutch did that the treaty had never been official, Britain acted swiftly: before the Netherlands could join the Armed Neutrality, Britain declared war on her neighbor. As a neutral carrier through St. Eustatius, by which she shipped supplies and contraband to America and to France and Spain, the Netherlands was a bigger threat to England than as an enemy. If the Dutch joined the Armed Neutrality, the Netherlands would receive protection from the League. Hence, Britain needed to declare war on the Dutch; she used Laurens' papers as an excuse.

Now that war had begun, the tide of Dutch national feeling changed from one of indecision and turmoil over neutrality to one of considerably more firmness and open sympathy for the American side. With grateful heart Adams received gestures of good will from those who immediately after publication of Laurens' papers had ignored him. He now believed the time had ripened for him to announce his powers as minister plenipotentiary to the Netherlands with power to make a treaty of amity and commerce. Realizing that he could never make a treaty or a loan until the Dutch had recognized America, Adams retired to draw up a memorial to the States-General containing news of his powers as minister plenipotentiary. He produced a masterful document. Appealing to common historical, religious, governmental and commercial roots, he marshaled every argument to persuade the States-General to recognize him and, of consequence, recognize the United States.[12] Completing and signing the document on April 19, he went immediately to The Hague to inform the French ambassador, the Duc de la Vauguyon, of what he had done. He later recounted this momentous little combustion in his *Correspondence in the Boston*

Patriot.[13] Knowing that la Vauguyon would have been instructed by Vergennes to do all in his power to prevent Adams from communicating his character as minister with power to make a treaty of amity and commerce, and yet bound by his instructions to consult with the French ambassador, Adams perceived the interview would not be pleasant.

For two hours la Vauguyon tried to dissuade Adams from presenting his credentials. For two hours Adams listened politely, answering all his questions. "But, as is usual, neither was convinced; and I took my leave with as full a determination as ever to pursue my plan," Adams said.

Not to be bested so easily, la Vauguyon, the next morning at eight o'clock, appeared at Adams' lodgings, when "he went over all the ground we had trod the day before and ran about all Europe, especially the northern maritime confederation, to find arguments against the step I proposed to take." This time la Vauguyon detained him some four or five hours; yet Adams knew his arguments "to be mere pretexts."

Finding Adams unconvinced, la Vauguyon suggested that Adams postpone his talk with the president of the States-General until la Vauguyon could write to Vergennes for an opinion.

"By no means," Adams returned. La Vauguyon wanted to know why.

"Because I know beforehand the Count's opinion will be point blank against me; and I had rather proceed against his judgment, without officially knowing his opinion, than with it, as I am determined in all events to go." Well, then, la Vauguyon asked, would Adams join him in writing to Vergennes? Or, he suggested, he would himself write to Vergennes, asking for permission to unite with Adams in trying to gain recognition of his character at the Dutch court. Again, Adams refused. Annoyed, la Vauguyon again asked why.

"Because, Monsieur le Duc, if I must speak out in plain English or plain French, I know the decision of the King's council will be directly and decidedly against me; and I am decidedly determined to go to the president, though I had a resolution of the King in council against me and before my eyes. Besides, the moments are critical, and there is no time to be lost; whereas, the correspondence and negotiations you propose may be spun out for years. Moreover, I think that neither the King nor his ministers ought to commit themselves in this business."

"What!" la Vauguyon exclaimed, "Will you take the responsibility of it upon yourself?"

"Indeed, Monsieur le Duc, I will; and I think I alone ought to be responsible and that no other ambassador, minister, council, or court, ought to be answerable for anything concerning it."

"Are you willing to be responsible, then?"

"Indeed I am; and upon my head may all the consequences of it rest."

"Are you then determined?"

"Determined, and unalterably determined, I am."

Thus, seeing that he could not budge this short piece of New England granite, la Vauguyon smiled and assented pleasantly, "Well, I can say no more. If you are determined, and actually go to the States-General, though it will be against my opinion and advice, and although I can give you no assistance in my official capacity, yet, as a man and an individual, I will give you all the countenance in my power." Adams thanked him with equal affability, agreeing that la Vauguyon could not compromise his court or his public character.

Adams then sent copies of his memorial to Van Bleiswyck, grand pensionary of the province of Holland, the most influential of the seven provinces and most favorable to the American cause; and to Baron Lynden van Hemmen, president of the week of the States-General. Though neither man officially received the memorial, neither of them refused it. Adams' friend Dumas then had the memorial printed in Dutch, French and English, distributing it throughout the provinces.[14] With his memorial acclaimed by the Patriot party, Adams surged hopefully forward in his campaign to gain, first, recognition of his public character, which would be tantamount to recognition of American independence, and, second, possession of a loan. Having labored single-handedly to convert the

Dutch and to swerve around French opposition, Adams had accomplished as monumental a task in Holland as Franklin had in France.

However, Vergennes was about to trim the sails of this dangerously independent American. The man who was presently in America carrying out the instructions of the foreign minister was the large, jovial Chevalier de la Luzerne, a man who had so ingratiated himself with the members of Congress that inch by inch he was establishing larger control over American foreign policy than any foreigner has ever had. Time and time again Vergennes wrote to his ambassador, impressing upon him that Adams was unsuited for his job as minister to treat for peace with Britain. Over and over Vergennes pushed the chevalier to have Congress redraw Adams' instructions, recall him, or at least add several other members to the peace commission who might be more willing tools in French hands.

Hence, la Luzerne began to persuade Congress in the winter of 1781 that its peace demands were too strenuous, that it ought to alter the peace commission. Meanwhile, Vergennes at this point was playing with the possibility of a mediation by Russia and Austria on the basis of the *uti possidetis*—a truce based on the territory each side held at the end of hostilities. Realizing that Adams would never approve such a plan—which would doom American independence—Vergennes pressed harder to have him replaced or checked. Direct Congress to give the French court the power to rein in Adams whenever the Braintree lawyer became too obstinate, Vergennes wrote to la Luzerne.

Accordingly, la Luzerne requested that Congress form a committee to whom he might relay his orders. To this pro-French committee he gave a discreet word, telling them that the mediators might suggest an *uti possidetis* truce but never leaking the information that France might choose to agree to it.

What la Luzerne now succeeded in doing was to persuade this gullible, credulous committee, inexperienced in foreign affairs, to alter Adams' instructions of 1779 and 1780. One member of the committee was General John Sullivan of New Hampshire, leader of the pro-French party, a man in financial straits who took secret payments from la Luzerne to break the anti-Gallican faction. When the committee returned its report, several important members of the anti-Gallican party, like Sam Adams, had left for their states. Thus, ignorant that Vergennes now strongly favored an *uti possidetis* truce, Congress passed a resolution that instructed the peace commissioner to make candid and confidential communications upon all subjects to the ministers of the King of France, to do nothing in the negotiations without their knowledge and agreement, and, in general, to act according to their advice. Designed to put the negotiations totally in the hands of the French court, this resolution dealt a death blow to Adams' laborious attempts to render America less dependent upon France, less at the mercy of the winds of European politics.

La Luzerne, realizing that Adams would never consent to be putty in the hands of Vergennes, now gained another success. He managed to get John Jay, Henry Laurens, Benjamin Franklin and Thomas Jefferson named as a plural commission with Adams, with decisions to be made by a majority of the members. These additional men, la Luzerne congratulated himself, were satisfactorily pro-French; they would offset Adams' pugnacious independence. As events turned out, la Luzerne had misjudged his men.

Meanwhile, summer arrived without word to Vergennes of la Luzerne's victory in Philadelphia. So far as Vergennes knew, Adams was still sole peace minister. Nor had Adams yet received new instructions. Proposals for a Russian-Austrian mediation had advanced to the point that Vergennes, however unwilling, found it necessary to call Adams from Holland to Paris for consultation.

Maria Theresa of Austria, knowing that her French ally could not bear up under a long conflict with England, had been the first European monarch to offer to mediate a peace. Her impulsive and brilliant son, Joseph II, though not so inclined toward peace as his mother, hoped that Austria in the position of mediator could right the balance that now slightly favored France. After the war with Prussia that ensued when Joseph had invaded Lower Bavaria, France and Russia had mediated a peace between the combatants, resulting in some diplomatic points for France.

Catherine of Russia, though she believed that England could do little else but make peace with her colonies, hesitated to allow England to sink too low in the power scale and thus give France the upper hand. However, Vergennes had initiated a rapprochement between France and Russia, a development that Catherine greeted amicably. Seeing that by offering to serve as mediator she could not only increase her prestige but protect neutral rights on the seas, an interest that was dear to her heart, Catherine offered her services. Furthermore, in the summer of 1780 she received an unusual visitor—Joseph II, who suggested an alliance. Together the two posed a force for mediation that could not be ignored.

Vergennes had several times rebuffed the Austrian offer of mediation. Now, however, he feared that Spain and England were reaching a separate agreement without his participation. He would accept Catherine as mediator; she offered something for everyone. After declaring an armistice, the mediators could offer to partition America. Each state could be polled separately as to its preference: to become independent or to return to England. France would no longer be obliged to guarantee independence for those that chose to return. Perhaps the entire South might vote to return to Britain. Consequently, with this scheme England would retain some honor, and France could satisfy her agreement with America under terms of the alliance.

Vergennes refused Austrian mediation in favor of Russian. But now Britain surprised him by agreeing to a co-mediation. Since Joseph II suggested Vienna as a meeting place for a peace congress and since Catherine amiably accepted, there was little that Vergennes could do but to agree. Thus, expecting that a peace would be forged upon the basis of partition or an *uti possidetis* truce, Vergennes now called Adams to Paris. He had misread the picture, of course, for he had rated too low American resolution to secure independence for the Confederation and he had rated too high the British military position in America. He underestimated, as well, Adams' insistence upon preservation of American independence.

Adams had already written to Congress that he would "dread a negotiation for a general peace at this time, because I should expect propositions for short truces, *uti possidetis*, and other conditions, which would leave our trade more embarrassed, our union more precarious, and our liberties at greater hazard than they can be in a continuance of the war; at the same time, it would put us to as constant, and almost as great an expense."[15] If British troops were to be left in America in a truce settlement, Adams knew that would doom independence. Until the mediators should recognize American independence he could never consent to an armistice. The objections to an armistice "are as numerous as they are momentous and decisive." He could say, further, "that as there is no judge upon earth of a sovereign power but the nation that composes it, I can never agree to the mediation of any powers, however respectable, until they have acknowledged our sovereignty, so far at least as to admit a minister plenipotentiary from the United States as the representative of a free and independent power." After that, he admitted, "we might discuss questions of peace or truce with Great Britain, without her acknowledging our sovereignty, but not before."

"Peace," he pointed out, "will only be retarded by relaxations and concessions, whereas firmness, patience and perseverance will insure us a good and lasting one in the end. The English are obliged to keep up the talk of peace, to lull their enemies, and to sustain their credit. But I hope the people of America will not be deceived. Nothing will obtain them real peace but skillful and successful war."[16] He repeated the same sentiments to Vergennes in an angry letter on July 13, 1781.[17] There then followed a series of protesting, threatening missives from Adams and insults from Vergennes. Furthermore, Adams' sharp ears had caught rumor of the partition proposal, an inadmissible suggestion, he warned, since it would be contrary to the constitution of the American Confederation.[18]

Eager to return to Holland, where he felt his efforts would achieve better results than in Paris, he waited anxiously for a reply from Vergennes. No word came from the foreign minister, who now took the tactic of keeping Adams in the dark about his feelings on the mediation. Though justly infuriated, Adams took pride in the series of letters with which he had overwhelmed Vergennes. He had "the satisfaction to believe" that they "defeated the profound and magnificent project of a congress at Vienna, for the purpose of chicaning the United States out of their independence." Moreover, it established "the principle that *American ministers plenipotentiary were not to appear without their public titles and characters, nor to negotiate but with their equals, after an exchange of full powers.*"[19] Meanwhile, la Luzerne sounded out Congress as to an *uti possidetis* truce and a separate polling of the states on the question of independence. They were repulsed by such an idea. In the meantime, Britain no longer cared for mediation. Hence, the scheme for an imperial mediation died on the vine, both sides preferring to negotiate between themselves.

Adams returned to Amsterdam in the final days of July. With anguished and heavy heart he watched his two boys, his source of consolation in this lonely business, depart for far-flung destinations —John Quincy to St. Petersburg to serve as private secretary to Francis Dana at the Russian court, and the homesick Charles, too young to be so long from his mother, to Braintree. Adams now fell victim to a serious fever, a debilitating misery from which he did not recover until October. Having heard of the plural peace commission, he thought he might be excused from his duties; consequently he asked Congress to recall him so that he might return home to recuperate. They did not heed his request.

However, by the beginning of the year 1782 Adams' mission in the Netherlands looked more successful. Applying for recognition at The Hague, he at last received, on April 19, acknowledgment by the States-General as minister plenipotentiary to the Netherlands. Three days later he gained audience with the Stadholder. In May he moved into new lodgings at The Hague, the Hôtel des États-Unis, which he had purchased through Charles Dumas as the first American legation building in Europe. So well did Adams like and trust Dumas that he invited him and his family to move into the Hôtel with him. Madame Dumas then took over as an efficient housekeeper and charming hostess. Dumas, more than any other man, had aided, advised, translated, reported—and, in short, labored with utmost diligence for the success of Adams' Dutch mission. From now until his death in 1796 he would act as chargé d'affaires at The Hague, a devoted servant to the America that he so admired.

Having trimmed off one branch of his mission in Holland, Adams now snipped off another. After months of discouraging, futile efforts, he negotiated a loan with a syndicate of Amsterdam bankers. It was a skillful victory, indeed, won single-handedly and with perseverance. All in all he obtained 5,000,000 guilders, raised by Wilhem and Jan Willink, Nicolaas and Jacob van Staphorst, Jacobus de la Lande and Hendrik Fynje, at five per cent interest with four and a half per cent commission to the bankers. Repayment was to begin after ten years, to be completed in fifteen. And this was only the first of four loans that Adams would obtain, providing almost the only support for weak American credit under the Confederation. Were it not for these loans the Confederation could never have limped along until the Constitution was ratified and a new government recognized. Adams secured in these four loans a sum of 9,000,000 guilders, or $3,500,000.[20]

Finally, Adams moved along in his work to agree upon a treaty of amity and commerce. He went at noon on October 8 to the Statehouse at The Hague, where, in an elaborate room emblazoned with large paintings, he signed the treaty.[21]

Now ready to return to Paris, where the wheels of the peace negotiations were starting to turn, Adams finished his work in the Netherlands, signing papers and sending dispatches.[22]

"It is hard work to sign one's name 1600 times after dinner," he complained, but it was a joyful task, nevertheless, signalizing a successful end to two years of exhausting toil.

Of the five members of the plural peace commission only three —Franklin, Adams and Jay—participated in the negotiations. Jefferson did not sail from America in time to participate. Laurens, though he was finally released from the Tower on bail, did not appear until immediately before the preliminary signing.

After the surrender of Cornwallis at Yorktown, Lord North had been forced to resign. King George, obstinately opposed to granting independence, still had to bow to the loss of his favorite minister. He now offered the government to Lord Shelburne, a man who had not favored independence. But Shelburne, knowing that he lacked support, refused. For that reason, on March 22, 1782, the government went to Rockingham, the only man who could rally any strength. Even so, since the King refused to see Rockingham directly, Shelburne—in his post as Secretary of State of the Southern Department in charge of home, Irish and colonial affairs—had to act as middleman. Charles James Fox, Shelburne's bitter rival, now acted as Secretary of the Northern Department in charge of foreign affairs. The peace negotiations, however, were Shelburne's domain until independence of the states should be recognized.

With everyone in Britain but King George ready for a peace, Shelburne sent an elderly Scotsman, Richard Oswald, to talk with Franklin in Paris in April, 1782, about the time Adams was concluding his business in the Netherlands. Though Oswald had been a slave trader, he had lived for a while in his youth in Virginia and was patient, moderate and inclined toward the philosophy of free economy. In fact, it had been Adam Smith who had introduced him to Shelburne, also a disciple of the new idea of laissez faire. Oswald got on remarkably well with Franklin, making it clear that he thought Britain's financial condition had been so strained by war that peace was indispensable. Despite the fact that Americans had failed to capture Canada in 1775, Franklin suggested that Britain cede Canada to the United States as a safeguard against future friction and bitterness. Surprisingly, Oswald took up the idea, relaying it to Rockingham and Shelburne, who both seemed to receive it with equanimity. Fox expressed shock at the proposal. Feeling that by rights he ought to have charge of the negotiations, he persuaded the cabinet to let him send to Paris his own man, Thomas Grenville, to deal with matters concerning a general peace. Oswald continued in his station as negotiator with the Americans. The two men lacked a unified purpose; working on two different and somewhat opposing levels, they presented a weakened front that the Americans could use to advantage.

Troubled by infirmities, Franklin could not manage the negotiations alone. He called Jay from Madrid, who gladly left his dismal, fruitless mission in the land where for two and a half years he had never been recognized in his official character. When he departed from Spain, Jay was anything but the man la Luzerne had anticipated, for with his ferociously independent spirit he now combined intense suspicion of the Spanish court with almost equal conviction of the unreliability of the court at Versailles. Indeed, Jay had reason for his distrust: because French and Spanish forces had not succeeded in capturing Gibraltar and because Spain still insisted on the Rock as her prize, Vergennes hoped to pacify Floridablanca with a guarantee to Spain of the land between the Alleghenies and the Mississippi River. It was in the interest of France for America to gain independence from Britain, but equally in the interest of France to prevent the United States from growing too powerful. Consequently, Vergennes did not object to Britain's remaining in Canada, to Spain's insisting upon tighter American boundaries, nor to limitation of American fishing rights. Vergennes was prepared to gratify Spain by allowing the United States to be restricted to the territory east of the Alleghenies, cutting off ambitions of the large landholding states that owned territory in the Mississippi Valley. To that end Vergennes dispatched his secretary Rayneval on a secret trip to London to arrange for a quick settlement. Alert to danger, Jay caught wind of the plot, immediately conveying his suspicions to Franklin. Though Franklin did not share Jay's alarm, Jay could not stand to let the matter go. Instead, without the knowledge of Franklin, he determined to scotch the French scheme by opening separate negotiations with Britain. Thus, he sent a special messenger to London.

Meanwhile, Rockingham had died, Shelburne had become prime minister and Fox had resigned, ending the feud of the latter two men. Since Shelburne had all along aimed to cleave America from her French ally, he agreed right away to Jay's proposal.

At this point Adams entered the picture. Arriving in Paris on October 26, he went immediately to see Jay. These two formidably independent fellows met in complete accord. Adams was moved to write spiritedly, "Nothing that has happened since the beginning of the controversy in 1761 has ever struck me more forcibly or affected me more intimately than that entire coincidence of principles and opinions between him and me."[23] Jay's motto, "to be honest and grateful to our allies, but to think for ourselves," suited Adams exactly. Both were convinced that independence must be a precondition of negotiations. Moreover, they both were convinced now that only one course remained for them: to continue separate negotiations with Britain and to disobey their instructions regarding full communication of their moves to the French ministry. As Adams wrote to Congress, "I find a construction put upon one article of our instructions by some persons, which I confess I never put upon it myself. It is represented by some as subjecting us to the French ministry, as taking away from us all right of judging for ourselves and obliging us to agree to whatever the French ministers shall advise us to do, and to do nothing without their consent.

"I never supposed this to be the intention of Congress," he continued hotly; "If I had, I never would have accepted the commission; and if I now thought it their intention, I could not continue in it. I cannot think it possible to be the design of Congress; if it is, I hereby resign my place in the commission and request that another person may be immediately appointed in my stead."[24]

After his talk with Jay, Adams drove out to Passy to discuss matters with Franklin. Throughout the evening Adams orated impulsively, telling the doctor "without reserve my opinion of the policy of this court and of the principles, wisdom and firmness with which Mr. Jay had conducted the negotiation in his sickness and my absence, and that I was determined to support Mr. Jay to the utmost of my power in the pursuit of the same system." The reticent Franklin bore Adams' monologue with patience but, in his circumspect manner, remained silent.[25]

Yet at the next conference with Oswald, Franklin made an unexpected announcement. Turning to Jay, the doctor declared, "I am of your opinion and will go on with these gentlemen in the business without consulting this court."[26] No doubt he wished to present a front of unanimity with his other two colleagues. Even so, he himself had made some separate overtures to Oswald, even before Jay's action; he was not so tied to the French court as Adams imagined.

Now in harmony, the peace commissioners signed a preliminary peace treaty with Britain on November 30, 1782.

As might be expected, Vergennes received the preliminary articles with a gesture of irritation. Yet it was merely a gesture. His agents doubtless had relayed news to him of what the Americans were doing. But he had not objected, for in fact these events relieved him of his obligation to continue the war in order that Spain might win Gibraltar. With Britain and America already undertaking separate negotiations, Vergennes could now expect that Spain would drop her unobtainable demand and settle for some other prize. When Adams, Franklin, Jay, and David Hartley, the Englishman, signed the definitive treaty on September 3, 1783, they did so with the complete acquiescence of France.

By the definitive articles, which were nearly the same as the preliminary ones, Britain swallowed the hard pill of independence, acknowledging the United States to be free and sovereign states, relinquishing all claim to them. Second, the United States received actually more territory than she held at the end of the war. Her new boundaries on the north were approximately what they are today; the Mississippi River bounded the west; the southern boundary lay just north of Spanish East and West Florida. Britain kept Gibraltar, giving Minorca and the Floridas to Spain. France came off poorly with only Tobago in the West Indies and Senegal in Africa.

Article III was Adams' brainchild. As a New Englander long intimate with the zeal with which his neighbors guarded their fishing rights, he formulated a successful guarantee of those rights. Although it is sometimes difficult to understand the concern that colonial New Englanders had for their fishing privileges, the fisheries, in Adams' words, served two purposes: they were a "nursery of seamen" and a "source of profit."[27] Hence Adams stood adamant in his demand that Americans be able to retain their ancient privilege of fishing in all the waters they had traditionally covered. They could not, however, dry and cure fish on the coasts of Newfoundland. The unsettled parts of Nova Scotia, the Magdalen Islands and Labrador remained open for drying.

Adams, moreover, had a great deal to do with Article IV, by

which creditors on both sides should be able lawfully to recover their debts. At the opening of the war many Americans had owed sizable sums to British merchants; they hoped that the war would dissolve their debts. Adams insisted that everyone on both sides be paid his due.

Although there was naturally no affection for the Loyalists among the American commissioners or their people back home, the British continued to demand that these people be given compensation for their property that had been confiscated and the abuse they had received. Consequently, the commissioners agreed upon an innocuous article that salvaged British honor but required little of America. It merely recommended to the state legislatures that they provide for restitution of confiscated Loyalist properties. Both sides knew that probably nothing would come of the article; yet Britain could rest with the assurance that she had paid tribute to the Americans who had kept allegiance to her. And, according to the treaty, there would be no further confiscations or prosecutions of Loyalists.

All prisoners were to be set free. The British forces were to evacuate every garrison in the country. Finally, in another significant provision, navigation of the Mississippi River from its source to its mouth was to be free and open to the subjects of Britain and the citizens of the United States.

The American commissioners had achieved a magnificently liberal treaty. They had gained much, conceded only small points. After the preliminary treaty, Britain was angry with Shelburne. A strange Fox-North coalition succeeded Shelburne's ministry, but could get no better terms. Thus, the final treaty insured no more for Britain than had the preliminary one. Even so, Britain did not emerge from the Peace of Paris the pitiful, broken old matron that she might have been. Britons believed the end of their empire had come. Yet they still had the makings of a second empire, this time centered in the East.

As for France, she had indeed managed to isolate Britain. She had severed Britain from her American colonies, a large triumph. Nevertheless, she gained little else. Despite the craftiness of Vergennes, despite his artful contrivances, he had acquired nothing but a colossal pile of debts. Indeed, France had not fared so well as Spain, which, although she had failed to get Gibraltar or to pen up the United States behind the Alleghenies, had secured valuable territory in the Floridas. The Comte de Vergennes, so thoroughly schooled in Old World balance-of-power diplomacy, had exerted himself almost superhumanly for very limited ends. He did not prevent Britain's star from rising again, nor had he willing allies now to help him stop Catherine II from annexing the Crimea. Still, even if Vergennes had often proved hazardous to the Americans, he had done them one unforgettable good turn—the Franco-American alliance that won them the Revolution had been his work.

The Americans, at the final curtain, deserved the bouquets. Green, unseasoned, unaccustomed to European chessboard diplomacy, they came through with cool heads, the most highly developed sophistication, the quickest reflexes, and the only real perception of just what the American Revolution signified, not only for America but for all of Europe. Vergennes, Floridablanca and George III could not shake their Old World blinders; they could not realize that the Americans were not to be moved by what amounted, in the scale of things, to frivolous diplomatic parries. Europeans had long been used to waging wars for dynastic purposes —personalities not principles were most often the subjects of their wars. They could not conceive that these Americans waged war and waged diplomacy for constitutional reasons, for ideas that they believed to be objectively true.

Moreover, the Americans were a gutsy crew who could play upon the European power struggles. Because Britain was at war with three European nations and she greatly needed peace, the Americans benefited by a generous settlement. Never would they have won such a victory, however, had they not defied their instructions. Some may have thought the commissioners were morally bound to heed their instructions; they themselves believed they were morally bound to break them. As Adams said, Congress had put them all "under guardianship. Congress surrendered its own sovereignty into the hands of a French minister. Blush, blush, ye guilty records! Blush and perish! It is glory to have broken such infamous orders. Infamous, I say, for so they will be to all posterity. How can such a stain be washed out? Can we cast a veil over it and forget it?"[28]

As for Adams himself, he had seen the conflict through from beginning to end. He had witnessed James Otis in the writs of assistance case in 1761; he witnessed the peace ceremonies in Paris in 1783. The path from the Braintree cottage and the Boston law office to the European peace palace had been a long one. Adams, though still blunt and tender-skinned, had acquired a cosmopolitan character. His associates no longer were Braintree farmers but worldly courtiers. As ever, he philosophized upon the world. To the Conde de Aranda, Spanish ambassador at Paris, he remarked that "history was but a series of revolutions. Nature delighted in changes, and the world was but a string of them."

"But," he added, "one revolution is quite enough for the life of a man." He hoped "never to have to do with another."[29]

CHAPTER XI

A YANKEE GOES TO COURT

As autumn came on in Paris, Adams suffered once again from a fever nearly as severe as the one that had struck him two years before in Amsterdam. His secretary, John Thaxter, had sailed for America with the definitive treaty; there was no one to offer him more homely comfort than his physician and a collection of French servants. In the Place du Carousel outside the Hôtel du Roi, where he had apartments, carriages clattered furiously from five in the morning until two at night. Thoroughly ill, dejected, lonely, and utterly frayed by the constant roar outside his windows, Adams gratefully accepted Consul General Thomas Barclay's offer of apartments in his house at Auteuil.[1]

The Hôtel de Rouault near the Bois de Boulogne, with its graceful, quiet gardens filled with statuary, proved a soothing balm. From the windows of his chamber he could view the village of Issy, the Castle Royal of Meudon, the Palace Belle Vue, the Castle of the Duc d'Orléans at St. Cloud, and Mont Calvaire.[2]

The waters of Bath would benefit his ailment, Adams was advised, and so on October 20, 1783, he and John Quincy set out for London and Bath. Before embarking from Calais they put up at the Hôtel d'Angleterre operated by Pierre Dessin, a fellow whom Laurence Sterne had made famous as a character in *A Sentimental Journey*.[3]

Despite a harrowing voyage across the Dover Straits which made them helplessly seasick, the Adamses were struck by the huge white cliffs of Dover. One of them gave "an appearance of danger that the rocks at top might split off by their own weight and dash to pieces some of the small brick houses at its foot."[4]

In London, a postboy carried John and John Quincy to the fine Adelphi Hotel in the Strand, on the way pointing out to them John's Street, Adams' Street, and, finally, John Adams' Street. (Some of the streets surrounding the Adelphi buildings had been named for the Adams brothers who built them.)[5]

Though no longer an Englishman, Adams deemed this first journey to London a sort of homecoming. These Englishmen whom he had first loved, then argued with, and finally cursed were still his kin. His quarters at the Adelphi were more to his taste than any in Paris, "because they are more like what I have been used to in America."[6] Curiosity prompted him "to trot about London as fast as good horses in a decent carriage could carry me."[7]

David Hartley introduced him to the Duke of Portland, to Edmund Burke and Charles James Fox, "but finding nothing but ceremony here," Adams "did not ask favors or receive anything but cold formalities from ministers of state or ambassadors."[8] He found, a little to his surprise, that the American painters were more influential at court than almost anyone else. Benjamin West received permission from the King and Queen to show Adams and Jay, who was also in London, not only "the originals of the great productions of his pencils, such as Wolfe, Bayard, Epaminondas, Regulus," and so forth, which were displayed at Buckingham Palace, but, indeed, the whole palace. Thus, while the royal family was away at Windsor, the visitors could gawk unhampered at every apartment, even the Queen's bedchamber, where a German Bible attracted Adams' attention. Adams much admired the King's library, where he "wished for a week's time. . . . The books were in perfect order, elegant in their editions, paper, binding, and so forth, but gaudy and extravagant in nothing. They were chosen with perfect taste and judgment; every book that a king ought to have always at hand, and, as far as I could examine and could be supposed capable of judging, none other." There were "maps, charts, etc., of all his dominions in the four quarters of the world and models of every fortress in his empire."

All in all, the house appeared to Adams tasteful, elegant, simple, "without the smallest affectation, ostentation, profusion or meanness." He could not help contrasting it with Versailles "and not at all to the advantage of the latter." Having seen many a country mansion in France and Holland, he judged that "the interior of this palace was perfect," but the exterior fell below that of Versailles and many of the country estates.

As for the paintings of West, both Adams and Jay, who had examined a good many of the art treasures of Europe, "gazed at the great original paintings of our immortal countryman . . . with more delight than on the very celebrated pieces of Van Dyke and Rubens and with admiration not less than that inspired by the cartoons of Raphael."[9]

John Singleton Copley, a Boston painter whom Adams had known for many years, showed equal hospitality to his fellow countrymen. Both he and West had lived in London since before the Revolution. Copley delighted Adams by obtaining for him a place in the House of Lords to hear the King's speech at the opening of Parliament and to see introduced the Prince of Wales, now come of age. Adams was even more pleased that "the great Lord Mansfield" had done Copley the favor. Though he had not always approved of Mansfield's opinions, indeed detesting his stand on American affairs, Adams, since he had been a youth in the study of law, had admired the "learning, talents and eloquence of Mansfield. . . ." Now Adams "found more politeness and good humor in him than in Richmond, Camden, Burke or Fox." On the appointed day, November 11, Adams stood in the lobby of the House with "a hundred of the first people of the kingdom. . . ." Suddenly Sir Francis Molineux, "the gentleman usher of the black rod," appeared with his long staff, bellowing in a huge voice, "Where is

Mr. Adams, Lord Mansfield's friend?" Acknowledging himself, Adams was conducted to his place. Next day a gentleman commented to Adams, "How short a time has passed since I heard that same Lord Mansfield say in that same House of Lords, 'My Lords, if you do not kill him, he [Adams] will kill you.' "[10]

Always fascinated by museums and exhibits, Adams visited Sir Ashton Lever's natural history museum, where he saw a collection of American birds, insects "and other rarities" that must have produced a nostalgic pang for the familiar wildlife of his New England countryside. He thought it quaint that in the garden of the museum Sir Ashton and a group of knights practiced the ancient art of archery, hitting their mark as skillfully as any sharpshooting American rifleman.

Josiah Wedgwood's factory delighted Adams. He found the pottery an elegant substitute for porcelain and was impressed with a "rich collection" of artifacts and furniture from the ruins of Herculaneum, which demonstrated once again, he thought, the graceful artistry of the Greeks "in the mechanic arts no less than in statuary, architecture, history, oratory and poetry."

With cut glass coming into vogue, some gentlemen introduced Adams to its manufacture. The American declared it did as much honor to England as the mirrors, the china or the Gobelin tapestry did to France—"it seemed to be the art of transmitting glass into diamonds."

Nor did Westminster Abbey, St. Paul's and the Exchange escape Adams' tourist enthusiasm. He visited Richard Penn and old Governor Thomas Pownall at Richmond Hill, but to his disappointment he missed seeing the grotto where Swift, Bolingbroke, Arbuthnot, Gay, Prior, "and even the surly Johnson and the haughty Warburton" held forth.

At Windsor he viewed the castle, Eton School, and enjoyed comparing the forest with what he remembered of Pope's Windsor Forest.

Still ailing after his visit to London, Adams decided to go on to Bath. Yet he had not been twenty minutes in the hotel there before a distant cousin, John Boylston, accosted him with the offer of showing him around the public buildings, card rooms, assembly rooms, dancing rooms. Caring no more for seeing these curiosities than for the "bricks and pavements," Adams nevertheless went along with a polite face.[11] The Bath interlude ended in a hurry, however, for he received sudden word that congressional drafts had exhausted all of the first loan he had arranged and that many bills had already been presented and protested for non-acceptance. He must return to Amsterdam to try for another loan, a goal for which his bankers gave him little hope.

"It was winter; my health was very delicate; a journey and voyage to Holland at that season would very probably put an end to my labors. I scarcely saw a possibility of surviving it. Nevertheless, no man knows what he can bear till he tries," Adams wrote, and so he went. Returning to London, he and John Quincy journeyed to Harwich, where they found the packet delayed by bad winds and a severe storm. There they remained for three days, in poor quarters, bored, "without society and without books," grumpy over their interrupted vacation, apprehensive about the ensuing voyage.

When the packet finally departed on the fourth day, the "tremulous, undulating, turbulent kind of irregular tumbling sea" made the Adamses as sick as they had ever been. For three days every passenger, worn out by continual storms and lack of sleep, was laid low. Finally the captain announced that they could not make their destination of Hellevoetsluis, that they would have to land on the island of Goeree in the province of Zeeland. Once landed, the voyagers found that the only habitation on this desolate shore was a lone fisherman's hut. It was five or six miles to the town of Goeree, the fisherman told them, and there was no wagon to take them.

Never had John Adams been so ill, so weak and exhausted. He sincerely doubted that he could ever walk through violent weather, through ice and snow for several miles. Yet glancing at John Quincy, he saw that his son received this news of impending adventure with actual gaiety. The sight determined Adams to pull body and soul together and walk into town.

The only route, the party was informed at the inn, was to cross the island of Goeree, then cross an arm of the sea to the island of

Overflakkee, across that island to the ferrying point, whence they could get across a wide expanse of sea to the continent. With the water frozen, they would have to take ice boats across the sea. Consequently, they all piled into a boor's or peasant's wagon, the only conveyance available. No springs or cushions softened the wooden seats. Clinging to their hard benches, the Adamses jolted over a nearly impassable clay road that the rainy weather had made "as soft and miry as mortar." Horses' hooves and wagon wheels had rutted the clay during the rains; then freezing weather had transformed it into hard rocks. "Over this bowling green" the wagon rattled and skipped to the ferrying point, where warmed at last by good fires and Dutch cheer, the Adamses collapsed into cozy, comfortable beds.

Ice boat pilots demanded high prices for providing passengers with a wet, freezing excursion over a broad arm of sea. The Adamses were forced to pay dearly to be rowed in the water to the ice, where the skipper and his men leaped out, hauled the boat up onto the ice and skated the boat on its runners. Passengers disembarked, too, picking their way along the ice. When the ice became thin, the boat plunged into the water; all hopped in and rowed until they reached more ice. When they finally reached the mainland, Adams looked exactly as he felt—"like a withered old worn-out carcass." Compassionately, the skipper eyed him, saying he "pitied the old man." Once ashore, the skipper declared he "must come and take the old man by the hand and wish him a safe journey to The Hague." How sorry he was that the old fellow had suffered so much in the passage.[12]

Adams arrived on January 12 at the Hôtel des États-Unis at The Hague, but he did not tarry there. He rushed on to Amsterdam where, much beyond his own expectations, he obtained a loan adequate to save the credit of the United States. He signed a contract on March 9 for a second loan, this time for 2,000,000 guilders to be repaid by 1807.[13]

Nearly four and a half years had passed since Adams had seen his wife. For two such devoted people the separation had posed an almost unbearable burden. Letters saved them. Yet even these faithful, indefatigable writers could not overcome the inadequacy of mere letters. Hearts ached, nerves were strained, imaginations wondered.

". . . you are neither of an age or temper to be allured by the splendor of a court or the smiles of princesses," Abigail wrote, as if to convince herself. "I never suffered an uneasy sensation on that account. I know I have a right to your whole heart, because my own never knew another lord; and such is my confidence in you, that if you were not withheld by the strongest of all obligations, those of a moral nature, your honor would not suffer you to abuse my confidence."[14] Though she would go through the dreary absence again—and willingly—if she had to, Abigail still could not help but consider her husband's honors "as badges of my unhappiness." It was true that "the unbounded confidence I have in your attachment to me and the dear pledges of our affection has soothed the solitary hour and rendered your absence more supportable; for, had I loved you with the same affection, it must have been misery to have doubted." Even so, "a cruel world too often injures my feelings by wondering how a person possessed of domestic attachments can sacrifice them by absenting himself *for years.*"[15]

As early as 1782 Abigail had asked to come to Europe, but Adams, thinking the final peace treaty would soon be signed, told her that he would soon be coming home himself. He wrote saying that he had asked Congress to allow him to resign and that if he did not soon hear, he would come home without it. "Don't think, therefore, of coming to Europe. If you do, we shall cross each other, and I shall arrive in America about the same time that you may arrive in Europe."[16] But with the delay of Hartley's arrival in Paris, the signing could not take place until September, 1783. Congress in the meantime had begun proposals for negotiation of a commercial treaty with Great Britain. Adams then wrote immediately to Abigail telling her to come and bring Nabby with her. Nabby's coming, her parents hoped, might put an end to her romance with Royall Tyler, a young Harvard graduate and lawyer who had settled in Braintree and whose rather erratic emotional behavior made

John and Abigail wonder if he were the right man for their daughter. When Abigail received final word that Congress in May had elected her husband a joint commissioner with Franklin and Jefferson (who succeeded Jay) to negotiate commercial treaties with twenty-three European and African powers, she arranged passage on the *Active* for herself and Nabby and two reliable servants, John Briesler and Esther Field. The two younger boys, Charles and Tom, were to stay with their Aunt Betsy Shaw in Haverhill.

The ocean voyage sorely tried the novice passengers. There was no "inducement sufficient to carry a lady upon the ocean,"Abigail declared, "but that of going to a good husband and kind parent." The captain, Abigail observed, was an excellent seaman but paid "little attention to anything besides his sails and his ropes." The cook could only be classed as "miserable." She thought the mate "a droll being; swears for all the rest of the ship." With his diverting stories told with a comical face, he was "a right tar in his manners."

So poorly supplied was the ship that Abigail's silver porringer was in constant service, the only bowl on board. "I should not have been in this condition if I had not been assured that the ship supplied everything," she wrote with annoyance in her journal of the trip. "I think the price we paid entitled us to better accommodations. In short I have been obliged to turn cook myself and have made two puddings, the only thing I have seen fit to eat. I have been obliged to order and direct sick, as I have been to the cleaning out of the cabin every day. It is a great misfortune that Esther is so sick. I have been obliged to see to the cleaning of the milk pail, which has been enough to poison anybody. If we do not die of dirt now, we shall at least eat our peck."[17]

By July 21, Abigail and Nabby were settled in a hotel in Covent Garden, from which they moved to the Adelphi. Adams, beside himself with anticipation over their arrival, had sent John Quincy in May to meet them in London. But when a month passed and they still had not arrived, John Quincy returned to The Hague. Abigail's letter informing John that she had arrived made him "the happiest man upon earth"; he felt twenty years younger. He was mortified, he wrote, that he could not come for her himself, but he would explain when he saw her the variety of reasons that prevented him. In his stead he was sending her an excellent son who was "the greatest traveler of his age." Finally receiving word that John Quincy had reached his mother in London, Adams impatiently canceled his commitments, dashing off a note to "stay where you are until you see me."[18]

Adams said little of his reunion with his wife, only recording on August 7, 1784, "Arrived at the Adelphi buildings and met my wife and daughter after a separation of four years and an half. Indeed after a separation of ten years, excepting a few visits. Set off the next day for Paris."[19] But it is safe to say that the forty-nine-year-old Adams met his beloved with a heart full of intense relief, joy, a touch of sadness at time irrecoverably lost, a shade of unbelief, a bit of shock over the painful realization that a loved one had aged. Abigail, too, must have sensed every tender and complicated feeling as she and her husband, perhaps a little awkwardly after so long a separation, once again met each other and their two attractive grown-up children.

Adams felt fortunate that he could rent the Hôtel de Rouault at Auteuil. Four miles from the "putrid streets of Paris,"[20] it provided a pleasant, serene dwelling where Adams could enjoy his newly regained family. Finding the graceful sprawl of Auteuil a challenging change from her Braintree cottage, Abigail bustled about the management of her new domain, puttering with a peace of heart long unknown, soothing her cranky husband with the deft hand that only she possessed. Nabby observed with delight every beribboned frock, every dazzling jewel, every handsome gentleman, thriving upon the elegant, sophisticated Parisian scene that alternately thrilled her and made her blush. John Quincy, though always the object of fatherly pride, had led in a way a stern, lonely existence these last few years. Now a manly seventeen, he doubtless rejoiced in the obvious admiration with which his mother and sister made much of him.

Jefferson became an honored visitor at Auteuil. Deliberating with him on the commercial treaties, Adams developed a brotherly fondness for this stimulating intellectual companion. He felt a real kinship with the Virginian whose interests were as wide-ranging as his, whose sharp mind matched his, whose zeal for political debate was equally keen, who loved farming as much as he did. Their minds operated differently—Adams' more profound, creative, more fascinated by the study of human nature and more attuned to history; Jefferson's more all-encompassing, liberal, eclectic and scientific—but they meshed together with invigorating harmony. The Adamses welcomed Jefferson as one of the family, Abigail no doubt feeling a maternal compassion toward this widower with two daughters in his care. Adams, in his impulsive, boyish manner, beamed upon his friend the affection that he reserved for intimates.

For his part, Jefferson had once remarked of Adams that "his dislike of all parties, and all men, by balancing his prejudices, may give the same fair play to his reason as would a general benevolence of temper."[21] Fortunately, he came to view his colleague with a kindlier eye, looking upon him with genuine fondness. However, his natural restraint and coolness never allowed him to adopt in his letters the familial warmth that Adams exhibited.

Adams had drafted a commercial treaty with the Prussian minister in the Netherlands, Baron von Thulemeier. Though it was not signed until 1785, it served in a revised version as a model for treaties with Portugal, Denmark, Tuscany and Morocco. The British would not accept any part of it, however.

Early in 1785, the American diplomatic corps in Europe underwent a change. In February Congress named Adams as first American minister to the Court of St. James's, a post he had dearly coveted. In fact, he was criticized for expressing so openly his desire to receive the appointment. Jefferson was named minister to Versailles, permitting Franklin to take a long-sought retirement. Adams and Jefferson were to retain their joint commission on commercial treaties.

The Adamses regretted leaving Auteuil—all the more because in May they bade farewell to John Quincy, now almost eighteen and ready to embark for America to study at Harvard. After parting with John Quincy and leaving their friends, John, Abigail and Nabby made a "rather triste" journey to London.[22]

Leaving behind her garden and her weeping domestics, Abigail felt low, she wrote Jefferson, but especially did she regret leaving behind "the only person with whom my companion could associate with perfect freedom and unreserve: and whose place he had no reason to expect supplied in the land to which he is destined."[23]

Installed at the Bath Hotel in Piccadilly, Adams immediately upon his arrival announced himself to Foreign Secretary Lord Carmarthen. He received an audience with George III on June 1.

It meant a great deal to Adams to be the first independent American to receive audience with the King. Vain enough to consider this appointment as minister to St. James's as the epitome of his diplomatic career, yet eager, now that independence was won, to begin to heal the breach between Britain and the United States, he prepared for his audience with exceeding pains and nervous agitation. Several European diplomats in London advised him to deliver a complimentary speech, and Vergennes had told Jefferson that a speech was the custom. Thinking that he would simply present his credentials silently to the King and then withdraw, Adams now saw that he must work up a short speech.

At one o'clock on Wednesday, June 1, Sir Clement Cotterell Dormer, master of ceremonies, called for Adams, accompanying him to Carmarthen's office in Cleveland Row. Lord Carmarthen received them there, introducing Adams to the undersecretary, Mr. Fraser, a veteran who had held his post for thirty years. Kindly, Fraser told Adams that he would arrange for his things to be imported duty-free from Holland and France. Carmarthen and Adams then stepped into his lordship's coach.

When they arrived at court, Adams stood in the antechamber with Sir Clement, while Carmarthen went to receive the instructions of the King. Ministers of state, lords, bishops, courtiers of every sort crowded the antechamber, spilling over into the adjacent bedchamber of the King. Feeling every eye upon him, Adams gratefully received the pleasantries of the Swedish and Dutch ministers, who quieted his nerves with their engaging conversation during the wait. Lord Carmarthen then returned, announcing to Adams that it was time to meet the King. Through the levee room they went

—into the King's closet. The door shut behind them; Adams found himself alone with Carmarthen and King George. Meeting his foe of more than twenty years, Adams sensed the overwhelming historical significance of the moment. Here before him sat the man who represented all that he had chosen to reject but who undeniably symbolized, as well, the roots from which he came. Here sat the symbol of political oppresson—yet here also sat the bulwark of the British law and Constitutions that Adams, of all men, knew must form the basis for the independent American government. Adams felt moved beyond words. He bowed to the King the customary three times—first at the door, then half-way, and again before him. As Adams began to speak, tension reinforced the sincerity of his words.

"Sir," he commenced, "the United States of America have appointed me their minister plenipotentiary to Your Majesty and have directed me to deliver to Your Majesty this letter which contains the evidence of it." Congress had the utmost desire "to cultivate the most friendly and liberal intercourse between Your Majesty's subjects and their citizens. . . . " The appointment of a minister from the United States to the King's court would begin a new epoch in the history of England and America.

"I think myself more fortunate than all my fellow-citizens," he went on—and he meant it—"in having the distinguished honor to be the first to stand in Your Majesty's royal presence in a diplomatic character; and I shall esteem myself the happiest of men, if I can be instrumental in recommending my country more and more to Your Majesty's royal benevolence and of restoring an entire esteem, confidence, and affection, or in better words, the old good nature and the old good humor between people, who, though separated by an ocean, and under different governments, have the same language, a similar religion, and kindred blood."

Finally he said, "I beg Your Majesty's permission to add that although I have some time before been entrusted by my country, it was never in my whole life in a manner so agreeable to myself."

King George, with royal dignity but with considerable emotion, listened attentively to every word. Adams knew not whether it was the nature of the meeting or his own visible uneasiness that touched the King. At any rate, when King George began to answer him, he did so with a more evident tremor in his voice than Adams had shown.

"Sir," said the King distinctly, but hesitating for long painful interludes between sentences, "the circumstances of this audience are so extraordinary, the language you have now held is so extremely proper, and the feelings you have discovered so justly adapted to the occasion, that I must say that I not only receive with pleasure the assurance of the friendly dispositions of the United States, but that I am very glad the choice has fallen upon you to be their minister. I wish you, sir, to believe, and that it may be understood in America, that I have done nothing in the late contest but what I thought myself indispensably bound to do, by the duty which I owed to my people. I will be very frank with you. I was the last to consent to the separation; but the separation having been made, and having become inevitable, I have always said, as I say now, that I would be the first to meet the friendship of the United States as an independent power. The moment I see such sentiments and language as yours prevail, and a disposition to give to this country the preference, that moment I shall say, let the circumstances of language, religion, and blood have their natural and full effect."

Since he was so apprehensive himself, Adams could not swear that the King had spoken these precise words, he wrote to John Jay, but they were the King's words as he had understood and recollected them.

King George then inquired whether Adams came directly from France. "He put on an air of familiarity and laughing said, 'There is an opinion among some people that you are not the most attached of all your countrymen to the manners of France.'"

Adams heard this remark with surprise, thinking it "an indiscretion and a departure from the dignity." Though he was a trifle embarrassed, he was "determined not to deny the truth on one hand, nor leave him to infer from it any attachment to England on the other." Consequently, in a light tone he replied, "That opinion,

sir, is not mistaken; I must avow to Your Majesty, I have no attachment but to my own country."

"As quick as lightning" the King shot back, " 'An honest man
will never have any other.' " Then uttering a low word to Carmarthen, he turned and bowed to Adams—the signal to retire. Still
facing the King, Adams bowed himself out, joined Sir Clement
outside the door, and went down to his carriage, hearing himself
announced by Sir Clement's booming voice.[24]

The whole of Britain, however, did not receive an American
minister with charitable grace. Abigail kept Jefferson informed on
their reception in England, writing that the *London Public Adver-
tiser* had groaned disgustedly, "An ambassador from America!
Good heavens, what a sound! The gazette surely never announced
anything so extraordinary before, nor once on a day so little expected. This will be such a phenomenon in the Corps Diplomatique
that 'tis hard to say which can excite indignation most, the insolence of those who appoint the character, or the meanness of those
who receive it. Such a thing could never have happened in any
former administration, not even that of Lord North."[25]

Adams attended the King's birthday, an ordeal he wondered that
the King and Queen were able to survive. How this royal pair could
sustain small talk with four or five thousand people in one day he
could not fathom. Standing next to the Spanish minister, Don
Bernardo del Campo, Adams marveled that the King could converse in good French for nearly half an hour with Don Bernardo.

"You would die of ennui here," Adams wrote Jefferson, "for
these ceremonies are more numerous and continue much longer
here than at Versailles."[26]

Abigail's expeditions to find a house soon paid off; in June,1785,
Adams leased from the Hon. John Byron of Purbright a house at
the northeast corner of Grosvenor Square, to be the first United
States legation in London.

Though Adams obtained an interview with the younger Pitt, now
prime minister, and talked with Carmarthen about the ever-present
problems—western posts still occupied by British soldiers, British
trade restrictions, slaves captured by the British during the war,

American debts owed to British creditors—negotiations proceeded nowhere. Not until the Jay Treaty of 1794 would these difficulties be resolved.

Arrangements with Baron von Thulemeier for an American-Prussian commercial treaty went ahead, however. After angling for such a treaty with the Baron since March, 1784, Adams signed, in August, 1785, a treaty of amity and commerce between America and Frederick the Great. Franklin and Jefferson had signed it in Paris in July.

Jefferson made his first and only visit to London in March of the following year. He and Adams hoped to negotiate treaties with Portugal and the piratical Barbary state of Tripoli and to make one last effort at a British treaty.

The venture proved a total disappointment. Britain remained imperturbable; Portugal signed but did not ratify the treaty. Adams and Jefferson, working through Thomas Barclay, an American consul general in France, managed to obtain a treaty with Morocco, but Spanish Consul John Lamb's toil to get a similiar treaty with Algiers, most powerful of the Barbary states, collapsed amidst demands of the Dey of Algiers for high tribute money.

Adams and Jefferson eased their gloom with a pleasant tour in April of English country seats. These two companions set off in a spirit of congeniality, a short, ruddy-faced stout fellow and a tall, angular spare one. Edgehill and Worcester they found curious and interesting, "as scenes where freemen had fought for their rights." These friends of liberty were dismayed to find the inhabitants of Worcester ignorant of their town's heritage. No doubt Jefferson kept still, yet Adams typically felt provoked to advise them, "And do Englishmen so soon forget the ground where liberty was fought for? Tell your neighbors and your children that this is holy ground, much holier than that on which your churches stand. All England should come in pilgrimage to this hill once a year." The Englishmen appeared pleased with this interest shown in their neighborhood; their awkwardness, Adams surmised, perhaps stemmed from "their uncertainty of our sentiments concerning the Civil Wars."[27]

At Stratford-upon-Avon the literary enthusiasts visited the birthplace of Shakespeare. With the credulity of tourists they viewed the "old wooden chair in the chimney corner where he sat," from which "we cut off a chip, according to the custom." A mulberry tree said to have been planted by the Bard had been cut down "and is carefully preserved for sale." Unfortunately, the home where he died was gone; there was not even a name on his tombstone, nothing preserved worth knowing—"nothing which might inform us what education, what company, what accident turned his mind to letters and the drama."[28]

After they had seen the sights of Surrey, Berks, Bucks, Warwick and Shropshire, the friends journeyed through Oxford back to London.

Adams and Jefferson gathered about them in London an entertaining little group of Englishmen and Americans. Besides the painters Copley, West and Trumbull, there was William Vans Murray, a young man from Maryland studying at the Middle Temple, a friend of John Quincy and a fledgling political devotee of John Adams. One day he would be a Federalist member of Congress and successor to John Quincy as minister to The Hague. The late Thomas Hollis, Adams' friend, editor of the London publication of the *Dissertation on Canon and Feudal Law* and a benefactor of Harvard, had bequeathed his estate to Thomas Brand. After receiving his inheritance, Brand added the name Hollis to his name; he was an antiquarian, dissenter, and pro-American who lectured amiably upon both liberal political principles and his architectural mentor, the sixteenth-century Italian Andrea Palladio. Richard Price of Newington Green, another ardent pro-American, wrote political pieces and was a dissenting minister. He regularly held forth at Hackney, where the Adamses went to hear him every Sunday while they were in London. Finally, Adams became acquainted with Joseph Priestley, another dissenting minister and political radical, discoverer of oxygen, and writer upon disparate subjects, as was so usual with eighteenth-century men. Priestley later would move to Philadelphia during Adams' Vice Presidency.[29]

Yet most significant to the Adamses of all the London group was Colonel William Stephens Smith, Adams' secretary, a native of

New York City, a graduate of Princeton, who had studied a little
law but became a Continental Army officer in 1776. He had served
under Sullivan, Lee, Lafayette and, finally, Washington. After supervising the British evacuation of New York City, he had left the
army in 1783 to become secretary of legation to Adams.[30] Both
John and Abigail liked Colonel Smith well enough, thought him a
young man of good manners and conduct. All the same, though
they spoke of him in complimentary fashion, they never seemed to
offer extraordinary praise of him. He appeared to be a pompous,
humorless fellow, but good-looking with a dapper air. Nabby,
meanwhile, began to find that Colonel Smith was supplanting
Royall Tyler in her affections. For a while after her arrival in
Europe the romance with Tyler flowered, yet at last it fell upon hard
times, finally blowing up in a misunderstanding that separation
made it impossible to patch up. Colonel Smith made an elegant
proposal, John and Abigail gave their blessings, and plans began for
a wedding. Since dissenting ministers had no authority to perform
marriages, Jonathan Shipley, bishop of St. Asaph and somewhat
pro-American, officiated on June 12 at the wedding in the legation.
Colonel Smith took his bride to a house in Wimpole Street. Smith's
long absences from home and precarious financial speculation
would one day cause Nabby and her parents untold heartache, but
for the moment the newlyweds glowed in the first bliss of married
life.

In July the Adamses and Smiths visited Thomas Brand-Hollis
and his maiden sister, Miss Brand, at their palatial museum-home,
The Hyde, in Essex. From there John and Abigail made a sentimental excursion to Braintree, yet saw to their disillusionment that it
was a poor little place, rather dirty, with very ordinary houses.
Rummaging through the churchyard, they discovered no names on
the tombstones to indicate that any Braintree, Massachusetts, families had emigrated from Braintree, England.[31]

Immediately upon his return from Essex, Adams found that Congress had at last ratified the commercial treaty with Prussia. With
no Prussian minister in either London or Paris, Adams decided to

travel at once to The Hague, to which he was still minister, and exchange ratifications with Baron von Thulemeier. Leaving on August 3, he took Abigail with him, going through Harwich, Hellevoetsluis, and Rotterdam.

After accomplishing his official business with von Thulemeier, Adams showed his wife around the Netherlands, visiting Utrecht, where, in a great constitutional reform victory for the Dutch Patriots, new magistrates were being sworn into office.[32]

"We were present at Utrecht at the august ceremony of swearing in their new magistrates," Adams wrote Jefferson. "In no instance of ancient or modern history have the people ever asserted more unequivocally their own inherent and unalienable sovereignty."[33]

The constitutional reforms gained by the Patriots in the Netherlands served as partial inspiration, in fact, for Adams' largest literary work, *A Defence of the Constitutions of Government of the United States of America*, which he began writing after he and Abigail returned to London. Though he had little time during his diplomatic career to continue his political writing, he managed during this ten-year period to turn out two of his most significant contributions to political thought—the Massachusetts Constitution of 1780 and the *Defence*.

The Massachusetts Constitution stood as Adams' monument as a framer of government, evidence that his theories, based on traditional English and colonial constitutional principles, could be transferred from paper to practice. Containing no surprises, it followed naturally from the previous course of his thought that had culminated in the *Thoughts on Government*. Again, it demonstrated how consistent was Adam's thought, how it evolved but changed little in substance.

During the period of the Revolution, the states faced the dilemma of rebuilding the governments they had devastated. With the congressional resolution of May 10, 1776, they began one by one to respond to the challenge of constitution-making. In this fascinating period they could make one of those rare beginnings in political history. They could make whatever innovation they chose.

The states had never before possessed so much power as during this Confederation period; they would never possess so much again.

Connecticut and Rhode Island felt satisfied to retain their old corporate charters under the new title of state governments. Among the other states three types of governments came into being. Prestigious Virginia came first with a Declaration of Rights and Constitution drafted by the illustrious George Mason. The Declaration of Rights, a magnificent embodiment of ancient English rights, served not only as a model for Jefferson's Declaration of Independence but for all the other state bills of rights and the first ten amendments to the United States Constitution. The Virginia Constitution itself took a back seat in brilliance to the Declaration of Rights. Following Locke's maxim of legislative supremacy, the Virginia Constitution provided for a governor, council and judiciary elected jointly by both houses of the legislature. Such a constitution lacked wisdom in making governor, council and judiciary responsible to the legislature rather than to the people, but since Virginia was so highly respected, most states followed her lead.

Most democratic and most radical of the state goverments was that of Pennsylvania, sanctioned by Benjamin Franklin, a unicameral type imitated by Georgia and Vermont. Artisans, farmers, and frontiersmen upset the Quakers in a bitter struggle and set up a unicameral assembly open to anyone of the Christian religion and apportioned according to population. An elected council, limited by rotation of office, took the place of a governor. The only semblance of a governor was the president of this council, chosen jointly by the council and assembly. In strife-torn Pennsylvania, where factions rode rampant, the workers and farmers of the assembly excluded Quakers from the vote, generally ruling with a tight and intolerant hand. Though much touted in Europe as an example of constitutional perfection, this government lasted only until 1790, when disgusted Pennsylvania instituted a bicameral legislature and regular governor.

In contrast to these legislative-supremacy and unicameral types was the Massachusetts Constitution, a mixed government as well balanced as Adams could make it. It was the most conservative type of constitution, as well as the one most like the later Federal Constitution. Moreover, apart from that of New Hampshire, it was the only state constitution adopted through the most popular and peaceful means of creating a new government—Adams' pet institution—the constitutional convention. All other states adopted their constitutions through their state legislatures.

After the last General Court session under Crown government had ended in 1774, an extra-legal provincial congress without constitutional authority operated an interim government for several years. This congress in September, 1776, asked the people of Massachusetts to give it power to make a new constitution. Given this authority, the assembly appointed a committee to work up a draft. A convention in turn accepted the draft. But when the constitution was submitted to the towns, they rejected it flatly, objecting that it had no bill of rights, among other things. Again in 1779, the congress asked for authority to call a constitutional convention. By a vote open to all freemen over twenty-one, a convention met in 1780. Adams, home from France after his first sojourn abroad, was elected to attend, along with Sam Adams, John Hancock and James Bowdoin. Appointed to the drafting committee, Adams was chosen to write the constitution. His draft drew the approval of the committee and then, with only a few changes, of the convention. After the towns debated it clause by clause and accepted it, the constitution became law in June, 1780.[34]

Though Adams realized that no writers of constitutions could possibly foresee every emergency, he did feel proud of his work.

"There never was an example of such precautions as are taken by this wise and jealous people in the formation of their government," he wrote. "None was ever made so perfectly upon the principle of the people's rights and equality. It is Locke, Sidney, and Rousseau and De Mably reduced to practice in the first instance."[35]

He seemed to get carried away with rhetoric here, for it was not Locke, Sidney, Rousseau and De Mably so much as Polybius and Harrington. It was a conscious effort to reconcile the monarchic, aristocratic and democratic elements of society in a balance of power, an attempt to prevent any one of society's inevitable factions from seizing control. Here was highly responsive government republican style, with the seat of sovereignty firmly in the people. All branches of government reported directly to the people, but none reported to another branch, as was the case with some other state constitutions.

"The end of the institution, maintenance, and administration of government," stated the preamble, "is to secure the existence of the body politic; to protect it, and to furnish the individuals who compose it with the power of enjoying, in safety and tranquillity, their natural rights and the blessings of life. . . . " If these objects were not obtained, then the people had the right of revolution—Adams would hope by the peaceful means of a constitutional convention.

Adams in the preamble paid a token nod to the eighteenth-century penchant for social compact theory. In a very real way this new constitution, as a product of a popularly elected convention, was indeed a contract and solemn covenant among the people—a contract in an actual sense not usually true of government. Yet to the notions then in vogue of man contracting himself out of a state of primitive nature Adams did not subscribe. Like Aristotle he believed that man was a social animal from the beginning, never come at some remote time from a wilderness state outside society.

In the Declaration of Rights following the preamble Adams borrowed heavily from George Mason. Adams in fact had borrowed Mason's phrase that all men are born "equally free and independent." This phrase appeared to Adams to clarify that devilish problem of equality, a concept with which he was much concerned. Here was the distinct meaning that men are born equal under natural and human law. Unfortunately the convention chose to substitute for "equally free and independent" the muddled words "free and equal." With the phrase "free and equal" it was possible to mire down in the notions that to Adams seemed absurd—that men might be equal in talent, merit, wealth, manners, charm, beauty and so on. As Adams wrote Article I of the Declaration it read, "All men are born equally free and independent, and have certain natural, essential, and unalienable rights, among which may be reckoned the right of enjoying and defending their lives and liberties; that of acquiring, possessing, and protecting their property; in fine, that of seeking and obtaining their safety and happiness."

Adams never felt that he could come up with a satisfactory article on religious freedom. Consequently, the article in the Declaration pertaining to religion was not his work. It was an ambiguous statement, endorsing the principle of no favored denomination while at the same time retaining a state religion.[36]

Adams elaborated in the Declaration the principle of sovereignty of the state of Massachusetts except in matters expressly delegated to the central government in Congress assembled. He stated the principle of magistrates and legislators as agents of the people; of the error of divine right of magistrates; of equal protection of the laws; of the right to alter government; of free elections; of deprivation of private property only by consent through a representative body. He brought forth the rights of individuals as enumerated in the Magna Carta, Petition of Right and the English Bill of Rights. He clearly set forth freedom of speech and press. He provided for judges' terms according to good behavior. Finally, he wrote in the well-known Article XXX, "The judicial department of the state ought to be separate from, and independent of, the legislative and executive powers." In the most significant change made by the convention, this article was made to read, "In the government of this commonwealth, the legislative department shall never exercise the executive and judicial powers, or either of them; the executive shall never exercise the legislative and judicial powers, or either of them; the judicial shall never exercise the legislative and executive powers, or either of them, to the end it may be a government of laws and not of men."[37]

The convention revision that read so strictly as to exclude the executive from any part in the legislative misconstrued Adams' concept of balance of powers. Adams wanted separation of legislative, executive and judicial branches. But within the legislative branch the executive with his veto power exercised an essential function. Even though the executive had no other powers of legislation, the one authority of the veto made him an indispensable member of the legislative, Adams believed.

In the beginning of the section entitled "The Frame of Government," Adams had merely stated, "In the government of the Commonwealth of Massachusetts, the legislative, executive and judicial power shall be placed in separate departments, to the end that it might be a government of laws, and not of men." As a pointed illustration of how men of the eighteenth century felt about the political theory of James Harrington, one member of the convention suggested that the word "Oceana" be substituted for "Massachusetts" in this particular clause.[38]

The constitution provided for a legislative composed of a senate and house of representatives, the senate to represent property, the house to represent the populace, "the principle of equality." Senators were elected from districts apportioned on the basis of taxable wealth. Representatives were to be elected according to population from every corporate town. Each house was to have a veto on the other; the governor, as well, possessed an absolute veto on the other two houses. Adams always believed absolute executive veto necessary to the preservation of independence of the executive and judicial branches. However, the convention changed this provision to provide for the governor's veto to be overridden by a two-thirds vote of both houses. All elections were annual. Property qualifications were necessary for both voting and office-holding.

The Massachusetts Constitution gave less power to the legislature and more to the governor than did other constitutions which, except for Massachusetts, New York and South Carolina, deprived the governor of the veto. But at the same time Massachusetts and some other New England states, as well as New York, were the only states in which the people themselves elected their governor. In the Virginia type of constitution he was elected by the legislature, making him responsible not to the people but to the legislature. In this regard, then, the Massachusetts Constitution was more responsive to the people than some of the others.

Senators and representatives by joint ballot elected a council, which was to advise the governor. Members of the judiciary held their offices by appointment and during good behavior.

A particularly interesting section of the constitution granted favored status to Harvard College, continuing the ancient practice of including the governor, lieutenant governor, council and senate among the overseers of the college.

Finally, in a section original with him, Adams provided for the "Encouragement of Literature, etc."[39] Remembering the museums and philosophical societies of Europe, which he felt sure could be equally successful in Boston, Adams hoped to introduce the same kind of thing in his own state. It had long been one of his themes that education and virtue were essential to the people of a republic; consequently, he thought it natural to provide a section on literature and learning in his constitution.

Because "wisdom and knowledge, as well as virtue, diffused generally among the body of the people" were "necessary for the preservation of their rights and liberties, and as these depend on spreading the opportunities and advantages of education in the various parts of the country and among the different orders of the people," it was the duty of the legislators and magistrates "to cherish the interests of literature and sciences, and all seminaries of them, especially the university at Cambridge, public schools and grammar schools in the towns. . . ." It was their duty to promote private societies and public institutions, agriculture, arts, sciences, commerce, trade, manufacture, "and a natural history of the country," and "to countenance and inculcate the principles of humanity and general benevolence, public and private charity, industry and frugality, honesty and punctuality in their dealings, sincerity, good humor, and all social affections and generous sentiments among the people."

In this section on encouragement of literature Adams displayed once again his distinctive emphasis on the classical concept of virtue—a term that embraced wisdom and goodness, charity, thrift, integrity, even a sense of humor—indeed, all those characteristics that humanize man.

Finally, Adams provided, as some state constitution-makers did not, that the constitution might be revised.

He hoped desperately that his constitution would be ratified. "I am persuaded we never shall have any stability, dignity, decision, or liberty without it," he wrote Elbridge Gerry.[40] Foreshadowing Madison's essay on factions in Number Ten of the *The Federalist,* Adams believed that "we have so many men of wealth, of ambitious spirits, of intrigue, of luxury and corruption, that incessant factions will disturb our peace without it, and, indeed, there is too much reason to fear, with it. The executive, which ought to be the reservoir of wisdom, as the legislative is of liberty, without this weapon of defense [a negative upon the laws], will run down like a hare before the hunters."

After the constitution had been adopted, Adams told Edmund Jenings with relief that he took "a vast satisfaction" in its passage. "If the people are as wise and honest in the choice of their rulers as they have been in framing a government, they will be happy, and I shall die content with the prospect for my children, who, if they cannot be well under such a form and such an administration, will not deserve to be at all."[41]

As an old man in his retirement, Adams recalled that he had taken a copy of the proposed Massachusetts Constitution when he returned to France in 1780.[42] Dr. Franklin, as well, had taken a copy of the Pennsylvania Constitution when he had gone to France in 1776. Proclaimed by French intellectuals to be the brainchild of Franklin, the Pennsylvania pact, Adams knew, was even more the work of the radicals Timothy Matlack, James Cannon, Thomas Young, and Thomas Paine. Yet the *philosophes* Turgot, Condorcet, the Duc de la Rochefoucauld and others became enamored of it, a fact that contributed to the downfall, Adams believed, of the latter two men.

With speculation on the nature of government much in style, the *philosophes* enjoyed the game of contrasting the two constitutions, always to the discredit of the Massachusetts plan. Several years later Adams would defend his constitution; it would cost him three volumes.

CHAPTER XII

THE *DEFENCE*

D R. Richard Price, ever an enthusiast of political theory, published in 1784 a small pamphlet entitled *Observations on the Importance of the American Revolution and the Means of Making It a Benefit to the World*. As an appendix he included a letter that Turgot had written him back in 1778, in which the Frenchman objected to the constitutions of the American states as being too imitative, so he thought, of the British system in their separation of powers, asserting that greater centralization of power was the only answer for these states. By the time Dr. Price published the Turgot letter, the Massachusetts Constitution, of course, was already in effect.

Adams probably would have let the matter drop had not news been pouring in from his home state regarding affairs in western Massachusetts that led to Shay's Rebellion in the fall of 1786. Western farmers, in financial straits after the war, hoped to persuade the legislature to relieve them of some of their obligations as debtors. Though little blood was shed, there were skirmishes all through the fall. A newly elected legislature answered some of these popular demands; furthermore, an upturn of prosperity in 1787 put a quick end to the little uprising. Nonetheless, all of America had received news of the rebellion with genuine alarm. An infant government could not afford these disruptions of order. Abigail expressed the same horror as most other Americans when she wrote Jefferson: "Ignorant, restless desperadoes, without conscience or principles, have led a deluded multitude to follow their standard, under pretense of grievances which have no existence but in their imaginations. Some of them were crying out for a paper currency, some for an equal distribution of property, some were for annihilating all debts, others complaining that the Senate was a useless branch of government, that the Court of Common Pleas was unnecessary, and that the sitting of the General Court in Boston was a grievance." There was no question that "these mobbish insurgents are for sapping the foundation and destroying the whole fabric at once."[1]

When the delegates to the Federal Convention gathered in Philadelphia in the summer of 1787, they recalled the Shays episode as a dangerous popular threat to republican government. Most of them, like the Adamses, detested one of the results of that uprising: a call for simple democratic government in a unicameral assembly.

Hence, it was the Shays' Rebellion, with its attendant pressure for unicameral government, that convinced Adams of the urgent necessity to answer these attacks on his republican constitution. The Turgot letter offered him a vehicle for argument.

Immediately after his return from the Netherlands in September, 1786, Adams began reading for his *Defence*. Pushed for time, hurrying to remind the people of his state that they had adopted the best form of government and ought to preserve it, he swallowed whole everything he read. Then he spewed it upon paper, interspersed with his own comments. Time seemed more important than careful documentation. Moreover, men of his era paid little attention to footnotes and scholarly trappings. And so, he paraphrased or quoted verbatim from an overwhelming number of authors, sometimes acknowledging his source, sometimes not. By today's standards it would be a careless job, but the hasty, faulty documentation, the jerky, slung-together text, lacking in continuity, really did not matter. Despite the defects of the *Defence*, its rough-hewn grandeur displayed Adams' mind in full maturity. Here was the culmination of years of thought and study, the only full-scale discussion of his political structure that Adams had ever attempted. Faults and all, the *Defence* insured him a place in American thought as a political theorist of considerable magnitude.

The first volume of the *Defence* appeared in January, 1787, and although it was not designed to do so, it influenced the delegates to the Constitutional Convention who gathered in Philadelphia that summer. Adams turned out another volume in September and a third in 1788. As he himself explained, he did not have in mind the Federal Constitution but only the state constitutions when he wrote the *Defence*.[2]

Adams apologized for "so hasty a production." Yet "the disturbances in New England" had forced him to write immediately, "in order to do any good." He was "no great scholar," he told his brother-in-law Cranch, "and have had but a few months' time; but I hope the men of genius and science in America will pursue the subject to more advantage." Admittedly, "by the hurry and precipitation with which this work was undertaken, conducted and completed," he had "been obliged to be too inattentive both to method and the ornaments of style for the present taste of our countrymen. . . ." Nonetheless, he did not apologize for the thoughts contained within his work.

"I am myself as clearly satisfied of the infallible truth of the doctrines there contained as I am of any demonstration in Euclid," he made plain, "and if our countrymen are bent upon any wild schemes inconsistent with the substance of it, the sooner they remove me out of their sight the better; for I can be of no service to them in promoting their views."[3]

The Turgot letter to which Adams replied called for a simple democracy with sovereignty in a vague center, "that of the nation," an absolute democracy uniting legislative, executive and judicial powers in one assembly. Since republics were "formed upon the equality of all the citizens," an equilibrium of powers of government was irrelevant, serving only as a "source of divisions." Moreover, Turgot declared he was tired of hearing "that threadbare sentiment of the greatest class of even the most republican writers, that *liberty consists in being subject only to laws,* as if a man oppressed by an unjust law was free."[4]

In the three volumes of the *Defence,* Adams once again built a case for mixed government embodying "representations, instead of collections, of the people; a total separation of the executive from the legislative power, and of the judicial from both; and a balance in the legislature, by three independent, equal branches. . . ." These, after all, were ". . . perhaps the only three discoveries in the constitution of a free government since the institution of Lycurgus."[5] But in the *Defence* Adams, more than ever before, explained *why* a balanced form is the best government. Several recurring and clearly identifiable themes permeated his *Defence.* His appeal to law and history; his declaration of the imperfectibility of man and the necessity to form government accordingly; his insistence upon equilibrium between the three orders of the legislative—monarchic, aristocratic and democratic, or executive, upper house and lower house; his attention to the relation between power and property; his horror of uncontrolled factions as the antithesis of law and the root of despotism; his emphasis upon written constitutions that insure continuance of law through all transfers of power; his zeal for rotation of office to protect against an hereditary senate and executive—all these themes ran powerfully through the *Defence,* appearing again and again.

Adams in the *Defence* confronted squarely the fundamental political problem of how to combine freedom and order, freedom and law. He answered that freedom and law are completely compatible; in fact, he thought, freedom exists only *in* law. The republican writers, Adams objected, never made the foolish statement that Turgot attributed to them, namely, that liberty consists in being subject only to laws. Rather, there would be liberty only where there were *equal* laws, made by common consent for the general interest. Certainly there could be no liberty where there were no fixed, known laws. Liberty under law—that is, equal laws, true law in harmony with right reason—was the goal of political society. Proper government must "form an equilibrium between the one, the few, and the many, *for the purpose of enacting and executing*

equal laws, by common consent, for the general interest. . . ."[6]
Liberty and law were inseparable, for, as Adams would say in later
years, liberty lay in doing as you would be done by,[7] a concept
based on justice and quite apart from license. The vehicle for accomplishing this goal of liberty under law, this enactment, execution and judgment of equal laws by common consent for the general
interest was, of course, establishment of a balance between the
three orders of society, monarchic, aristocratic, democratic. Rule
of equal laws was the goal, balance of power the means. Consequently, the principle of free republican government could only
consist "in a strict execution of the laws and an equilibrium of
estates or orders."[8] In order to secure liberty under law it was
crucial to maintain equilibrium of power. Balance or despotism—
there was no alternative. So unflinchingly convinced of this fact was
Adams that he hewed to it more doggedly as the years went by,
although pained by accusations of those who questioned his motives. In his own day some people decried Adams as a monarchist;
in modern times they have sometimes labeled him a materialist or
a utilitarian. But he was none of these—not materialist or
utilitarian, not monarchist or democrat ever—but a republican always.

"The great question before us is," Adams stated in the *Defence*,
"what combination of powers in society, or what form of government, will compel the formation, impartial execution, and faithful
interpretation of good and equal laws, so that the citizens may
constantly enjoy the benefit of them, and may be sure of their
continuance. The controversy between M. Turgot and me is
whether a single assembly of representatives be this form. He main-
tains the affirmative. I am for the negative."[9]

From his Grosvenor Square study Adams poured forth a crushing weight of sources to prove his point—Swift, Price, Machiavelli,
Sidney, Montesquieu, Harrington, Polybius, Plato, Aristotle, Cicero, Locke, Milton, Hume, and strings of others. He delved back
into the histories of tiny states—the Swiss cantons, San Marino—
and large ones, ancient and modern. He spent the entire second
volume digging into the Italian Renaissance republics. The third

volume, a fascinating piece with an original twist, he devoted to a critical analysis of pamphleteer Marchamont Nedham's *The Excellencie of a Free State*, a work published in the seventeenth century but reprinted in 1767 by Thomas Hollis and given to Adams some twenty years later by Thomas Brand-Hollis.

Adams was in too much of a hurry to finish the *Defence* and little inclined by temperament to present his republican thought in a thoroughly systematic structure. However, so often did he state his themes in the *Defence* that it is possible to formulate from these a sketch of his theoretical system.

In the first place, he began with a concept of the law of nature, a divine scheme of objective moral truth. Classicist and Puritan, he ever referred to a moral essence in human nature, a justice, a conscience by which men could apprehend right and wrong. In the mainstream of classical and Christian thought on the subject of moral law, he never attempted, as the *philosophes* did, to subject this implicit moral sense in man to the laws of another sphere, that of physical nature. He never tried, in other words, to make ethical principles discoverable by the mathematics of discursive reasoning. That sort of method would be to judge man by tools that belonged to the mechanical sphere. Pure reason could never get anywhere in the study of human nature, a nature not only reasoning but impassioned. History, however, was a tool peculiarly adapted to the study of human nature; it was the one Adams used.

Contrary to the eighteenth-century Frenchmen, Adams remained in the ancient tradition, specifying that man intuitively and immediately apprehends right and wrong. Right reason his mentor Coke had called it. Self-evident truth his friend Jefferson had said. The law written in men's hearts, said Paul in the Epistle to the Romans.

Adams in the *Defence* did not often speak formally of the moral law. Most of the time he implied rather than explicitly expressed such a law; he took it as a precondition for his discussion. He did write, however, "All nations, from the beginning, have been agitated by the same passions. The principles developed here will go a great way in explaining every phenomenon that occurs in the history of government. The vegetable and animal kingdoms, and those heavenly bodies whose existence and movements we are as yet only permitted faintly to perceive, do appear to be governed by laws more uniform or certain than those which regulate the moral and political world."[10] If he did not always express exactly a moral law, he discoursed many times on the subject of that law, human nature. Keenly aware of the ethical and religious drama of every moment, he was always captivated by the nature of man. Unfailingly fascinated by the immutable eternal principles that govern human action, he knew that the "first inquiry" in his study of government "should be what kind of beings men are."[11]

Because he so firmly believed in a moral law for human nature, because the study of justice occupied his whole life, he felt the exceeding importance of virtue. Virtue was right action, right reason in response to moral law. Virtue in political life meant that "men should endeavor at a *balance* of affections and appetites under the monarchy of reason and conscience within, as well as at a balance of power without."[12] Hence, political virtue required not only balance of powers in the structure of government, but also each man's discipline of his own passions and adherence to the precepts of justice. Adams believed that a corrupt people could not long remain free. Freedom was not license. An immoral man could not be free but was instead a slave to unreasoning passion. Only the man who disciplined himself to act according to the highest dictates of the law of human nature could be free and happy—all because he acted in the most truly human way. Tough, uncompromising moralist that he was, Adams demanded strict balance, or discipline; excellence; supreme integrity, as characteristics of republican men. But he also had the common sense to realize that all men would not act according to those standards. For that reason, good government must foster virtue in its citizens. In fact, good government probably caused virtue to a certain extent. "The best republics," said Adams, "will be virtuous and have been so; but we may hazard a conjecture that the virtues have been the effect of the well-ordered constitution rather than the cause."[13]

In regard to human nature Adams believed one must take it as it is. He was quite willing to fit government to real man, not a remodeled version. Though no one appreciated more than Adams the heights often attained by human reason, no one more than he knew that reason could never attain perfection. Further, no one more than he, a man of enormous passion, felt the dangers should unshackled power be given to passionate, unreasonable human nature. If reason made men godlike then passion made them animals. Because Adams accepted the two aspects of man, he held a realistic but not vicious view of humanity. He admired the view of life expressed in Sterne's *Tristram Shandy* more than in Mandeville's *Fable of the Bees*, Butler's outlook more than Hobbes'.

"It is weakness rather than wickedness which renders men unfit to be trusted with unlimited power," he thought. "The passions are all unlimited; nature has left them so; if they could be bounded, they would be extinct; and there is no doubt they are of indispensable importance in the present system. They certainly increase, too, by exercise, like the body." Every ambition grows with indulgence, particularly those most subtle of passions, the love of gold and the love of praise.

It is imperative that men try to balance their passions and appetites with reason and conscience. Fortunately, "they were intended by nature to live together in society and in this way to restrain one another, and in general they are a very good kind of creatures; but they know each other's imbecility so well that they ought never to lead one another into temptation." A passion continually indulged feeds upon itself, eventually warping the owner's inherent capacity to judge right from wrong. Men entrusted with unlimited power thrive upon their passions. "The passion that is long indulged and continually gratified becomes mad," Adams thought; "it is a species of delirium; it should not be called guilt, but insanity. But who would trust his life, liberty, and property to a madman or an assembly of them? It would be safer to confide in knaves. Five hundred or five thousand together, in an assembly, are not less liable to this extravagance than one. The nation that commits its affairs to a single assembly will assuredly find that its passions and desires augment as fast as those of a king. And, therefore, a constitution with a single assembly must be essentially defective."[14]

Basically, it was this view of man governed by both reason and appetite, of man subject to moral law, that separated Adams from the *philosophes*. Turgot, Condorcet, Rousseau, Diderot, D'Alembert, Voltaire removed man from the sphere of moral law. True, they did think him subject to law, but instead of traditional moral law, they now believed they could apply to him, as Descartes had done, the mathematical rules of physical nature. Several implications led from the two opposing suppositions about life. On the one hand, from Adams' view came naturally the assumption that human nature throughout history remains the same; men are not perfectible, and every generation meets the same old human problems—simply because the essence of human nature is the same as at the beginning.

"All nations, from the beginning," Adams said, "have been agitated by the same passions. . . . Nations move by unalterable rules. . . ." It is not to be inferred from this point that men never make improvements. They do improve their institutions. ". . . education, discipline, and laws," Adams believed, "make the greatest difference in their accomplishments, happiness, and perfection."[15] Indeed, the accoutrements of civilization—government, education, literature, and so on—can be distinctly improved. They make life bearable. They ameliorate the bestial in man, emphasize his definite metaphysical, religious and ethical inclinations. Even so, the essential nature of man can never really improve. Although each individual man can improve himself in his own lifetime, or at least make enough right decisions to make himself a force for good rather than evil, his children are all born with the same human faculties of reason, the same human tendency to succumb to passion. When it comes to the ultimate question, it is an individual rather than a group fight, and although a man may discipline his passions through education, he can never get rid of them. The institutions of society serve as instruments to check what cannot be changed. Through the study of history, Adams' favorite tool, one may discover two things—first, more about the essential nature of man and, second, what kinds of institutions are most in keeping with that nature. Adams was most interested to learn what ordering of the powers of government could best preserve liberty under law. He looked to history to find out.

On the other hand, from the *philosophes'* rejection of moral law sprang their theory of the perfectibility of man. Applying instead the laws of physical nature to man, it is possible to deduce a whole set of mathematical principles regarding the thought and behavior of man, the machine. It is not too hard, then, to use these principles to control and perfect human nature. For instance, if, according to Locke's psychology, the mind is a *tabula rasa* at birth, a blank tablet that absorbs knowledge only through sense impressions, then it remains only to make sure that the right objects for impressions are put before the tablet. Though Locke himself did not go so far, the logical outcome of his psychology is that men are wholly conditioned by their environment, education and experience. There is little place for free will. Some of Locke's followers, such as Condillac, did go so far as to say that man is a mechanism, operating entirely through the laws of cause and effect. David Hartley believed man consisted of vibrating particles. Helvétius thought man lived according to a pleasure-pain principle. Later *philosophes* began to combine this notion of mechanical man with perfectible man. If man is shown to be conditioned, and if he is thought to be innately good, then it follows that he becomes bad only through his environmental influences. Rousseau exemplified such a view in his novel *Émile*, a salute to the man of nature undefiled by society; Diderot carried out the same theme in a dialogue between a European and a man of Tahiti. The doctrine of unbounded progress, as expounded by Condorcet, flowed directly from these theories of man's goodness and his indestructible reason. Education is all that is needed to create perfection. Moreover, there must be a rejection of history. What is most modern is most perfect, so there is little call to look at what is past. The *philosophes* were profoundly antihistorical. Institutions formed in the past were to be detested as hateful barriers to progress; society was too cluttered with these cobwebs of tradition. Furthermore, since all knowledge of man could be gathered from scientific data, there was no point to the study of history.

One particularly explosive issue evolved from the theories of the *philosophes*. Although the *philosophes* retained the doctrine of natural rights, they divorced it from moral law. Hence, these rights lost their spiritual base; they became liberty without law—in other words, license. Severed from law these rights became subject to irresponsible claims; they were expanded from the traditional trio of life, liberty, and property to include a fourth—equality. Adams had a great deal to say on this subject of equality.

For him, as for so many theorists before him, there were three rights immutable under moral law—life, liberty and property. Long rooted in English and colonial law, these rights carried the authority of constitutional tradition. All other historic rights extended from these primary three. But during the latter part of the eighteenth century, property as a basic right began to be called into question. Adams, ever convinced that the right to acquire property is the very tool by which men secure their life and liberty, declared his opposition to this new trend of thought. "Property," he said, "is surely a right of mankind as really as liberty. . . . The moment the idea is admitted into society, that property is not as sacred as the laws of God and that there is not a force of law and public justice to protect it, anarchy and tyranny commence. If THOU SHALT NOT COVET, and THOU SHALT NOT STEAL, were not commandments of Heaven, they must be made inviolable precepts in every society, before it can be civilized or made free."[16] Adams perceived sharply the intimate relation between liberty and property. He believed that without the right to acquire property, life and liberty are totally without protection and are mere abstract phrases. He believed that the right to property without liberty to acquire it is a term equally empty. Indeed, when defining a republic, Adams referred to Cicero's concept of a *Respublica*, meaning wealth, riches or property of the people. The very name republic implied, Adams agreed, "that the property of the people should be represented in the legislature and decide the rule of justice."[17] According to this classical notion of a republic, the "property of the people predominated and governed. . . . It signified a government in which the property of the public, or people, and of every one of them, was secured and protected by law." Adams realized that "this idea, indeed, implies liberty; because property cannot be secure unless the man be at liberty to acquire, use, or part with it, at his discretion, and unless he have his personal liberty of life and limb, motion and rest, for that purpose. It implies, moreover, that the property and liberty of all men, not merely of a majority, should be safe; for the people, or public, comprehends more than a majority; it comprehends all and every individual; and the property of every citizen is a part of the public property, as each citizen is a part of the public, people, or community [he meant here property of each citizen individually and not commonly held]. The property, therefore, of every man has a share in government and is more powerful than any citizen, or party of citizens; it is governed only by the law."[18] The right to acquire property means a concrete way to secure liberty; at the same time, liberty is necessary to attain and dispose of property. In a republic, property and, consequently, liberty are subject only to law.

Adams and his generation have been criticized many times for limiting franchise and office-holding to those who possessed a nominal amount of property. But they believed there was adequate reason for this provision. The husbandman, merchant or artificer who held some small property could "be supposed to have a judgment and will of his own, instead of depending for his daily bread on some patron or master. . . ." Hence, a man with a little property was independent, a freeman, "a sufficient judge of the qualifications of a person to represent him in the legislature." These men of little property, represented in the lower house of the legislature, formed an essential branch of republican government without which free government would have been impossible. Frequent elections of this house of commons held the key to assuring these men their proper weight in the legislature. And quite obviously, "The moral equality that nature has unalterably established among men gives these an undoubted right to have every road opened to them for advancement in life and in power that is open to any others."[19]

According to Adams, then, life, liberty, property are natural rights, but equality is not—men are morally equal, of course, but not equal in merit, wealth, talent, and so on. Turgot had said in his letter to Dr. Price that since republics were founded on the equality of all citizens, then orders and equilibriums were unnecessary, only causing disputes.

"But what are we to understand here by equality?" Adams demanded. "Are the citizens to be all of the same age, sex, size, strength, stature, activity, courage, hardiness, industry, patience, ingenuity, wealth, knowledge, fame, wit, temperance, constancy, and wisdom? Was there, or will there ever be, a nation whose individuals were all equal in natural and acquired qualities, in virtues, talents, and riches? The answer of all mankind must be in the negative. It must then be acknowledged that in every state, in the Massachusetts, for example, there are inequalities which God and nature have planted there, and which no human legislator ever can eradicate."

With his obsession for law equally applied to every citizen, Adams held no truck with interest groups; he advocated "a moral and political equality of rights and duties among all the individuals. . . ." Moreover, he always remained inviolably opposed to all "artificial inequalities of condition"—hereditary titles, magistracies, legal distinctions. He heartily disapproved of "established marks, as stars, garters, crosses, or ribbons," grumbling and glowering at the Society of the Cincinnati, the group of Continental officers who patterned their organization after the Roman soldier who retired to private life. Nevertheless, without a doubt, there were present in the members of society natural inequalities "of great moment in the consideration of a legislator, because they have a natural and inevitable influence in society."[20]

Continually interested in fitting his form of government to human nature, Adams listed some of these natural inequalities. In addition to such distinctions as talent, merit, wisdom, beauty, knowledge and so on, there are the two highly important ones of wealth and birth. In any society there are always people who have a large amount of wealth, either by dint of inheritance or hard work, others who have a medium amount and some who have little or none. Those with property naturally have others working for them in trades and manufactures, dependent upon them for their living. Others, such as professional men, while not dependent upon these men of property for a living, might, however, be attached to them through acquaintance, conversation and so forth.[21] Now, of course, the propertied must not be deprived of their wealth, for ". . . it must be remembered, that the rich are *people* as well as the poor; that they have rights as well as others; that they have as clear and as *sacred* a right to their large property as others have to theirs which is smaller; that oppression to them is as possible and as wicked as to others; that stealing, robbing, cheating are the same crimes and sins, whether committed against them or others."[22]

Secondly, there is inequality of birth. Recognizing that America had no inherited titles, Adams nevertheless warned, "Let no man be surprised that this species of inequality is introduced here." It is inevitable that some people come from families of greater wealth, intelligence, or admiration in the community than others. "Will any man pretend," Adams inquired, "that the names of Andros and that of Winthrop are heard with the same sensations in any village of New England? Is not gratitude the sentiment that attends the latter and disgust the feeling excited by the former?" Adams knew that one "cannot presume that a man is good or bad, merely because his father was one or the other"; yet, it is probable that the child of a substantial family will profit by better education and example. Emulation, Adams believed, is a powerful force to shape character. Thus, birth is an inequality to be recognized, although of less influence than wealth.

Adams pondered all his life over this factor of inequality. Quite obviously it existed, a plain fact that could not be done away with and so had to be accepted. To correspond to the reality of human nature, then, government must embrace this fact.

"These sources of inequality," Adams wrote soberly, "which are common to every people and can never be altered by any because they are founded in the constitution of nature, this natural aristocracy among mankind, has been dilated on because it is a fact essential to be considered in the institution of government. It [natural aristocracy] forms a body of men which contains the greatest collection of virtues and abilities in a free government, is the brightest ornament and glory of the nation, and may always be made the greatest blessing of society, if it be judiciously managed in the constitution. But if this be not done, it is always the most dangerous; nay, it may be added, it never fails to be the destruction of the commonwealth."[23]

Furthermore, in addition to their natural inequalities of talent, birth and wealth, men contain a passion that resists equality. They simply do not want to be like all the others, but yearn for distinction. "Every man hates to have a superior," Adams believed, "but no man is willing to have an equal; every man desires to be superior to all others." A man is not satisfied for others to be on the same level; rather, he wishes for others to be even below him. "When every man is brought down to his level, he wishes them depressed below him; and no man will ever acknowledge himself to be upon a level or equality with others, till they are brought down lower than him."[24]

"We may look as wise," Adams realized, "and moralize as gravely as we will; we may call this desire of distinction childish and silly; but we cannot alter the nature of men; human nature is thus childish and silly; and its Author has made it so, undoubtedly for wise purposes; and it is setting ourselves up to be wiser than nature and more philosophical than Providence to censure it."[25] In his discussions of human nature, Adams often showed himself to be an astute psychologist. Man's yearning to be singled out, to rise to his full capabilities and be recognized for them, to gain love and admiration, bore considerable affiliation with his spiritual inclinations. It was human to hope that a small corner of the world was made a little different because one had lived there. A human soul felt violently repelled at the thought of sinking into oblivion amidst a mass. It was peculiarly like Adams that he should dwell upon man's desire for distinction; he had only to look into his own character to find a powerful, unquenchable passion to excel, to be made much of. Put to good use such a desire could produce the loftiest achievements; allowed to run undisciplined and unchecked it inevitably became a thirst for power.

Adams concerned himself so closely with inequality in men because he believed, with Harrington, that property, the most crucial of those inequalities, forms the base of power. Both a principle of authority and a principle of power compose government—the first includes virtues of the mind and heart, wisdom, prudence, courage, temperance, justice and so forth; the second is made up of the goods of fortune, such as riches, birth, reputation, education. Of all these characteristics none equals property in importance.

"Riches will hold the first place," Adams emphasized, "in civilized societies, at least, among the principles of power and will often prevail, not only over all the principles of authority, but over all the advantages of birth, knowledge, and fame."[26] Empire, that is, power, follows the balance of property, Harrington had preached, and Adams agreed. Whoever owns most of the property of the country likewise holds the reins of power. Sovereignty lies in the hands of the one, few, or many, according to which of the three orders of society owns the balance of property.

It is an unfailing principle of fundamental law, Adams thought, that these three orders are natural to society. "All independent bodies of men seem naturally to divide the three powers of the one, the few, and the many. A free people met together, as soon as they fall into any acts of civil society, do of themselves divide into three ranks."[27]

First of all, one man is sure to rise above all the others, whether because of great fame, wisdom, riches, valor, or a variety of other reasons. Next there will be a small group somewhat like this first man, although not quite so great. Finally, in the last group will be all the rest of the people. Unquestionably rivalries arise within and between these groups. The few wrestle among themselves to gain favor with the chief or even to surpass him; they likewise contend with each other to curry favor of the many attached to them. At the same time, the many struggle to become part of the few. Meanwhile, the chief fights to maintain his first place.

Of these groups the one that owns the most property will have the most power. Because the many owned the balance of property in the United States, they were sovereign.

"In America," Adams pointed out, "the right of sovereignty resides indisputably in the body of the people, and they have the whole property of land. There are no nobles or patricians."[28] In each state commoners held nineteen-twentieths of the property, meaning that "the sovereignty, then, in fact, as well as morality, must reside in the whole body of the people."[29] Nonetheless, it did not follow that simply because many individuals rather than one or a few happened to own most of the land in America, Americans would not, like all men everywhere, tend to form three orders of society. Though Americans possessed moral and political equality, though they were a democratic republic in which many people owned property, they were still separated by the natural distinctions that, when men gathered together in any group, caused them to fall naturally into three types. First, there would always be one great man who would rise eventually to the surface. A little way below would be a small group of men of talent, birth or wealth. Those remaining would fall into a large group of men very nearly on a par in understanding and fortune. For that reason, it was just as essential in a democratic republic as in any other government to maintain a careful balance among these three orders.

That balance had indeed been established in most of the American constitutions. "Our people are undoubtedly sovereign," Adams wrote proudly; "all the landed and other property is in the hands of the citizens; not only their representatives, but their senators and governors, are annually chosen; there are no hereditary titles, honors, offices, or distinctions; the legislative, executive, and judicial powers are carefully separated from each other; the powers of the one, the few, and the many are nicely balanced in the legislatures; trials by jury are preserved in all their glory, and there is no standing army; the *habeas corpus* is in full force; the press is the most free in the world. Where all these circumstances take place, it is unnecessary to add that the laws alone can govern."[30]

To relinquish this government by laws, to create a single assembly of representatives without a governor and without a senate, as Turgot suggested, would be to admit the country to the worst tyranny. Because all simple governments, that is, governments without checks on power, become corrupt, so would this one degenerate. Just what would occur?

In a nutshell, factions would run rampant. Due to the distinctions among men and the three orders of society, factions were to be expected, but the problem lay in making them equally obedient to law: "All nations, under all governments, must have parties; the great secret is to control them."[31] Since wealth is the most significant factor of distinction, it would most often be the source of faction. "In every society where property exists," Adams asserted, "there will ever be a struggle between rich and poor. Mixed in one assembly, equal laws can never be expected. They will either be made by numbers, to plunder the few who are rich, or by influence, to fleece the many who are poor. Both rich and poor, then, must be made independent, that equal justice may be done and equal liberty enjoyed by all."[32]

It is certainly true, Adams felt, that "the people are the best keepers of their own liberties," the only keepers who can be trusted. Thus, "the people's fair, full, and honest consent to every law, by their representatives, must be made an essential part of the constitution. . . ." Yet the people themselves are no keepers of their liberties when they hold either collectively or by representation the executive, judicial and all three branches of the legislative. History has taught the inviolable principle that in such cases the people "instantly give away their liberties into the hand of grandees, or kings, idols of their own creation."[33] Feeding upon the insatiable passion of uncontrolled power, corrupted by the headiness of license without law, the people dissolve into factions that snatch the wealth from the propertied by imposing unequal laws upon them. These men, disseized of their wealth, will in turn rob those who robbed them. In such a vicious circle, there will shortly be no rule but that of the majority, now become a lawless band, totally unprincipled, in which "it becomes more profitable and reputable, too, except with a very few, to be a party man than a public-spirited one."[34]

Because the majority operate in their own interest, they form a faction. "It may sound oddly," Adams acknowledged, "to say that the majority is a faction; but it is, nevertheless, literally just. If the majority are partial in their own favor, if they refuse to deny a perfect equality to every member of the minority, they are a faction; and as a popular assembly, collective or representative, cannot act or will but by a vote, the first step they take, if they are not unanimous, occasions a division into majority and minority, that is, into two parties, and the moment the former is unjust it is a faction."[35] Moreover, if the majority is a faction and the majority is the government, then "the government itself is a faction and an absolute power in a party, which, being without fear and restraint, is as giddy" in a simple democracy as it is in any other simple form.[36]

It is wrong "to flatter the democratical portion of society" into believing that although kings and grandees might use uncontrolled power for their own benefit, the people themselves would not. After all, "there is no reason to believe the one much honester or wiser than the other; they are all of the same clay; their minds and bodies are alike." And "as to usurping others' rights, they are all three equally guilty when unlimited in power. No wise man will trust either with an opportunity; and every judicious legislator will set all three to watch and control each other." History offers lesson after lesson "that the people, when they have been unchecked, have been as unjust, tyrannical, brutal, barbarous, and cruel, as any king or senate possessed of uncontrollable power. The majority has eternally, and without one exception, usurped over the rights of the minority."[37]

Once in the majority in a single assembly, Adams believed the men of small property would begin to usurp the right of property of those with more. Perhaps, he remarked, they would feel restrained at first by habit, shame, principle, fear and so on, but soon they would invent pretexts by which they could seize and divide the property among themselves or at least share it equally with the present possessors. "Debts would be abolished first, taxes laid heavy on the rich and not at all on the others, and at last a downright equal division of everything be demanded and voted." This would be morally wrong, of course, for it would deprive a man of his intrinsic right to retain the fruits of his industry. But in addition, these attempts to equalize, to redistribute property would not even effect their desired end. Because the more those plunderers gained the more they would want, they would never remain satisfied with the first act of equalization. "The idle, the vicious, the intemperate," Adams emphasized, "would rush into the utmost extravagance of debauchery, sell and spend all their share, and then demand a new division of those who purchased from them. The moment the idea is admitted into society, that property is not as sacred as the laws of God and that there is not a force of law and public justice to protect it, anarchy and tyranny commence."[38] Hence, on both moral and practical grounds such redistribution would be objectionable. And this insidious invasion of property rights would occur just as certainly in a simple democracy as in a simple monarchy or aristocracy. Wherever the people had shared, as in a democracy, in the executive or in more than their one-third of the legislative power, they had always rendered property insecure. Their unbalanced government formed "as real a tyranny as the sovereignty of a hereditary senate, or thirty tyrants, or a single despot."[39] No one's property, large or small, could be secure in such a government, for those who had just stolen another's property would have no guarantee that someone else would not do the same to them. A small mechanic had every moral right to the rewards of his labor; a large merchant or landowner had every right to his —these were precepts of justice. It was to the advantage of both, then, to support a balanced government where the laws applied equally to everyone, where each man could be sure that he could not only retain his present fruits but work for more.

In this uncertain scheme of majority tyranny, where factions jousted daily to become the majority in the next vote, anarchical conditions would provide a perfect vehicle for another manifestation of simple democracy—the rise of "some one overgrown genius, fortune, or reputation. . . ." A single assembly would not operate in this awkward, unwieldy form without becoming "at once a simple monarchy in effect." Taking advantage of the confusion, a single man would soon appear, "a despot who rules the state at his pleasure, while the deluded nation, or rather a deluded majority, thinks itself free; and in every resolve, law, and act of government, you see the interest, fame, and power of that single individual attended to more than the general good." Whether this single genius were elected for a long term or short term or for life would make no difference; the people would cheerfully, willingly vote him in, waxing stronger in their praise of him with each successive election. While the people supposed him to be caring for their interests, he would be supervising his own self-interest, all "with the acclamations and hosannas of the majority of the people."[40] Unwittingly prophesying the outcome of the French Revolution, Adams warned solemnly against the dangers of a man on horseback. If there were no balance in a government where the people had a voice, that government would undergo "everlasting fluctuations, revolutions, and horrors, until a standing army, with a general at its head, commands the peace. . . ."[41]

There was another alternative to majority tyranny in this struggle among the factions of a simple assembly. That possibility was oligarchy, a corruption of aristocracy. If the poor did not plunder the rich, then the rich would rob the poor, ever widening the gulf between the two orders. Even though in America the many held most of the property, in a simple assembly the few who had greater ambition, talent, merit, birth, or wealth might find it dangerously easy to grasp the balance of property and power from the many. Growing more greedy day by day, these oligarchs would unite against their natural enemies, the people and the first magistrate. History had many times shown that oligarchs, "increasing every day in a rage for splendor and magnificence, will annihilate the people, and, attended with their horses, hounds, and vassals, will run down the King as they would hunt a deer, wishing for nothing so much as to be in at the death."[42]

Despite whatever path to corruption that factions took in a simple assembly, one fact stood clear: unbalanced government failed in the necessary task of controlling factions. With no means but despotism to order government, there was neither liberty nor law. Law was what the ruling faction said it was—mere ill-conceived legislation. Consequently, without fixed and permanent protection of the tool which is basic to preserve life—property—there was no liberty either.

What remained to remedy this disordered tyranny? A balance of the three orders of the legislative in separate bodies to force them to check and watch each other. The three orders must be removed from one assembly and put into three bodies. First of all, the people must have a bulwark for their liberties; they will gain that through a representative assembly. The few require the same protection, which they will have in an independent senate. A strong executive vested with an absolute veto will reinforce the other two bodies, an insurance to both that their rights are guaranteed.

With the people reserving to themselves one essential branch of the legislature, in which they keep absolute control of the purse and make inquest of grievances and state crimes, the interests of the many would be safe, provided they have no executive power and provided the aristocracy is separated into another body.[43]

Isolated in their own body, the aristocratical few would, first, be prevented from running roughshod over the many; and, second, would be protected from encroachments by the envious many.

"The only remedy," as Adams saw it, "is to throw the rich and the proud into one group, in a separate assembly, and there tie their hands; if you give them scope with the people at large or their representatives, they will destroy *all equality and liberty, with the consent and acclamations of the people themselves.* They will have much more power, mixed with the representatives, than separated from them. In the first case, if they unite, they will give the law and govern all; if they differ, they will divide the state and go to a decision by force. But placing them alone by themselves, the society avails itself of all their abilities and virtues; they become a solid check to the representatives themselves, as well as to the executive power, and you disarm them entirely of the power to do mischief."[44]

To control rival factions, then, that divide on the basis of the natural inequalities of talent, birth and wealth—to solve this problem a wise people will establish a carefully balanced government through which the rule of law can prevail.

Since Adams was much concerned that the law be constant, perpetual, and known to every citizen, without which, of course, it would be not law but edict or whim, he specified that the constitution ought to be written. A written constitution stood as the final assurance that laws, not men, would rule, that every personal whim, every passion of people or magistrates must bow before the impartial hand of the law: ". . . it is the laws alone that really love the country, the public, the whole better than any part. . . ." That form of government that unites its citizens "in a reverence and obedience to the laws is the only one in which liberty can be secure and all orders, and ranks, and parties compelled to prefer the public good before their own; that is the government for which we plead."[45] Adams felt extraordinarily pleased to be able to close his *Defence* with reference to two such frames of government that had just been devised.

"It is now in our power to bring this work to a conclusion with unexpected dignity," he said. "In the course of the last summer, two authorities have appeared, greater than any that have been before quoted, in which the principles we have attempted to defend have been acknowledged."[46] These were, first, that greatest accomplishment of the Confederation Congress, the Northwest Ordinance of July 13, 1787, a plan for the government of the Northwest Territory, and second, the draft adopted by the Constitutional Convention of 1787.

As usual, Adams expected an unfavorable reaction to his *Defence*. With his typical pessimism regarding the anticipated public reception of his work, he declared to James Warren, "Popularity was never my mistress, nor was I ever, or shall I ever be a popular man. This book will make me unpopular." Nevertheless, he would "deliver the book up to the mercy of a world that will never show me much mercy, as my confession of political faith."[47]

Yet, this cheerless forecast missed its mark. Much to Adams' surprise, Americans greeted the *Defence* with effusive exclamations of praise. Members of the Federal Convention had time to read the first volume before they took up session; many of them did read it and referred extensively to it during debates. For that reason, even though he was not present, Adams made his influence felt in the convention that was to produce the Constitution of the United States.

Dr. Price wrote to say how much he approved of Adams' answer to Turgot's letter. He agreed with Adams' view.[48]

Jefferson had read the book "with infinite satisfaction and improvement." It would "do great good in America," he felt sure. "Its learning and its good sense will, I hope, make it an institute for our politicians, old as well as young."[49] Though he offered one criticism,[50] he agreed with Adams that "the first principle of a good government is certainly a distribution of its powers into executive, judiciary, and legislative and a subdivision of the latter into two or three branches." Adams should now undertake a work on the nature of confederations, he suggested.[51] Immediately Jefferson set to work to have the *Defence* translated into French.

From New York John Jay encouraged Adams: "Your book circulates and does good." It shed much light on a subject "with which we cannot be too intimately acquainted, especially at this period, when the defects of our national government are under consideration. . . ."[52]

Richard Henry Lee read the first volume "with great pleasure. . . ." Adams' "judicious collection" of sources and examples with his "just reflections" had "reached America at a great crisis and will probably have their proper influence in forming the federal government now under consideration. Your labor may, therefore," he offered generously, "have its reward in the thanks of this and future generations." Government in a triple balance, Lee believed, would prevail in the new constitution.[53]

Even before he had published the last two volumes of the *Defence*, Adams had decided to terminate his diplomatic career. He had determined to do that several times before, but this time he would not be put off. Nearly ten years had passed since he had seen his favorite corner of the world; that was long enough to pay any man's debt to public service. He deserved to go home to Braintree. Thus, as early as January, 1787, he wrote to Congress asking for recall from his mission to Great Britain, due to expire in February, 1788, and from his mission to the Netherlands and from his joint mission with Jefferson to the Barbary states. He expected to be able to sail for home early in 1788.

Jefferson, who had developed real attachment to the Adamses as kindred lonely Americans in Europe, learned "with real pain" of his friend's resolution to go home. "Your presence on this side of the Atlantic gave me a confidence that if any difficulties should arise within my department, I should always have one to advise with on whose counsels I could rely. I shall now feel bewidowed." Perhaps Adams might wish to go to Holland to improve the American financial situation there, he suggested hopefully.[54]

"My resolution of quitting Europe," Adams answered firmly, "has been taken upon mature deliberation. . . ." Not only did he choose to return to America, but he felt that it was a matter of necessity, as well. Until Britain should send a minister to America, Congress could not with dignity renew his commission. "As to a residence in Holland," he could never stand the climate; he was sure, too, that "it would be fatal to her on whom depends all the satisfaction that I have in life."

However, he faced with some perturbation the prospect of the circumstances he would meet in the United States. "For a man who has been thirty years rolling like a stone, never three years in the same place," he reflected dejectedly, "it is no very pleasant speculation to cross the seas with a family, in a state of uncertainty what is to be his fate; what reception he shall meet at home; whether he shall set down in private life to his plough; or push into turbulent scenes of sedition and tumult; whether be sent to Congress, or a convention, or God knows what." He often felt "a violent disposition" to "take a vow to retire to my little turnip yard and never again quit it." Yet common sense told him that "it is best to preserve my liberty to do as I please according to circumstances."

Only two things did he regret leaving—first, the access to any books he might desire for research and, second, the interruption of his close correspondence with Jefferson, "which is one of the most agreeable events in my life." These he would leave with genuine sadness, but, as he summed up, "I am not at home in this country."[55]

Waiting for their recall, the Adamses whiled away the time with a new grandson, born April 2, 1787, and christened by Dr. Price as William Steuben Smith. The baby monopolized the household, intriguing his parents and refreshing his grandparents. Abigail later proudly described "Master William" to her sister as "the very image of his mamma at the same age, except that he has a great share of vivacity and sprightliness, the merest little truncheon that you ever saw, very pleasant and good-humored."[56]

However, in May Adams was jolted out of these small pleasures. Receiving notice that America could not meet a heavy interest payment, he was obliged to journey to Amsterdam to negotiate a third loan. He arrived just in time to sign a contract on June 1 for a loan of a million guilders at five percent interest, redeemable in 1798-1802. Distressed by anti-Patriot rioting in the city, he nonetheless set about the grim task of signing 2,000 American obligations before he returned to London.[57]

As summer came on in Grosvenor Square, Abigail mothered Jefferson's lonely, frightened little daughter Polly, en route to meet her father in Paris. Terrified by the recent ocean voyage and the expectation of joining her father and older sister, from whom she had been absent so long that they seemed like strangers, Polly hovered under Abigail's comfortable wing, refusing to leave London until she received an outright command from her father, and declaring she was as unhappy to leave Abigail as she had been to depart from her Aunt Eppes. For her part, Abigail felt sad to give up the little girl, as did John, who in all his life "never saw a more charming child."[58]

In midsummer Adams took his family on an excursion to western England, during which they went ten miles out of their way to take a sentimental look at Weymouth. Returning to London, the Adamses began to think about the more practical aspects of going home. Unquestionably, their spacious accommodations at Auteuil and Grosvenor Square had spoiled them for settling again in their tiny cottage. The fine tastes and elegant possessions they had acquired in Europe had grown much too large for their simple cottage. Consequently, through the medium of Cotton Tufts and Thomas Welsh, Adams arranged to buy for £600 the John Borland house, a place once briefly owned by Royall Tyler but now in the possession of Leonard Vassall Borland, son of John and Anna Vassall Borland.

Both Adams and Jefferson waited expectantly for tidbits of news about the Federal Convention. Jefferson was "sorry they began their deliberations by so abominable a precedent as that of tying up the tongues of their members"; yet he felt that the motives of the delegates were innocent, "that all their other measures will be good and wise." Impressed by the caliber of the men who attended the convention, he proclaimed that they were "really an assembly of demigods."[59]

As soon as Elbridge Gerry sent him a copy of the proposed Constitution, Adams forwarded a copy to Jefferson. On the whole Adams approved of it, commenting that "it seems to be admirably calculated to preserve the union, to increase affection, and to bring us all to the same mode of thinking." But he did not approve of the Senate's participation in the executive power of selection of civil officers. "I think that senates and assemblies should have nothing to do with executive power," he insisted; however, he still hoped that "the Constitution will be adopted and amendments be made at a more convenient opportunity."

"What think you of a declaration of right?" he added, anticipating the most general complaint against the Constitution. "Should not such a thing have preceded the model?"[60]

Jefferson had already read the Constitution, writing to Adams about the same time, "How do you like our new Constitution? I confess there are things in it which stagger all my dispositions to subscribe to what such an assembly has proposed." The House of Representatives, he asserted, would be inadequate to manage either foreign or federal affairs. Moreover, he complained that "their President seems a bad edition of a Polish king. He may be reelected from four years to four years for life. Reason and experience prove to us that a chief magistrate, so continuable, is an officer for life."

The President would become the object, Jefferson thought, of every sort of foreign intrigue. "Once in office, and possessing the military force of the union, without either the aid or check of a council, he would not be easily dethroned, even if the people could be induced to withdraw their votes from him." Jefferson wished "that at the end of the four years they had made him forever ineligible a second time." In fact, he declared, "All the good of this new Constitution might have been couched in three or four new articles to be added to the good, old, and venerable fabric" of the Confederation, "which should have been preserved even as a religious relic."[61]

On the other hand, Adams dreaded the power of the Senate to advise and consent on appointment of civil officers. "You are afraid of the one," he answered Jefferson, "I, of the few. We agree perfectly that the many should have a full, fair and perfect representation. You are apprehensive of monarchy; I, of aristocracy." Fearing the factional power of the Senate as a threat to the House, he would "have given more power to the President and less to the Senate." Ever believing that a strong executive stood as a buffer for the House against an aristocratical Senate, he would have given to the President the entire power of nomination and appointment of officers, "assisted only by a Privy Council of his own creation, but not a vote or voice would I have given to the Senate or any senator, unless he were of the Privy Council. Faction and distraction are the sure and certain consequence of giving to a Senate a vote in the distribution of offices."

Furthermore, Adams did not share Jefferson's apprehension toward unrestricted reelection of the President. "You are apprehensive the President, when once chosen, will be chosen again and again as long as he lives," he said in a statement indicating he had relinquished his former allegiance to the idea of annual elections. "So much the better as it appears to me." Perhaps less intrigue and conniving would center around one figure often elected than many figures elected but once.

"Elections, my dear sir," said Adams, "elections to offices which are great objects of ambition I look at with terror. Experiments of this kind have been so often tried and so universally found productive of horrors that there is great reason to dread them." But despite his objections to the Constitution, he predicted a fairly sanguine future under the Constitution. ". . . and now, as we say at sea," he announced merrily, "huzza for the new world and farewell to the old one."[62]

Meanwhile, grave political dislocations began to rumble throughout Europe—but they were of quite a different variety from what was transpiring in America. A French assembly of notables, a consultative body, had been dissolved early in 1787. The French *parlements*, especially the *parlement* of Paris, refused to register the reforms proposed by Loménie de Brienne, minister of finance. Public opinion urged Louis XVI to recall the Estates General, last summoned in 1614, an action that the King would be forced to take in 1789.

In Prussia the great Frederick, ruler for forty-six years, was dead. Yet his League of the German Princes against Emperor Joseph II continued in force. In the Austrian Netherlands and Hungary, opposition to Joseph's high-handed constitutional reforms ran high.

After several years of conflict with the Patriot Party in the Netherlands, Stadholder Willem in 1787 called in Prussian troops to restore his authority. Adams sadly watched these developments.

"My worthy old friends, the Patriots in Holland, are extremely to be pitied," he wrote Jefferson; "and so are their deluded persecutors. That country, I fear, is to be ruined past all remedy."[63] He observed, "All Europe resounds with projects for reviving states and assemblies, I think: and France is taking the lead. How such assemblies will mix with simple monarchies is the question." The fermentation ought to bring some improvements, he felt. Even so, would not "essential ideas be sometimes forgotten in the anxious study of brilliant phrases? Will the Duke of Orléans make a sterling patriot and a determined son of liberty? Will he rank with posterity among the Brutuses and Catos?"

"Corrections and reformations and improvements are much wanted in all the institutions of Europe, ecclesiastical and civil," he remarked, "but how or when they will be made is not easy to guess. It would be folly, I think, to do no more than try over again experi-

ments that have been already a million times tried. Attempts to
reconcile contradictions will not succeed, and to think of reinstitut-
ing republics as absurdly constituted as were the most which the
world has seen would be to revive confusion and carnage, which
must again end in despotisms." With some relief he added, "I shall
soon be out of the noise of all these speculations in Europe. . . ."[64]

Adams spent the usual frustrating wait for permission from Congress to come home. With so many of its delegates sitting in the
Federal Convention, Congress had shrunk to a pathetic number,
not getting around to action on Adams' request until October. At
last, in December Adams received instructions to return—but without the specific letters of recall that protocol required. Embittered
by this slight on the part of Congress, this deliberate disregard, as
he felt, of his request for formal letters of recall, he decided to write
his own letters, memorials to the Stadholder and States-General.
But, to his humiliation, Secretary Hendrik Fagel wrote that he
could not accept the memorials without letters of recall.[65]
Wounded and angry that the years of monumental work were to be
rewarded by such callous ingratitude on the part of Congress,
Adams wrote to Jay, "There is no alternative now left for me; home
I must go and leave all Europe to conjecture that I have given
offense in Holland; and, in England, that I have misbehaved abroad,
though my conduct has been approved at home. When the public
shall hear that I have gone home without taking leave, there will
be no end of criticism, conjectures, and reflections."

"To a man who has taken the utmost pains to do his duty," he
finished in a mortified tone, "and to fulfill every obligation to the
smallest punctilio, nothing can be more disagreeable than such
disappointments, especially as, in all my letters, I have so expressly
and repeatedly requested regular letters of recall."[66]

But he soon discarded the idea of departing without formal notice, realizing that once more he must make the hateful winter
voyage across the North Sea to Hellevoetsluis in order to take
official leave from The Hague. It was fortunate that he did decide
to make the trip, for he found upon arrival that he had additional
business in Amsterdam. Urgently encouraged by Jefferson, who

met him in Amsterdam for a few days in March, Adams negotiated a fourth and final loan with the Willinks and Van Staphorsts, this time for 1,000,000 guilders at five percent interest, entirely redeemable in fifteen years. Though he undertook the loan without congressional instructions, Congress speedily ratified the transaction. American credit would now be safe during the crucial infancy of the federal government.

When he returned to London, Adams discovered that Abigail in her efficient manner had carted the household off to the Bath Hotel in Piccadilly to make way for the packing job at the legation. The Colonel, Nabby, and little William had already left for Falmouth, planning to sail from there for New York.

At long last, John and Abigail set off on March 30, 1788, from Grosvenor Square. And, like a scene from a novel, John at the very moment of departure received his oft-requested official letters of recall. He could leave now with a light heart. Dispatching one letter to Lord Carmarthen and the other to the Dutch ambassador in London, he stepped into his coach and rode off to Portsmouth.[67]

He and Abigail with their servants, John Briesler and Esther Field, who had married during their stay abroad, boarded the *Lucretia* at Cowes on Sunday, April 20. Bad winds delayed their departure for more than a week, but just before the end of April they set sail from Portland Harbor. A decade had passed, an era in European history had rolled to an end, and John Adams was going home.

CHAPTER XIII

THE VICE-PRESIDENCY

PORTLY little Ambassador Adams and his wife could be sentimental—especially over the applause of their countrymen, and, more particularly, of Bostonian Americans. These accolades they received in measure full enough to satisfy the proudest heart when in June of 1788 the *Lucretia* brought them home. Saluting cannon, an enthusiastic crowd of greeters, a reception from the Secretary of State, a formal welcome at Governor Hancock's mansion, a cascade of church bells all day long—these gestures of appreciation could not but ease the usual Adams complaint that he labored unnoticed for his country.

He went before the General Court the day after his arrival for more congratulations. Already he had been elected a Massachusetts delegate to the First Congress of the United States. But though he accepted, he was never to serve.

As he came back to Braintree in this summer of 1788 he pondered his future course. An urge for still more public life nagged him, but he had resolved to till again the rocky soil in the occupation he loved almost above all others. For the moment it was a complete restorative—the return to the life of a Braintree farmer.

"Peacefield," as the Adamses named their new home—or "Stonyfield," as they sometimes called it—stood as Leonard Vassall had built it in 1731.[1] They soon grew much attached to their clapboard gambrel-roofed house, a gentle, charming example of clean-lined eighteenth-century New England architecture. In the garden at the west side of house Abigail planted rose bushes. John leisurely unpacked his books and enthusiastically resumed farming.

Above all Adams reveled in the reunion with his boys. John Quincy, a man of nearly twenty-one, he had not seen for three years. Charles and Tommy he had not seen for seven and nine years respectively. Charles, eighteen now, and Tom, almost sixteen, were like strangers, reared by their mother and good aunts and uncles, deprived of their father's guidance during their most formative years. For the past four years they had even been without their mother. It must have pained Adams to realize he did not know his two younger sons—he who believed so completely in the instructive example of parents, in the duty of parents to their children. He had bidden farewell years ago to little boys—now here in his household were young men. But if there was any temporary awkwardness it soon faded. The Adamses spent a relaxed, happy summer, learning to be a family again, settling themselves in their new home, making improvements on the farm.

Balmy, puffy-clouded summer days slipped into golden, long-shadowed days and crisp nights of autumn. Adams, sweating in the fields with his hired hands, moving stone fences, ordering new cows bought, piling manure, transacting for new salt marsh acres, proudly inspecting his orchards, felt as happy as he had at any time of his life. Braintree, his farm, his family: this was contentment, all he required in life, except—he dared not admit it even to himself—he gravitated toward politics like a moth to a lantern. As many times in his life as he had vowed to retire he could never force himself to swear off politics for long. Frustrated and angry as practical politics made him, he loved it every bit as much as he did political theory. Fortunately for Abigail, politics long ago had caught fire for her, too; she thrived on it as much as did her husband. Yet more than pure love of politics drew Adams to the public scene. Duty ranked high in his Puritan character, a sense of responsibility that overcame every revulsion at subjecting himself to the inevitable public criticism so painful to his large pride. Some men, like Washington, mellowed with age—they refined their edges, subdued their most troublesome passions. But Adams never toned down. He was proud; he despised and yet dreaded censure as only a man of tremendous pride can fear it. At the same time, Puritanlike, he saw pride as the hateful nemesis of mankind, a demon to be purged by humility. Thus, when pride got the better of him, he became humble, lapsing into pessimism and despondency. Perhaps plunging into the political fires, where condemnation was inevitable, purified him of pride and vanity. Whatever the case, pride, on the one hand, and humility, on the other, had tumbled Adams from one pillar to another for fifty-three years, never allowing him to settle into complacent comfort. To his overwhelming surprise and gratitude, he had been blessed with a wife who knew every cranny of his complicated mind, who not only tolerated but rejoiced to put up with his vanity, his restlessness, his constant struggle to subdue his warring traits that refused to soften with middle age.

His code of honor prohibited him from actively seeking office in the new national government now being formed. Much as he loved politics, he considered it beneath him to behave in the manner of politicians. His public service, he always emphasized, had been in response to duty and not to some shortsighted political gain. Above all, he considered himself an independent man who must be true first of all to himself. Petty factional fights and unstatesmanlike caballing were for glad-handing politicians like Hancock whose every motivation was political advantage. Much as Adams would have to admit to himself that he wanted a high office in the new government, he could not consent to lower himself to campaign for it. Such behavior would be un-republican, un-classical, un-Roman. If the people wanted to entrust him with an office, then they must seek him out; he would accept because it was his duty.

He had, of course, no small estimate of his abilities and of his worthiness to receive high office. The Presidency he did not expect —that would and should go, he thought, to Washington. Yet he believed that he deserved a place not far below that. To Theophilus Parsons, a lawyer of Newburyport, he stressed firmly that he would not accept the post of senator from Massachusetts.

"I have long revolved in an anxious mind," he wrote, "the duties of the man and the citizen; and, without entering into details at present, the result of all my reflections on the place of a senator in the new government is an unchangeable determination to refuse it."[2]

He made plain to Benjamin Rush, who felt sure that Adams would have a place in the new government, that "the choice will be in the breasts of free men, and if it falls upon me, it will most certainly be a free election." To Rush's suggestion that Adams' labors were just beginning, he replied, "Seven and twenty years have I labored in this rugged vineyard and am now arrived at an age when man sighs for repose." His thoughts now were for Nabby on Long Island, for John Quincy in his study of the law, and for Charles and Tom at Harvard, whose interests he had sacrificed to public service.[3]

He delightedly told Thomas Brand-Hollis about his farm, "not large . . . but the farm of a patriot," where there were "two or three spots from whence are to be seen some of the most beautiful prospects in the world." As for politics, he could not speak very optimistically about that. The people had "discarded from their confidence almost all the old, staunch, firm patriots who conducted the Revolution in all the civil departments" and had "called to the helm pilots much more selfish and much less skillful." All in all, though, the elections in the new government were going well. "You may have the curiosity to ask what share your friend is to have," Adams wrote. "I really am at a loss to guess. The probability at present seems to be that I shall have no lot in it." In a jocular tone he concluded, "I am in the habit of *balancing* everything. In one scale is vanity, in the other comfort. Can you doubt which will preponderate? In public life I have found nothing but the former; in private life I have enjoyed much of the latter."[4] Hence, with his determination not to tussle for office, Adams had to sit back and wait.

Meanwhile, heads more intent on political maneuvering got together. Without a doubt Washington would be President. Adams was a possibility for Vice-President, along with Hancock, Governor George Clinton of New York, and John Jay, secretary of foreign affairs from the old government. If the President were from Virginia, then the Vice-President ought to be a New Englander, Hamilton and Madison decided, considering Adams but hesitating over the unfounded rumors that he was unfriendly to Washington. General Benjamin Lincoln of the Massachusetts militia, who had come to support Adams as Vice-President, questioned Washington as to his choice and learned that the Mt. Vernon planter had no objection to Adams. Washington had some thought that he might resign when the government got going; Adams would be a responsible man with whom to leave things. Certainly Washington would never endorse the Antifederal Clinton. Hearing that Adams would probably be the choice for Vice-President, Washington wrote approvingly to Henry Knox, Secretary of War, "He will doubtless make a very good one; and let whoever may occupy the first seat, I shall be entirely satisfied with that arrangement for filling the second office."[5]

Factions had already sprung up; Alexander Hamilton had risen to head the Federalist ranks. Adams, he surmised, was too tough a fellow to be led; consequently, Hamilton would prefer a more flexible Vice-President. His motives unknown to Adams, he sent Knox to Braintree with the intimation that the New Englander was too great a figure himself to serve second to Washington. But Knox returned to New York with the information that Adams, if he were asked, could not be moved from accepting the Vice-Presidency. Hamilton saw no alternative now but to support Adams.

As early as October, 1788, Hamilton had written to Theodore Sedgwick, former delegate to the Continental Congress and presently speaker of the Massachusetts House, that he felt that Adams, rather than Clinton, would have the votes of New York for Vice-President. His "only hesitation" was a "suggestion by a particular gentleman" that Adams was "unfriendly in his sentiments to General Washington." Furthermore, Hamilton feared a cabal of the Adamses and the Lees of Virginia that would embarrass the administration.

"What think you of Lincoln or Knox?" he added in a "flying thought."[6]

But Sedgwick sought to ease Hamilton's fears regarding Adams' reputed hostility to Washington. It was simply that "Mr. Adams was formerly infinitely more democratical than at present," Sedgwick explained, and consequently had opposed placing unlimited power in the hands of the Commander-in-Chief, an action toward which Congress then had seemed inclined.

"Mr. Adams is not among the number of my particular friends," Sedgwick pointed out, "but as a man of unconquerable intrepidity and of incorruptible integrity, as greatly experienced in the interests and character of this country, he possesses my highest esteem. His writings show that he deserves the confidence of those who wish energy in government, for although those writings are tedious and unpleasant in perusal, yet they are evidently the result of deep reflection and as they encounter popular prejudices are an evidence of an erect and independent spirit." Sedgwick tossed aside the notion of Lincoln or Knox; it was too late to push them, he said; Massachusetts had fixed on either Adams or Hancock.[7]

Several weeks later Sedgwick wrote Hamilton again, declaring that if the electors were to be chosen by the legislature, "Mr. Adams will probably combine all the votes of Massachusetts." Emphatically Sedgwick noted that "I am very certain that the suggestion that he is unfriendly to General Washington is entirely unfounded."[8]

Thus assured of Adams' loyalty to Washington, Hamilton promised support of the man from Braintree. "Mr. A.," he wrote Sedgwick, "to a sound understanding has *always* appeared to me to add an ardent love for the public good; and as his further knowledge of the world seems to have corrected those jealousies which he is represented to have once been influenced by, I trust nothing of the kind suggested in my former letter will disturb the harmony of the administration."[9]

To Madison, Hamilton gave his reasons for supporting Adams. First of all, Adams was "a declared partisan of referring to future experience the expediency of amendments" to the Constitution. Although Hamilton did not entirely agree with this view, it was much nearer his own than some other recent doctrines. Second, Adams was "a character of importance in the Eastern states." If he were not Vice-President, then Hamilton could foresee that "one of two worse things" would happen—"either he must be nominated to some important office for which he is less proper, or will become a malcontent and possibly espouse and give additional weight to the opposition to the government."

All the same, Hamilton, the natural intriguer, though he wanted Adams as Vice-President, could not bear to allow him the power of a full vote. Unwilling to permit even a threat to his own position as head of the Federalist party, he sought to siphon off to other candidates some of Adams' votes. Until the Twelfth Amendment was added to the Constitution in 1804, electors simply voted for two men, not indicating which man they wanted for President and which for Vice-President. The man who received the most votes was to be President and the man with the second largest number of votes was to be Vice-President.[10] Thus, Hamilton wrote letters to key men in each state, suggesting that perhaps their electors ought to vote for Washington and then throw away some votes for the second man by casting ballots for someone other than Adams. Hamilton pointed out in his letter to Madison "the possibility of rendering it doubtful who is appointed President." Certainly ". . . it would be disagreeable even to have a man treading close upon the heels of the person we wish as President."[11]

James Wilson, back in his Philadelphia law practice after coaxing the Constitution through the Pennsylvania ratifying convention, received a similar letter from Hamilton. "We all feel of how much moment it is that Washington should be the man," Hamilton stressed, "and I own I cannot think there is material room to doubt that this will be the unanimous sense. But as a failure in this object would be attended with the worst consequences, I cannot help concluding that even possibilities should be guarded against."

Everybody was aware, he said, "of that defect in the Constitution which renders it possible that the man intended for Vice-President may in fact turn up President. Everybody sees that unanimity in Adams as Vice-President and a few votes insidiously withheld from Washington might substitute the former to the latter. And everybody must perceive that there is something to fear from machinations of Antifederal malignity. What in this situation is wise?"

From all accounts Hamilton had every reason to think that Adams would carry the North unanimously. He had heard that New Jersey, Pennsylvania, Delaware and Maryland would probably vote for Adams. The Southerners talked of no alternative, except that South Carolinians favored their own man, John Rutledge, and Virginia seemed to prefer Clinton. At least, Hamilton pointed out, there was "a *chance* of unanimity in Adams." Nothing would cause that unanimity more than for the electors to hear that "the current sets irresistibly towards him." Men were "fond of going with the stream." If personal caprice or hostility moved a mere dozen or so electors to withhold votes from Washington—"What may not happen? Grant there is little danger. If any, ought it to be run?"

Hence, Hamilton concluded to Wilson that it would be "prudent to throw away a few votes, say seven or eight. . . ." He had proposed to his Connecticut friends, he told Wilson, that they throw away two, to Jerseyites that they throw away an equal number, and now he asked Wilson whether it might not be wise for Pennsylvania "to lose three or four." Wilson's advice from the South should guide him, of course—"but for God's sake let not our zeal for a secondary object defeat or endanger a first." Hamilton realized that some men might oppose his plan with the wish "particularly to avoid disgust to a man who would be a formidable head to Antifederalists." These men might believe that "it is much to be desired that Adams may have the plurality of suffrages for Vice-President. . . ." Nonetheless, he himself asked, "If risk is to be run on one side or on the other can we hesitate where it ought to be preferred?"[12]

Meanwhile, Adams suspected no part of this plot, for as late as July, 1789, he would pay Hamilton the compliment of asking him to take Charles as a clerk in his law office—which Hamilton did.[13]

Benjamin Rush wrote to his friend Adams in January, 1789, saying that both his affection and his judgment favored "that form of government which you have proved from so many authorities to be the only one that can preserve political happiness." Pennsylvania's unicameral constitution ranked even below a democracy—

it was a mobocracy, a wheelbarrow, a balloon. Every time that "self-balanced legislature" met, Rush expected to see a group of men "ascending in one of those air vehicles without sails or helm." He then went on to say that his Philadelphia friends had "not been idle in preparing an honorable seat for you in the federal Senate." Friendship, he said in a statement that must have pleased Adams, had much less to do with his own efforts to get the New Englander elected Vice-President "than a sincere desire to place a gentleman in the Vice-President's chair upon whose long-tried integrity, just principles in government, and firm opposition to popular arts and demagogues such a dependence could be placed as shall secure us both from a convention and from alterations falsely and impudently called by some of our state governors *amendments.* "[14]

Elbridge Gerry wrote from New York on March 4 to notify Adams that he had been elected Vice-President. Though Dr. Rush called his election "the capstone of our labors respecting the new government,"[15] for Adams it was a rather joyless victory, only thirty-four out of sixty-nine votes, while Washington's had been unanimous. Those states that had not voted unanimously for Adams had been "apprehensive," Gerry said, "that this was a necessary step to prevent your election to the chair [the Presidency]."[16]

Adams took his half-vote as a personal affront, another rejection of the public service in which he had toiled for so many years. "I have seen the utmost delicacy used towards others, but my feelings have never been regarded," he wrote in an injured tone to John Trumbull of Hartford.[17] Nonetheless, Adams had every approbation of Washington, who wrote Secretary of War Knox that "to hear that the votes have run in favor of Mr. Adams gives me great pleasure."[18] Apprehensive and glum over the crushing burden he had accepted, dubious of his capacity to handle this yet hardest task, Washington gratefully acknowledged a Vice-President who had shown himself to be a sturdy friend of the new Constitution.

After receiving official word of his election on April 12, Adams left the next day for Boston. He departed without Abigail, who still felt worn out after her winter's trip to New York to attend Nabby and a new baby. A troop of light horse accompanied Adams to Boston, where church bells acclaimed him and crowds cheered him along King Street. When Adams arrived with the Roxbury Light Horse at Governor Hancock's mansion, the Governor outdid himself in elaborate welcome. After a splendid feast, Adams proceeded along the Connecticut road, heralded by musket volleys. The people of Hartford and New Haven celebrated his passage; the Westchester Light Horse met him at the New York line to escort him to the temporary capital at New York City and his new residence at Richmond Hill.

Just as soon as the government began to function, factions leaped forth more vigorously than ever, clicking into operation Adams' principle that rivalries were inevitable. Never able to agree on the nature of government, people were prepared to be contentious from the start. Men like George Clinton of New York and Patrick Henry of Virginia, who had fought ratification the whole way, still called loudly for a new constitutional convention. Men like these were radical Antifederalists, while men such as Richard Henry Lee and William Grayson of Virginia were moderately Antifederal. In the House of Representatives alone, factions almost immediately began to line up behind two philosophically influential figures—James Madison of Virginia and Fisher Ames of Massachusetts. Madison, an enigmatic little man of mammoth reasoning, a profound student of political thought, was a match for Adams—being a most thoroughly trained man in classical politics. Probably the most important man in the Federal Convention, Madison had guided the debates with his flawless logic and extensive legal knowledge. After the Convention he had joined Hamilton and Jay to write *The Federalist Papers*, leading the battle for ratification in Virginia, whose ratification in turn prompted New York to ratify. Certainly no one during this crucial period of constitution-making and ratification had been more Federalist in his sympathies than Madison, although he did believe that he must, in accordance with the wishes of many of his state, gain passage of a Bill of Rights. But shortly after institution of the new government, Madison began to move toward a more Antifederalist point of view. After barely winning a House seat from Antifederalist Virginia, he began to side more with the rights of the states against the federal government. Eventually, of course, he and Jefferson would become the most powerful leaders of the Democratic-Republican party.

On the other hand, Fisher Ames, scarcely past thirty, a Dedham man of great likeableness and oratorical talent, asserted leadership of the Federalist faction in the House. He deplored democracy in favor of a rather narrow concept of aristocracy, unfortunately looking a little too closely to the interests of his own section of the country. As the years passed, Ames, always in poor health, gave in to his gloomy, reactionary cast of mind, failing to realize the brilliant promise of his early years in the House. He, along with Hamilton and Adams, became symbols of the Federalist party, but he was as different from the nationalistic, almost monarchical Hamilton as Adams was from either. Of the three, Adams most defied being stuffed into Federalist pigeonholes.

In the Senate, as well, factions lined up according to inclinations toward power centered in the national or in the state governments. Adams, presiding officer of the Senate, supported the Constitution as providing, on the whole, a well-balanced distribution of power. His chief objection all along had been what he thought was a dearth of power in the executive. Of the many failings of the Confederation, one of the most serious had been its nonexistent executive; Adams now hoped that the executive could maintain enough power to prevent the Constitution from falling prey to eleven jealous states. (North Carolina and Rhode Island remained recalcitrant outsiders.) After all, the national government at this stage of its development was a weak little infant indeed, esteemed far below the state governments. It was indicative of the regard with which most people held the federal government that the majority felt that a place in the state government was much more of a plum than one in the national. Senators such as Tristram Dalton of Massachusetts, Adams' old friend and Harvard classmate; Caleb Strong, also of Massachusetts; Oliver Ellsworth of Connecticut; Charles Carroll of Maryland and Robert Morris of Pennsylvania tended to share Adams' point of view. Opposing them were such men as Pierce

Butler, a charging, radical Antifederalist, and his fellow South
Carolinian, Ralph Izard; William Johnson of Connecticut; John
Langdon and Paine Wingate of New Hampshire.

Yet there was no stronger Antifederalist, no more vocal pugilist
in the factional debates than William Maclay of the Pennsylvania
frontier. A Scottish lawyer and land speculator who farmed near
the backwoods town of Harrisburg, Maclay first had been pointed
out to Adams by Dr. Rush, who claimed him as "one of my early
and most intimate friends . . . a scholar, a philosopher, and a
statesman."[19] A large man with badly rheumatic knees, Maclay
loved his family, his Pennsylvania farm and his democratic principles. Though Rush had ascribed Federalist sympathies to him, he
was no Federalist but a committed democrat who preferred prac-
ticalities to theory, simplicity to form, Pennsylvanians to New Englanders. At the opposite pole from Adams, whom he did not
understand and came to despise as a monarchist, he feared that the
Constitution would "turn out the vilest of all traps that ever was set
to ensnare the freedom of an unsuspecting people." The Constitution, he felt, was "meant to swallow all the state constitutions by
degrees. . . ."[20] Since the Senate then did not make its sessions
public, Maclay provided a valuable service by keeping a detailed
journal of his term of office from 1789 to 1791. Just as Adams often
felt that he stood alone, so did Maclay labor under the dreary
conviction that no one else was on his side; consequently, few men
of the new government escaped Maclay's blistering censure. Particularly did Adams become the subject for his waspish, vitriolic
sketches.

Since Adams reached New York before Washington did, he was
sworn into office ahead of the President. On April 20 Caleb Strong
and Ralph Izard conducted Adams to the Senate chamber in the
remodeled City Hall at the corner of Wall and Nassau Streets,
where John Langdon, president pro tem, met him on the Senate
floor and escorted him to the chair. Adams had prepared a short
speech. He had taken his post out of duty, he said, believing that
at such a time the prosperity of the country and the liberty of the
people required "the attention of those who possess any share of

the public confidence." He congratulated the people of America "on the formation of a national constitution and the fair prospect of a consistent administration of a government of laws; on the acquisition of a House of Representatives, chosen by themselves; of a Senate, thus composed by their own state legislatures; and on the prospect of an executive authority in the hands of one whose portrait I shall not presume to draw." He paid high compliment to Washington who, Adams was sure, would discharge his "present exalted trust on the same principles, with the same abilities and virtues which have uniformly appeared in all his former conduct, public or private." In no other nation had the first magistrate been a man "whose commanding talents and virtues, whose overruling good fortune have so completely united all hearts and voices in his favor, who enjoyed the esteem and admiration of foreign nations and fellow citizens with equal unanimity." These "qualities, so uncommon, are no common blessings to the country that possesses them."

Finally, Adams concluded with a telling admission of what his own greatest problem would be as President of the Senate. It was "necessary to make an apology for myself." Though he was "not wholly without experience in public assemblies," he had "been more accustomed to take a share in their debates than to preside in their deliberations. It shall be my constant endeavor to behave towards every member of this most honorable body with all that consideration, delicacy, and decorum which becomes the dignity of his station and character. But if, from inexperience or inadvertency, anything should ever escape me inconsistent with propriety, I must entreat you, by imputing it to its true cause, and not to any want of respect, to pardon and excuse it."[21]

This was a brief confession but a plain effort to withhold nothing from view, a demonstration that in spite of his pride and vanity he was also moved by inner humility. It was more of an admission than perhaps even Adams realized. His every instinct keyed him for debate—his wit, his sharpness, his penetrating, unyielding line of attack schooled by long years in a courtroom. He rose to his full powers in the midst of debate. Much as he loved to be in the thick of a fight, he could never restrain himself to be an onlooker. His years as presiding officer would prove a miserable torture. When he was not free to plunge into the fray with flailing words, to watch an opponent wither before an exquisitely placed rapier of argument, he was a wretched soul. Time after time he could not check himself, rushing into action with both fists up; time after time he simply could not keep his mouth shut. Unfortunately, his precipitous moments were more apparent to the Senators than the countless times when he *did* manage to harness himself. For the next eight years he was to chafe in a job to which, for the only time in his life, he was really unsuited. So entirely did his instincts go against this task that he could not conquer them. He made himself disliked, maligned, misunderstood, accused of believing things he really did not believe. And right at hand to record every slip was William Maclay.

The job of instituting the new government posed a problem for every official. With no established protocol, no judiciary as yet, no departments, no fixed tradition of handling business, no one knew exactly what to do. Adams realized the patterns set now would direct the future course of the government. He knew that this was a time for careful consideration, for prudence, caution, mature deliberation. Moreover, he believed that the esteem in which people held the new government, the zeal with which they would obey its laws, depended on the government's ability to command their respect. For this reason, he launched into a campaign for titles and ceremonies that would fit the estimable character of the new government. In retrospect it may seem puzzling, even humorous, that Adams should have harped so relentlessly upon so inconsequential a matter. Yet to him it was a weighty concern.

Inconspicuously and modestly as he had always lived and dressed, much as he had always scorned ostentatious display, he nevertheless appreciated the form which men attached to their cherished objects of veneration. Men required tangible forms with which to associate their highest concepts. Hence, some meaningful form became essential to religion, to patriotism, to orderly society. Having just spent ten years in Europe, the home of proprieties, Adams found it natural to assume that some of these decencies should be observed in the United States. The members of the Senate, however, found these suggestions wearisome, absurd, impractical—and, worst of all, monarchical.

Adams succeeded in getting appointed a committee on titles, much to Maclay's disgust. "Ceremonies, endless ceremonies," Maclay reported on April 25, were "the whole business of the day." Adams "as usual, made us two or three speeches from the chair." One of these talks concerned the subject of how Washington would be received in the Senate on the day of his inauguration.[22]

April 30 had been set for Washington's inauguration. After the President had been sworn in, he was to address both houses of Congress in the Senate chamber. Adams intended to do all in his power to bring off the occasion with proper dignity. "This son of *Adam*," Maclay remarked, "seemed impressed with deeper gravity. . . . He often in the midst of his most important airs—I believe when he is at loss for expressions (and this he often is, wrapped up, I suppose, in the contemplation of his own importance)—suffers an unmeaning kind of vacant laugh to escape him. This was the case today, and really to me bore the air of ridiculing the farce he was acting." When Washington addressed Congress, Adams asked of the Senators how should they receive the speech —standing or sitting?

A flurry of comment then followed—from Lee, who referred to the House of Commons, then the House of Lords, the King, and then Commons again; from Izard, who told how he had seen it done in Parliament; from Adams, who listed his remembrance of Parliament, and from Carroll, who "got up to declare that he thought it of no consequence how it was in Great Britain." Suddenly during this exchange the secretary whispered to Adams that the clerk from the House was outside the door with a communication. How should this clerk be received? More debate. Then word came that members of the House were outside the chamber waiting to come in. Confusion reigned in the Senate. Members left their seats, babbling unintelligibly. Finally the Speaker and the Representatives were simply admitted and introduced. All sat, then, for an hour and ten minutes awaiting the President, because Lee, Izard and Dalton had failed to meet him on time.

When Washington arrived in the chamber, he bowed to the members of both houses. Adams gave him the chair, attempting to greet him with a little speech. But Adams appeared to Maclay to have forgotten his lines, for he stood vacantly for an embarrassed pause, then simply bowed formally, indicating that Washington was now to take the oath. The President moved out into the gallery, where he took the oath, administered by Chancellor Robert R. Livingston of New York. As Washington bowed to them, the crowd outside cheered wildly. The President then came back into the Senate chamber. He took the chair but rose when he was to give his address. The members of Congress rose, too.

"This great man," Maclay recorded, "was agitated and embarrassed more than ever he was by the leveled cannon or pointed musket." His dark brown suit was plain homespun, relieved only by the metal buttons decorated with eagles, the white stockings, bag and polished sword. So severely did his hands tremble that he could barely read his paper, fidgeting his speech from one hand to the other and his hands in and out of his pockets. An attempted flourish with his right hand came off awkwardly. "I sincerely, for my part," Maclay said, "wished all set ceremony in the hands of the dancing-masters and that this first of men had read off his address in the plainest manner, without ever taking his eyes from the paper, for I felt hurt that he was not first in everything."[23]

The dispute over ceremonies and titles continued unabated, Maclay objecting angrily to Washington's inaugural address being termed "his most gracious speech," deploring attempts to pin upon Washington a glorious royal title. Adams, on the other hand, scorned the simple title of President—there were presidents of fire companies and cricket clubs.[24]

Adams argued, "What will the common people of foreign countries, what will the sailors and the soldiers say, 'George Washington, President of the United States'? They will despise him *to all eternity.*"[25]

In beating his dead horse of titles, Adams showed peculiar insensitivity to the general temper of the Senate. His incessant speeches irritated the senators, his intense concern for ceremony gave them the impression that he himself sought a title.

"His grasping after titles has been observed by everybody," Maclay noted, adding that Izard had taken to referring to Adams as "His Rotundity."[26] It was an unfortunate cause for Adams to espouse, for this position, probably more than any he took in his life, made him the target of accusations that he was a monarchist. The fact that he had preached and acted in favor of republicanism all his life, that he had helped lead the Revolution against monarchy, for the moment made no difference. In this era of touchiness on the subject of monarchy, Adams began to be suspect. His *Discourses on Davila* would seal his indictment in the public mind.

Revenue posed the thorniest problem of the new administration —how to raise money to allow the government to function and to pay off the debt at home and abroad, how to prevent the new republic from falling into the pit of mistakes of the Confederation. Consequently, the first big debate in Congress concerned a tariff, an issue that even this early split Federalists and Antifederalists along sectional lines. As Madison had put it, not only were there divisions in the new government between Federalists and Antifederalists, but between Northerners and Southerners. In the sectional split, New England battled Virginia, which allied with Pennsylvania and a group of New Yorkers. Furthermore, the delegates displayed in the tariff fracas another root of party debate—their sympathies for either France or Britain. Henceforth, labels of Francophile or Anglophile would be hurled between opponents.

Once the means of revenue was finally agreed upon, the task then remained to establish a framework of government. The Judiciary Act became law on September 24, 1789. Next the bills for departments specified a department of foreign affairs, or state, and departments of war, treasury and justice. For Secretary of State, Washington had little choice; of the three most qualified diplomats, Franklin was too old and sick, Adams was Vice-President, and so Jefferson, still minister to France in Paris, became the first Secretary of State. Though Jefferson did not relish the job at all and declined, Washington persisted. When he returned home in 1790, Jefferson, feeling almost commanded to accept, took the post.

Though Washington asked Robert Morris, financier of the Revolution, to be Secretary of the Treasury, he declined. Alexander Hamilton then became the choice for a job perfectly in tune with Hamilton's capabilities. Henry Knox continued as Secretary of War, Edmund Randolph, former governor of Virginia, accepted the post of Attorney General.

Out of the bills on the departments emerged a debate on interpretation of the Constitution. The President could make official appointments with the advice and consent of the Senate. But what about removal of officers? The Constitution stood silent. Men such as Madison, Ames and Adams believed that the President ought to do his own firing; that might be assumed since the Constitution did not specify. Yet Maclay, Izard, and Butler preached that whomever the Senate advised and consented to appoint they should likewise advise and consent to remove.

Adams actually did not believe that the Senate should approve either appointment or removal. Those powers both belonged to the executive. In one of three letters to Roger Sherman of Connecticut on the United States Constitution, in which he expressed his principles of balanced government, Adams gave his reasons for objecting even to the right of the Senate to advise and consent upon appointments. First, he wrote, it would lessen the responsibility of the executive for his officials, diffusing the seat of blame until neither executive nor Senate would accept censure for an unworthy official; it would turn "the minds and attention of the people to the Senate, a branch of the legislature, in executive matters," posing a dangerous unity of executive and aristocratic elements. It would have "a natural tendency to excite ambition in the Senate," prompting influential Senators to plump certain candidates; it would introduce corruption; it would induce formation of "a court and country party," perhaps even leading to schism of the United States into two or three nations.[27]

Senate debate raged on July 16 over the Presidential removal power. When the issue came to a vote, ten stood against, ten stood in favor. Beside himself with excitement, Adams cried, "It is not a vote!" and cast his vote in favor of Presidential removal, one of

the major occasions when he settled a tie. Maclay felt dismal:
"What avowed and repeated attempts have I seen to place the
President above the powers stipulated for him by the Constitu-
tion!" he groaned.[28]

Adams hastily sought to free himself from a charge made by his
Massachusetts friend, James Lovell, that he had given the casting
vote because he himself wanted the Presidency. "You insinuate
that I am accused 'of deciding in favor of the power of the prime
because I look up to that goal,' " he wrote Lovell. That he did look
to that goal sometimes, he readily admitted; in fact, he was bound
by duty to do so, for "there is only the breath of one mortal between
me and it." During the recent serious illness of Washington, Adams
had looked up to it "with horror." If, indeed, he had been looking
to the Presidency, he would have voted the popular way, against
the removal power, he argued. But there was not, "to be serious,
the smallest prospect" that he would ever become President. "Our
beloved chief is very little older than his second, has recovered his
health, and is a much stronger man than I am," Adams insisted. "A
new Vice-President must be chosen before a new President."
Rather than being a painful thought, this was a pleasant one, "for
I know very well that I am not possessed of the confidence and
affection of my fellow citizens to the degree that he is. I am not of
Caesar's mind. The second place in Rome is high enough for me,
although I have a spirit that will not give up its right or relinquish
its place. Whatever the world, or even my friends, or even you, who
knows me so well, may think of me, I am not an ambitious man.
Submission to insult and disgrace is one thing, but aspiring to higher
situations is another. I am quite contented in my present condition
and should not be discontented to leave it."[29]

Despite attempts then and since to discredit his loyalty to the
President, Adams strongly admired Washington. "No man, I believe, has influence with the President. He seeks information from
all quarters and judges more independently than any man I ever
knew."[30] Here was the supreme compliment Adams could pay another man, a tribute to his justice and independence, to his integrity.

With Abigail now at Richmond Hill, the Adamses socialized with Washington and his lady. Abigail felt warm toward the President, "a singular example of modesty and diffidence" with a "dignity which forbids familiarity mixed with an easy affability which creates love and reverence." A real friendship soon developed between Abigail and Martha, two women who held their husbands' welfare above all else. Of the two Abigail was by far the more intellectual, but both women were kind-hearted, generous, practical, unpretentious. "Mrs. Washington," Abigail found, "is one of those unassuming characters which create love and esteem. A most becoming pleasantness sits upon her countenance and an unaffected deportment which renders her the object of veneration and respect. With all these feelings and sensations I found myself much more deeply impressed than I ever did before Their Majesties of Britain."[31]

Washington could not have selected for the key secretaries in his Cabinet two men more at antipodes than Hamilton and Jefferson. Physically, they looked entirely different, the one much younger, short, erect, quick, of clean-cut physique, a ladies' man; the other tall, shambly, haphazardly groomed, of disconnected, lounging gait. Intellectually, too, they had nothing in common. Hamilton, on the one hand, expressed his genius in an immensely practical fashion. With an uncanny facility to visualize projected financial schemes in operation, he fortunately realized that establishment of credit must be the building stone of the new government. Propelled by dazzling energy and his marvelous executive ability to translate plans into fact, he almost single-handedly gave the weakling America an economic strength that in a few short years gained respect for her throughout the world. Hamilton's paragon was England, his economic philosophy a mixture of laissez faire and mercantilistic protectionism. He honored property as the most basic of rights; he intended to protect those people in society who most possessed that good. He despised democrats and, hence, the French Revolution. He understood that the national government must be given a sturdy framework that would prevent another disastrous Confederation. Yet for all his financial wizardry, he failed to perceive that American industrialization was developing on a different model from the British. Nor could he understand the principle of federalism—that it tends toward centralization even without help. Finally, this native of the West Indies could never sympathize with the traditional, long-ingrained reverence for their native states and local customs that motivated deeply rooted men like Adams and Jefferson. To Hamilton, the nationalist, states' rights were a mysterious, impenetrable notion to which he could not relate.

On the other hand, Jefferson was an American equivalent of a French *philosophe*. Viewing humanity in the same benevolent spirit as the Frenchmen, Jefferson believed men were essentially good, rational and perfectible. To protect the liberty of the virtuous people, he demanded a limited government based on an agrarian democracy. The innate virtue of the people was best preserved, Jefferson felt, when life was decentralized in a rural atmosphere where life remained simple. He could only fear Hamilton's concept of an urban, industrialized society dominated by merchants and investors. Jefferson, like so many Virginia planters, did not understand money; the economy of his entire state had long been based upon tobacco, a commodity which planters generally used as money in this loose-credit section of the country. Indeed, more than mere philosophy separated Hamilton and Jefferson; as the party system began to assume definite shape, the chief difference between them and their parties came to be based upon the economy of geographic sections.

It was these two men whom Adams would one day face as enemies—one a member of his own party, the other a favorite friend. The first would come to be the only man that Adams ever hated; with the second he would be reunited one day in the old sentimental ties, but only after much discord.

Meanwhile, when the second session of the First Congress convened in January, 1790, issues began to crystallize as Hamilton proposed his financial program. In order to support public credit, Hamilton recommended, first of all, that the foreign and floating domestic debt should be funded at face value. The old debts of the war would be paid off by creating a new debt; six percent bonds would be issued in exchange for the old securities and certificates. Import duties and excise taxes would pay the interest of these bonds and, eventually, the principal as well. Second, the federal government would assume the debts of the states—this action would consolidate state and national interest, Hamilton felt. In order to stabilize government security prices, a sinking fund, of which Adams was to be a commissioner, would buy up these securities if they fell too much below par. Finally, later in the year, Hamilton suggested a Bank of the United States modeled after the Bank of England.

Adams welcomed Hamilton's plan, knowing from his European experience in attempting to get loans how necessary it was for the new government to settle upon a solid credit footing. Madison, he was dismayed to see, fought to substitute for the funding bill a plan to compensate the original purchasers, complaining that funding at par would encourage speculators. Although Jefferson approved the funding bill, he did not accept assumption of state debts. However, in the loud debate over location of the national capital, Jefferson bartered with Hamilton to support assumption in return for removal of the capital from New York to Philadelphia for ten years. After that time it would be moved to Washington on the Potomac.

While John Adams watched the United States stumble along toward a surer foundation, at the same time he gravely contemplated the fast-moving events in France. A Paris mob had stormed and destroyed the Bastille on July 14, 1789. Peasants had rioted in the provinces; provisional governments had been set up. Representatives of the nobles had relinquished all feudal rights, privileges and titles. A declaration of the rights of man had been issued, borrowing from English and American documents but also from the theories of the *philosophes.* Mobs had raged through Paris and on to Versailles, forcing the royal family to flee. A unicameral constitution now prevailed.

The French Revolution with its slogan of equality was finding ready sympathizers in America, where Antifederalists took up the banner of French revolutionaries. To a man such as Maclay,

" . . . France seems travailing in the birth of freedom. Her throes and pangs of labor are violent. God give her a happy delivery! Royalty, nobility and vile pageantry, by which a few of the human race lord it over and tread on the necks of their fellow-mortals, seem likely to be demolished with their kindred Bastille, which is said to be laid in ashes." Indignantly, Maclay considered "the late attempts of some creatures among us to revive the vile machinery! O Adams, Adams, what a wretch art thou!"[32]

But to Adams, long a student of government, long a first-hand observer of the European scene, the Revolution was neither so simple nor so pleasing. He feared these cries for equality would begin a train of tragic repercussions; he knew what a weight of ancient tradition and custom the revolutionaries proposed blithely to toss away. He received on the first day of February, 1790, a discourse on love of country from Dr. Price, a piece which incidentally inspired Burke to write his *Reflections on the Revolution in France.* Much impressed with the discourse, Adams wrote to thank Dr. Price, saying that he loved "the zeal and the spirit which dictated this discourse" and that he admired its sentiments. "From the year 1760 to this hour," he went on, "the whole scope of my life has been to support such principles and propagate such sentiments. No sacrifices of myself or my family, no dangers, no labors, have been too much for me in this great cause." Thus, he could not be indifferent to the French Revolution, yet he had "learned by awful experience to rejoice with trembling." It was a ponderous thought to ". . . know that encyclopedists and economists, Diderot and D'Alembert, Voltaire and Rousseau," men with whom he little agreed, "have contributed to this great event more than Sidney, Locke, or Hoadly, perhaps more than the American Revolution; and I own to you, I know not what to make of a republic of thirty million atheists." The French constitution was "but an experiment and must and will be altered. I know it to be impossible that France should be long governed by it. If the sovereignty is to reside in one assembly, the King, princes of the blood, and principal quality will govern it at their pleasure as long as they can agree; when they differ, they will go to war and act over again all the tragedies of

Valois, Bourbons, Lorraines, Guises, and Colignis two hundred years ago." Adams felt convinced that "too many Frenchmen, after the example of too many Americans, pant for equality of persons and property. The impracticability of this God Almighty has decreed, and the advocates for liberty who attempt it will surely suffer for it."

As for the American government, he told Price, it was another "attempt to divide a sovereignty"; it would "prevent us for a time from drawing our swords upon each other, and when it will do that no longer, we must call a new convention to reform it. The difficulty of bringing millions to agree in any measures, to act by any rule, can never be conceived by him who has not tried it. It is incredible how small is the number in any nation of those who comprehend any system of constitution or administration, and those few it is wholly impossible to unite." Bleakly, he observed, "I am a sincere inquirer after truth, but I find very few who discover the same truths." The King of Prussia had once expressed a truth with which Adams could agree: " 'That it is the peculiar quality of the human understanding that example should correct no man. The blunders of the father are lost to his children, and every generation must commit its own.' " Adams had "never sacrificed my judgment to kings, ministers, nor people, and I never will. When either shall see as I do, I shall rejoice in their protection, aid, and honor; but I see no prospect that either will ever think as I do, and therefore I shall never be a favorite with either. I do not desire to be; but I sincerely wish and devoutly pray that a hundred years of civil wars may not be the portion of all Europe for want of a little attention to the true elements of the science of government."[33]

Troubled about the outcome in both his own country and in France, Adams ached for man muddling in the chaos of blind ignorance. His pen itched to advise, to warn, to teach. It now found an occasion to set to work. Condorcet had recently published *Four Letters of a Bourgeois of New Haven*, a defense of Turgot's position on unicameral government. Hence, with this as his take-off point, Adams began publishing in Fenno's *Gazette of the United States* in Philadelphia his *Discourses on Davila*, a series that ran from

April, 1790, until April, 1791.[34] By the end of that time such a tide
of fury had risen against the articles that Adams at Fenno's request
was forced to cease writing. The *Discourses* were a sequel to the
Defence, a continued plea for balanced government, but more outspoken on the subject of equality than anything Adams had ever
written. With equality and the French Revolution such idols of
public opinion, Adams could not have chosen a less propitious time
to publish his articles. He was not always very prudent, however,
or primarily interested in his political livelihood. Often he took a
kind of obstinate joy in uttering the politically unfavorable comment; he thereby demonstrated to the world, he thought, that he
cared little for public adulation, that he was an independent man.
Yet in his position as Vice-President he did act unwisely in publishing the *Discourses*. He held, after all, a job to which some nonparti-
sanship ought to be attached. Nonetheless, he had no idea that his
articles would meet such outraged opposition; to him it seemed that
the truth he spoke would mollify the Francophiles. Even he himself,
however, eventually admitted that the publication of the *Discourses*
had been inopportune.

Later, as a crusty old character of seventy-seven, unafraid to
reveal himself, he could write of the *Discourses*, "This dull, heavy
volume still excites the wonder of its author—first that he could
find, amidst the constant scenes of business and dissipation in
which he was enveloped, time to write it; secondly, that he had the
courage to oppose and publish his own opinions to the universal
opinion of America, and, indeed, of all mankind. Not one man in
America then believed him. He knew not one and has not heard of
one since who then believed him. The work, however, powerfully
operated to destroy his popularity. It was urged as full proof that
he was an advocate for monarchy and laboring to introduce a
hereditary President in America."[35]

CHAPTER XIV

DISCOURSES ON DAVILA

SCARCELY anyone in America had heard of the Italian historian, Enrico Caterino Davila. But Adams, the insatiable reader, owned a French translation of Davila's *History of the Civil Wars of France*, a commentary on the intrigues and wars of sixteenth-century France, when unrestrained rivalries between the great noble houses had plunged the nation into a blood bath.

Taking as his theme, as he had suggested in the *Defence*, that men are unequal and so imperfectible by nature as never to be made equal, Adams urged France not to repeat the mistake of the civil wars—that of failing to balance rivalries that inevitably resulted from the distinctions between men. At the same time, he admonished the United States not to follow the French into the pitfalls of equality but to support a reasonable, balanced government under the Federal Constitution. France had never determined the seat of power in her government; for that reason, she had never effectively controlled rivalries. Without such control, despotism certainly resulted— that despotism formerly had been absolute monarchy, but now just as surely tyranny would prove to be rooted in the unicameral National Assembly.

As a basis for his argument against equality, Adams analyzed man's passion for distinction. Perfectly in step with man's social nature, this passion for distinction was "a desire to be observed, considered, esteemed, praised, beloved, and admired by his fellows . . . one of the earliest, as well as keenest dispositions discovered in the heart of man." Every man hoped to be singled out, distinguished, ". . . to be seen, heard, talked of, approved and respected by the people about him and within his knowledge." Even if he tried, he could never by reason or will rid himself of this passion; instead, the more he yearned for others to notice him, the more he feared their neglect.[1]

This passion for distinction manifested itself in various ways. First, when it was desire to excel another through industry and virtue it was called emulation. When it sought power, it was ambition; when fearful that one who was now inferior might become superior, it was jealousy. Envy aimed to bring a superior down to one's level or below. Vanity gave a man a false opinion of his own importance. In fact, "this propensity" to seek distinction "in all its branches is a principal source of the virtues and vices, the happiness and misery of human life; and . . . the history of mankind is little more than a simple narration of its operation and effects."[2]

Now, of course, Adams agreed, simple benevolence, an affection for the good of others, did truly exist in human nature. Yet by itself benevolence could not offset the selfish passion. Thus, nature had added to benevolence the desire of reputation, in order to make men good members of society. Nature had ordained this passion for distinction "as a constant incentive to activity and industry, that, to acquire the attention and complacency, the approbation and admiration of their fellows, men might be urged to constant exertions of beneficence."[3] Indeed, this desire to be esteemed became the means by which society could exist, ". . . the only adequate instrument of order and subordination in society and alone commands effectual obedience to laws, since without it neither human reason nor standing armies would ever produce that great effect." Consequently, it was a principal end of government to regulate this passion which, in its turn, made government possible.[4]

Although the wise and just man realized that he must judge others on the basis of merit and virtue, the world generally assessed people on other considerations, too, namely birth and wealth. A well-born man or man of riches attracted the attention and congratulations of mankind. On the other hand, "the poor man's conscience is clear; yet he is ashamed. His character is irreproachable; yet he is neglected and despised." It was not that he was censured or disapproved—"*he is only not seen.*" Yet even a poor man lived in a little circle of people with whom he tried to distinguish himself. Somewhere, Adams suggested, there must be one "who is the last and lowest of the human species. But there is no risk in asserting that there is not one who believes and will acknowledge himself to be the man. To be wholly overlooked, and to know it, are intolerable." Adams again recounted the story he had told in the *Defence* in which a starving man refused to kill his dog for food, asking "Who will love me then?" Putting his finger on a truth of human nature, Adams pointed out, "In this *'who will love me then?'* there is a key to the human heart, to the history of human life and manners, and to the rise and fall of empires. To feel ourselves unheeded chills the most pleasing hope, damps the most fond desire, checks the most agreeable wish, disappoints the most ardent expectations of human nature." The wish to be regarded, beloved, admired, Adams felt, was an inescapable fact of human nature, an unchangeable reality, as strong a passion as the need for food, a social passion that gave men incentive to do good works in society.[5]

Adams summed up the importance of this passion: "The language of nature to man in his constitution is this — 'I have given you reason, conscience, and benevolence; and thereby made you accountable for your actions and capable of virtue, in which you will find your highest felicity. But I have not confided wholly in your laudable improvement of these divine gifts. To them I have superadded in your bosoms a passion for the notice and regard of your fellow mortals, which, if you perversely violate your duty and wholly neglect the part assigned you in the system of the world and the society of mankind, shall torture you from the cradle to the grave.'" Furthermore, nature had taken care of her own work: "She has wrought the passions into the texture and essence of the soul and has not left in it the power of art to destroy them." As Adams

had stated again and again in his writings, man had reason, conscience, benevolence, or a desire to do good, but with all that, he
also had passions—irremovable passions. "To regulate and not
eradicate them," Adams thought, "is the province of policy. It is
of the highest importance to education, to life, and to society, not
only that they should not be destroyed, but that they should be
gratified, encouraged, and arranged on the side of virtue."[6] "In
short," he believed, "the theory of education and the science of
government may be reduced to the same principle and be all comprehended in the knowledge of the means of actively conducting,
controlling, and regulating the emulation and ambition of the citizens."[7]

Emulation, a desire not only to imitate and to equal but to excel,
was "so natural a movement of the human heart that, wherever men
are to be found, and in whatever manner associated or connected,"
the results could be seen in rivalry.[8] Every kind of rivalry existed
between every type of men, group, nation, a perfectly natural and,
so long as it was balanced by other rivalries, healthy and harmless
state of affairs. "Nature . . . has ordained that no two objects shall
be perfectly alike and no two creatures perfectly equal. Although,
among men, all are subject by nature to *equal laws* of morality, and
in society have a right to *equal laws* for their government, yet no
two men are perfectly equal in person, property, understanding,
activity, and virtue, or ever can be made so by any power less than
that which created them; and whenever it becomes disputable,
between two individuals or families which is the superior, a fermentation commences, which disturbs the order of all things until it is
settled and each one knows his place in the opinion of the public."[9]
The French civil wars had been nothing but "a relation of rivalries
succeeding each other in a rapid series. . . ."[10] Thus, the French
government had failed in an essential task, effective control of
rivalries.

"There is a voice within us," Adams declared, "which seems to
intimate that real merit should govern the world; and that men
ought to be respected only in proportion to their talents, virtues and
services." But how were the best men to emerge from these count-

less rivalries? How would they be discovered and judged? How would they be made members of government?[11]

Adams answered, predictably, that only a well-balanced constitution could insure that the most distinguished men came to the fore. Only a balanced government could control rivalries. Since there were no limits to the passions, "and as the world, instead of restraining, encourages them, the check must be in the form of government." Unfortunately the world encouraged those perversions of the passion for distinction—ambition and avarice. "That world, for the regulation of whose prejudices, passions, imaginations, and interests governments are instituted, is so unjust," Adams felt, "that neither religion, natural nor revealed, nor anything but a well-ordered and well-balanced government has ever been able to correct it, and that but imperfectly."[12] For that reason, Americans who had been unfriendly or lukewarm toward the Constitution should recognize that "emulations of a serious complexion" existed in the United States—between cities and universities, between North and South, between Middle and North, Middle and South, between one state and another, between state governments and the national government. Americans ought to inquire whether the natural remedy to inconveniences and dangers of these rivalries existed in a "well-balanced constitution such as that of our Union purports to be. . . ." Americans ought to support their Constitution ". . . as our only hope of peace and our ark of safety, till its defects, if it has any, can be corrected."[13]

Now even a balanced constitution could not erase the inequalities and distinctions among people. Americans had been told that the French National Assembly had abolished all distinctions. "But be not deceived, my dear countrymen," Adams warned. "Impossibilities cannot be performed. Have they leveled all fortunes and equally divided all property? Have they made all men and women equally wise, elegant, and beautiful? Have they annihilated the names of Bourbon and Montmorency, Rochefoucauld and Noailles, Lafayette and La Moignon, Necker and De Calonne, Mirabeau and Bailly? Have they committed to the flames all the records, annals, and histories of the nation? . . . Shall we believe the

National Assembly capable of resolving that no man shall have any desire of distinction; or that all men shall have equal means of gratifying it? Or that no man shall have any means of gratifying it?"[14]

Because the National Assembly had no check on its power, the rival parties among its members would churn wildly until one strongest managed to seize control. Shackles would be laid upon the free press; riots and seditions would "at length break men's bones, or flay off their skins." Lives would be lost; "and when blood is once drawn, men, like other animals, become outrageous. If one party has not a superiority over the other, clear enough to decide everything at its pleasure, a civil war ensues."

"The men of letters in France," Adams asserted, "are wisely reforming one feudal system; but may they not, unwisely, lay the foundation of another? A legislature in one assembly can have no other termination than in civil dissension, feudal anarchy, or simple monarchy."[15]

Adams watched soberly as "the first empire of the world" broke "the fetters of human reason" and exerted "the energies of human liberty." But Frenchmen and Americans both "should remember that the perfectibility of man is only human and terrestrial perfectibility. Cold will still freeze, and fire will never cease to burn; disease and vice will continue to disorder and death to terrify mankind." Emulation "next to self-preservation" would continue to be the mainspring of human action; only "the balance of a well-ordered government" could "prevent that emulation from degenerating into dangerous ambition, irregular rivalries, destructive factions, wasting seditions, and bloody civil wars."[16]

Distinctions among men were a fact of life that no *philosophes* or revolutionaries could dissolve—they could only regulate and live with them. "The controversy between the rich and the poor, the laborious and the idle, the learned and the ignorant, distinctions as old as the creation and as extensive as the globe, distinctions which no art or policy, no degree of virtue or philosophy can ever wholly destroy, will continue, and rivalries will spring out of them." These rival parties had to be represented in the legislature, where they must be balanced, "or one will oppress the other." Probably no other method of keeping equilibrium would ever be found than putting the two basic types, rich and poor, into two independent houses of the legislature, with a third, independent member, an executive, "such as that in our government," to arbitrate between them. "Property must be secured or liberty cannot exist," Adams maintained. "But if unlimited or unbalanced power of disposing property be put into the hands of those who have no property, France will find, as we have found, the lamb committed to the custody of the wolf. In such a case, all the pathetic exhortations and addresses of the National Assembly to the people to respect property will be regarded no more than the warbles of the songsters of the forest."

Adams always restated his theme of government—the theme of the *Defence*—to him the most viable truth of politics: "The great art of lawgiving consists in balancing the poor against the rich in the legislature and in constituting the legislature a perfect balance against the executive power, at the same time that no individual or party can become its rival. The essence of a free government consists in an effectual control of rivalries." Because the executive and legislative were natural rivals, neither could be allowed control over the other or the stronger would swallow up the weaker. Hence, "the nation which will not adopt an equilibrium of power must adopt a despotism. There is no other alternative. Rivalries must be controlled or they will throw all things into confusion; and there is nothing but despotism or a balance of power which can control them."[17]

Finally, Adams broached the subject of religious principles, a matter the *philosophes* scorned. "Is there a possibility," he asked, "that the government of nations may fall into the hands of men who teach the most disconsolate of all creeds, that men are but fireflies and that this *all* is without a father? Is this the way to make man, as man, an object of respect? Or is it to make murder itself as indifferent as shooting a plover, and the extermination of the Rohilla nation as innocent as the swallowing of mites on a morsel of cheese?" If this was so, then better to return to the gods of the

Greeks, to the systems of Athanasius and Calvin—even to the popes and hierarchies, Jesuits and Benedictines.[18]

Adams in the *Discourses* had recited two favorite themes—first, that distinctions among men are natural, impossible to abolish; no amount of wishing, planning or renovating can rid society of that basic truth; second, that rival parties arising from these distinctions must be directed to virtuous activity—and can be, providing they are represented in a well-ordered constitution that keeps them all in balance. With such a balance all men of rival parties might live under liberty and law.

"It has been said," Adams admitted, "that it is extremely difficult to preserve a balance. This is no more than to say that it is extremely difficult to preserve liberty." Perhaps, he said, a perfect balance had never existed or if it had, never been long maintained. Even so "... such a balance as has been sufficient to liberty has been supported in some nations for many centuries together; and we must come as near as we can to a perfect equilibrium, or all is lost."[19]

Even before Adams published his *Discourses*, his tirade on titles had left him accused of being a monarchist. In March, 1790, on his way to New York City to become Secretary of State, Jefferson visited Dr. Rush in Philadelphia. Avowing himself a republican, Jefferson "deplored the change of opinion upon this subject in John Adams, of whom," Rush said, Jefferson "spoke with respect and affection as a great and upright man." At the same time, Jefferson claimed that Madison was " 'the greatest man in the world.' "[20] Writing a most cordial letter to Adams, Rush mentioned that he had seen Jefferson on March 17, when both he and Jefferson had "deplored your attachment to monarchy and both agreed that you had changed your principles since the year 1776." The proof of that change, Rush argued, derived from an old letter of Adams to William Hooper of North Carolina, a signer of the Declaration of Independence, upon the subject of a form of government for North Carolina. The letter, Rush declared, had been published in Philadelphia.[21]

In some dismay, Adams replied, "To the accusation against me which you have recorded in your notebook of the seventeenth of March last, I plead not guilty. I deny an attachment to monarchy, and I deny that I have changed my principles since 1776." In fact, no letter of his to Hooper had ever been printed that he knew about. "Indeed," he answered, "I have but a very confused recollection of having written him any letter." He had, of course, written up a plan of government for Hooper which he had reproduced in a letter to George Wythe. That letter had been published as *Thoughts on Government*, in which he had advocated a three-branch legislature, "and to such a legislature I am still attached." He admitted that at that time he "understood very little of the subject, and, if I had changed my opinions, should have no scruple to avow it." And he had changed one detail of his thinking. In the letter to Wythe he had recommended very frequent elections, but now, with reading and experience, he felt convinced "that Americans are more rapidly disposed to corruption in elections than I thought they were fourteen years ago."

Adams went on, "My friend Dr. Rush will excuse me if I caution him against a fraudulent use of the words *monarchy* and *republic*. I am a mortal and irreconcilable enemy to monarchy. I am no friend to *hereditary limited* monarchy in America. This I know can never be admitted without an hereditary Senate to control it, and a hereditary nobility or Senate in America I know to be unattainable and impracticable. I should scarcely be for it if it were. Do not, therefore, my friend, misunderstand me and misrepresent me to posterity." Adams, as always, was "for a balance between the legislative and executive powers," for an executive capable of maintaining a balance between Senate and House, "or, in other words, between the aristocratical and democratical interests." Moreover, Adams was "for having all three branches elected at stated periods...." He hoped these elections would continue "until the people shall be convinced that fortune, Providence, or chance, call it which you will, is better than election." If the time should come when elections became corrupt, as well as full of intrigue and maneuver, "and produce civil war, then, in my opinion, chance will be better than choice for all but the House of Representatives." Such was

Adams' explicit denial of charges of monarchical sympathies.

His letter to Rush ended on a sour note. He lamented the "deplorable condition" of the country, "which seems to be under such a fatality that the people can agree upon nothing." Certain changes could be made for the better—with the exception of a change of the President. As for the Vice-President, he wished "very heartily that a change of Vice-President could be made tomorrow." He had been "too ill-used in the office to be fond of it," elected "in a manner that made it a disgrace." He would "never serve in it again upon such terms."[22]

At the same time that Adams was denying charges of monarchism, he was publishing the *Discourses* and sending out publicly and in letters warnings on the French Revolution. One day late in April he cornered Maclay in the Senate chamber before the day's business commenced, telling the Pennsylvanian how many pamphlets he had received lately from England, how the French Revolution agitated English politics, how he himself cared only for the recent book of Burke, and how "this same Mr. Burke despised the French Revolution."

"Bravo, Mr. Adams!" Maclay recorded caustically in his journal. "I did not need this trait of your character to know you."[23]

Adams declared to Alexander Jardine that he had noticed from his experience that revolutions often brought forward "the most fiery spirits and flighty geniuses" rather than men of sense. He feared that was taking place in France. Yet he agreed that the French Revolution came as no surprise. "Abuses in religion and government" had so long oppressed the people, government and church pensionaries had grown to such numbers that the commoners could not bear up under the weight of supporting them. France had too long suffered under the disasters of unbalanced government.[24]

Adams could see the hand of Providence working in the French Revolution, he told Thomas Brand-Hollis—"working, however, by natural and ordinary means, such as produced the Reformation in religion in the sixteenth century." Men themselves were carrying out this revolution. "That all men have one common nature is a principle which will now universally prevail," Adams expected, "and equal rights and equal duties will in a just sense, I hope, be inferred from it. But equal ranks and equal property never can be inferred from it, any more than equal understanding, agility, vigor, or beauty. Equal laws are all that ever can be derived from human equality."

Laws could only remain equal so long as neither the rich nor the poor were ever permitted to be masters over the other. Both should have equal power to defend themselves; an independent mediator between them should make certain that their power stood intact, otherwise equal laws could never be made or enforced.

"You see," Adams explained, "I still hold fast my scales and weigh everything in them. The French must finally become my disciples, or rather the disciples of Zeno, or they will have no equal laws, no personal liberty, no property, no lives."

In the United States, he feared, "the pendulum has vibrated too far to the popular side, driven by men without experience or judgment, and horrid ravages have been made upon property by arbitrary multitudes or majorities of multitudes." Both America and France would find "that to place property at the mercy of a majority who have no property" was the gravest folly. "If you are not perfectly of my mind at present," Adams closed with a dash of humor, "I hereby promise and assure you that you will live to see that I am precisely right. Thus arrogantly concludes your assured friend."[25]

In addition to his earnest concern for the condition of government in America and France, Adams worried over family matters. John Quincy had joined Thomas Welsh's household in Boston, where he was practicing law; Charles would practice in New York; Thomas was to go into a Philadelphia law office. Remembering the agonies of starting a practice, of attempting to make the world notice him, Adams was flooded with sympathy for the present hardships of his boys. He wrote to Dr. Welsh enjoining him to teach John Quincy the difficult lesson of entering politics only by way of amusement, not allowing it to interfere with his profession. "I recollect the painful years I suffered from 1758, when I was sworn at

Boston, to the year 1761, too perfectly not to sympathize with John," wrote his father. "Do not let him flatter himself with hopes of a run of business, which is neither to be expected, nor would be beneficial. His business is to study and be constant to his office and in court. Causes and clients will come soon enough for his benefit, if he does that." Applying Gridley's precept to attend to the study of the law rather than the gain of it, Adams insisted that although he could "ill afford to maintain my sons at their studies," he had rather do that "than have them overwhelmed with a run of business at first, which must put an end to their studies."

Speaking, he admitted, with the partiality of a parent, he thought that John Quincy was "as great a scholar as this country has produced at his age"; his father knew that "he possesses a spirit that will not stoop to dishonorable practice or conduct." Adams was "therefore perfectly at ease in my mind about his success. Whether his reputation spreads this year, or two or three years hence, is indifferent to me, provided his anxiety does not injure his health. I have seen too many flashing insects in my day glitter and glare for a moment and then disappear to wish that my sons may add to the number."[26]

In addition to the difficulties of his sons, Adams had Nabby on his mind. Colonel Smith suddenly flitted off to England on some speculative venture, leaving Nabby and their young children in New York to stay with in-laws. John and Abigail felt all the more distressed since they themselves moved in the fall of 1790 from New York to Bush Hill outside Philadelphia, now that the government had been relocated. Nabby, "poor girl," Abigail wrote Mary Cranch, "is called to quite a different trial from any she has before experienced, for though the Colonel was once before absent, she was in her father's house. Now she writes that she feels as if unprotected, as if alone in the wide world."[27]

Compared to Richmond Hill, which had been the sublime, Bush Hill was the beautiful, Abigail told her sister. The present house had a better interior but the other had been grand in its architecture, "and the avenue to it perfectly romantic." Abigail was indignant that "the British troops robbed this place of its principal glory by cutting down all the trees in front of the house and leaving it wholly naked." A grove of trees behind the house somewhat compensated. Abigail had heard that for eight months of the year Bush Hill was "delicious." Now, however, it was January; the roads were bad, and they were two and a half miles from the city.[28]

In the following spring of 1791, shortly after Adams had discontinued publication of his *Discourses*, he fell into a political tangle with Jefferson that caused him everlasting heartache. In answer to Burke's *Reflections*, Thomas Paine had written his *Rights of Man*, a piece drawing parallels between the American and French revolutions and declaiming against the English government as a reactionary instrument working against revolution. Rather by accident, Jefferson's endorsement of Paine's work as a cure for "the political heresies" that had sprung up among the American people was published as the introduction to the *Rights of Man*. Jefferson had sent to the printer a borrowed copy of Paine's pamphlet along with a note expressing his approval, and the printer, without permission, printed the note as an introduction. Severely embarrassed, since everyone immediately assumed the "political heresies" to refer to Adams' *Discourses*, Jefferson hastened to write Washington an explanatory letter. There was little Jefferson could do to alleviate the tenseness, however, for he admitted that indeed he had meant the *Discourses*.

"I am afraid the indiscretion of a printer has committed me with my friend, Mr. Adams," wrote Jefferson to Washington, "for whom, as one of the most honest and disinterested men alive, I have a cordial esteem, increased by long habits of concurrence in opinion in the days of his republicanism; and even since his apostasy to hereditary monarchy and nobility, though we differ, we differ as friends should do." Jefferson confessed as a "certain" fact that when he referred to "political heresies" he had in mind the *Discourses*, "but nothing was ever further from my thoughts than to become myself the contradictor before the public. To my great astonishment, however, when the pamphlet came out, the printer had prefixed my note to it, without having given me the most distant hint of it. Mr. Adams will unquestionably take to himself the charge of political heresy, as conscious of his own views of drawing the present government to the form of the English constitution, and, I fear, will consider me as meaning to injure him in the public eye." Nevertheless, Jefferson would not take back anything he had said in his introduction to Paine's pamphlet, for " . . . this popular and republican pamphlet, taking wonderfully, is likely at a single stroke to wipe out all the unconstitutional doctrines which their bellwether Davila has been preaching for a twelve-month."

"I certainly never made a secret of my being anti-monarchical and anti-aristocratical," he added, "but I am sincerely mortified to be thus brought forward on the public stage, where to remain, to advance or to retire, will be equally against my love of silence and quiet and my abhorrence of dispute."[29]

Outraged that his father's *Discourses* should have been so misunderstood, disgusted that even friends had stumbled in the rough going of the *Discourses*, failing to study it thoroughly, John Quincy, eager to vindicate his parent, now leaped into the controversy. Beginning on the eighth of June, he published in the *Columbian Centinel* his articles signed "Publicola," attacking Paine's *Rights of Man* and defending the English and American constitutions.[30] So much did "Publicola" bear the Adams stamp that everyone, including Jefferson, simply took for granted that the elder Adams had written the articles.

Meanwhile, Adams, wounded by this breach with Jefferson, which he would have gone to all lengths to prevent, kept his own pen silent. The well-meaning Henry Knox, sensing Adams' injury, attempted to soothe him. "Perhaps the 'political heresies' mentioned in the preface to the American edition of Paine's pamphlet, as coming from a more respectable quarter, may occasion some uneasiness," Knox wrote the Vice-President. "But the author has assured me that the note he wrote to the printer never was intended for publication, but as a sort of apology for having detained the book, which was a borrowed one, longer than the impatience of the printer would admit."[31]

At length, Jefferson decided there was no way out of his dilemma but to explain to Adams himself. In mid-July he sat down to write to Adams, who was at home in Braintree.

"I have a dozen times taken up my pen to write to you," began Jefferson, "and as often laid it down again, suspended between opposing considerations. I determine, however, to write from a conviction that truth, between candid minds, can never do harm."

He then explained the circumstances of the ill-fated note, that he had "thought so little of this note" that he had not even kept a copy —"nor ever heard a little more of it till the week following," when he was "thunder-struck with seeing it come out at the head of the pamphlet." He had hoped it would not attract notice. But returning from a month's trip, he had found that "Publicola" had written articles "attacking not only the author and principles of the pamphlet, but myself as its sponsor, by name." Then had come other writers on Paine's side, indicting Adams as the author of "Publicola." "Thus were our names thrown on the public stage as public antagonists," Jefferson wrote ruefully. "That you and I differ in our ideas of the best form of government is well known to us both: but we have differed as friends should do, respecting the purity of each other's motives and confining our difference of opinion to private conversation. And I can declare with truth in the presence of the Almighty that nothing was further from my intention or expectation than to have had either my own or your name brought before the public on this occasion. The friendship and confidence which has so long existed between us required this explanation from me, and I know you too well to fear any misconstruction of the motives of it." Though some people had assumed that he had been the author of various newspaper articles that had recently appeared under pseudonyms, Jefferson concluded, he could assure Adams that he had never in his life had a sentence "inserted in a newspaper without putting my name to it; and I believe I never shall."[32]

Adams almost immediately replied with a telling letter. The old warm esteem for Jefferson glowed forth in willingness to heal a misunderstanding. The hurt at having been misrepresented was not cloaked before this friend; there was a repeated effort to clarify political views. But more than that, the letter expressed sadness that the contention between friends had occasioned mischievous quarreling between factions.

Adams had received Jefferson's "friendly letter . . . with great

pleasure." He gave "full credit to your relation of the manner in
which your note was written and prefixed to the Philadelphia edition of Mr. Paine's pamphlet on the *Rights of Man. . . .* " Nonetheless, "the misconduct of the person who committed this breach of
your confidence by making it public, whatever were his intentions,
has sown the seeds of more evils than he can ever atone for."
Adams minced no words. The pamphlet, with its "striking" recommendation bearing Jefferson's name, had been reprinted everywhere, said Adams, "and was generally considered as a direct and
open personal attack upon me, by countenancing the false interpretation of my writings as favoring the introduction of hereditary
monarchy and aristocracy into this country." The question on
everyone's lips naturally was what political heresies had the Secretary of State meant in his introduction. To which the newspapers
had glibly answered, "the Vice-President's notions of a limited
monarchy, an hereditary government of King and Lords, with only
elective Commons." A writer in the *New Haven Gazette*, reprinted
in New York, Boston and Philadelphia papers, had held up the
Vice-President "to the ridicule of the world for his meanness," an
object to be detested "for wishing to subjugate the people to a few
nobles." Sam Adams, Lieutenant Governor of Massachusetts, had
followed with a formal speech to the state legislature cautioning the
people against the danger of hereditary powers, "as if they were at
that moment in the most imminent danger of them." (Only the year
before Sam and John had exchanged a series of letters debating the
nature of government, Sam advocating democracy and John explaining the virtues of mixed government in a three-power balance.)[33] At the same time, Lieutenant Governor Adams and Governor Hancock had shown "marked neglect" of the Vice-President.
Further, sympathizers of the old Shays' Rebellion and Pennsylvanians who had lost the fight over a new state constitution of 1790,
with bicameral legislature, regarded Vice-President Adams' writings as a "cause of their overthrow" and had resolved to hunt down
Adams "like a hare, if they could." In this state of affairs, "Publicola" began to write his articles.

Adams then told Jefferson specifically that he was not the author of these pieces—"I neither wrote nor corrected 'Publicola.' The writer in the composition of his pieces followed his own judgment, information and discretion, without any assistance from me."

Jefferson in his letter had stated that he and Adams knew that they differed in their ideas of the best form of government. "But, my dear sir," objected Adams, "you will give me leave to say that I do not know this. I know not what your idea is of the best form of government. You and I have never had a serious conversation together that I can recollect concerning the nature of government. The very transient hints that have ever passed between us have been jocular and superficial, without ever coming to any explanation." Again he said plainly, "If you suppose that I have or ever had a design or desire of attempting to introduce a government of King, Lords and Commons, or, in other words, an hereditary executive, or an hereditary senate, either into the government of the United States or that of any individual state, in this country, you are wholly mistaken." If anyone could find such a thought contrary to that statement in any of Adams' writings, let him quote the chapter and verse. If Jefferson had put such a construction on anything Adams had written, let Adams convince him otherwise. Many people had read Adams' works, yet great numbers had not read them. "Of the few who have taken the pains to read them, some have misunderstood them and others have willfully misrepresented them, and these misunderstandings and misrepresentations have been made the pretense for overwhelming me with floods and whirlwinds of tempestuous abuse, unexampled in the history of this country."

Adams took time to deplore the "unbridled rivalries" in the country, "the most melancholy and alarming symptoms" that he had ever seen in America. He had heard, for instance, that Hancock's faction was plotting to have Governor Hancock replace Adams as Vice-President, leaving Sam Adams to be governor of Massachusetts, so that a democratic faction would "be sure of all the loaves and fishes in the national government and the state government. . . ."

Finally, Adams thanked Jefferson for writing to him. "It was high time that you and I should come to an explanation with each other.

The friendship that has subsisted for fifteen years between us without the smallest interruption, and until this occasion without the
slightest suspicion, ever has been, and still is, very dear to my heart.
There is no office which I would not resign, rather than give a just
occasion to one friend to forsake me. Your motives for writing to
me, I have not a doubt were the most pure and most friendly; and
I have no suspicion that you will not receive this explanation from
me in the same candid light."[34]

When Jefferson received this reciprocation of eagerness to make
amends, he should have let well enough alone. But instead he took
up his pen again, this time to convince Adams that the note had not
really had the virulent effects that Adams imagined. The controversy had only become controversy, Jefferson argued, when "Publicola" had attacked Paine's pamphlet. Only then had the Paineites
retaliated with their angry articles. "To 'Publicola,' then, and not
in the least degree to my note, this whole contest is to be ascribed
and all its consequences," Jefferson insisted. This was a weak point
at best; considering the present newspaper venom pointed at him,
Adams must have felt disheartened to read it. Furthermore, in view
of the positive tone with which Jefferson had assured Washington
that he had meant Adams' *Discourses* when he referred to "political
heresies," the additional point now made by Jefferson rang hol-
lowly. It had been impossible that his note should bring into question Adams' name, wrote Jefferson, "for so far from naming you,
I had not even in view any writing which I might suppose to be
yours, and the opinions I alluded to were principally those I had
heard in common conversation from a sect aiming at the subversion
of the present government to bring in their favorite form of a King,
Lords and Commons."

"Thus, I hope, my dear sir," he continued, "that you will see me
to have been as innocent *in effect* as I was in intention. . . . The
business is now over, and I hope its effects are over and that our
friendship will never be suffered to be committed, whatever use
others may think proper to make of our names."

He finished with a remark on the King's flight from Paris and his
recapture. Jefferson had still not changed his mind, he said, "as to

the favorable issue of that Revolution, because it has always rested on my own ocular evidence of the unanimity of the nation and wisdom of the patriotic party in the National Assembly."[35]

Although their correspondence continued on a businesslike basis after this episode, the friendship of Adams and Jefferson had suffered a harsh blow. It became more and more obvious to both that their political views did differ. Moreover, Adams could easily perceive that Jefferson was beginning to assert leadership of the democratic party. Nor did Jefferson keep silent about his exchange with Adams over the Paine pamphlet. In a few days he mentioned to Hamilton that he had received a letter from Adams denying that he was "Publicola" and denying that he ever wished to bring the United States under a hereditary executive or senate. Hamilton, upon hearing this, then spoke critically to Jefferson of Adams' writings, the *Discourses* in particular, "as having a tendency to weaken the present government. . . ." It was his own opinion, said Hamilton, though he did not air it publicly, that the present American government would never be able to maintain stability and that it would "probably be found expedient to go into the British form." But since Americans had undertaken this course, he was for giving it a fair trial. The success they had met so far, he confessed, far exceeded anything he had ever expected; and even if the present form did not succeed, there were all sorts of improvements that might be innovated before giving up on the republican form. After all, thought Hamilton, ". . . that mind must be really depraved which would not prefer the equality of political rights which is the foundation of pure republicanism, if it can be obtained consistently with order." Consequently, "whoever by his writings disturbs the present order of things is really blamable, however pure his intentions may be," and Adams' intentions were pure, he was certain.[36]

Publicly, however, Hamilton defended Adams in his writing of the *Discourses*. In the "Catullus to Aristides" letters published the following year in the *Gazette of the United States*, Hamilton, while sidestepping the charge of hereditary distinctions, nonetheless spoke of Adams as "pre-eminent for his early, intrepid, faithful, persevering, and comprehensively useful services to his country—

a man pure and unspotted in private life, a citizen having a high and solid title to the esteem, the gratitude, and the confidence of his fellow-citizens."[37]

On the other hand, Jefferson, much as he had taken pains to explain an embarrassing situation to Adams, had almost at the same time written to Monroe, implying he thought Adams had written the "Publicola" papers. In order to deny authorship, said Jefferson, Adams would have to disavow both the *Discourses* and the *Defence*.[38] To William Short in Paris, Jefferson denounced not only Adams but Hamilton, Jay and Knox, accusing them of being monarchists.[39]

In the jotted notes later known as *Anas*, part of which was his sketch of the conversation with Hamilton concerning Adams, Jefferson set down that ". . . Mr. Adams had originally been a republican." But influenced by his sojourn in Europe he had come to believe in monarchy. With his politics made known through the *Defence*, he had been taken up on his return home by the "monarchical Federalists," who influenced him to think that Americans generally favored monarchy. He then wrote his *Davila*.[40]

Even Benjamin Rush, to whom Adams had so emphatically denied charges of monarchism, remained unconvinced of Adams' republican allegiance. Rush had not changed his mind in 1795 when he wrote Horatio Gates, inviting him and his wife to visit the Rushes in Philadelphia. "Let us feast once more," wrote Dr. Rush, "before we are parted by the grave, upon the republican principles and maxims with which our bosoms glowed in the years 1774, 1775, and 1776. We will fancy Richard H. Lee and Samuel Adams are part of our company. John Adams, who once took the lead in our republican conversations, shall not be of our party. We will still respect him for his integrity, while we deplore his apostasy from his first love."[41]

Adams had never anticipated the harshness of the denunciation that would shower upon him, first, because of his views on honoring men of position with titles, and, second, because of his *Discourses* — and even because of the *Defence*, which now was often dragged into criticism. The outrage with which the democrats reviled him stunned, shocked, and angered Adams, who increasingly felt that the country he had long served had turned its back upon his loyalty. Further, it only confirmed his faith that only a balanced government could control vicious factions. For years to come, Adams would be hounded as a monarchist, an aristocrat, an advocate of unrepublican pomp and an hereditary executive and senate. Though he exonerated himself at every turn, his explanations fell upon deaf ears that preferred to listen to voices more pleasing to their sentiments. To some extent Adams had brought such stricture upon himself. He spoke out too often, too plainly. He was too intellectual for most politicians. who could not fathom his disinterested, nonpartisan spirit, let alone his heavy writings steeped in history that they neither understood nor cared about. Moreover, his enemies could ask for no juicier bait with which to snag him than his own works—his own works read carelessly, then passed around by word of mouth. By his writings, unfolded before the eyes of unknowledgeable enemies—and friends, too—Adams did himself harm. His mind ranged too deep, too far backward into history, too far forward into the future, for most men. And so they took what they could of him—often to the detriment of the real meaning of his works.

But in addition, another factor blew Adams' writings into the gales of debate—that was the party spirit, which during the 1790's roared as wildly as at any time in United States history. With Massachusetts as the Federalist home base and Virginia the democrat and the Middle States as the object of a tug of war between them, the country swayed perilously before each fresh blast of factional fury. By the summer of 1792, factions had become parties, even beginning now to call themselves Federalists and Republicans.[42] The French Revolution, first, strongly influential in all of Europe, and, second, Hamilton's financial policies divided Federalists and Republicans more than any other two issues. Almost to a man Federalists favored England over France in foreign affairs, fearing the French Revolution, and advocated Hamilton's policies. Republicans viewed the French Revolution as an offspring of their own, England as the seedbed of aristocracy and monarchy, Hamilton's innovations, particularly the Bank, as an odious club for Northern speculators to brandish over Southern heads. Philosophy played only a small part in these party divisions—sectional economics meant much more. Merchants, sea traders, investors, mostly Northern, but also in coastal towns south to Charleston, lined up as Federalists, whereas planters and farmers with their wealth primarily in land declared themselves Republicans. Where men of both economic interests lived, as in New York and Pennsylvania, there were hot disputes between the parties. Local politics, as usual in America, played a role, too, explaining why planter-hating frontiersmen of the Shenandoah Valley could remain Federalist and some rural New Englanders could join the Republicans.

The President hesitated to run again in the election to take place in November, 1792. But Hamilton realized no other man but Washington could unite both parties. Jefferson sensed his own party was still too weak to put forth a candidate. After the two secretaries had persuaded Washington to seek a second term, the question of candidacy devolved to the Vice-Presidency. Once again, Adams did not intend to pant for office. He would remain in Quincy (the northern parish of Braintree had separated and been renamed Quincy) until he heard the outcome of the election. He knew that Clinton would be his competitor—that grasping Clinton who had run for governor against Jay, lost, demanded a recount, and won upon dubious statistics. He knew that Sam Adams and John Hancock were Clinton men—and, sadly, that his friend, Dr. Rush, had become a Clinton backer. Clinton had in mind no doubt to combine New York's governorship with the Vice-Presidency. Nonetheless, Adams refused to fight for office.

Hamilton, so firmly the Federalist leader that he no longer feared Adams in office, acknowledged Adams was the logical Vice-Presidential candidate. Hamilton could not afford to let Adams lose the election to Clinton. Accordingly, Hamilton wrote to Adams in September advising him in the plainest terms to hurry on to Philadelphia.

"I learn with pain that you may not probably be here till late in the session. I fear that this will give some handle to your enemies to misrepresent, and though I am persuaded you are very indifferent, personally, to the event of a certain election, yet I hope you are not so as regards the cause of good government." He added even more strongly, "Permit me to say it best suits the firmness and elevation of your character to meet all events, whether auspicious or otherwise, on the ground where station and duty call you. One would not give the ill-disposed the triumph of supposing that an anticipation of want of success had kept you from your post."[43]

But Adams, troubled by bad teeth and inflamed eyes and by Abigail's poor health, refused to budge. Finally, as November edged to a close, he set off for Philadelphia.

When the election results came in, Adams saw reason to feel gloomy over a second failure to receive a large percentage of electoral votes. Washington took all 132, of course; but for the second position Adams received 77; Clinton got 50 in a New York–Virginia–North Carolina coalition; the new Republican state of Kentucky cast four for Jefferson; Republican Senator Aaron Burr of New York, who had formed a benevolent group, the Society of Tammany, into a powerful machine to rival Hamilton, got one vote from South Carolina.

Adams' second administration as Vice-President meant another painful term in the passive role of presiding rather than debating. He felt ungracious and grumpy over the acid campaign the Republicans had waged against him. He viewed sorrowfully the increasingly caustic party collisions that racked the country more violently than in its first four years. All the same, he could take some melancholy comfort in the fact that to some extent, at least, the monkey of the public eye had leaped from his own to the backs of Hamilton and Jefferson, who snarled in unceasing party debate. Though the Republicans still denounced him as a monarchist, Adams wrote no more political treatises to reinforce their wrath. For a little while the greatest thrust of public censure fell upon other men.

With news in America that the French National Convention had declared war on Austria and Prussia and had abolished the mon-

archy, proclaiming the country a republic, American Francophiles
rejoiced exuberantly. A French fever so seized the nation with
affection for a sister republic that even Bostonians took to address-
ing each other as "Citizen" and "Citizeness." Everyone but himself, it seemed to Adams, hailed the magnanimity of the French
Convention in promising to assist all countries that wanted to overthrow their kings.

But in April, 1793, came crashing news—not only had France
declared war on Britain, Spain and Holland but had guillotined
Louis XVI. The rightist party, the Girondists, now in power had
decided to send Citizen Edmond Genet to America as minister
from France.

Washington met immediately with his cabinet, initiating a fresh
hostility between his two top secretaries. Although both Hamilton
and Jefferson agreed upon the necessity to maintain neutrality, they
diverged upon the question of the Franco-American alliance of
1778. That alliance had bound the United States to guarantee
French possession of her West Indian islands in case they were
attacked, a promise that Hamilton hoped to escape, fearing it would
precipitate a disastrous American war with Britain. Jefferson, on
the other hand, although he knew the United States could ill afford
a war with anyone, felt the government should honor the terms of
the alliance. Washington saw that neutrality was imperative; consequently he issued on April 22, 1793, the controversial Neutrality
Proclamation, after which the Neutrality Act of 1794 was modeled.
The Proclamation voiced the favorite American doctrine that "free
ships make free goods"—which meant that enemy goods not spe-
cially designated as contraband could not be seized when carried
in neutral ships. Americans always insisted that as neutrals they
could rightfully carry enemy goods. Britain, however, would never
tolerate America's supplying her enemies and consistently overlooked the American slogan.

Citizen Genet now came upon the scene to begin an episode that
would result in mischief for the American government and embarrassment for Jefferson, who all this time had fostered popular enthusiasm for France. Genet from the start acted in unorthodox

fashion. First of all, he landed in Charleston rather than Philadelphia; he immediately outfitted privateers against the British—
then proceeded triumphantly to Philadelphia, so feted and acclaimed along the way that he surmised that Americans were even
greater French lovers than he had expected. Wherever Genet went,
Americans were prompted to organize Jacobin clubs, or Democratic Societies, modeled after the Jacobin Society of Paris, dedicated to cultivation of "rational liberty," republican government
and ardor for the French cause. Communicating through committees of correspondence, these societies, the Federalists believed,
presaged nothing but trouble for the American Constitution.

Genet intended to obtain, as his instructions dictated, every
American aid in the war against Britain. Besides sending out privateers from America to prey upon British commerce, he planned to
pry Louisiana from the hands of Spain, a British ally. To execute
this scheme, Genet took George Rogers Clark and others into his
pay in a private French army. Fortunately for American neutrality,
Washington and his cabinet caught wind of this plot that would
have put America at war with Spain. Furthermore, Hamilton
nipped in the bud Genet's intention to finance his plan by obtaining
advance payments on the American debt to France.

Finding that the administration thwarted his designs, Genet decided that if he could not achieve his ends through the government,
then he would go over its head to the people by pressing for a
convocation of Congress. But he overestimated his popularity. By
this time Washington and his cabinet, even Jefferson, had become
so thoroughly disgusted with the young Frenchman that they requested his recall. Robespierre, who with the leftist Mountain Party
had replaced the Girondists, readily acquiesced. Rather than send
the Girondist Genet home to the executioner, however, Washington allowed him to remain in America, where he eventually married
Governor Clinton's daughter, assuming the life of a Hudson Valley
farmer.

To Adams, who had always tried to apply to political problems
experience and the principles of human nature, the worship of pure
reason that engulfed the French Revolutionaries and their Ameri-

can sympathizers seemed the most dangerous folly. When men under the egoism of pride threw aside history in favor only of the recent manufacture of their own reason, they almost certainly headed for failure. To see that so many Americans marched under the banner of the cult of reason alarmed Adams all the more when he observed that Robespierre was leading the Revolution into the Reign of Terror. Adams had read too much history not to perceive sinkingly that the dark panther of tyranny slunk ominously through this revolution.

In the meantime, Washington's cabinet was cleft so deeply over the French question and the Genet affair that Jefferson, on the last day of 1793, resigned his secretaryship. Free from the open broils of political warfare, he could now take his ease at Monticello, bolstering his party indirectly from his position in the wings. Adams rather envied Jefferson his shelter from the tumult, writing him in April, 1794, "I congratulate you on the charming opening of the spring and heartily wish I was enjoying of it as you are upon a plantation, out of the hearing of the din of politics and the rumors of war."[44]

Jefferson replied that he had returned to farming "with an ardor which I scarcely knew in my youth," that he had let his studying slide, putting off answering his letters "farmerlike, till a rainy day. . . ." He added then, "My countrymen are groaning under the insults of Great Britain," meaning the British seizures of American ships carrying goods to the French West Indies. "I hope," continued Jefferson, "some means will turn up of reconciling our faith and honor with peace; for I confess to you I have seen enough of one war never to wish to see another."[45]

The continued seizures of American ships had put Congress in a bellicose mood. After putting an embargo on the seaports, their spirit grew more inflamed when they heard rumors that British officials were offering promises of aid to the Indians if they would drive the Americans south of the Ohio River. Realizing that Congress was angry enough to risk war, the British foreign minister revoked the order-in-council that allowed English ships to capture American vessels in the French West Indies.

Washington then appointed Jay as envoy to Britain to negotiate a treaty. The President had considered Adams and Jefferson, as well, but Hamilton urged him to choose Jay. Adams looked favorably upon Jay's appointment, hoping the Chief Justice could avert war. He himself had just done what he could to that end by giving the deciding vote against a bill that would have ended commercial traffic with Britain.

"The President has sent Mr. Jay to try if he can find any way to reconcile our honor with peace," Adams wrote to Jefferson. "I have no great faith in any very brilliant success: but hope he may have enough to keep us out of a war. Another war would add two or three hundred millions of dollars to our debt, raise up a many-headed and many-bellied monster of an army to tyrannize over us, totally disadjust our present government, and accelerate the advent of monarchy and aristocracy by at least fifty years.

"Those who dread monarchy and aristocracy and at the same time advocate war are the most inconsistent of all men."[46]

Adams presumably found the results of Jay's Treaty as satisfying as he could expect. Even though tempers flared throughout the nation in vehement protestation that Jay had sold his country, Jay actually had accomplished something solid. America had stayed out of war, gained a promise of British evacuation of Northwest posts, obtained permission for some American trade with the British West Indies, kept American territory intact, gained access to the West, and referred the Maine boundary to the work of commissions. Jay's Treaty, however, would inflict a headache upon Adams, for it would figure as a major issue in the Presidential election of 1796.

Hamilton, meanwhile, was becoming as exasperated a cabinet member as Jefferson had been. Insulted and angered by a congressional investigation into his public finances—which, as well as his private ones, were always impeccably scrupulous, even though some of his aides engaged in questionable schemes—Hamilton resigned as Secretary of the Treasury in January, 1795.

The cabinet now took shape in a form that would bedevil Adams in his Presidency—all Federalist, all Hamilton apostles. To replace

Hamilton, Washington named Oliver Wolcott, then first auditor of the Treasury. James McHenry was Secretary of War. Timothy Pickering had been named Secretary of State in the stead of Edmund Randolph, who had resigned in disgrace. Hamilton had gone home to practice law—but the specter of his influence did not leave Philadelphia. Adams would feel it until almost the end of his Presidency.

CHAPTER XV

THE PRESIDENCY

WHOEVER won the 1796 Presidential election would inherit a pot of boiling party animosities that not even Washington in a third term could have quieted. The Jay Treaty debate of the spring of 1796 provided the bitter ingredient to keep the soup seething. Republicans, both convinced that the treaty would make America a British servant and blocked by a heavy Federalist majority in the Senate, initiated acrimonious controversy in the House. Proposals flew back and forth to give the House a voice in the treaty-making process and to cut off appropriations necessary to put the treaty into effect. Adams predicted to Abigail, however, that the treaty would pass.[1] He proved correct; the treaty did pass, a tormenting thorn in the side for the Republicans—and for the French Directory, which saw it as an Anglo-American confederation. The next Presidential administration would begin office burdened with this grim French disapproval.

Washington, weary and disillusioned, determined to retire to Mount Vernon at the end of his term. That meant serious consequences for Adams, who speculated "what my duty will demand of me." Admittedly, it was "no light thing to resolve upon retirement," for he saw that "my country has claims, my children have claims, and my own character has claims upon me; but all these claims forbid me to serve the public in disgrace." He loved his country "too well to shrink from danger in her service"; yet, he ought to have "a reasonable prospect" of serving to his nation's "honor and advantage." If he thought that he lacked either abilities or public confidence to a sufficient degree, then he ought to decline the Presidency. In any case, he would certainly never serve as Vice-President under anyone else but Washington, particularly if the new President were of the opposite party. It would be "a dangerous crisis in public affairs," he thought, anticipating the snags of the Constitution's electoral system, "if the President and Vice-President should be in opposite boxes."[2]

Washington apparently expected that Adams would succeed him. He invited Adams to dine with him several times, prompting the Vice-President to remark in jocular confidence to his wife, "I am, as you say, quite a favorite. I am to dine today again. I am heir apparent, you know, and a succession is soon to take place." Then more seriously he added, "But whatever may be the wish or the judgment of the present occupant, the French and the demagogues intend, I presume, to set aside the descent."[3]

As a personal matter, the question for Adams stood simply, or so he thought—"between living at Philadelphia or at Quincy, between great cares and small cares." Regardless of how the issue resolved itself, he felt satisfied that he had faced it squarely, finding no shameful deeds to hide: "I have looked into myself and see no meanness nor dishonesty there. I see weakness enough, but no timidity."

Nonetheless, so many conflicting emotions swarmed upon him when he thought about the Presidency. "I hate to live in Philadelphia in summer," he told Abigail, "and I hate still more to relinquish my farm. I hate speeches, messages, addresses and answers, proclamations, and such affected, studied, constrained things. I hate levees and drawing rooms. I hate to speak to a thousand people to whom I have nothing to say. Yet all this I can do. But I am too old to continue more than one, or, at most, more than two heats; and that is scarcely time enough to form, conduct, and complete any very useful system."[4] Ambition beckoned him toward the summit of public honor in America; love of home and farm pulled him toward the comfort of Quincy. Duty required that he submit "to the voice of the people in this case, which is the voice of God."[5]

With Washington out of the picture in this election, the Republicans sensed that for the first time they might have a chance of victory. With a pugnacious snarl they dashed into the race, glad for opportunity to stretch their electioneering legs in behalf of their unquestioned favorite, Jefferson. They received competent aid in Pierre Adet, new French minister, who entered more actively into an American election than any representative of a foreign power before or since. Adet had Benjamin Bache publish in the Philadelphia *Aurora* four explosive diplomatic notes specifying, first, that France would have its way with American shipping, regardless of American pretensions to neutral status; second, that French citizens in the United States should don the French tricolor; third, that full French diplomatic relations with America would be suspended; and, finally, that Jefferson was a man of high republican principle. When Secretary of State Pickering, hawk-nosed French hater, answered Adet in a furious open letter, the French minister replied with a similar document in which he campaigned frankly for Jefferson.

Since Jay's name had been so vilified in the treaty debate, the Federalists could not boast such a complete favorite as Jefferson. Thus, Adams, depicted as more moderate than either Jay or Hamilton, appeared the obvious candidate. Some Republicans even played with the notion of running Jefferson for President and Adams for Vice-President. Again, however, Hamilton hatched a scheme different from anyone's.

Hamilton, disliking Adams even as he did, grudgingly admitted that the bulk of Federalists, particularly in New England, supported him for President. Adams' high achievements in the service of his country and his prestige among fellows of his party precluded the Federalists from choosing any other candidate. The problem, then, rested on the selection of a Vice-Presidential candidate. Just as the Republicans hoped to win some northern support by running Aaron

Burr of New York as their second man, Hamilton and the lieuten-
ants of his wing of the party, looking to the South for votes, resolved
upon Thomas Pinckney of South Carolina as their second candidate. Pinckney, who had just returned from Europe with a successful Spanish treaty that brought the acclaim of the South and West,
had earned the praise of southern congressmen. Hamilton perceived that here was a man who, if anyone could, might break the
Republican hold on the South. He further saw that if both northern
and southern electors voted for Pinckney as their second candidate,
then neither Adams nor Jefferson would win the Presidency, but
instead Pinckney would gain that prize. Hence, while outwardly
declaring Pinckney for Vice-President, Hamilton and his followers
furtively pushed him for President.

This time Hamilton did not try to deceive Adams, who realized
what a trap the Hamiltonians were attempting to spring.

"If Colonel Hamilton's personal dislike of Jefferson does not
obtain too much influence with Massachusetts electors," he commented to Abigail, "neither Jefferson will be President nor Pinckney Vice-President."

"I am not enough of an Englishmen, nor little enough of a
Frenchman for some people," he continued in an astute observation
of what would be his dilemma for the next four years. "These would
be very willing that Pinckney should come in chief. But they will
be disappointed." Perhaps Adams knew the hearts of New England
Federalists better than did Hamilton. He felt, moreover, that
Republicans who caught wind of the Hamiltonian scheme against
him bent a little in his favor. William Branch Giles, Madison's ally
in the House, had gone so far as to declare, Adams told his wife,
" 'The point is settled. The V. P. will be President. He is undoubtedly chosen. The old man will make a good President, too. . . . But
we shall have to *check* him a little now and then. That will be all.' "

"There have been maneuvers and combinations in this election
that would surprise you," Adams concluded. "I may one day or
other develop them to you."

"There is an active spirit in the Union," he said, referring to
Hamilton, "who will fill it with his politics wherever he is. He must

be attended to and not suffered to do too much."[6]

Yet despite his careful strategy, Hamilton's plan backfired. That New Englanders were a clannish group he had failed to recognize in all its intensity. Adams had never been especially popular (and would grow less so) with the Essex Junto, the top Massachusetts Federalists who came mainly from Essex County—such men as Fisher Ames, George Cabot, Stephen Higginson, John Lowell Sr., and Timothy Pickering. Nonetheless, he managed strong favor among the rank and file of Massachusetts Federalists—and what would the Federalist party be without Massachusetts—as well as among a considerable group in other New England strongholds. Hamilton seemed to forget that Adams had twice come in second only to the great Washington in number of electoral votes. Furthermore, by failing to realize the vigor with which New Englanders balked at voting for a Southerner, Hamilton instigated a split in the Federalist party that, rather than submerging Jefferson, would set him up in the second spot, in perfect vantage to succeed as President in 1800.

The senior Oliver Wolcott, governor of Connecticut and patriarch of his state's politics, exemplified the reaction to the Pinckney plot by the core of New England Federalists. Advised by his son, young Oliver, to vote for Adams and Pinckney, the governor explained how the electors had voted unanimously for Adams and had split their second vote between Pinckney and Jay. When he himself had gone to Hartford, the governor had intended to vote for Adams and Pinckney. Feeling "a strong repugnance" to the possibility of Pinckney's winning the Presidency, he still had thought voting for the two men a necessary risk. Other electors, however, voiced "a strong propensity . . . to secure, if possible, Mr. Adams' election as President." At length, they all decided "that we ought to run very considerable risk, rather than not secure, if possible, the election of Mr. Adams, and that it would be expedient to lessen Mr. Pinckney's vote to the amount of four or five."

The elder Wolcott's "strong wish that Mr. Adams might be elected President" arose from the Vice-President's "knowledge of all the public characters of his country" and from his experience.

On the other hand, Pinckney's acquaintances were "people whose political opinions we do not approve of. . . ." His stay abroad might have jaded his firmness or given foreign courts too intimate a knowledge of his vulnerable points. His election would mean "a partial triumph of the French and their traitorous American partisans"; Adams would never serve under him; and, finally, Pinckney, as a relative newcomer to the public scene, probably lacked "facility" and "intuitive perception." Last, Wolcott finished with a pronouncement that after the retirement of so esteemed a President as Washington, he knew ". . . of no southern character who can secure more than a small part of that confidence [of the northern states] in case of a war. . . ."[7] Plainly, New Englanders were not about to allow a southerner to slip in as President.

Still, even though Hamilton's scheme missed its end, it seriously cut down the vote awarded to Adams. It was a close election indeed —71 electoral votes for Adams, 68 for Jefferson, 59 for Pinckney. Adams claimed the rather humiliating distinction of being a President by three votes, a fact for which he never forgave Hamilton. All the same, by this time he was used to small victories. He had been handed a duty; he took it with matter-of-fact acceptance.

"John Adams must be an intrepid to encounter the open assaults of France and the secret plots of England in concert with all his treacherous friends and open enemies in his own country," he wrote Abigail. "Yet, I assure you, he never felt more serene in his life."[8] Abigail, too, felt the same resolution to duty. From Quincy she congratulated him upon his election: "My feelings are not those of pride or ostentation upon the occasion. They are solemnized by a sense of the obligations, the important trusts and numerous duties connected with it. That you may be enabled to discharge them with honor to yourself, with justice and impartiality to your country, and with satisfaction to this great people shall be the daily prayer of your A. A."[9]

Adams bore trouble upon his shoulders from the very outset of his administration. In the first place, he found himself in the impossible situation of being a plain man following a hero. Ambitious though he was, he knew better than to think that he could assume the commanding stance of a Washington. He inherited Washington's problems without the magic of Washington's name to help solve them. The great man's shadow overlay his administration, binding him to men and methods with which he might have preferred to dispense. Yet, even had he himself possessed the heroic magnetism of Washington, he undoubtedly would have lost the struggle to unify parties, because by 1796 parties had become an undeniable political fact of life.

In the second place, until a year before the end of his administration Adams contended with disloyalty among his own ranks. For several reasons he felt required to continue with Washington's cabinet, but he did not know until too late that Pickering, Wolcott and McHenry secretly took their orders from Hamilton. With no precedent for a change of cabinet with a change of President, most people seemed to assume that members of the cabinet remained in office until they chose to retire. At any rate, only Wolcott offered a resignation, which Adams refused. Further, Adams, like Washington, faced a grave patronage problem. If he fired these present men, who would replace them? After Randolph's downfall, not even Washington had been able to find a Secretary of State.

"Happy is the country to be rid of Randolph," Adams had commented at the time, "but where shall be found good men and true to fill the offices of government?" Washington had been refused by William Paterson of New Jersey, Charles Cotesworth Pinckney of South Carolina, Thomas Johnson of Maryland, Patrick Henry of Virginia and Rufus King of New York before he finally received a yes from Pickering. C. C. Pinckney, Pickering, John E. Howard of Maryland and Edward Carrington of Virginia had rejected invitations to the War Department, leaving him with McHenry. Adams had not blamed the men who had refused. "The expenses of living at the seat of government are so exorbitant, so far beyond all proportion to the salaries, and the sure reward of integrity in the discharge of public functions is such obloquy, contempt, and insult that no man of any feeling is willing to renounce his home, forsake his property and profession for the sake of removing to Philadelphia, where he is almost sure of disgrace and ruin."[10]

But Adams' most important reason for retaining Washington's cabinet lay in the fact that as a President by three votes he could not afford to risk splitting the party by firing them. Such small enthusiasm had been shown for his leadership that he felt bound to tread lightly to keep essential peace within the party.

Meanwhile, except for two Adams men, Attorney General Charles Lee and Benjamin Stoddert, the latter who would come into office a little later as Secretary of the Navy, Hamilton from his New York law office directed the cabinet members and the high Federalist wing of the party.

No one in Adams' cabinet was a brilliant man. Pickering, a hard-working, honest member of an old Salem family, had been an Indian agent and Postmaster General. More obligated to Washington than to Hamilton for his advancement, the fierce-tempered Secretary of State, even if following Hamilton's instructions, catered less to him than did either Wolcott or McHenry. In fact, Hamilton preferred to deal indirectly with Pickering through either of the other two.

Wolcott, as former auditor of the Treasury, had been under Hamilton's influence all along. Yet he exercised his own mind at times and was able, surprisingly enough, to play successfully both to Hamilton and Adams. Indeed, he alone of the three Hamiltonian cabinet members escaped dismissal by Adams in 1800.

Finally, James McHenry, who had served under Washington during the Revolution, was simply in over his head in his job with the War Department. Washington only as a last resort had asked him to serve and had found him exasperatingly incompetent. More a tool of Hamilton than any of the three men, McHenry appeared so bewildered in his job that he referred to Hamilton on every question.

Although Adams had gained a reputation for irascibility, he showed uncommon patience with his cabinet. Finally suspecting their allegiance to Hamilton rather than to himself, he nonetheless sought as long as he could to soothe troubled waters. Consequently, far from being his somewhat intolerant self, he actually used too easy a hand on his men. Elbridge Gerry, unpopular with the Essex Junto but always faithful to Adams, warned his chief about Pickering. He added further that Hamilton had tried to bring in Pinckney as President by surprise.[11] Adams replied, "Pickering and all his colleagues are as much attached to me as I desire. I have no jealousies from that quarter." If he actually believed, as he professed, that the Hamiltonians had simply been frightened by thoughts of Jefferson's possible victory into supporting Pinckney, meaning no dishonesty, an Albany friend a few days later convinced him otherwise, providing conclusive evidence that the Hamiltonians had secretly undermined Adams' position.[12]

In addition to the difficulties of being the man to follow Washington and contending with disloyalty among his cabinet, Adams confronted a foreign issue that whirlwinded into the major domestic issue of his administration. French depredations had increased American shipping losses. Shippers demanded redress for such arrogant disregard of neutral rights. France, the greatest world power, apparently yearned for war. How, then, was Adams to continue Washington's neutral policy, a policy he himself heartily endorsed —yet show France that he meant business without at the same time allowing America to become a British puppet? How, moreover, was this task to be accomplished without men, money, or, most of all, a strong navy? Firmness, insistence upon observance of American rights, prudence backed by a resolute spine was the only attitude he felt he could honorably take. To John Quincy at The Hague, about to go on to Lisbon as the new Portuguese minister appointed by Washington, Adams wrote:"My entrance into office is marked by a misunderstanding with France, which I shall endeavor to reconcile, provided that no violation of faith, no stain upon honor is exacted. But if infidelity, dishonor, or too much humiliation is demanded, France shall do as she pleases and take her own course. America is not *scared.*"[13]

Adams' guiding principle of foreign relations was the one that he had advocated as minister to France, Holland and Britain—"that we should make no treaties of alliance with any European power;

that we should consent to none but treaties of commerce; that we should separate ourselves as far as possible and as long as possible from all European politics and wars."[14]

However, a domestic fact complicated the picture. The Republican party, more than any party at any time in American history, identified itself with a foreign power. So intertwined were the French and Republican causes that the resulting hatred between parties nearly plunged the country into war with France.

Adams' attempted answer to these touchy problems typified his old theory of government arbitrated by the executive. In both foreign and domestic issues he sought to preserve the mediating role of the executive. He did not always succeed, of course, but even so he believed that he must pursue a moderate course through the thicket of party fighting.

Adams dreaded a situation in which President and Vice-President should be "in opposite boxes." He hoped at the beginning of his administration that he and Jefferson could work together. Never a hidebound party man anyway, Adams would have utilized the resources of men of both parties if he had had his way. Jefferson apparently shared some of these thoughts, for on December 28, 1796, just before all the election results were in, he had written Adams a cordial letter demonstrating that two eighteenth-century gentlemen of honor, who took their public service as a duty, could not be entirely separated by diverse political alliances.

"The public and the public papers have been much occupied lately in placing us in a point of opposition to each other," he wrote. "I trust with confidence that less of it has been felt by ourselves personally." News from Philadelphia, he went on, seemed to confirm what Jefferson had always anticipated—that Adams had been elected President. "I have never one single moment expected a different issue: and though I know I shall not be believed, yet it is not the less true that I have never wished it." He regretted the subtle election tricks of Hamilton, "who has been able to make of your real friends tools to defeat their and your just wishes."

When Adams should receive the Presidency, "no one," Jefferson assured him, "then will congratulate you with purer disinterestedness than myself." Jefferson would value the share that he himself had had in the vote, "as an evidence of the share I have in the esteem of my fellow citizens." But he would be relieved not to have to assume public office. "I have no ambition to govern men," he said, explaining:

> It is a painful and thankless office. Since the day, too, on which you signed the Treaty of Paris our horizon was never so overcast. I devoutly wish you may be able to shun for us this war by which our agriculture, commerce and credit will be destroyed. If you are, the glory will be all your own; and that your administration may be filled with glory and happiness to yourself and advantage to us is the sincere wish of one who, though in the course of our voyage through life various little incidents have happened or been contrived to separate us, retains still for you the solid esteem of the moments when we were working for our independence, and sentiments of respect and affectionate attachment.[15]

Unfortunately, Adams never received the letter. Jefferson enclosed it in another letter to Madison, directing Madison to decide whether it should be sent on to Adams. Thinking that the sentiments Jefferson expressed in the letter might put him in an embarrassing situation should Adams in the future advocate a policy that Jefferson could not accept, Madison kept the letter and so informed its writer.[16]

Even without this letter, a rapprochement between the two men still was a possibility in the early days of the administration. On March 3, the day before his inauguration, Adams called upon Jefferson. Washington had replaced the Anglophobe James Monroe with Charles Cotesworth Pinckney as minister to France. But Pinckney was suffering a bad reception in Paris. What did Jefferson think, Adams now inquired, of sending either a replacement for Pinckney or a new man or two to reinforce him? Adams asked about the possibility of either Jefferson or Madison serving as envoy, perhaps with Pinckney and Gerry. However, not only did Jefferson think that the Vice-President ought to remain in the country, but he detested the thought of another wearisome sojourn in Europe. Neither did he believe that Madison would consent to

leave. Adams agreed with Jefferson's opinion that his office required the Vice-President to stay home. After discussing other
possible men, Adams recorded, "We parted as good friends as we
had always lived; but we consulted very little together afterwards.
Party violence soon rendered it impracticable, or at least useless,
and this party violence was excited by Hamilton more than any
other man."

Adams then went to Secretary Wolcott, whom, he made clear,
he "had no thoughts of removing"; indeed, he "had then no objection to any of the secretaries." To the suggestion that Madison be
sent to France, either alone or with others, Wolcott replied heat-
edly, "Sending Mr. Madison will make dire work among the passions of our parties in Congress, and out of doors, through the
states!"

"Are we forever to be overawed and directed by party passions?"
Adams returned. He had approached the secretary in good humor,
but now Wolcott, expression distraught, blurted, "Mr. President,
we are willing to resign." Adams received this unexpected statement with veiled surprise, for he had not anticipated that the mere
mention of Madison's name would engender such resistance.
"Nothing was farther from my thoughts than to give any pain or
uneasiness," Adams declared. With tact unusual for him, he merely
answered, "I hope nobody will resign; I am satisfied with all the
public officers."[17]

After questioning the other cabinet members, Adams realized
that Madison's appointment would meet with so much opposition
that the Senate would doubtless veto him even if Adams should
name him. Consequently, Adams found himself in the embarrassing circumstance of having to tell Jefferson that he had changed his
mind on the question of Madison. Much as he wanted to take
advantage of Madison's abilities, ". . . the violent party spirit of
Hamilton's friends, jealous of every man who possessed qualifications to eclipse him, prevented it. I could not do it without quarreling outright with my ministers, whom Washington's appointment
had made my masters, and I gave it up. Yet Hamilton himself
intrigued in a curious manner. . . ."[18]

With so much cabinet opposition to Madison's appointment, the possibility for an entente between Adams and Jefferson ended. The President realized that if he were to keep any peace within his administration, he must consult the cabinet before mentioning proposals to Jefferson. The high Federalists of his cabinet and his Republican Vice-President were never likely to agree, it seemed obvious. Moreover, a letter of Jefferson's criticizing the May 16 speech the President would make to Congress soon leaked into Adams' hands. Adams received this news as ". . . a motive, in addition to many others, for me to be upon my guard," as "evidence of a mind soured, yet seeking for popularity and eaten to a honeycomb with ambition, yet weak, confused, uninformed, and ignorant. I have been long convinced that this ambition is so inconsiderate as to be capable of going great lengths."[19]

Adams' cabinet originally had strongly opposed the idea of Madison as envoy—and, indeed, of a new mission to France altogether. They found, however, that they must gulp down their recalcitrance, for Hamilton, they now discovered, approved of such a mission. Hamilton wrote to Wolcott on March 30, mentioning that he had heard rumors "that the actual administration . . .," that is, the secretaries, were "not averse from war with France. How very important to obviate this."[20]

Wolcott protested that he could never adopt "the idea of a commission consisting of Mr. Madison, or anyone like him . . . without the utmost reluctance"; he had "no confidence in Mr. Madison." Hamilton calmed him with the reply that Madison in combination with Pinckney and George Cabot would be a safe choice.[21] Hamilton, who at this time advocated a conciliatory policy toward France, knowing that America could ill afford war, recognized that Republicans would hardly put up with an all-Federalist mission; hence, for the sake of unity he intended to combine two Federalists with a Republican or political neutral. His views at this stage coincided with Adams'—a fact that made it possible for the President to receive approval from the cabinet. In later years Adams, knowing that these early days of harmony resulted merely from an accidental likeness of mind with Hamilton, accepted this fact with ill grace, declaring that Hamilton had copied his idea to beguile his way into public favor.

When Adams learned in April, 1797, that Paris had ousted C. C. Pinckney and had delivered the warning that "free ships, free goods" was no longer neutral policy, he requested from his cabinet answers to a list of questions on the French crisis. All but Charles Lee then turned to Hamilton for guidance. The cabinet agreed to a mission— but quarreled on the subject of who should go. John Marshall of Virginia and Pinckney they agreed upon—then pushed for Cabot. Adams preferred his Massachusetts friend, Justice Francis Dana. When Dana refused, Adams would hear of no one else but Elbridge Gerry. Gerry's nomination got through the Senate, much to the discomfiture of the high Federalists, accomplishing a bipartisan mission after all.

In the meantime, Adams had called a special session of Congress that convened on May 15. The next day he delivered his speech to Congress. Hearing the message, Jefferson and his Republicans grew more somber with what they believed to be each war-filled word. Adams gave a firm speech; not only did he inform Congress of Pinckney's humiliating dismissal and the Directory's March 2 proclamation to ignore neutral shipping rights, but he proposed a series of recommendations for strengthening of naval forces, for greater coastal defenses, increased artillery and cavalry regiments in the army, and finally, a provisional army. Adams intended to show France by these measures that he meant business; but that was all he intended to do. He had unmasked his entire program of emergency measures, the full list of actions he considered necessary to meet this crisis. To the Republicans his speech was tantamount to a declaration of war. To the Federalists it was proper resistance to disgraceful arrogance on the part of France. What neither party realized was that Adams had chosen to show his whole hand in the beginning. When the Hamiltonians urged stricter measures and a much larger army, Adams would fight these proposals both as an inevitable lead-up to war and a foolish barb with which to jab the Republicans. His May 16 speech expressed his first and final program.

After Pinckney had been rebuffed by the Directory and Adams had delivered his May 16 speech, war clouds hung ominously over the nation. Republicans, particularly, thought outright war was imminent. However, appointment of the three-man bipartisan peace mission ameliorated the situation for the time being.

Nonetheless, any optimism vanished within a few months, for the envoys spent a frustrating winter of 1797-1798 at the hands of the French Directory. President Adams received on March 4, 1798, grim news of the events that had transpired in France from October to January. The envoys reported in coded dispatches that they, too, had never received official recognition—in fact, that they had been expected to deal with unofficial agents who had demanded bribes as a prelude to negotiation. These monumental bribes were to consist of a United States loan to help France conduct her European war, as well as a direct grant to the Directory of a quarter of a million dollars. The shocked envoys refused to barter on these grounds.

Consequently, Talleyrand in March directed Marshall and Pinckney to return to America. But, thinking the third member of the commission more amenable to agreement, he urged Gerry to stay. Thrown into an awkward position, Gerry ultimately decided to remain as a private citizen, hoping to avoid complete suspension of diplomatic relations.

On the very day after he and the cabinet had received the envoys' dispatches, Adams announced to Congress that the trio had been turned away without hope of being received. Then, on March 19, when the dispatches had been fully decoded, Adams again told Congress that he could "perceive no ground of expectation that the objects of their mission can be accomplished on terms compatible with the safety, honor, or the essential interests of the nation." For that reason, he asked again for prompt defense measures. Finally, toward the end of the month he recalled the envoys.

Republicans, alarmed at events which seemed to be moving directly toward war, demanded that the papers of the envoys be made public. Federalists, anticipating that revelation would enhance their anti-French campaign, chimed in with requests for exposure of the documents. Thus, Adams on April 3 complied with the cries for revelation, releasing the dispatches to Congress but substituting for the names of the three unofficial French agents simply the letters X, Y and Z.

In the midst of the furor initiated by disclosure of the XYZ papers, John Marshall returned home. (Pinckney had taken his daughter on a tour of Europe.) Adams allowed Gerry to remain privately in Paris, provided that he would consent to no loans—"and therefore," Adams concluded, "the negotiation may be considered at an end."

"I will never send another minister to France," he declared to Congress, "without assurances that he will be received, respected, and honored as the representative of a great, free, powerful, and independent nation."[22] Surely, he thought, an honorable nation could take no other position—despite the woeful fact that it found itself in a near state of war with the most powerful country in the world.

This quasi-war with France meant profound domestic results for the United States. First of all, a militant anti-French spirit sent sympathy for the Republicans tumbling downward. Exuberance for national honor and resistance to French offenses rallied the public around the Federalist cause. With France a symbolic ogre, Republican party propaganda that had so long preached the kinship of the American and French revolutions with their common cause of liberty and democracy received only sneers and jest. The return of Marshall to America heightened the antipathy toward France. During the spring and summer of 1798 Congress established a navy under a separate department headed by Benjamin Stoddert, gave the President power to create a provisional army of ten thousand men (Hamilton, who had now grown militant, called for 50,000 men), did away with all treaties with France, passed the Alien and Sedition laws, provided for revenue for the defense program through a direct tax to be levied on the basis of land, houses and slaves. The Federalists held firm control and intended to keep it. To prevent the Republicans from recovering any of their lost ground, the high Federalists, if necessary, would declare war on France. If war would keep them in power and the Republicans properly in the shadow, then war it would be. As Fisher Ames wrote to Wolcott, the Federalists in Congress ought to go to "every proper length" to get their measures passed, "as no time seems to promise such success to rendering the Jacobin members obnoxious before another election." Further, though Ames did "not wish Congress to *declare* war, I long to see them wage it."[23]

The second result of the XYZ crisis was the remarkable popularity of Adams. Never a strong favorite of either his countrymen or the rulers of his party, Adams now received a flattering, gratifying rush of support.

From spring through the fall of 1798, Adams found himself deluged with the job of answering countless petitions and resolutions of individuals and groups of citizens who pledged their loyalty. Abigail wrote to her sister that "the public opinion" in Philadelphia was "changing here very fast, and the people begin to see who have been their firm unshaken friends, steady to their interests and defenders of their rights and liberties." Philadelphia merchants had prepared "an address of thanks to the President for his firm and steady conduct as it respects their interests." People had left off wearing the French cockade in their hats "and the common people say if Jefferson had been our President, and Madison and Burr our negotiators, we should all have been sold to the French...."[24] Addresses poured in from a group of 500 merchants, traders and underwriters, "highly approving the measures of the executive." Similar addresses arrived from the grand jurors of Philadelphia, from the people of Yorktown, from the mayor, aldermen and common council of Philadelphia, "a very firm and manly address." Others came from New York, Baltimore and Boston.[25]

Never so popular during all his years in the federal government, Adams, who relished glory despite lifelong protestations that he did not yearn for fame, was not one to turn aside from this opportunity. Always a patriot, always a writer whose pen thrilled to the chance to preach, particularly love of liberty and virtue, the President in his answers to the addresses called forth every zealous word in his

vocabulary. To the inhabitants of Bridgeton, New Jersey, he promised never to purchase neutrality "with bribes, by the sacrifice of
our sovereignty and the abandonment of our independence, by the
surrender of our moral character, by tarnishing our honor, by violations of public faith, or by any means humiliating to our own
national pride, or disgraceful in the eyes of the world. . . . "[26] To
the young men of Philadelphia he wished lives "long, honorable
and prosperous in the constant practice of benevolence to men and
reverence to the Divinity, in a country persevering in liberty and
increasing in virtue, power and glory." America , he said, "will look
to our youth as one of our firmest bulwarks."[27] By and large these
replies to the petitions contained noble, inspiring sentiments, full of
healthy vigor of a writer who warmed to his subject. Sometimes,
however, they wandered down an inflammatory alley, giving just
cause to those who have criticized Adams for fanning the already
incensed mood of the nation, providing an atmosphere for the
passage—even though he did not recommend them—of such fac-
tionally based measures as army-expansion, the direct tax and the
Alien and Sedition laws.

". . . I know of no government ancient or modern that ever
betrayed so universal and decided a contempt of the people of all
nations as the present rulers of France," Adams wrote to the Sons
of the Cincinnati of South Carolina. "They have manifested a settled opinion that the people have neither sense nor integrity in any
country, and they have acted accordingly." Likewise, he showed
imprudence, for example, in his reply to the grand jury of Dutchess
County, New York, in which he pointed out that distress in that
state, "if this has been owing to the influx of foreigners, of discontented characters . . . ought to be a warning. If we glory in making
our country an asylum for virtue in distress and for innocent industry, it behooves us to beware that under this pretext it is not made
a receptacle of malevolence and turbulence for the outcasts of the
universe."[28]

The Hamiltonian Federalists, however, rejoiced in the strong
tone of Adams' answers. George Cabot reported that "all men,
whose opinions I know, are unbounded in their applause of the

manly, just, spirited, and instructive sentiments expressed by the President in his answers to the addresses."[29] Yet Hamilton himself, realizing there must not be a slip in the Federalist program to preserve the newly won national unity, directed Wolcott that "there are limits which must not be passed, and from my knowledge of the ardor of the President's mind. . . I begin to be apprehensive that he may run into indiscretion. This will do harm to the government, to the cause, and to himself. Some hint must be given, for we must make no mistakes."[30]

All the same, Hamilton was far more disturbed by the more extreme statements that the impolitic Pickering handed out. Adams refrained from going so far as Pickering and, in fact, felt it improper to draw upon some of Pickering's suggested papers due to their radical expression. To avoid driving Adams down a path of diplomacy more independent of the high Federalist line, to which the President would move inevitably if he continually felt obliged to reject Pickering's papers, Hamilton rushed to shore up his own influence by curbing the Secretary of State.

Another important domestic effect arose immediately from the XYZ affair. That, of course, was passage of the infamous Alien and Sedition laws. Advanced by such high Federalists of the second session of the Fifth Congress as Senator James Hillhouse of Connecticut and Representatives Harrison Gray Otis of Massachusetts, John Allen of Connecticut and Robert Goodloe Harper of South Carolina, the Alien and Sedition laws were ill-conceived measures designed to muzzle the Republican party which the Federalists so feared and equated with the French effort. Caused both by the frantic terror with which the Federalists viewed a possible Republican accession to power and the vicious dagger thrusts by the newspapers of both parties, the laws sprang out of the white heat of public indignation that followed release of the XYZ papers.

The first piece of legislation, the Naturalization Act, revised the Naturalization Law of 1795, which had lengthened to five years the period of residence that foreigners must spend in the United States before becoming citizens. Distressed by the numbers of foreigners who joined Republican ranks, the Federalists in the 1798 act extended the residence requirement to fourteen years, five of those in the state where the alien intended to live. Moreover, five years before citizenship, he must declare his intention to be naturalized. Finally, the act put all white aliens under a system of national registration.

Two alien laws were passed in 1798. One, the Alien Enemies Act, received both Federalist and Republican support as a measure to be put into effect during wartime. After the President proclaimed a state of war, alien enemies, or citizens of the enemy power, should be apprehended and removed from the country.

The most controversial of the alien laws, the Alien Friends Act, applied both to peacetime and wartime. Supported only by Federalists, this bill was a temporary two-year action intended to cover the possibility that war might not be declared. Regardless of whether the country was at peace or war, any alien, by order of the President, could be arrested and deported by federal marshals. The President received enormous discretion, for he could deport not only those he judged to be dangerous to the national safety but those he *suspected* were involved in some treasonable activity. The President was to give notice of the time allowed for departure. But although an alien could present evidence in his own behalf, he could not do so until after he had been ordered to depart. He could, however, take his property with him. If the alien could prove to the President that he had not engaged in secret or treasonable activity, then the President might issue him a license to remain. Numerous tags were attached to the license, nevertheless; the President, for instance, could revoke it at will. If an alien were found at large after his allotted time for departure ended, then he could be deported bodily or tried for failure to obey the deportation order. If convicted, he might receive a three-year imprisonment and be forever excluded from citizenship. Finally, masters of all vessels were to list entering aliens and file the list with customs collectors.

Since the United States did not declare war during the Adams administration, the Alien Enemies Act never went into force. Even though President Adams signed several blank deportation warrants, nobody was deported under the Alien Friends Act, either.

Last came the Sedition Law, harshest and most notorious of all. Anyone conspiring against operation of the federal laws could be punished by not more than five years' imprisonment and a fine of not more than $5,000. Further, anyone who wrote, printed, uttered or published any false, scandalous and malicious statements against the government, Congress or President, with intent to defame the government or the President or to excite against them the hatred of the people of the United States, could be punished by a fine of not more than $2,000 and by not more than two years in prison. Some twenty-five men were arrested under this law; of those, ten were convicted and jailed or fined.

The Alien and Sedition laws arose from several sources. First, Federalist judges seemed to show sympathy for such laws. Chief Justice Francis Dana of Massachusetts and Supreme Court Justices James Iredell and Samuel Chase occasionally had expressed their agreement.

Second, the doctrine that the common law of England was part of the law of the United States was widespread among Federalists and a major argument for the Alien and Sedition laws. Chief Justice Jay, Justices Wilson and Peters had all upheld that doctrine as early as 1793; Chief Justice Oliver Ellsworth would do likewise in 1799. The theory directed that if Congress had not legislated on a specific question, then the federal courts could apply the common law answer whenever the matter became a federal question or came under federal jurisdiction. Consequently, this theory that the common law was already in force on the alien and sedition subject would, in Federalist opinion, actually make specific statutes unnecessary. Even before the Sedition Law went into force, there were already instances of arrest under the common law ruling on sedition. For this reason, Federalists were able to argue that the Sedition Law in fact did nothing more than to enact into statutory law the common law of seditious libel. The new statute allowed the defendant to offer truth as a valid defense against libel conviction. Thus, the Federalists declared, the Sedition Law actually softened the harshness of the common law ruling already in force. The

Federalists looked upon Republicans as Whigs had considered Tories during the Revolution. By doing so, they argued that the Alien
and Sedition laws were actually more lenient than the laws that
Congress had passed on the subject of Tories during the Revolution.

Whereas the Federalists argued that the common law on seditious libel was already in force, the Republicans rejected this opinion as opposing their idea that federal jurisdiction should be limited
to the delegated powers under the Constitution. Because of their
notion of limited jurisdiction, they further objected to trying cases
of libel in federal rather than state courts. Questions of libel had
formerly been tried in state courts. Vesting such jurisdiction in the
federal courts gave the Federalists a greater handle of censorship.

Both parties, furthermore, turned the issue upon the First
Amendment. With the common law already in force, according to
the Federalists, the Constitution gave Congress power to regulate
the press. The First Amendment simply reinforced that fact, said
the Federalists. On the other hand, the Republicans believed that
just in case the Constitution had allowed the remote possibility that
Congress could regulate the press, the First Amendment specifically denied that it could. Moreover, the First Amendment introduced something new; not only did it do away with prior
censorship, but it guaranteed free public discussion, a liberty surely
violated by the alien and sedition legislation.

In addition to the influence of Federalist judges and the doctrine
that the common law already ruled on the alien and sedition question, a third source of this legislation was the hue and cry of Federalist editors that their Republican opposition be put down.

Besides, British legislation and common law offered a precedent
for American alien and sedition legislation. The French Revolution
had cast a pall of horror in Britain as well as the United States.
During the 1790's the Pitt ministry had pushed through laws to
repel the shadow of the French Revolution. The American Alien
Friends Act, for example, was modeled after a similiar British law.

Finally, Adams' answers to popular addresses set a tone for passage of the Alien and Sedition laws. He could speak of "domestic

treachery" or of "divisions, sedition, civil war, and military despotism."[31] He, too, seemed to believe that the common law already applied in matters of aliens and sedition.

Because the Alien and Sedition laws ordinarily have been considered a blot on the Adams administration, there arises the question of how much Adams had to do with them. His grandson, Charles Francis Adams, who defined the Alien and Sedition laws as "acts borrowed from the extravagant apprehensions entertained in Great Britain of the spread of the revolutionary spirit, which proved of no practical value whatever to America, whilst they furnished an effective handle for attack against their authors,"[32] maintained that President Adams, beyond signing the bills, played no role in their passage and enforced them unenthusiastically. It is true that the high Federalists suggested and passed the legislation without consulting Adams. Moreover, although Pickering offered for Adams' speech of May 16, 1797, the idea of an alien law, Adams never, in any speech or in writing, recommended alien and sedition legislation.[33] Indeed, he scarcely ever mentioned the laws in any part of his writings.

A "gag law," he later called the Sedition Act in a letter to John Taylor of Caroline, Virginia.[34] On the other hand, he stated in later years to Rush that he had believed the Alien and Sedition laws "to have been constitutional and salutary, if not necessary."[35] Yet he wrote to Pickering in August, 1799, that he thought the Alien Law would never be effective.[36] He appeared, on the whole, to have borne no constitutional objections to the laws, having thought of them as in keeping with the common law tradition and the right of government to preserve itself. At the same time, he seemed to have considered them unwise and incapable of proper enforcement. He would one day write to Jefferson, ignoring the fact that the Vice-President voted only in case of a tie, "As your name is subscribed to that [Alien] law as Vice-President and mine as President, I know not why you are not as responsible for it as I am. Neither of us were concerned in the formation of it. We were then at war with France; French spies then swarmed in our cities and in the country. Some of them were intolerably turbulent, impudent and seditious. To check these was the design of this law. Was there ever a government which had not authority to defend itself against spies in its own bosom? Spies of an enemy at war? This law was never executed by me in any instance."[37]

Adams later attributed the Alien and Sedition laws to Hamilton's recommendation, saying, "Nor did I adopt his idea of an alien or sedition law. I recommended no such thing in my [May] speech. Congress, however, adopted both these measures. I knew there was need enough of both, and therefore I consented to them. But as they were then considered as war measures and intended altogether against the advocates of the French and peace with France, I was apprehensive that a hurricane of clamor would be raised against them, as in truth there was, even more fierce and violent than I had anticipated."[38]

Adams could sputter in annoyance over such a man as the Irishman William Duane, successor to Bache as editor of the *Aurora*, saying that "the matchless effrontery of this Duane merits the execution of the Alien Law. I am very willing to try its strength upon him."[39] Yet the President exhibited a marked reluctance to carry the Alien and Sedition laws into action. He showed leniency in a number of instances.[40] A particularly notable case involved a Pennsylvania German, John Fries, charged with treason and found guilty in the armed resistance to the direct tax that occurred in Northampton County, Pennsylvania, in the spring of 1799. Pickering urged that Fries be executed as an example to ward off future insurrection, commenting to Adams, ". . . painful as is the idea of taking the life of a man, I feel a calm and solid satisfaction that an opportunity is now presented in executing the just sentence of the law to crush that spirit, which, if not overthrown and destroyed, may proceed in its career and overturn the government."[41] But Adams' attention was arrested by a remark that Wolcott made in his explanation of the case, saying that the defense lawyer had insisted that Fries' offense did not amount to treason. Moreover, Fries had declared that greater men than he had been behind the insurrection.[42] Immediately, Adams requested of Attorney General Lee a list of reasons why the defense counsel had been of that opinion.

"The issue of this investigation has opened a train of very serious contemplations to me," he wrote Pickering on the same day, "which will require the closest attention of my best understanding and will prove a severe trial to my heart."[43] He bombarded Wolcott with questions—Was Fries a native or a foreigner? A man of property or in debt? Was he industrious or idle, sober or intemperate? "It highly concerns the people of the United States," he concluded, "and especially the federal government that, in the whole progress and ultimate conclusion of this affair, neither humanity be unnecessarily afflicted nor public justice essentially violated, nor the public safety endangered."[44] The court ordered a retrial for Fries; the jury again convicted him and two other men. Encouraged again by his cabinet to order execution, Adams instead pardoned all three men.[45]

In addition to public enthusiasm for war, the popularity of Adams and passage of the Alien and Sedition laws, there was one final domestic effect of the quasi-war with France—the most significant of all, the breach between Adams and the Hamiltonians over defense measures. John Quincy, who himself later left the Federalist party altogether, ascribed the beginning of that party's demise to the dispute over the army during 1798-1799. In the story of the fall of the Federalist party the split over the army meant more than any other issue of the four years of John Adams' administration.

Adams had outlined his full program for defense at the beginning of his administration. He had shown at that time that he considered these steps emergency actions to convince France that the United States would not stand for a flagrant abrogation of the 1778 treaty. If these measures brought war, then the United States would accept that consequence. Yet Adams made clear that he intended his policy to be defensive rather than offensive. After introducing his program all at once, he clung to his original plan. Adams stubbornly contested attempts by the Hamiltonians to intensify the scope of the program. Although he always championed a strong navy, once the threat of French invasion had subsided, he saw little need for a large provisional army. Especially after he began to suspect, in the fall of 1798, that the French would soon accept an American minister, Adams resisted attempts to strengthen the army.

But Hamilton, from the early days of defense planning, advocated a much heavier program. Whereas Adams proposed a provisional army of 20,000 men, a temporary unit with purpose only to deter invasion, Hamilton sought from the beginning to obtain a 50,000 -man force of permanent standing. He suggested to Pickering as early as March 17, 1798, that the President ought to recommend these measures to Congress: to arm merchant vessels; build frigates and sloops-of-war; provide the President with power to equip ships-of-the-line in case of "open rupture" with any foreign power; increase the regular army to 20,000 and the provisional army to 30,000, in addition to the militia; fortify the principal ports; suspend treaties with France; and, to finance this program, extend taxation and float a loan.[46] Three months later he amplified his revenue proposal to include, in addition to the $2,000,000 land tax, stamp duties on such items as hats and taxes on other property, as well as a loan of $10,000,000 with interest high enough to insure the loan at par.[47]

Adams, who urgently enough requested Congress to outfit the country for military emergency, had asked for a larger army, especially in artillery and cavalry. Even harder he had pushed for a navy, which he considered America's natural defense. He had agreed, too, to nullify the French treaties. Yet the Alien and Sedition laws, direct taxes, high interest loans, and a 50,000-man regular and provisional army had not been his suggestions. True, he had not vetoed any of these measures, but he had strongly opposed the taxes and the large standing army.

"The army was none of my work," he explained later. "I only advised a few companies of artillery to garrison our most exposed forts, that a single frigate or picaroon privateer might not take them at the first assault. Hamilton's project of an army of 50,000 men, 10,000 of them to be horse, appeared to me to be proper only for Bedlam. His friends, however, in the Senate and the House embarrassed me with a bill for more troops than I wanted."[48] Hamilton's army scheme had seemed to him "to be one of the wildest extravagances of a knight-errant," proving that "Mr. Hamilton knew no more of the sentiments and feelings of the people of America than he did of those of the inhabitants of one of the planets." The same question occurred to Adams as to the Republicans: Of what purpose would such an army be after the danger of invasion had passed? "Such an army without an enemy to combat would have raised a rebellion in every state in the union. The very idea of the expense of it would have turned President, Senate, and House out of doors." So substantial, however, was the Hamiltonian weight in Congress that, Adams remarked bitterly, "without any recommendation from the President, they passed a bill to raise an army, not a large one, indeed, but enough to overturn the then federal government."

As for Hamilton's tax program, Adams declared, "Seizing on all the taxable articles not yet taxed to support an army of 50,000 men at a time when so many tax laws, already enacted, were unexecuted in so many states, and when insurrections and rebellions had already been excited in Pennsylvania on account of taxes, appeared to me altogether desperate, altogether delirious."[49]

The high Federalists strove for a large standing army because, in fact, they needed war. In order to prevent the Republicans from recovering the public support they had lost after the XYZ incident, the Federalists felt they must push themselves further into a warlike posture. To Hamilton, Representative Uriah Tracy of Connecticut, Pickering, Sedgwick and Cabot, war was a preferable alternative to loss of power. However, not mere obsession with power motivated their besetting desire to remain in office. Hamilton, before the XYZ crisis, had led the group to see honorable peace as a desirable end. But when the Federalists saw that France had no intention of receiving an American mission, they believed war to be the only answer for a country that wished to maintain its independence and respect in the eyes of Europe. They gloried, too, in the ill fortune that, when Republican and French causes so intermingled, consequently befell the Republicans after the XYZ affair. Yet, they genuinely feared that if the Republicans should ever replace them in power, it would be a victory for the French as well—a victory, in turn, for the leveling hand of democracy. Equality, the perfectibility of man, the redistribution of property—concepts of the French Revolution—were sure to be taken up in full force by the Republicans, once they stepped into power. Constitutionality, protections for property, respect for aristocracy would amount to bywords of the past. The Federalists honestly felt that a Republican rise to power would mean a disastrous finish to the American republic.

Hamilton was too intelligent a man to embrace the thought of war with all the zeal that some of his faction displayed. George Cabot perhaps more truly expressed the sentiments of the high Federalists when he wrote: "It is unfortunate that Congress did not declare war; the danger of French artifice would have been less. It is impossible to make the people feel or see distinctly that we have much more to fear from peace than war; that peace cannot be real, and only leaves open a door by which the enemy enters, and that war would shut him out; that the French are wolves in sheeps' clothing, entreating to be received as friends, that they may be enabled to destroy and devour. But war, open and declared, would not only deprive our external enemy of his best hopes, but would also extinguish the hopes of internal foes. The rights and duties of every citizen in a state of war would be known and regarded; traitors and sedition-mongers who are now protected and tolerated would then be easily restrained or punished. I hope, therefore, we shall not long persist in pacific war, with one part of our citizens against us and another part neutral."[50]

Stephen Higginson even more outspokenly encouraged war, believing that "nothing short of this will depress effectually the French faction, or discourage the Directory from continuing their efforts to support their partisans in our country or councils." In short, "nothing but an open war can save us, and the more inveterate and deadly it shall be, the better will be our chance for security in future."[51]

The army issue became so violent in Federalist ranks that it resulted inevitably in a split. To Adams and like-minded Federalists, who detested standing armies and who intended to leave a door open for negotiation with the French, the use for a large army died away when the invasion danger withered. Republicans whispered in a feverish terror that the army would be used to suppress political opponents, and even Adams suspected that possibility. Even though no one ever proved that the Hamiltonians expected to use the army to squelch domestic violence rather than to repel invaders, the Republicans were well aware of Hamilton's faith in a standing army as a requisite for preservation of the law and order of government. Furthermore, some New Englanders firmly believed that southern Republicans were on the point of civil war; they would not have hesitated to use the army to put down rebellion. Hamilton pointed out to Harrison Gray Otis that any reduction of the actual army would suggest to the enemy that American resources were small. But in addition, "with a view to the possibility of internal disorders alone, the force recognized is not too considerable. The efficacy of militia for suppressing such disorders is not too much to be relied upon."[52]

After passage of the Virginia and Kentucky Resolutions that attempted to nullify the Alien and Sedition laws, Hamilton proposed several stringent actions to consolidate the strength of the national government, such as internal improvements, increased indirect taxes, expansion of the legal powers of the federal government by subdividing the larger states and, finally, stronger sedition laws. "Vigor in the executive is at least as necessary as in the legislative branch," he emphasized; "if the President requires to be stimulated, those who can approach him ought to do it."[53]

A further peculiar aspect complicated the army issue. Rufus King, American minister to Britain, felt that when France invaded Spain, as she was expected to do, the Spanish American colonial empire would collapse. Francisco de Miranda, who had waited for years in the pay of Britain for such an opportunity to liberate Venezuela from Spain, was to lead an army through South America. King and Hamilton concocted visions of grandeur of collaborating with Britain to provide an Anglo-American force that would swoop down from Louisiana to join Miranda in ousting the Spanish. Hamilton, who seemed to have hopes of leading the army himself, anticipated gaining East and West Florida and Louisiana from Spain. Adams heartily disapproved of the little he could surmise of the scheme, only to be embarrassed some years later by the participation with Miranda of his son-in-law William Stephens Smith and his grandson William Steuben Smith. What Adams knew of the proposed South American venture led him to think that it could not help involving the United States in a war with Spain.

The final breach between Adams and the Federalists over the army resulted, however, when high Federalists forced him to appoint Hamilton second after Washington in command of the army. Adams, gravely concerned over the threat of war, decided in June of 1798 that he should invite Washington to command the army. "I have no qualifications for the martial part" of Presidential duties, Adams wrote to Washington, "which is like to be the most essential. If the Constitution and your convenience would admit of my changing places with you, or of my taking my old station as your lieutenant civil, I should have no doubts of the ultimate prosperity and glory of the country." It was a mistake to call out Washington, Adams later conceded. Even greater was his misjudgment in agreeing that no one would be appointed to the general staff without Washington's consent.

"In forming an army," Adams mused to Washington, "whenever I must come to that extremity, I am at an immense loss whether to call out all the old generals, or to appoint a young set."[54] After accepting Adams' request to head the army, Washington made plain that he thought ". . . it will not be an easy matter. . . to find among the *old set* of generals men of sufficient activity, energy and health, and of sound politics, to train troops to the *quick step*, long marches and severe conflicts they may have to encounter. . . ."[55]

Though he advanced no higher than colonel in the Revolution, Hamilton was Washington's choice for second in command. Adams now found himself in an embarrassing squeeze, for what of the faithful old generals such as Knox, who as former Secretary of War would most certainly take offense at being bypassed? Knox did indeed feel degraded when he discovered that Washington had listed him as third of the major generals, after Hamilton and Charles Cotesworth Pinckney.[56] Adams, too, insisted that Knox be placed second to Washington, only to be stymied by Washington himself, who angrily protested, "In the arrangement made by me with the Secretary of War, the three major generals stood Hamilton, Pinckney, Knox; and in this order I expected their commissions would have been dated. This, I conceive, must have been the understanding of the Senate. And certainly was the expectation of all those with whom I have conversed. But you have been pleased to order the last to be first and the first to be last."[57] Four long months the struggle over the major generals continued; Adams refused to consent to having a man he despised handed so much authority in his own administration, but ultimately, when Washington threatened to resign and the Hamiltonian faction—which meant the Senate as well—demanded Hamilton, he relented. Nonetheless, that he had had to overlook the old Revolutionary generals who had shared with him that glorious period that he always viewed with patriotic sentiment, that Knox had been so angered as to refuse his appointment, stung him with mortification all the rest of his life. "I ought to have said no," he told Rush, "to the appointment of Washington and Hamilton and some others; and yes to the appointment of Burr, Muhlenberg, and some others. I ought to have appointed Lincoln and Gates and Knox and Clinton, and so forth. But if I had said yes and no in this manner, the Senate would have contradicted me in every instance. You ask what would have been the consequence. I answer Washington would have been chosen President at the next election if he had lived, and Hamilton would have been appointed commander-in-chief of the army. This would have happened as it was if Washington had lived, and this was intended. With all my ministers against me, a great majority of the Senate and of the House of Representatives, I was no more at liberty than a man in a prison, chained to the floor and bound hand and foot. . . . Washington ought either to have never gone out of public life, or he ought never to have come in again. . . . "[58]

Adams had long since found that he could not make any appointments contrary to the wishes of the Hamiltonians without their being vetoed in the Senate.

". . . I soon found myself shackled. The heads of departments were exclusive patriots. I could not name a man who was not devoted to Hamilton without kindling a fire. The Senate was now decidedly Federal. . . . And prosperity had its usual effect on Federal minds. It made them confident and presumptuous. I soon found that if I had not the previous consent of the heads of departments and the approbation of Mr. Hamilton, I ran the utmost risk of a dead negative in the Senate."[59]

This irked Adams, for he had high hopes of uniting the country through bipartisan appointment of officers.[60] Consequently, he did all in his power to build up the navy while frustrating Federalist attempts to build up the army. Believing so strongly that the navy was the proper defense for America, he told Abigail, "The English have exhibited an amazing example of skill and intrepidity, perseverance and firmness at sea. We are a chip of that block, and we could do as we pleased, at least as we ought upon the watery element, if it were not that we shall excite jealousy in the English navy. We must, however, stand for our right."[61] Adams worked with Stoddert to establish a navy with all possible haste. But he deliberately stalled on the appointment of army officers. To McHenry's urging that the President come to Philadelphia in October to discuss setting up the new military forces, Adams replied that his wife's serious illness kept him in Quincy until the opening of Congress. Abigail had indeed been almost at the point of death for several months.

"As to recruiting service, " Adams added, "I wonder whether there has been any enthusiasm which would induce men of common sense to enlist for five dollars a month, who could have fifteen, when they pleased, by sea or for common work at land."

Furthermore, he stated, "There has been no national plan that I have seen as yet formed for the maintenance of the army. One thing I know, that regiments are costly articles everywhere, and more so in this country than any other under the sun. If this nation sees a great army to maintain, without an enemy to fight, there may arise an enthusiasm that seems to be little foreseen. At present there is no more prospect of seeing a French army here than there is in Heaven."[62] Nine months later he wrote irritably to McHenry, "As it is an excellent principle for every man in public life to magnify his office and make it honorable, I admire the dexterity with which you dignify yours by representing an army, and means adequate to its support, as the first thing necessary to make the nation respected." As to the difference McHenry had with Stoddert, Adams stated clearly: "It would not be necessary for me to decide the controversy between you; if it should be, I should be at no loss. My answer would be ready."[63] His own allegiance was to the navy.

Hamilton, meantime, had become almost another member of the cabinet. From his post as Inspector General of the army, he led the inept McHenry along the path he wished him to take. Pickering and Wolcott, too, continued to do his bidding. Wolcott, relating sorrowfully to Hamilton that McHenry "does the best in his power, yet his operations are such as to confirm more and more a belief of utter unfitness for the situation," put in as well that the President refused to cooperate with the military program. "The President has been informed of the disorders in that department, yet there appears no disposition to apply any correction." Wolcott concluded with the offer to Hamilton that "if anything can and ought to be done, and I can be of any service, I will do it, however unpleasant."[64]

No longer, however, was Adams unaware of the power that manipulated his cabinet. From the beginning of the army wrangle, he had suspected the hand of Hamilton behind his difficulties. Sedgwick reported as much to Hamilton himself. One evening early in February Sedgwick called upon the President, who was alone. They discussed the military. After Sedgwick had expressed his views, Adams answered, "As to the Virginians, sir, it is weakness to apprehend anything from them [such as a rebellion]; but, if you must have an army, I will give it to you; but remember, it will make the government more unpopular than all their other acts. They have submitted with more patience than any people ever did to the burden of taxes, which has been *liberally laid on*, but their patience will not last always."

"During the time that I was with him," Sedgwick continued, "the bill before the Senate for the organization of the army was mentioned. He asked me what additional authority it was proposed to give the commander-in-chief. I answered, none; that all that was proposed was to give him a new title—that of general. 'What!' said he, 'are you going to appoint him general over the President? I have not been so blind but I have seen a combined effort among those who call themselves the friends of government to annihilate the essential powers given to the President. This, sir (raising his voice), my understanding has perceived and my heart felt.' After an expression of surprise and a declaration of belief that he was mistaken, with *all humility* I prayed him to mention the facts from which he had made this inference. He answered that if I had not seen *it*, it was improper for him to go into detail."[65]

By their direct taxes and their Alien and Sedition laws, upon which they had not consulted Adams, by their sympathies for war, their emphasis upon an army, particularly a standing army, rather than a navy and, finally, their elevation of Hamilton to the rank of Inspector General, second only after Washington, the Federalists had intended to drive down the Republicans. But they succeeded only in driving off their President from one faction of his party. He who prided himself upon his independence and who felt, moreover, a keen attachment to the concept of executive as mediator, arbitrator and champion of the people's liberties in the face of an encroaching House and Senate could no longer tolerate being someone else's errand boy. When he discovered that Hamilton was brandishing the whip; when he suffered the humiliation of being forced to accept Hamilton as an acknowledged, titled power in his administration; when he began to suspect that a conspiracy was afoot to raise Hamilton above his own head; and when he began to believe that the relish for war of Hamilton and his faction eclipsed both the danger of war and the popular support for it, he declared his independence. Seeking the advice of no one, he threw open the doors to a French peace.

CHAPTER XVI

A DECLARATION
OF INDEPENDENCE

JOHN ADAMS on February 18, 1799, did a notable and, to the Hamiltonians, a shocking thing. Without consulting his cabinet or anyone else, without a warning to anybody, he nominated William Vans Murray, minister to Holland, as commissioner to negotiate a new peace with France. This wholly unexpected move startled Republicans and Federalists alike. Hamiltonian Federalists greeted the nomination with offended anger that the President would act independently to wound their war program. More moderate Federalists were pleased but puzzled. Republicans were suspicious.

But for Adams this was no hasty decision. He had weighed this step for over four months—in fact, ever since Elbridge Gerry had returned from France on the first of October. Although Adams had allowed Gerry to remain in Paris, his friend's stay on unofficial grounds had embarrassed him. Now, however, much to the annoyance of the Hamiltonians, who did their best to discredit Gerry, the unofficial commissioner visited the President's home in Quincy. With cautious but interested ear Adams heard out Gerry. Talleyrand, Gerry insisted, was ready to make some kind of amends; the Directory had let up in its tough attitude toward America.

Far more significantly, Adams only a week after Gerry's return received dispatches from William Vans Murray reporting that France appeared to be worried that Britain was gaining support among the anti-French parties in Europe.[1] Because Adams had to send the dispatches to be deciphered, Pickering, too, was aware of the possibility of a softened French attitude. Moreover, Adams wrote to Pickering on October 20, inquiring whether the Secretary thought that the President, in case he received assurances that a minister would be received, should appoint such a minister to France.[2] Pickering never answered the letter nor acknowledged it.

At the same time, Rufus King wrote to Hamilton from London on September 23, and this letter would have arrived by early winter at the latest.

"You will have no war!" King declared. "France will propose to renew the negotiation upon the basis laid down in the President's instructions to the envoys—at least, so I conjecture."[3]

Even so, when Adams arrived in Philadelphia toward the end of November, 1798, he was met by a cabinet in a mood for war. Many of the party at this time pushed for a specific declaration of war. Some of the leading generals, including Hamilton and Pinckney, had gathered ahead of time to prepare the draft for part of a speech that they hoped Adams would deliver to Congress. They chose Wolcott to present the President with the recommended draft.

Adams had announced in June, 1798, that he never again would send a minister to France without assurances of his being received. He did not intend now to back down from that resolution. Nonetheless, when Wolcott showed him the proposed draft of the speech, there was one passage with which Adams could not concur. "... *the sending another minister to make a new attempt at negotiation would,*" the cabinet had written, "*in my opinion, be an act of humiliation to which the United States ought not to submit without extreme necessity. No such necessity exists.* It must, therefore, be left with France, if she be indeed desirous of accommodation, to take the requisite steps. The United States adhere to the maxims by which they have been governed. They will sacredly respect the rights of embassy. Their magnanimity discards the policy of retaliating insult in bar of the avenues of peace, *and if France shall send a minister to negotiate, he will be received with honor and treated with candor.*"[4]

Instead, Adams stated in the speech which he delivered on December 8, ". . . to send another minister without more determinate assurances that he would be received would be an act of humiliation to which the United States ought not to submit. It must, therefore, be left to France, if she is indeed desirous of accommodation, to take the requisite steps."[5] Not only did he allow France the opportunity to make those "assurances," but he relieved her of the necessity of being the first to send a minister. Ten years in Europe had taught him that France was a proud power who, if expected to make the first official overtures, would rather allow the half-war with America to continue indefinitely. And the United States, Adams realized, was probably more harmed by the "war" than France.

Pickering, meanwhile, did not cease his obnoxious behavior toward his chief. When Adams asked him on January 15, 1799, to draft a treaty and consular convention which the United States might accept, Pickering again ignored the direction. Dealings between the two men continued according to official civilities but grew increasingly cold and stiff.

All the while, William Vans Murray supplied Adams with further dispatches. In January both Pickering and Adams received copies of an amazing letter from Talleyrand to Pichon, French secretary of legation at The Hague, agreeing in the very words Adams had specified that if the United States should send an envoy to France, he would be received as the emissary of a free, powerful and independent nation.[6] Thomas Boylston Adams now arrived home from Europe with direct copies of the letter for his father, reinforcing Murray's assurances that Talleyrand had changed his mind. At the same time, John Quincy, who was now in Berlin as minister to Prussia and had already acquired the reputation of being the finest diplomat in the American corps, voiced his conviction that France would receive an American minister.

Adams made up his mind. Knowing that he would receive nothing but delays and arguments from his cabinet, he transmitted directly to the Senate on February 18 the Talleyrand-Pichon document together with the nomination of Murray as minister to France.[7] The turbulent protest with which the Hamiltonians received Adams' decision strained his patience but did not lessen his positive state of mind. He wrote to Abigail, "Your sickness last summer, fall, and winter has been to me the severest trial I ever endured. Not that I am at this moment without other trials enough for one man. I may adopt the words of a celebrated statesman, whom, however, I should not wish to resemble in many things. 'And now, good judge,' says he, 'let me ask you whether you believe that my situation in the world is perfectly as I could wish it; whether you imagine that I meet with no shock from my superiors, no perverseness from my equals, no impertinence from my inferiors. If you fancy me in such a state of bliss, you are wide from the mark!' "[8]

The great bulk of the Federalist party, the moderates, approved of Adams' action. Henry Knox wrote Adams saying that ninety-nine out of a hundred persons would share this approval but that the President should beware of the "hundredth part," those persons "who have an influence over the mind of that part and who affect to suggest to, correspond with, and even to influence the conduct of certain characters in the executive departments," who would "loudly fault the measure of the nomination." He himself thought that Adams' decision had been "one of the most dignified, decisive, and beneficial ever adopted by the chief magistrate of any nation, soaring above all prejudice and regarding the happiness of the nation as the primary object of his administration, and in the pursuit of which he nobly hazards his reputation until the mists of ignorance of party shall subside."[9]

The enraged Hamiltonians, however, now set about stalling the new mission. Sedgwick dashed off a note to Hamilton on the day after the announcement: "This measure, important and mischievous as it is, was the result of Presidential wisdom, without the knowledge of or any intimation to anyone of the administration. Had the foulest heart and the ablest head in the world been permitted to select the most embarrassing and ruinous measure, perhaps

it would have been precisely the one which has been adopted."
Hamilton returned an answer immediately—the Senate should try
to have the commission increased to three: "The step announced,
in your letter just received, in all its circumstances would astonish,
if anything from that quarter could astonish.

"But as it has happened, my present impression is that the
measure must go into effect with the additional idea of a commission of three.

"The mode must be accommodated with the President. *Murray*
is certainly not strong enough for so immensely important a mission."

Pickering wrote to Hamilton in utter despair. "We have all been
shocked and grieved at the nomination of a minister to negotiate
with France," he stated. "There is but one sentiment on the subject
among the friends of their country and the real supporters of the
President's administration. Pains have been taken to ameliorate the
measure by throwing it into a commission. But the President is
fixed. The Senate must *approve* or negative the nomination. In the
latter event, perhaps he will name commissioners. I beg you to be
assured that it is wholly *his own act*, without any participation or
communication with any of us." The foundation for Murray's
nomination, Pickering concluded, had been laid in Adams' speech
at the opening of Congress, in which he had "peremptorily determined (against our unanimous opinions) to leave open the door for
the degrading and mischievous measure of sending another minister to France, even without waiting for *direct* overtures from her."[10]

After holding off the President for a couple of days, the Senate
referred Murray's nomination to a Federalist commission of five,
headed by Sedgwick. The committee then made a rather irregular
call upon the President to try to persuade him to postpone the
nomination. Sedgwick outlined the visit for Hamilton's benefit. The
senators met with a stone wall, for throughout the conversation
Adams "declared repeatedly that to defend the executive against
oligarchic influence, it was indispensable that he should insist on a
decision on the nomination; and he added, 'I have, on mature
reflection, made up my mind, and I will neither withdraw nor

modify the nomination.' " Nonetheless, he was not opposed to a
joint commission—in fact if the Senate rejected Murray, then he
would propose a joint commission. Ultimately, the Senate did accept a commission of Murray, Chief Justice Oliver Ellsworth and
Patrick Henry. When Henry later declined, Adams nominated
Governor William R. Davie of North Carolina. "That," Sedgwick
mournfully told Hamilton, "is everything which, under the circumstances, could be done."[11]

If the Hamiltonians could not prevent the commission then they
hoped at least to delay it as long as possible. Throughout the summer and fall Pickering did his best to subvert the mission, an effort
made the more possible by the fact that Adams left Philadelphia
before the expected yellow fever epidemic and went home to spend
the summer in Quincy. Before leaving, however, he decided with
his cabinet the three points or *ultimata* that the United States
would consider as necessary to be accepted by France if negotiations should recommence—first, that France should pay indemni-
ties for spoliations upon American commerce; second, that
American vessels could not be seized for not having on board what
the French called a *rôle d'equipage*, and third, that the United
States would no longer promise, as she had by the 1778 treaty, to
guarantee the French West Indies. After Adams had left for
Quincy, Pickering put off as long as he could setting these instructions into formal shape.

Benjamin Stoddert now wrote Adams from Trenton, where the
cabinet had been forced to flee by the threatened yellow fever,
hinting that the President should come to Trenton.[12] With Abigail
again ill, Adams did not care to leave Quincy unless he had to. But
only a short time later he received a strange letter from Pickering,
stating that news from France indicated "that the dictatorial power
of the Directory is overturned," that a king might possibly be
returned to the throne, and that "the question of *suspending the
mission* seems to the heads of department to merit serious consideration."[13] Then Ellsworth wrote almost at the same time requesting
that if "the present convulsion in France" should persuade Adams,
"as many seem to expect," to postpone the mission, he would like

early notice of that fact so that he could conduct his circuit court.[14]

Recognizing that a plan brewed at Trenton, Adams announced that he was on his way and departed. He arrived at Trenton on October 10; Hamilton showed up, too. Throughout the ensuing showdown, Adams moved with what was for him astonishing coolness. If the cabinet were concerned about a turn of events in France, then he would consent to a delay until the last of October for departure of the mission. Yet when the cabinet began to talk exuberantly of recent British victories being sure to cause restoration of a Bourbon to the French throne, Adams realized that in their talk of postponement they aimed in fact for complete abandonment of the mission. He invited them to a cabinet meeting on the evening of October 15, to which they came expecting to hear that the mission would be called off. Instead, the President merely discussed some points of difficulty in the instructions to the commissioners. Eleven o'clock came and went; the cabinet had nothing to do but to approve the instructions and go home. Next morning, two of them received before breakfast the surprising directive from the President to make out the papers for the commissioners and to have a frigate prepared for them. The commissioners were to leave on or before the first of November. The cabinet had lost the battle to suspend the French mission; Ellsworth and Davie sailed on November 5 to join Murray in Europe.

With Adams' February 18 announcement to send a new mission, the split in the Federalist party had become a known public fact; when the commissioners sailed, it confirmed the breach in the party. Sometimes criticized among later generations for lack of political astuteness, Adams had won the greatest battle of his administration. Convinced that the war program had faded from public support only a short while after the first explosion of post-XYZ enthusiasm; assured that the consequent high taxes and military organization had no excuse for being, and were a detriment to the country; positive that France would accept a peace mission in keeping with American honor; and finally, sure that his role as mediating executive required him to steer a moderate course, Adams decided against high Federalist militarism and heavy spending in favor of peace and his old principle of American neutrality. The majority of the Federalist party supported his judgment, for he was far more in the mainstream of general Federalist opinion than the Hamiltonians. Although the Hamiltonians may have been the noisiest members of the party, they were not the most numerous.

Adams' cabinet thought they had been able to dominate him— and for some time they had deceived him. Yet for all their talk they had never been able to control him; ultimately he took a course completely opposed to the one which they and their chief, Hamilton, prescribed. In March of 1799 Adams had written a revealing comment to Attorney General Lee: "The nomination of Murray has had one good effect, at least. It has shown to every observing and thinking man the real strength or weakness of the Constitution, and where one part of that weakness resides. It has also produced a display of the real spirit of the parties in this country and the objects they have in view. To me, it has laid open characters. Some of these will do well to study a little more maturely the spirit of their stations. But vanity has no limits; arrogance shall be made to feel a curb. If anyone entertains the idea that because I am a President of three votes only I am in the power of a party, they shall find that I am no more so than the Constitution forces upon me. If combination of senators, generals, and heads of department shall be formed, such as I cannot resist, and measures are demanded of me that I cannot adopt, my remedy is plain and certain. I will try my own strength at resistance first, however."[15] He had tried his own strength at resistance and had won, but at length he decided that he must take the plain and certain remedy of firing the Hamiltonians in his cabinet. After the commissioners left for France in November, it could not be long until Adams got rid of Pickering and McHenry. Wolcott had done a better job of playing the part of middleman. Moreover, as Secretary of the Treasury he had felt the financial pinch inflicted by the military organization; hence he opposed a standing army.

McHenry, generally agreed by all to have served miserably in his post, felt his own inadequacy for his job. As early as November, 1799, McHenry expected that he would be fired.[16] Consequently, he finally wrote in May, 1800, asking to resign. Adams immediately granted his resignation. At the same time, Adams offered Pickering a chance to resign. When Pickering, however, answered that he did "not feel it to be my duty to resign," Adams promptly fired him.[17] He appointed to replace Pickering and McHenry two moderate Federalists—John Marshall, most powerful Federalist in the South and an opponent of the Alien and Sedition laws, as Secretary of State and Samuel Dexter of Massachusetts as Secretary of War.

The election of 1800 stood close at hand. Washington had died in December of 1799, the last force to bind the Federalist factions together. Typically, Hamilton intrigued to bring in another candidate over Adams. But Adams could boast a number of friends in the rank and file of the party—Gerry, Knox, Benjamin Lincoln, Marshall, Henry Lee, Stoddert, Charles Lee and now even Harrison Gray Otis, who pressed for his nomination. Massachusetts, the taproot of Federalist power, remained loyal to its native son. In addition, even some of the first-rung party leaders decided finally to support Adams. Thus, caucuses in Congress had selected Jefferson and Aaron Burr for the Republicans, Adams and Charles Cotesworth Pinckney for the Federalists. This time Hamilton planned to have Pinckney gain a slight edge over Adams, even at the risk of Jefferson's winning the Presidency. Referring to Adams, Hamilton wrote to Sedgwick:

> Were I to determine from my own observation, I should say *most* of the most *influential men* of that party consider him as a very unfit and incapable character.
>
> For my individual part, my mind is made up. I will never more be responsible for him by my direct support, even though the consequence should be the election of *Jefferson*.
>
> If we must have an *enemy* at the head of the government, let it be one whom we can oppose, and for whom we are not responsible, who will not involve our party in the disgrace of his foolish and bad measures. Under *Adams*, as under Jefferson, the government will sink. The party in the hands of whose chief it shall sink will sink with it; and the advantage will all be on the side of his adversaries.
>
> 'Tis a notable expedient for keeping the Federal party together, to have at the head of it a man who hates and is despised by those men

of it who, in time past, have been its most efficient supporters. If the cause is to be sacrificed to a weak and perverse man, I withdraw from the party and act upon my own ground, never certainly against my principles, but in pursuance of them my own way. I am mistaken if others will not do the same. The only way to prevent a fatal schism in the Federal party is to support General Pinckney in good earnest.[18]

Hamilton further enforced his expression of dislike for Adams in a letter to Charles Carroll: "That this gentleman ought not to be the object of the Federal wish is, with me, reduced to demonstration. His administration has already very materially disgraced and sunk the government. There are defects in his character which must inevitably continue to do this more and more. And if he is supported by the Federal party, his party must in the issue fall with him. Every other calculation will, in my judgment, prove illusory.

"Doctor *Franklin,* a sagacious observer of human nature, drew this portrait of Mr. Adams: 'He is always honest, *sometimes* great, but *often mad.'* I subscribe to the justness of this picture, adding as to the first trait of it this qualification—'as far as a man excessively *vain* and *jealous* and *ignobly* attached *to place* can be.' "[19]

Hamilton enhanced these statements with publication at the end of the summer of 1800 of an impolitic paper in unforgivably bad taste—a *Letter from Alexander Hamilton, concerning the Public Conduct and Character of John Adams, Esq., President of the United States*—in which he attacked the fitness of Adams to be President.

With the party splintered by such murderous infighting, the Federalists lost the election of 1800 and John Adams failed to gain the second term he sought. Yet the prize was so closely contested that the outcome hung in the balance until the last state was counted. The closeness of the balloting, moreover, failed to yield evidence to those who thought they saw in the results some revolutionary move toward a more democratic era. This was clearly not the case and even Jefferson admitted as much.

Rather, Americans seemed to be deciding against three issues— the militarism so cleverly nurtured by the Hamiltonian wing, the high taxes this state of affairs exacted and the standing army it demanded, and the price being paid by the repressive Alien and Sedition laws. Sensing this public mood as the election approached, Adams moved adroitly in the aftermath of the 1799 peace mission to divorce himself from the militarists, vigorously denouncing Hamilton and taking his record directly to the public.

Although the country seemed to some to yearn for the change Jefferson offered, Adams was far from bankrupt of support. Buttressed by the rank-and-file backing of his party, he swept the New England states; he enjoyed about the same mid-Atlantic popularity as four years earlier, except in New York, where Aaron Burr's native son candidacy and expert maneuvering put that state into the Republican column by a narrow margin. The Jeffersonians, as expected, carried the South, leaving Adams, Jefferson and Burr all deadlocked at 65 electoral votes each with only South Carolina remaining. The Carolina candidate, Pinckney, held 64 votes; forces in his state now conspired to divide the ballots in such a way that would make their man President and Jefferson Vice-President, thus freezing out Adams. Pinckney, however, turned thumbs down on the scheme, avowing his loyalty to Adams. In the ensuing vote, the Republicans closed ranks, collecting all the South Carolina electors. Adams' fate was sealed.

The Republican aspirants stood tied for first place with 73 votes each, setting the stage for the tumultuous House struggle that ultimately gave Jefferson the Presidency over Burr by a majority of only two states.

For the bitter factional split of his administration and the subsequent loss of the esteemed prize of a second term as President, Adams blamed Hamilton. As an old man Adams still reserved for Hamilton castigations he would have pinned upon no other, for by that time he could still feel ". . . the blisters of Paine, Hamilton, and Callender."[20] Hearing that a life of Hamilton was in preparation, Adams wrote in 1808 to Dr. Rush, "Though the life of Hamilton will be a made-up picture, like Dean Swift's *Celia*, and rags will be contrived to prop the flabby dugs, lest down they drop, I shall be very glad to see it. I hope his famous letter which produced the army, the Sedition Law, and so forth, in which he recommended an army of 50,000 men, 10,000 of them horse, will not be omitted. . . ."[21]

He bitterly confided to Rush: "Although I read with tranquillity and suffered to pass without animadversion in silent contempt the base insinuations of vanity and a hundred lies besides published in a pamphlet against me [*Letter . . . concerning the Public Conduct and Character of John Adams*] by an insolent coxcomb, who rarely dined in good company where there was good wine without getting silly and vaporing about his administration like a young girl about her brilliants and trinkets, yet I lose all patience when I think of a bastard brat of a Scotch pedlar daring to threaten to undeceive the world in their judgment of Washington by writing an history of his battles and campaigns. This creature was in a delirium of ambition; he had been blown up with vanity by the Tories, had fixed his eyes on the highest station in America, and he hated every man, young or old, who stood in his way or could in any manner eclipse his laurels or rival his pretensions. . . ."[22]

Adams, of course, outlived Hamilton and so got the last word. "Although I have long since forgiven this arch enemy," he wrote in his *Autobiography*, "yet vice, folly, and villainy are not to be forgotten because the guilty wretch repented in his dying moments. . :. Nor am I obliged by any principles of morality or religion to suffer my character to lie under infamous calumnies because the author of them, with a pistol bullet through his spinal marrow, died a penitent. Charity requires that we should hope and believe that his humiliation was sincere, and I sincerely hope he was forgiven: but I will not conceal his former character at the expense of so much injustice to my own, as this Scottish Creolian Bolingbroke in the days of his disappointed ambition and unbridled malice and revenge was pleased falsely to attempt against it. Born on a speck more obscure than Corsica, from an original not only more contemptible but infamous, with infinitely less courage and capacity than Bonaparte, he would, in my opinion, if I had not controlled the fury of his vanity, instead of relieving this country from confusion as Bonaparte did France, he would have involved it in all the bloodshed and distractions of foreign and civil war at once."[23]

Crotchety, cranky as he might be, Adams ordinarily remained a kind man. Justice required him to treat both friend and foe with fairness; further than that, a streak of tenderness and a regard for men as individuals prompted him to act kindly toward the lowliest men. However, toward Hamilton he entertained animosity akin to genuine hatred. This was the man who not only had plotted against him in two Presidential elections, had assailed his character with a defamatory pamphlet, but had tried to usurp his power as chief executive and direct his administration along lines wholly out of tune with his own policy. In short, Adams blamed Hamilton for the problems of his administration.

But now that his administration had closed with his crowning achievement, a convention with France upon American terms, Adams turned his sights toward a serene retirement in Quincy. Sending Abigail on ahead from the President's House, later called the White House, where they had been the first residents, Adams took time only to appoint the famous last-minute Federalist judges, the "midnight judges" of whom he named John Marshall as Chief Justice. Rudely, he committed in his haste a great breach of etiquette, for he left Washington early on the morning of Jefferson's inauguration. He had left only a terse note for his successor, their only communication in four years, informing Jefferson that in order to save him the trouble and expense of purchasing new horses and carriages, Adams had kept in the stables "seven horses and two carriages with harness and property of the United States."[24]

Jefferson wrote to Adams again only to send unopened a private letter that had come to him by mistake. That letter contained the news that Charles Adams, lovable, charming second son of the President, had died a drunkard's death in New York City at the tragically young age of thirty. Charles left a young widow, Sarah, sister of Colonel William Stephens Smith, and two young children. Charles had been perhaps the most personable of Adams' children; he and his father had kept up an affectionate attachment and close correspondence.

"Had you read the papers enclosed," wrote Adams to Jefferson, "they might have given you a moment of melancholy or at least of sympathy with a mourning father. They relate wholly to the funeral of a son who was once the delight of my eyes and a darling of my heart, cut off in the flower of his days amidst very flattering prospects by causes which have been the greatest grief of my heart and the deepest affliction of my life. It is not possible that anything of the kind should happen to you, and I sincerely wish you may never experience anything in any degree resembling it."[25]

Adams wrote in the same vein to his Dutch friend Van der Kemp: "The affliction in my family from the melancholy death of a once beloved son has been very great and has required the consolation of religion, as well as philosophy, to enable us to support it. The prospects of that unfortunate youth were very pleasing and promising but have been cut off, and a wife and two very young children are left with their grandparents to bewail a fate which neither could avert, and to which all ought in patience to submit. I have two sons left, whose conduct is worthy of their education and connections. I pray that their lives may be spared and their characters respected."[26]

Nowhere more than in the trials and tragedies of life did Adams and his wife give evidence of their Puritan characters. A parent must do his best to instruct his children in righteousness; yet when all was said and done, his children, being weak as all men were, might disappoint him. Drunkenness in a son, like any sin, was a grievous burden for a man to bear, but one to accept with fortitude. A man's children stood no more immune to sin than anyone else. There was nothing to do, then, but to put up with the disgrace and forgive the erring child. Abigail reflected the same quiet acceptance as her husband.

"Mercy and judgment are the mingled cup allotted me," she wrote her sister just before Charles' death. "Shall I receive good and not evil? At New York I found my poor unhappy son, for so I must still call him, laid upon a bed of sickness, destitute of a home. The kindness of a friend afforded him an asylum. A distressing cough, an affection of the liver and a dropsy will soon terminate a life which might have been made valuable to himself and others. You will easily suppose that this scene was too powerful and distressing to me. Sally was with him, but his physician says he is past recovery ——I shall carry a melancholy report to the President, who, passing through New York without stopping, knew not his situation."[27]

But it was only human to grope for reasons for such grief. "Food has not been his sustenance," she pondered, "yet he did not look like an intemperate man—he was bloated but not red—he was no man's enemy but his own—he was beloved in spite of his errors, and all spoke with grief and sorrow for his habits. . . . Afflictions of this kind are a two-edged sword."[28]

The loss of a son and the loss of an election that he really wanted to win combined to make Adams' last days in the Presidency a gloomy interim before he could return to the balm of Quincy. Nonetheless, though he would one day refer jokingly to his Presidency as " 'a tale told by an idiot, full of sound and fury, signifying nothing,' "[29] he could look back upon the last four years knowing that he had accomplished something creditable, that he had done the best he could to translate his principles into action.

In foreign affairs, Adams had achieved by the Convention of 1800, with its mere commercial agreement and freedom from entangling alliances, the same neutrality for America that he had proposed during the Confederation. He had protected American commerce, revitalized the navy and relieved the country of the provisions of the 1778 treaty with France.

In domestic affairs he had woven a moderate course through a labyrinth of party rivalries. Believing that it was his task as an executive arbitrator to guide the country between the wolves, he attempted to balance the thrashings of parties. To those Republicans who had struggled to douse American internal affairs into the French Revolutionary inkpot, or to those Federalists who had sought to ignore both American public opinion and the sheer nonsense of raising a big army in order to further the spirit of party, Adams said no. For awhile he seemed to lose his battle with the high Federalists, but he reinstituted his Presidential power in time to ward off the devils of militarism, the besetting problem of his administration. That he did successfully buck the cries for war, that he did refuse to succumb to the base pleas of faction there could be no question. When he took the path he did, he endorsed the moderate policy of rank-and-file Federalism, not the frantic, last-gasp pitches and groanings of high Federalism. The panic-stricken, power-mad party of the high Federalists was not the party of Adams, if, indeed, Adams could be called a party man at all. He who had always cherished his independence, who had made a life-long study of government, whose chief credo was balance of rivalries, could not easily become a man of party.

He wrote to Benjamin Rush: ". . . I do not curse the day when I engaged in public affairs. I do not say when I became a politician, for that I never was. I cannot repent of anything I ever did conscientiously from a sense of duty. I never engaged in public affairs for my own interest, pleasure, envy, jealousy, avarice, or ambition, or even the desire of fame. If any of these had been my motive, my conduct would have been very different. In every considerable transaction of my public life, I have invariably acted according to my best judgment for the public good, and I can look up to God for the sincerity of my intentions. How, then, is it possible I can repent? Notwithstanding this, I have an immense load of errors, weaknesses, follies, and sins to mourn over and repent of, and these are the only afflictions of my present life. . . ."[30]

CHAPTER **XVII**

A LAST CAREER

JOHN ADAMS returned to the Quincy farm nursing the scars inflicted by a long, strenuous public life. After passing a few years with Abigail in philosophical serenity and deserved quiet, he expected to ease out of this life and on to a proper reward. But John Adams, who had never eased out of anything, could not quit his life so lightly. Amidst the tombs of his ancestors, the delights of his tilled earth, the esteem of old friends and neighbors, and the solace of grandchildren, nieces and nephews, he found nurture and invigoration to endure not only the anticipated few years but far more. Relatives and countrymen numbered his birthdays by years, then decades—seventy, eighty, ninety, until a quarter of a century after his retirement had passed before the old man of Quincy consented to die.

Some men of history quite mercifully are allowed an early death; their powers soar to a height of achievement in the fullness of young manhood; for them to remain, humiliated by dwindling capacities, would be torture. Yet different men, whose strength, rather than in daring or physical courage, lies in vision and judgment, rise in a crescendo of ability as maturity increases their wisdom. These make grand old men, patriarchs of civilization, and nature knows it. They remain, unsoftened, undaunted, relishing their antiquity, wearing years as a badge of honor, accepting infirmities with unembarrassed nonchalance. Children, contrasting their own newness with hoary age, view these men with awe; descendants venerate them as a bridge of continuity with history; the would-be conflagrators of society, who in every generation try to consume their world in favor of a new one they would build, look with discomfort upon these old men, these monuments to the wisdom of experience.

For these few men Shakespeare's seventh stage of life becomes not a period of helplessness but of nobility. In defiance of decay, the mind within the infirm body plumbs still more astonishing depths. Old age becomes an apogee, a culmination of power without which life could never achieve full brilliance. Such men end their lives in style, climaxed in the lofty exit of death.

Charles Francis Adams remembered his grandfather as such a man, an indomitable old figure, even at ninety. As time eroded physical strength, the mind still fired the old being with the vigor present in the Gilbert Stuart portrait or the Browere life mask. Eyes too weak to read and hands too palsied by a "quiveration" did not prevent the stout old man from sitting hour after hour with arms folded, one hand on his cane, just as Stuart painted him, expecting his offspring to read to him. He preferred philosophy or theology, but if the younger folk chose to read the currently popular fictions of Sir Walter Scott, Cooper's sea stories or Byron's romantic poetry, he readily assented, enjoying them almost as much as they did. He despised the thought of losing touch, going to all lengths to keep abreast of the latest literature. He loved to converse with anyone on any subject, falling guilty to "rodomontade," as he called it, but entertaining rather than boring his listeners with his enthusiasm, wit and fine bag of stories.[1]

As Adams wrote the elderly Christopher Gadsden, he was determined to ward off ennui, an affliction which, "when it rains on a man in large drops, is worse than one of our northeast storms." He counted on ". . . the labors of agriculture and amusement of letters" to "shelter me." His "greatest grief" was that it was too late for him to return to the bar—there he ". . . should forget in a moment that

I was ever a member of Congress, a foreign minister, or President of the United States."[2]

Agriculture and correspondence did indeed satisfy him for the next twenty-five years. No sooner had he set permanent foot in Quincy than he tramped off to his acres with the glee of a small boy let out of school. Abigail reported that he could always be found in his fields looking after his haymakers, gratified that ". . . where eight years ago we cut scarcely six tons, we now have thirty."[3]

But as the years slipped by, taking agility with them but leaving a distinctive thickness of body, the labor of farming fell to other hands. Letter writing then became his sustaining joy, directed to an ever widening circle of correspondents. Adams came to write to countless figures of his generation who had stepped into public life and many who had not. Whether he had ever crossed swords with them mattered little. He felt compelled to keep contact with his confrères of the Revolutionary era. The Revolution had begun long before the actual war for independence; Adams felt that it was not even yet finished. Mistaken notions of Revolutionary history had already become gospel—consequently, only these last living relics of their age could explain to the present generation what had really happened. It was crucial that this period in time be portrayed for posterity with absolute truthfulness. It was this motive, then, as well as the wish to part on peaceful terms with the world, that prompted Adams to renew old connections.

He decided to delay no longer writing to Thomas McKean, for example, "lest I should glide away where there is no pen and ink." They had been friends for thirty-eight years, he declared, agreed in principle except on one subject, the French Revolution, which McKean had thought to be a "minister of grace" and Adams had "fully believed it to be 'a goblin damned.'" At their time of life, however, there could be "no question of honor or profits, or rank or fame. . . . Personal friendship and private feelings are all that remain."[4]

But it was with Benjamin Rush and Thomas Jefferson that Adams conducted the most lengthy, significant and candid correspondence. The Adams-Jefferson correspondence, of course, did not strike up again until 1812. In fact, Rush was responsible for reuniting the two old patriots, by that time the two most famous fathers of their country, in one of the most extraordinary correspondences in American literary and political history.

Adams himself renewed the communication with Rush in 1805, when he wrote saying, "It seemeth unto me that you and I ought not to die without saying good-bye or bidding each other adieu." There were mighty questions on which to seek Rush's opinion—"Is the present state of the nation republican enough? Is virtue the principle of our government? Is honor? Or is ambition and avarice, adulation, baseness, covetousness, the thirst of riches, indifference concerning the means of rising and enriching, the contempt of principle, the spirit of party and of faction the motive and the principle that governs? These are serious and dangerous questions; but serious men ought not to flinch from dangerous questions."[5] The two men, friends since 1774, had been separated for a time by Rush's Republicanism. Yet Rush could not forget that Adams, though much criticized for the appointment, had helped him through financial straits by naming him Treasurer of the Mint at a time when Rush had been heavily attacked by the Federalist editors Cobbett and Fenno for his theories of treatment for yellow fever. Rush replied immediately to Adams' letter, initiating a friendly and spirited correspondence that ended only with Rush's sudden death in 1813. Any topic was legitimate stuff for discussion in these letters. They were frank enough that Rush, for example, in complaining that his daughter-in-law had persuaded his son to move to Washington in order to be close to her relatives, summarized, "There are two classes of female tyrants—termagants and sirens. My son's wife belongs to the latter class. . . ."[6]

While the letters between Adams and Rush continued almost one a month, Rush vainly attempted to persuade Adams to correspond with Jefferson. Not all contact between Peacefield and Monticello had ceased, however, because the outspoken Abigail had made it her business in 1804 to pass some private communication with Jefferson. The occasion had been the death, at the age of twenty-five, of Polly Jefferson Eppes, for whom Abigail had developed such an attachment when she had cared for her as a little girl in London. Feeling at first restrained from writing, Abigail finally acknowledged that "the powerful feelings of my heart have burst through the restraint and called upon me to shed the tear of sorrow over the departed remains of your beloved and deserving daughter, an event which I most sincerely mourn."[7]

When Jefferson thanked Abigail for her expression of sympathy, he assured her of his friendship, adding that he could "say with truth that one act of Mr. Adams' life, and one only, ever gave me a moment's displeasure. I did consider his last appointments to office [under the Judiciary Act of 1801] as personally unkind. They were among my most ardent political enemies. . . ."[8] Abigail pounced upon that last statement to defend her husband, concluding sharply that she would now "freely disclose to you what has severed the bonds of former friendship and placed you in a light very different from what I once viewed you in." She took it as "personal injury" that Jefferson had pardoned James Thomson Callender, a Scotsman who had violently attacked Adams' administration in his pamphlet of 1800, *The Prospect Before Us*, for which he was tried under the Sedition Law, fined $200, and sentenced to nine months in prison by Justice Samuel Chase. When Jefferson explained his action toward Callender, not altogether to Abigail's pleasure, she returned another complaint—Jefferson's removal of John Quincy as commissioner of bankruptcy. Jefferson's answer that Congress had ended the appointment satisfied her that he had meant no unkindness. Consequently she felt content to end the correspondence, not without a barbed comment that ". . . here, sir, may I be permitted to pause and ask you whether in your ardent zeal and desire to rectify the mistakes and abuses, as you may consider them, of the former administrations, you are not led into measures still more fatal to the Constitution and more derogatory to your honor and independence of character? Pardon me, sir, if I say that I fear you are." She felt, however, that "time, sir, must determine and posterity will judge with more candor and impartiality, I hope, than the conflicting parties of our day what measures have best promoted the happiness of the people . . . and to whom-

ever the tribute is due, to them may it be given." That Adams and
Jefferson were still too close to the violent feuds of the 1790's to
put away old wounds was evidenced by Adams' terse note at the
bottom of Abigail's final letter: "The whole of this correspondence
was begun and conducted without my knowledge or suspicion. Last
evening and this morning, at the desire of Mrs. Adams, I read the
whole. I have no remarks to make upon it at this time and in this
place."[9]

Possibilities of connection between Adams and Jefferson remained a dead letter until the summer of 1811, when Madison was
President. Edward Coles, secretary to Madison and an Albemarle
County neighbor of Jefferson, happened to stop in Quincy with his
brother John. The Adamses, who delighted to receive young visitors, accepted their letters of introduction from President Madison
and cordially entertained the brothers. For two days Adams remi-
nisced about his administration, talking plainly to the young men
about the 1800 election. He concluded, however, with compliments
on the character of Jefferson, saying, "I always loved Jefferson and
still love him." Naturally, the Coles brothers repeated this information to Jefferson, who, moved to try for a reconciliation with
Adams, wrote to Rush, recounting what the Coles had reported.
The middleman, Rush, in turn relayed Jefferson's words to Adams,
quoting the Virginian: " 'This is enough for me. I only needed this
knowledge to revive towards him all the affections of the most
cordial moments of our lives.' "

"And now, my dear friend," Rush exhorted Adams, "permit me
again to suggest to you to receive the olive branch which has thus
been offered to you by the hand of a man who still loves you."[10]
So rhetorical a letter had Rush written that Adams could not for-
bear to josh him out of his seriousness.

"I perceive plainly enough, Rush," he replied, "that you have
been teasing Jefferson to write to me, as you did me sometime ago
to write to him. You gravely advise me 'to receive the olive branch,'
as if there had been war; but there has never been any hostility on
my part, nor, that I know, on his. When there has been no war, there
can be no room for negotiations of peace." On the matter of repub-

licanism, he could see little about which they had ever disagreed, beyond the facts that Adams had preferred speeches to Congress, whereas Jefferson had liked messages; Adams had held levees once a week, yet "Jefferson's whole eight years was a levee"; Adams entertained large numbers of company for dinner once or twice a week, but Jefferson had "dined a dozen every day"; Jefferson approved of liberty and straight hair, although Adams "thought curled hair was as republican as straight."

For Rush to urge correspondence between him and Jefferson was "much ado about nothing." Of what use could it be? Nonetheless, Adams hinted that "time and chance, however, or possibly design, may produce ere long a letter between us."[11] Only a week later, on New Year's Day, 1812, Adams wrote to Jefferson to tell him that he was sending him "two pieces of homespun," the two volumes of John Quincy's *Lectures on Rhetoric and Oratory*, written while John Quincy occupied a professorship at Harvard.[12] Jefferson received the gift with joyful gratitude; the correspondence between the two retired Presidents had resumed.

This time the old friends refused to allow disquieting ghosts from a former age to "disturb," as Jefferson expressed it, "the repose of affections so sweetening to the evening of our lives." Not even publication in 1823 of the letters of Adams to William Cunningham could destroy the companionship that both correspondents had come to value so highly. Cunningham had requested of Adams facts that could be used to defeat Jefferson for reelection in 1804. Still scourged by raw political sores, Adams had burst out in a typically blunt, carelessly overstated indictment of Jefferson. Although he stipulated that Cunningham was not to publish the letters during Adams' lifetime, Cunningham committed suicide in 1823. His son immediately published the letters for the purpose of ruining John Quincy, a candidate for President in the 1824 election. But Jefferson magnanimously assured his friend ". . . that I am incapable of receiving the slightest impression from the effort now made to plant thorns on the pillow of age, worth, and wisdom, and to sow tares between friends who have been such for near half a century." Much relieved, Adams called Jefferson's epistle "the best letter that ever was written."[13] The loss to him of either Jefferson's or Rush's letters would have meant an irreparable blow. The correspondence, first with Rush and then with Jefferson, sustained him both spiritually and physically.

In the first place, the present political scene always came in as fair game for discussion. Having served so long in public life, all three men maintained an eager interest in current developments. But perhaps Adams, because of John Quincy's active role, felt closest to the political picture. Year after year John Quincy bore out Washington's impression of him as the most brilliant member of the young diplomatic corps. Only shortly after his parents' retirement, John Quincy delighted them by returning from Berlin with his charming, intelligent wife, Louisa Catherine Johnson. Thereafter the elder Adamses followed their son's career, first as United States senator, then as minister to Russia under Madison, then as one of the commissioners at Ghent to negotiate peace with Britain in 1814; as minister to Britain, just as his father had been; as Secretary of State under Monroe; and, finally, as President. Just as his father was, John Quincy was a strong-minded man of independence. He did not hesitate, in contrast to the sentiments of New England, to vote for the Jeffersonian embargo on American shipping (only as a temporary measure to avoid possible war with Britain), or to support Madison for President in the 1808 Republican caucus.

Although never again active in politics, John Adams even in retirement could not bury his head in private sands. "At your age and mine," he told Rush, "it would perhaps be better for our tranquillity if we could outlive all our public feelings. Yet the very thought of this strikes us both with horror. . . ." There was no doubt that "our obligations to our country never cease but with our lives."[14]

Adams' correspondence with Jefferson commenced at a moment when threats of war clouded the nation. After the long hassles over embargoes and non-intercourse agreements, the War of 1812 distressed Adams, for he had ". . . never approved of non-importations, non-intercourses, or embargoes for more than six weeks," he stated to Jefferson. What a shame, he particularly thought, that the navy had been neglected.[15]

At the same time, Adams felt disturbed to watch New England threatening to secede from the nation over the embargo, going so far as to call the Hartford Convention. "The union is still to me an object of as much anxiety as ever independence was," he maintained. In fact, he could not but express his fear to Jefferson that "there will be greater difficulties to preserve our union than you and I, our fathers, brothers, friends, disciples, and sons have had to form it."[16]

More and more, Adams and Jefferson, these two holdovers from the eighteenth-century Enlightenment, found that they had much in common with each other. Both of them believed, as Adams put it, that ". . . we may say that the eighteenth century, notwithstanding all its errors and vices, has been, of all that are past, the most honorable to human nature. Knowledge and virtues were increased and diffused; arts, sciences useful to men, ameliorating their condition, were improved more than in any former equal period."[17] Even Adams, who would never accept the theory that man was perfectible, would grant the fact that man could at least be freer under certain conditions than under others. As men of the Enlightenment, Adams and Jefferson considered the relationship of man to liberty as the paramount question. With history as their tool, they judged political developments in the light of how well they enforced man's struggle for freedom.

The nineteenth century, however, had made a doddering entrance in the theater of liberty. ". . . What are we to say now?" Adams questioned in dismay. "Is the nineteenth century to be a contrast to the eighteenth? Is it to extinguish all the lights of its predecessor?" As he had expected, the French Revolution had ended tragically.

"Poor Bonaparte! Poor devil!" Adams wrote. "What has and will become of him? Going the way of King Theodore, Alexander, Caesar, Charles XII, Cromwell, Wat Tyler and Jack Cade, i.e., to a bad end." Moreover, the Congress of Vienna, even with its leading negotiators of Europe, such as Metternich, Hardenberg and

Von Humboldt, Castlereagh and Wellington, Talleyrand, and even Czar Alexander of Russia, chose a bad solution to the dilemma. Adams and Jefferson looked askance at the work of the congress, a backward development, they believed, in the history of freedom. Since Napoleon had "imposed kings upon Spain, Holland, Sweden, Westphalia, Saxony, Naples, etc.," Adams remarked, the "combined emperors and kings are about to retaliate upon France by imposing a king upon her. These are all abominable examples, detestable precedents."[18]

Nonetheless, the congress could not altogether stifle the huge revolutionary impetus set in motion by the French Revolution. In the years after the Napoleonic wars, Adams and Jefferson observed attempts of South American countries to liberate themselves from Spain. Although Adams felt sure that these countries would win their independence, he was anxious for them. "But can they have free governments?" he wondered. Without any tradition of republican institutions, could they maintain more than a facade of self-government? What was more, "Can the Roman religion and a free government exist together?"[19] Jefferson shared the same doubts. "They will succeed against Spain," he thought. "But the dangerous enemy is within their own breasts. Ignorance and superstition will chain their minds and bodies under religious and military despotism." For that reason, he believed ". . . it would be better for them to obtain freedom by degrees only; because that would by degrees bring on light and information and qualify them to take charge of themselves understandingly. . . ." Yet, only they had the right to choose their own government; since they sought independence, he could only wish them well.[20]

In the same vein, the squelches by Austria of the Piedmontese and Neapolitan revolutions moved Adams to comment that "the art of lawgiving is not so easy as that of architecture or painting. . . . I may refine too much. I may be an enthusiast. But I think a free government is necessarily a complicated piece of machinery, the nice and exact adjustment of whose springs, wheels, and weights are not yet well comprehended by the artists of the age and still less by the people."[21]

As for their own country, both Adams and Jefferson realized the import of the slavery issue. The somber implications of transmitting slavery to the territories raised by the Missouri Compromise of 1820 caused Jefferson to observe, "From the Battle of Bunker's Hill to the Treaty of Paris we never had so ominous a question." Adams, too, shuddered over the fact that "slavery in this country I have seen hanging over it like a black cloud for half a century." He had "been so terrified with this phenomenon" that he had always said in former times to the Southern gentlemen, "I cannot comprehend this object; I must leave it to you. I will vote for forcing no measure against your judgments. What we are to see *God* knows, and I leave it to him and his agents in posterity."[22]

Being a New Englander, Adams felt repulsed by the whole institution of slavery. But in 1820 he was included in an event closer to his own understanding. This was his attendance at the convention to revise the Massachusetts Constitution of 1780, the document that had been peculiarly his own. The delegates invited the Quincy sage, now eighty-five, to be president of the convention, but Adams, acknowledging his age, declined in favor of younger minds. He did, however, with his characteristic interest in the advancement of liberty, offer an amendment to the Massachusetts Bill of Rights, one guaranteeing freedom of religion. Yet when the convention turned it down, Adams acquiesced in good humor. It had been forty years since he had engaged in public debate—the last time, in fact, had been at the first Massachusetts constitutional convention. "After a total desuetude for forty years," he confided to Jefferson, "I boggled and blundered more than a young fellow just rising to speak at the bar."[23] It had pleased him immensely, though, to be elected to the 1820 convention, the only time that he ventured into a public role during his retirement.

In addition to keeping abreast of present politics, Adams indulged as much as ever in speculation on the first principles of government. As an old man he had scarcely altered the fundamentals of his thought, still contending in behalf of fixed laws to secure liberty; balanced government to control rivalries caused by inevitable inequalities among men; the necessity to foster virtue as a means of preserving republican government. He still considered men "as free, moral, and accountable agents" and "as God has made them."[24]

At the same time, he grew sharper, clearer, more thoughtful. More than half a century of contemplation now bore fruit in some of his most precise, exact statements on government. For example, he offered Jefferson the concise pronouncement: "The fundamental article of my political creed is that despotism, or unlimited sovereignty, or absolute power is the same in a majority of a popular assembly, an aristocratical council, an oligarchical junto, and a single emperor. Equally arbitrary, cruel, bloody, and in every respect diabolical."[25]

He gave one of his most illuminating definitions of liberty to John Taylor of Caroline, the eccentric Virginian who published in 1814 a huge treatise of 650 pages entitled, *An Inquiry into the Principles and Policy of the Government of the United States*, which contained a running commentary on Adams' *Defence*. Taylor, a radical agrarian democrat, had been senator three times and had supported the Virginia and Kentucky Resolutions. Adams answered Taylor's work in a series of letters, dealing primarily with aristocracy, which finished the body of his political writings.

Liberty, he told Taylor, is an intellectual quality; it is defined as "a self-determining power in an intellectual agent." Because it presupposes choice by a being with moral faculty, who can choose good or evil, liberty can be no part of fate, chance, predestination. Although in itself it has no moral quality, it cannot be divorced from moral implications. Liberty "implies thought and choice and power; it can elect between objects, indifferent in point of morality, neither morally good nor morally evil. If the substance in which this quality, attribute, adjective, call it what you will, exists, has a moral sense, a conscience, a moral faculty; if it can distinguish between moral good and moral evil and has power to choose the former and refuse the latter, it can, if it will, choose the evil and reject the good, as we see in experience it very often does."[26] Since men are free, intelligent and have consciences, then their freedom relates directly to morality; thus, the lawgiver receives a responsibility: "This free-

dom of choice and action, united with conscience, necessarily implies a responsibility to a lawgiver and to a law and has a necessary
relation to right and wrong, to happiness and misery."[27]

All men, because of their moral sense, are under obligation to use
their intellectual liberty for the public good. In other words, they
are "under moral obligations to do to others as they would have
others *do to them;* to consider themselves born, authorized, empowered for the good of society, as well as their own good." All
sovereigns—whether the unlimited one of a despotism, the limited
one of a monarchy, the few of an aristocracy, the many of a democracy, or the variety of a mixed government—"are under the most
solemn and the most sacred moral obligations to consider their
trusts and their power to be instituted for the benefit and happiness
of their nations, not their nations as servants to them or their
friends or parties. In other words, to exert all their intellectual
liberty to employ all their faculties, talents, and power for the
public, general, universal good of their nations, not for their own
separate good or the interest of any party."[28]

If Adams still looked upon man as a free being, responsible for
making right choices, he likewise still advocated his *moral* equality
and his *natural* inequality as the basis for just laws to control
factions.

"That all men are born to equal rights is true," he declared in one
of his most memorable passages. "Every being has a right to his
own, as clear, as moral, as sacred, as any other being has. This is
as indubitable as a moral government in the universe. But to teach
that all men are born with equal powers and faculties, to equal
influence in society, to equal property and advantages through life,
is as gross a fraud, as glaring an imposition on the credulity of the
people as ever was practiced by monks, by Druids, by Brahmins,
by priests of the immortal Lama, or by the self-styled philosophers
of the French Revolution."[29]

From his theories of inequality, of course, came his concept of
aristocracy. He understood aristocracy simply as "all those men
who can command, influence, or procure more than an average of
votes." An aristocrat was "every man who can and will influence

one man to vote besides himself."[30] By this definition even a representative government was an aristocracy. Virtues, talents, learning, loquacity, taciturnity, frankness, reserve, face, figure—any number of qualities could enable a man to obtain that one vote in addition to his own, hence making him an aristocrat.

"You seem to think aristocracy consists altogether in artificial titles, tinsel decorations of stars, garters, ribbons . . . hereditary descents established by kings or by positive laws of society," Adams reminded Taylor. "No such thing! Aristocracy was from the beginning, now is, and ever will be, world without end, independent of all these artificial regulations, as really and as efficaciously as with them!"[31]

Jefferson, who also supported a theory of aristocracy, spoke of a natural aristocracy of talent and virtue and an artificial aristocracy of birth and wealth. That government was best which provided most effectively for selection to the offices of government of the natural aristocrats. Provision then must be made to keep the artificial aristocrats from dominance. As to how to prevent that ascendancy, he believed that he and Adams differed. On the one hand, Adams hoped to control those aristocrats by placing them in a separate legislative chamber so that two other bodies could restrain them. Jefferson, on the other hand, counted on the citizens through free elections to elect the good and wise.[32]

But Adams corrected his friend. His own definition of aristocracy was much broader—birth and wealth, even if less desirable qualities, were as much a part of natural aristocracy as talent and virtue. Beauty, wealth, birth, genius and virtue were the five pillars of aristocracy, he believed.[33] Natural aristocracy, Adams thought, meant ". . . those superiorities of influence in society which grow out of the constitution of human nature." Artificial aristocracy was inequality created by civil laws.[34]

"When aristocracies are established by human laws," observed Adams, "and honor, wealth, and power are made hereditary by municipal laws and political institutions, then I acknowledge artificial aristocracy to commence: but this never commences till corruption in elections becomes dominant and uncontrollable."

Corruption meant sacrifice of national interest to that of faction, and who could say that America had not had some corrupt elections? For that reason, Adams could not share Jefferson's optimism that the people would always elect the good and wise. Because of jealousies and rivalries, artificial aristocracy always led, Adams believed, to monarchy and then to despotism. And, sadly, all of these, beginning with artificial aristocracy, stemmed from what Jefferson called the natural aristocracy of virtue and talents. Far better, then, to isolate aristocracy in its own legislative body.

He and Jefferson really did not differ on the subject of aristocracy, Adams felt. "I dislike and detest hereditary honors, offices, emoluments established by law. So do you. I am for excluding legal hereditary distinctions from the U.S. as long as possible. So are you." Adams considered it an unfortunate condition, however, that mankind had never yet found any remedy to the seeming irresistibility of corruption in elections except to make offices of great power and profit hereditary.[35] Man could not seem to refrain from darting by successive rivalries from natural to artificial aristocracy and finally into despotism.

"We, to be sure, are far remote from this," he allowed. "Many hundred years must roll away before we shall be corrupted." But he just could not believe that "our pure, virtuous, public-spirited federative republic will last forever, govern the globe and introduce the perfection of man, his perfectibility being already proved by Price, Priestley, Condorcet, Rousseau, Diderot and Godwin."[36]

Just as Adams philosophized on government, he examined theological principles. Theology, always a favorite study with him, became a primary amusement of his later years, "the marbles and nine pins of old age. . . ." All the same, he thought it ridiculous to carry philosophical or theological speculation too far. Even though in former years he had labored through the works of Plato, he snorted to Jefferson that he had learned only two things from the Greek: "One, that Franklin's ideas of exempting husbandmen and mariners, etc., from the depredations of war were borrowed from him; two, that sneezing is a cure for the hiccups." He had long ago decided "that there is now, never will be, and never was but one being who can understand the universe. And that it is not only vain but wicked for insects to pretend to comprehend it."[37]

Theological controversies had always fascinated him, however; he had observed them so long that, typical of an eighteenth-century man, he felt that he could "now say I have read away bigotry, if not enthusiasm."[38] In the same eighteenth-century manner he prided himself on his liberal faith, his rational religion so skeptical of revelation that reason could not prove. When, for example, Jefferson complained of the "Platonic mysticisms" of the Trinity that three are one and one is three, a falsehood he believed to be fostered by "the craft, the power and the profit of the priests," Adams applauded him. The human understanding was one revelation from God "which can never be disputed or doubted. . . . No prophecies, no miracles are necessary to prove this celestial communication. This revelation has made it certain that two and one make three; and that one is not three; nor can three be one. We can never be so certain of any prophecy, or the fulfillment of any prophecy, or of any miracle, or the design of any miracle as we are from the revelation of nature, that is, nature's God, that two and two are equal to four."[39]

For both Adams and Jefferson Christianity was valuable to society mainly as an ethical system. Disclaiming the divine nature of Christ, both men took the morality of Jesus as useful and, indeed, necessary to civilization. Adams could summarize his own moral and religious creed in the simple motto, "Be just and good." Only religion kept the world a tolerable place in which to live. Without it, "this world would be something not fit to be mentioned in polite company—I mean hell." Since he refused to believe that anyone could ever be completely depraved, then even the worst scoundrel retained some shred of conscience. Thus, "while conscience remains, there is some religion."[40] Moreover, a belief in God, Adams felt, was essential to any understanding of liberty. Because the French *philosophes* had all been atheists, "the universe was matter only and eternal; spirit was a word without a meaning; liberty was a word without a meaning. There was no liberty in the universe; liberty was a word void of sense. Every thought, word, passion, sentiment, feeling, all motion and action was necessary. All beings and attributes were of eternal necessity. Conscience, morality were all nothing but fate." But, Adams questioned, "Why. . . should we abhor the word God and fall in love with the word fate? We know there exists energy and intellect enough to produce such a world as this, which is a sublime and beautiful one and a very benevolent one, notwithstanding all our snarling, and a happy one, if it is not made otherwise by our own fault." If man only used his freedom to choose the course of action dictated by conscience and Christianity, then he could assure his own happiness and that of society. This was, Adams felt, "upon the whole a good world."[41]

As far as Jefferson went in his religion, Adams solidly agreed with him; but the man of Quincy thought that he himself was committed to a more definite faith than Jefferson's simple assumption that belief is "the assent of the mind to an intelligible proposition."[42] Though he could never accept the perfectibility of man, saying that "human reason and human conscience, though I believe there are such things, are not a match for human passions, human imaginations and human enthusiasm";[43] though he often displayed slack confidence in man's ability to govern himself, Adams, by being an enthusiast for life itself, broke his own rule against enthusiasm. That God is good, benevolent, all-wise, providing immortal life for man, his creature whom he created out of love, Adams never doubted for one moment. Joy, enthusiasm were essential to the make-up of this eighteenth-century Adams who scorned enthusiasm as irrational, excessive fervor. This sometimes dour New Englander was, after all, an exuberant optimist who proclaimed his jubilant faith: "The love of God and his creation; delight, joy, triumph, exultation in my own existence, though but an atom, a molecule organic in the universe, are my religion. Howl, snarl, bite, ye Calvinistic, ye Athanasian divines, if you will! Ye will say I am no Christian; I say ye are no Christians, and there the account is balanced. Yet I believe all the honest men among you are Christians in my sense of the word." Never a predestinarian, Adams consequently could never be a misanthrope. Being himself a man, "I must hate myself before I can hate my fellow men; and that I cannot and will not do. No! I will not hate any of them, base, brutal and devilish as some of them have been to me." However some peevish old men might complain, Adams could cheerfully declare that he had "never yet seen the day in which I could say I have had no pleasure or that I have had more pain than pleasure."[44]

At the age of eighty, Adams wrote one of his most succinct summaries of his faith: "My religion is founded on the love of God and my neighbor; on the hope of pardon for my offenses; upon contrition; upon the duty as well as necessity of supporting with patience the inevitable evils of life; in the duty of doing no wrong, but all the good I can, to the creation of which I am but an infinitesimal part. . . . I believe, too, in a future state of rewards and punishments, but not eternal."[45] These were the words of a man whose cap of eighteenth-century religious liberalism sat peculiarly askew, revealing, whether he knew it or not, a lining of hard-core seventeenth-century faith.

While Adams kept up with current political events and continued to prime his mind with political and theological theory, at the same time he delved into the history of Colonial America and the early days of the republic. As an effect of both his Puritan heritage and his own personality, he felt bound to assess his own place in this period of history, to train the relentless eye of judgment upon his own acts. Even though divine judgment concerned him, he was equally taken up with his fame in the eyes of posterity. Nagged constantly by self-doubt so that he "never could bring myself seriously to consider that I was a great man or of much importance or consideration in the world," Adams nonetheless could not escape the torture of realizing that "the few traces that remain of me must, I believe, go down to posterity in much confusion and distraction, as my life has been passed." And, then, after such a display of desire for fame he characteristically chided himself, "Enough surely of egotism!"[46]

What his place in history would be was a question that Adams discussed more than any other with Benjamin Rush, who was just as fearful for his own historical reputation. Both men were convinced that the later generation had misinterpreted and misrepresented their part in the founding of the country. Sorrowfully but coldly Adams recognized that "mausoleums, statues, monuments will never be erected to me. I wish them not. Panegyrical romances will never be written, nor flattering orations spoken to transmit me to posterity in brilliant colors. No, nor in true colors." Yet he admitted that he expected he would not die unlamented. Had he not lived, America would never have retained her independence by making separate peace negotiations with Britain after the Revolutionary War. She would have been cut off from 300,000,000 acres of land that she now held; she would have relinquished the fisheries; ". . . the Massachusetts constitution, the constitution of New York, that of Philadelphia, and every other constitution in the United States which is fit for any but brutes to live under would never have been made." Adams' European loans had saved the American army; without his foresight there would be no American navy; ". . . and without my treaty in 1800 which I made by force against all the arts and opposition of those who pretended to be my friends, we should have been now involved in a foolish war with France and a slavish alliance with Great Britain. All this in my conscience I believe to be true." The first to admit to his own vanity, Adams still believed that he had outlined his correct claim to fame.[47] Prophetically, he surmised how history would contrast his reputation with that of Jefferson.

"Your character in history may be easily foreseen," he told Jefferson. "Your administration will be quoted by philosophers as a model of profound wisdom; by politicians as weak, superficial and short-sighted. Mine, like Pope's woman, will have no character at all." The *Defence of the Constitutions* and the *Discourses on Davila* had dug the sluices of unpopularity that had already deluged Adams. On the other hand, Jefferson's "steady defense of democratical principles and your invariable favorable opinion of the French Revolution laid the foundation" of his "unbounded popularity."[48]

More than mere selfish vanity motivated Adams' concern for fame. To a man so acutely aware of the movement of history, of man as an historical being, of his own public and personal history, it was essential to preserve the truth for posterity. Because truth partly reveals itself through history, truth and history are inseparable.

"Truth, justice, and humanity are of eternal obligation," thought Adams, "and we ought to preserve the evidence which can alone support them. I do not intend to let every lie impose upon posterity." Because he had "very solemn notions of the sanctity of history," he believed that historians, just as witnesses in court, should tell the truth, the whole truth, and nothing but the truth. Yet, men being fallible beings, Adams doubted, he told Rush, ". . . whether faithful history ever was or ever can be written. Three hundred years after the event it cannot be written without offending some powerful and popular individual family party, some statesman, some general, some prince, some priest, or some philosopher. The world will go on always ignorant of itself, its past history, and future destiny. If you were to write the history of our Revolution, how different it would appear from the histories we have!"[49]

Adams, with Jefferson and Rush, feared that posterity would never receive a true picture of the Revolution. As readers of history, intensely conscious of historical movements, they believed that they had lived through one of the most profound periods of mankind. The Revolution, they concluded, had been a tremendous phenomenon, a force still unfulfilled in America, with implications for all of Europe and, in fact, the world. Europe, however, had mistaken the real nature of the American Revolution. Why, for instance, mused Adams and Jefferson, had Europe acted on the principle that power is right, or power makes right?

"I know not what answer to give you but this," Adams suggested, "that power always sincerely, conscientiously, de très bon foi, believes itself right. Power always thinks it has a great soul and vast views beyond the comprehension of the weak; and that it is doing God service when it is violating all his laws." Human passions, ambitions, and so on, could subvert the intelligence and conscience into believing that what the emotions yearned for was actually true. For that reason, "power must never be trusted without a check."[50]

That Americans would not make the same ghastly mistake as Europe had, it was crucial, the three friends believed, that successive generations be made to understand the principles of the Revolution, the *"general principles,"* as Adams put it, "on which the fathers achieved independence. . . . And what were these *general principles?* I answer, the general principles of Christianity, in which all those sects were united; and the *general principles* of English and American liberty, in which all those young men united, and which had united all parties in America in majorities sufficient to assert and maintain her independence."

"Now I will avow," he went on, "that I then believed and now believe that those general principles of Christianity are as eternal and immutable as the existence and attributes of God; and that those principles of liberty are as unalterable as human nature and our terrestrial, mundane system. I could therefore safely say, consistently with all my then and present information, that I believed they would never make discoveries in contradiction to these *general principles."* Adams voiced the same conviction to Dr. Rush: "You and I in the Revolution acted from principle. We did our duty, as we then believed, according to our best information, judgment and consciences."[51]

Even though Adams felt that "America is in total ignorance or under infinite deception. . ."[52] about the Continental Congress, he knew that fleeting time made it daily more impossible to record a correct impression of the Revolution. The old patriots were dropping off so rapidly that at last only he and Jefferson remained. Together the pair of ancient revolutionaries combed through their memories and their papers, supplying for each other pieces of missing data, answering questions about old colleagues, airing the most private opinions. Both men lamented that they had not kept more complete records and dairies.

"Who shall write the history of the American Revolution?" Adams asked in despair. "Who can write it? Who will ever be able to write it?"

"The most essential documents, the debates and deliberations in Congress from 1774 to 1783 were all in secret and are now lost forever," he mourned.[53] Americans already had begun to confuse the Revolution with the actual war for independence. But, Adams believed, the war was really no part of the Revolution, for in the fifteen years before the Battle of Lexington the Revolution took place—in the minds and hearts of the people.[54]

To Adams' query of who would write the history of the Revolution, Jefferson could offer only a pessimistic reply. "Nobody," he said, "except merely its external facts. All its councils, designs and discussions having been conducted by Congress with closed doors and no member, as far as I know, having even made notes of them —these, which are the life and soul of history, must forever be unknown." He did present one consoling fact. Did Adams know that there existed in manuscript a group of historical records, "the ablest work of this kind ever yet executed—of the debates of the Constitutional Convention of Philadelphia in 1787? The whole of everything said and done there was taken down by Mr. Madison, with a labor and exactness beyond comprehension."

Adams heard this news with delight. "Mr. Madison's notes of the Convention in 1787 or 1788 are consistent with his indefatigable character," he glowed. "I shall never see them; but I hope posterity will."[55]

Setting straight the historical record stood as the primary task in the lives of these old men. "You and I ought not to die before we have explained ourselves to each other," Adams pointed out.[56] Nor could they die until they had attempted to explain themselves to posterity.

Posterity deserved a true impression of the principles upon which these patriarchs had fought their Revolution—in other words, why had it all been worth the struggle? Future generations should be made to understand, as well, what the fathers had thought of that other revolution, the vast social, political, economic, religious upheaval that took place in France.

That issue, in fact, Adams declared, had first divided him and Jefferson.

"You [were] well persuaded in your own mind," he wrote to the Monticello philosopher, "that the nation would succeed in estab-

lishing a free republican government; I was as well persuaded in
mine that a project of such a government. . ." in a country where
most of the people were illiterate "was as unnatural, irrational, and
impracticable as it would be over the elephants, lions, tigers, pan-
thers, wolves and bears in the royal menagerie at Versailles." The
equality that the *philosophes* of the French Revolution had tried to
establish had been mere ideology, Adams thought, borrowing the
word that Napoleon had coined. After all, "the golden rule, do as
you would be done by, is all the equality that can be supported or
defended by reason or reconciled to common sense."[57]

When Adams had been in Europe from 1778 to 1785, he commented to Jefferson, he had taken some hope that France was
advancing "by slow but sure steps towards an amelioration of the
condition of man in religion and government, in liberty, equality,
fraternity, knowledge, civilization and humanity." But to Adams
the French Revolution had been a dreadful turmoil—"because I
was sure it would not only arrest the progress of improvement, but
give it a retrograde course for at least a century, if not many centuries. The French patriots appeared to me like young scholars from
a college, or sailors flushed with recent pay or prize money,
mounted on wild horses, lashing and spearing, till they would kill
the horses and break their own necks." To what had the revolution
led?

"Let me now ask you very seriously, my friend," he said, "Where
are now in 1813 the perfection and perfectibility of human nature?
Where is now the progress of the human mind? Where is the amelioration of society? Where the augmentations of human comforts?
Where the diminutions of human pains and miseries? . . . When,
where, and how is the present chaos to be arranged into order?"[58]

The problem would never resolve itself, Adams knew, so long as
men remained improvable but imperfectible, so long as they must
grapple with the political problem of fallible beings—how to balance freedom with power.

Dr. Rush appreciated the lifelong efforts that Adams had devoted
to solution of this puzzle. Two years before he died he paid Adams
the touching compliment of suggesting that Adams compile those

proffered answers in a posthumous address to the American people to be delivered after Adams' death.

"The time cannot be very distant when you and I must both sleep with our fathers," Rush reminded his friend. "The distinguished figure you have made in life and the high offices you have filled will render your removal from the world an object of universal attention." Adams could be assured that the address would be well received. "You stand nearly alone in the history of our public men," Rush emphasized, "in never having had your *integrity* called in question or even suspected. Friends and enemies agree in believing you to be an honest man."

"Your name and fame have always been dear to me," he concluded. "I wish you to survive yourself for ages in the veneration, esteem, and affection of your fellow citizens and to be useful to them even in the grave. None but those persons who knew you in the years 1774, 1775 and 1776 will ever know how great a debt the United States owe to your talents, knowledge, unbending firmness, and intrepid patriotism."[59]

Adams cherished Rush's letter as one of the most sincere tributes he had received. When all was said and done had he "not been employed in mischief all my days? Did not the American Revolution produce the French Revolution? And did not the French Revolution produce all the calamities and desolations to the human race and the whole globe ever since?" Then he made a typical Adams statement: "I meant well, however. My conscience was clear as a crystal glass without a scruple or a doubt. I was borne along by an irresistible sense of duty. God prospered our labors; and awful, dreadful, and deplorable as the consequences have been, I cannot but hope that the ultimate good of the world, of the human race, and of our beloved country is intended and will be accomplished by it. . . ."[60]

As Adams watched the fulfillment of the Revolution in American history, he also waited with the patience of old age for the working out of his own personal history. Resigned with Puritan stoicism to the hardships imposed by Providence, he suffered two tragedies in his later years. In August of 1813, Nabby, his only living daughter and first-born child, died of cancer at the age of forty-nine, "a monument to suffering and patience." At her request, her husband and family brought her to Quincy to die in the old homestead.[61] Six times parents, John and Abigail Adams now felt the wrench of burying their fourth child. Only John Quincy and Thomas Boylston outlived their parents.

Then it was Abigail's time to succumb. She died of typhoid fever on October 28, 1818, at the age of nearly seventy-four. The unspeakable loss of Abigail, "the dear partner of my life for fifty-four years as a wife and for many years more as a lover," . . . shattered Adams as the ultimate blow of his life. Scarcely anything now could further twist the injured heart. The calm of waiting settled over him.

"All is now still and tranquil," he wrote to Jefferson. "There is nothing to try men's souls nor to excite men's souls but agriculture. And, I say, God speed the plough and prosper stone wall."[62]

But there was one thing more—a triumph. The pride of having a son elected to the same Presidency in which he himself served is a reward that history has allowed only one man, John Adams. Because no words could express the bond of affection and pride between this brilliant father and son, each man understated his own feelings. Enclosing the note of Rufus King announcing the election, John Quincy wrote to his father:

My dear and honored father,
    The enclosed note from Mr. King will inform you of the event of this day, upon which I can only offer *you* my congratulations, and ask your blessings and prayers.
    Your affectionate and dutiful son, John Quincy Adams.[63]

The elder Adams replied:

My dear son,
    I have received your letter of the ninth. Never did I feel so much solemnity as upon this occasion. The multitude of my thoughts and the intensity of my feelings are too much for a mind like mine in its ninetieth year. May the blessing of God Almighty continue to protect you to the end of your life, as it has heretofore protected you in so remarkable a manner from your cradle! I offer the same prayer

for your lady and your family and am your affectionate father, John
Adams.[64]

Knowing that death must be imminent, Adams pondered the
impenetrable absolute of the going out. He believed so firmly "in
God and in his wisdom and benevolence" that he could not "conceive that such a being could make such a species as the human
merely to live and die on this earth. If I did not believe a future state
I should believe in no God. This universe, this all, this totality,
would appear with all its swelling pomp a boyish firework."[65]

For that reason, Adams faced the end with peaceful serenity. As
Jefferson commented, "There is a ripeness of time for death, regarding others as well as ourselves, when it is reasonable we should
drop off and make room for another growth. When we have lived
our generation out, we should not wish to encroach on another."[66]
All the same, the two old friends, both in remarkable health, kept
their lively interest to the last.

"Though I cannot write, I still live and enjoy life," Adams scrib-
bled.[67] Furthermore, both men considered it the greatest blessing
that the other still survived.

"While you live," said Adams, "I seem to have a bank at Monticello on which I can draw for a letter of friendship and entertainment when I please."[68]

During the winter of 1825-1826 Adams for the first time began
to fall into seriously ill health. Distinctive of an old man, he always
detested the discomforts of winter, a time "as terrible to me as to
you," he told Jefferson, in which he always felt reduced ". . . to the
life of a bear or a torpid swallow."[69] Though he had once felt that
perhaps he would like to live over his life, this winter he could not
repeat that desire. "I had rather go forward and meet whatever is
to come," he declared. "I have met in this life with great trials. I
have had a father and lost him. I have had a mother and lost her.
I have had a wife and lost her. I have had children and lost them.
I have had honorable and worthy friends and lost them—and instead of suffering these griefs again, I had rather go forward and
meet my destiny."[70] He lasted, however, through the spring, con-

tinuing until April to keep up his correspondence with Jefferson.

As spring matured into the fullness of summer, the nation prepared for its celebration of the fiftieth anniversary of the Declaration of Independence. The two men who had presided at that moment of birth, Adams and Jefferson, were invited to attend the ceremonies. But Adams and Jefferson, now ninety-one and eighty-three, had grown too feeble in recent months to venture out, and so they simply were to send their toasts. After deliberating awhile, nothing elaborate satisfied Adams; consequently, he offered for the Quincy celebration the plain words, "Independence forever!" That done, he had no more duties. On the Fourth of July, as the gaiety of Quincy's merrymaking subsided at dusk, John Adams died. His last words, a friend reported, were "Thomas Jefferson still lives."[71] But Jefferson, too, had died, only a few hours earlier. For these two firm friends, ardent students of history and patriarchs of the nation's founding, it was an appropriately glorious end, a mighty coincidence in American annals.

Selected Bibliography

Adams Family Correspondence, ed. Lyman H. Butterfield and others, Cambridge, 1963—.

Adams, Henry, *The Birthplaces of Presidents John and John Quincy Adams in Quincy, Massachusetts*, Quincy, 1936.

Alexander Hamilton and the Founding of the Nation, ed. Richard B. Morris, New York, 1957.

Diary and Autobiography of John Adams, ed. Lyman H. Butterfield and others, Cambridge, 1961; 4 vols.

Familiar Letters of John Adams and His Wife Abigail Adams, during the Revolution. With a Memoir of Mrs. Adams, ed. Charles Francis Adams, New York, 1876.

Legal Papers of John Adams, ed. L. Kinvin Wroth and Hiller B. Zobel, Cambridge, 1965; 3 vols.

Letters of Benjamin Rush, ed. Lyman H. Butterfield, Princeton, 1951; 2 vols.

Letters of John Adams, Addressed to His Wife, ed. Charles Francis Adams, Boston, 1841; 2 vols.

Letters of Mrs. Adams, the Wife of John Adams. With an Introductory Memoir by Her Grandson, Charles Francis Adams, Boston, 1840.

Memoirs of the Administrations of Washington and John Adams, edited from the Papers of Oliver Wolcott, Secretary of the Treasury, ed. George Gibbs, New York, 1846; 2 vols.

New Letters of Abigail Adams, 1788-1801, ed. with introd. Stewart Mitchell, Boston, 1947.

Sprague, Waldo Chamberlain, *The President John Adams and President John Quincy Adams Birthplaces*, Quincy, 1959.

The Adams-Jefferson Letters, The Complete Correspondence Between Thomas Jefferson and Abigail and John Adams, ed. Lester J. Cappon, Chapel Hill, 1959; 2 vols.

The Autobiography of Benjamin Rush: His "Travels through Life," Together with His Commonplace Book for 1789-1813, ed. George W. Corner, Princeton, 1948.

The Earliest Diary of John Adams, ed. Lyman H. Butterfield and others, Cambridge, 1966.

The Journal of William Maclay, ed. Edgar S. Maclay; introd. Charles A. Beard, New York, 1927.

The Papers of Alexander Hamilton, ed. Harold C. Syrett and Jacob E. Cooke, New York, 1961—.

The Papers of Thomas Jefferson, ed. Julian P. Boyd and others, Princeton, 1950—.

The Political Writings of John Adams, Representative Selections, ed. with introd. George A. Peek Jr., New York, 1954.

The Selected Writings of John and John Quincy Adams, ed. with introd. Adrienne Koch and William Peden, New York, 1946.

The Spirit of 'Seventy-Six, the Story of the American Revolution as Told by Participants, ed. Henry Steele Commager and Richard B. Morris, Indianapolis, 1958; 2 vols.

The Spur of Fame, Dialogues of John Adams and Benjamin Rush, 1805-1813, ed. John A. Schutz and Douglass Adair, San Marino, 1966.

The Works of Alexander Hamilton, ed. John C. Hamilton, New York, 1850; 7 vols.

The Works of John Adams, Second President of the United States: with a Life of the Author, ed. Charles Francis Adams, Boston, 1850-1856; 10 vols.

The Works of Thomas Jefferson, ed. Paul L. Ford, New York, 1904; 12 vols.

The Writings of George Washington from the Original Manuscript Sources, 1745-1799, ed. John C. Fitzpatrick, Washington, 1931-1944; 39 vols.

The Writings of Thomas Jefferson, ed. Albert Ellery Bergh, Washington, D. C., 1907; 18 vols.

Warren-Adams Letters: Being Chiefly a Correspondence Among John Adams, Samuel Adams, and James Warren (1743-1814), Boston, 1917; 2 vols.

Notes to Chapter I

1. *Diary and Autobiography of John Adams*, ed. Lyman H. Butterfield and others, 4 vols., Cambridge, 1961, III, 256.
2. 2. *Diary and Autobiography*, III, 256.
3. For detailed descriptions of Deacon John's house and John Adams' house next door, better known as the John Adams and John Quincy Adams birthplaces, see Waldo Chamberlain Sprague, *The President John Adams and President John Quincy Adams Birthplaces* (Quincy, 1959) and Henry Adams, *The Birthplaces of Presidents John and John Quincy Adams in Quincy, Massachusetts* (Quincy, 1936).
4. He was born October 19 according to the old calendar, October 30 according to the Gregorian, adopted in England in 1752.
5. *Diary and Autobiography*, III, 257.
6. *Diary and Autobiography*, I, 63-64.
7. *Diary and Autobiography*, III, 257.
8. *Diary and Autobiography*, III, 258-259, n. 6.
9. *Diary and autobiography*, III, 257.
10. *Diary and Autobiography*, III, 257-258.
11. *Diary and Autobiography*, III, 258.
12. *Diary and Autobiography*, III, 259.
13. *Diary and Autobiography*, III, 259.
14. *Diary and Autobiography*, III, 259-260.
15. *Diary and Autobiography*, III, 260.
16. *Diary and Autobiography*, III, 261-262.
17. *Diary and Autobiography*, III, 262.
18. *Diary and Autobiography*, III, 260. Also n. 9.
19. *Diary and Autobiography*, III, 260.
20. *Diary and Autobiography*, III, 261.
21. *Diary and Autobiography*, III, 261.
22. *Diary and Autobiography*, III, 262-263.
23. *Diary and Autobiography*, III, 263.
24. The five points were unconditional election, atonement only for the elect, total depravity, irresistible grace, and perseverance of the saints

(that last point meaning that once a man is elected to salvation he can never fall from God's grace).

25. *Diary and Autobiography*, III, 262.
26. *Diary and Autobiography*, III, 263.

Notes to Chapter II

1. *Diary and Autobiography*, I, 16.
2. *Diary and Autobiography*, I, 92-93.
3. *Diary and Autobiography*, I, 61.
4. *Diary and Autobiography*, I, 25.
5. *Diary and Autobiography*, I, 36-37.
6. *Diary and Autobiography*, I, 12.
7. *Diary and Autobiography*, I, 23.
8. *Diary and Autobiography*, I, 100.
9. *Diary and Autobiography*, I, 9.
10. *Diary and Autobiography*, I, 13-14.
11. *Diary and Autobiography*, I, 26.
12. *Diary and Autobiography*, I, 27.
13. *Diary and Autobiography*, I, 42-43. Also n. 1, 44.
14. For the best explanation of the court system in colonial Massachusetts see the Introduction by L. Kinvin Wroth and Hiller B. Zobel in *Legal Papers of John Adams*, ed. Wroth and Zobel, 3 vols. (Cambridge, 1965), I, xxxviii-lii.
15. *Diary and Autobiography*, III, 274.
16. *Diary and Autobiography*, III, 286.
17. *Diary and Autobiography*, III, 264.
18. *Legal Papers*, I, liv.
19. *Legal Papers*, I, lviii.
20. *Diary and Autobiography*, I, 54. Also n. 3.
21. *Diary and Autobiography*, I, 54.
22. *Diary and Autobiography*, III, 271.
23. *Diary and Autobiography*, III, 271.
24. *Diary and Autobiography*, III, 271-272.

25. *Diary and Autobiography*, I, 55.

26. *Diary and Autobiography*, III, 272.

27. *Diary and Autobiography*, III, 272-273.

28. *Diary and Autobiography*, I, 56.

29. *Diary and Autobiography*, I, 56.

30. *Diary and Autobiography*, I, 57.

31. *Diary and Autobiography*, I, 58-59.

32. *Diary and Autobiography*, I, 59.

33. *Diary and Autobiography*, I, 224.

34. *Legal Papers*, I, lx-lxi.

35. Roscoe Pound, *The Development of Constitutional Guarantees of Liberty* (New Haven, 1957), 61-62.

Notes to Chapter III

1. *Diary and Autobiography*, III, 260-261.

2. *Diary and Autobiography*, I, 230, n. 1.

3. *Adams Family Correspondence*, ed. Lyman H. Butterfield and others, 2 vols. (New York, 1963), I, 2.

4. *Adams Family Correspondence*, I, 49.

5. *Adams Family Correspondence*, I, 111.

6. *Adams Family Correspondence*, I, 400.

7. *Adams Family Correspondence*, I, 401-402.

8. *Adams Family Correspondence*, I, 412-413.

9. *Adams Family Correspondence*, I, 288-289.

10. *Adams Family Correspondence*, I, 295.

11. *Adams Family Correspondence*, II, 144.

12. *Adams Family Correspondence*, II, 250.

13. *Adams Family Correspondence*, II, 258.

14. *Adams Family Correspondence*, II, 276-277.

15. *Adams Family Correspondence*, II, 301.

16. *Adams Family Correspondence*, II, 358-359.

17. *Adams Family Correspondence*, I, 145.

18. *Adams Family Correspondence*, I, 383-384.

19. *Adams Family Correspondence*, II, 271.
20. *Adams Family Correspondence*, I, 160.
21. *Adams Family Correspondence*, II, 234.
22. *Adams Family Correspondence*, I, 388.
23. *Adams Family Correspondence*, I, 286.
24. *Adams Family Correspondence*, I, 317.
25. *Adams Family Correspondence*, I, 329-330.
26. *Adams Family Correspondence*, I, 352-353.

Notes to Chapter IV

1. *The Works of John Adams, Second President of the United States: with a Life of the Author*, ed. Charles Francis Adams, 10 vols. (Boston, 1850-1856), X, 245.
2. *Works*, X, 244-249.
3. *Works*, X, 247-248.
4. *Legal Papers*, II, 107-108.
5. *Legal Papers*, II, 112-114.
6. *Legal Papers*, II, 141-142.
7. *Legal Papers*, II, 142-143.
8. *Legal Papers*, II, 143.
9. *Legal Papers*, II, 143-144.
10. *Legal Papers*, II, 127-128.
11. 8 *Coke's Reports*, 118a, 652.
12. *Works*, X, 276.
13. *Works*, X, 282.
14. *Works*, X, 282-283.
15. *Works*, X, 283.
16. *Works*, X, 283-284.
17. *Works*, X, 284.
18. *Works*, X, 284.
19. *First Institute*, Book I, Ch. II, 12.
20. *Diary and Autobiography*, I, 251.
21. *Diary and Autobiography*, I, 253.

22. *Works*, III, 447-464.

Notes to Chapter V

1. *Diary and Autobiography*, I, 260-261, and n. 2, 261.
2. *Works*, III, 465-468.
3. *Diary and Autobiography*, I, 263-265.
4. *Diary and Autobiography*, I, 266.
5. *Diary and Autobiography*, I, 266-267.
6. *Diary and Autobiography*, I, 267.
7. *Diary and Autobiography*, I, 270.
8. *Diary and Autobiography*, I, 273.
9. *Diary and Autobiography*, I, 281.
10. "Clarendon" to "Pym," No. III, *Works*, III, 477-483.
11. *Diary and Autobiography*, I, 294.
12. *Diary and Autobiography*, I, 307-308.
13. *Diary and Autobiography*, I, 309.
14. *Diary and Autobiography*, I, 312.
15. *Diary and Autobiography*, I, 324.
16. *Diary and Autobiography*, I, 338.
17. *Works*, III, 501-504.
18. *Diary and Autobiography*, III, 289-290.
19. *Diary and Autobiography*, III, 290-291.
20. *Diary and Autobiography*, III, 290.
21. *Diary and Autobiography*, III, 287-289.
22. *Legal Papers*, II, 173-210.
23. *Diary and Autobiography*, III, 306.
24. *Works*, III, 505-510.
25. *Diary and Autobiography*, I, 341.
26. *Diary and Autobiography*, I, 341-342. Also see n. 2, 342.
27. *Legal Papers*, II, 276-335.
28. *Legal Papers*, II, 335-351.
29. *Legal Papers*, all of vol. III.

30. Adams' account of the Massacre and his acceptance of the case, *Diary and Autobiography*, III, 291-294.
31. *Legal Papers*, III, 46-98.
32. *Legal Papers*, III, 98-314.
33. *Diary and Autobiography*, III, 296.
34. *Works*, IX, 551.
35. *Works*, IX, 352.
36. *Diary and Autobiography*, III, 294-295.
37. *Diary and Autobiography*, II, 54-55; III, 295.
38. *Diary and Autobiography*, III, 296.
39. *Diary and Autobiography*, II, 7.
40. *Diary and Autobiography*, II, 28.
41. *Diary and Autobiography*, II, 64.
42. *Diary and Autobiography*, II, 73-74.
43. *Diary and Autobiography*, III, 304-305.
44. *Diary and Autobiography*, III, 297.
45. *Diary and Autobiography*, II, 78.
46. Both men's articles are in *Works*, III, 511-574.
47. See *Diary and Autobiography*, III, 298-302, for a discussion of the question of the judges' salaries.
48. *Works*, X, 240-241.
49. *Works*, IX, 333.
50. *Diary and Autobiography*, II, 85-86.
51. *Legal Papers*, I, 106-140.
52. *Legal Papers*, I, 137.
53. *Diary and Autobiography*, II, 86.
54. *Legal Papers*, I, 140; *Adams Family Correspondence*, I, 131.

Notes to Chapter VI

1. *Diary and Autobiography*, II, 96.
2. *Diary and Autobiography*, II, 97.
3. *Diary and Autobiography*, II, 97, also n. 2, 97-98.
4. *Adams Family Correspondence*, I, 143.

5. *Adams Family Correspondence*, I, 145.

6. *Adams Family Correspondence*, I, 116, and *Diary and Autobiography*, III, 307.

7. *Diary and Autobiography*, II, 114-115, and III, 310.

8. *Diary and Autobiography*, II, 115.

9. *Diary and Autobiography*, II, 117.

10. *Diary and Autobiography*, II, 121.

11. *Diary and Autobiography*, II, 118-119.

12. *Diary and Autobiography*, II, 116.

13. *Diary and Autobiography*, II, 119.

14. *Diary and Autobiography*, II, 121.

15. *Diary and Autobiography*, II, 117.

16. *Diary and Autobiography*, II, 119-120.

17. *Diary and Autobiography*, II, 120.

18. *Diary and Autobiography*, II, 122-123.

19. *Adams Family Correspondence*, I, 150.

20. *Adams Family Correspondence*, I, 155.

21. *Diary and Autobiography*, II, 127.

22. *Adams Family Correspondence*, I, 159.

23. *Diary and Autobiography*, II, 134-135.

24. *Adams Family Correspondence*, I, 162-163.

25. *Adams Family Correspondence*, I, 165.

26. *Adams Family Correspondence*, I, 178-179.

27. *Adams Family Correspondence*, I, 177.

28. *Diary and Autobiography*, II, 143.

29. *Diary and Autobiography*, II, 140.

30. *Diary and Autobiography*, III, 309.

31. *Diary and Autobiography*, II, 128-129.

32. *Diary and Autobiography*, II, n. 1, 131.

33. *Diary and Autobiography*, II, 151.

34. *Diary and Autobiography*, III, 309.

35. As finally adopted, Article Four read: "That the foundation of English liberty, and of all free government, is a right in the people to participate in their legislative council; and as the English colonists are not represented, and from their local and other circumstances cannot be properly represented in the British Parliament, they are entitled to a free and exclusive power of legislation in their several provincial legis-

latures, where their right of representation can alone be preserved, in all cases of taxation and internal polity, subject only to the negative of their sovereign, in such manner as has been heretofore used and accustomed. But, from the necessity of the case, and a regard to the mutual interest of both countries, we cheerfully consent to the operation of such acts of the British Parliament as are *bona fide* restrained to the regulation of our external commerce for the purpose of securing the commercial advantages of the whole empire to the mother country and the commercial benefits of its respective members; excluding every idea of taxation, internal or external, for raising a revenue on the subjects in America without their consent." *(Works*, II, Appendix C, 538-539.) During the course of debate on the Declaration, John Dickinson appeared as a delegate to Congress and was named to the committee. He later said he wrote the final draft of the Declaration himself *(Diary and Autobiography*, II, n. 1, 151), but Adams also said that he did. At any rate, Dickinson must have had something to do with the final draft, as the language is somewhat milder than might be expected of Adams, who probably would have ended the first sentence with the word "polity." Dickinson's conciliatory mood prompted Adams to call him "very modest, delicate and timid."

36. *Diary and Autobiography*, II, 156.
37. See *Works*, IX, Appendix A, 641-643, for copy of Hawley's letter.
38. For the comments by Henry and Lee and Adams' assessment of Washington's opinion, see JA's letter to William Wirt, January 23, 1818, *Works*, X, 278-279.
39. *Diary and Autobiography*, II, 157.
40. See excerpts from the *Massachusettensis* essays in *The Political Writings of John Adams, Representative Selections*, ed. with introd. George A. Peek Jr. (New York, 1954), 26-79.
41. *Works*, IV, 124.
42. *Works*, IV, 121-122.
43. *Works*, IV, 99-100.
44. *Works*, IV, 106-107.
45. *Works*, IV, 102.
46. *Works*, IV, 107.
47. *Works*, IV, 105.
48. *Works*, IV, 117.
49. *Works*, IV, 113-114.
50. *Works*, IV, 176-177.

51. *Works,* IV, 140.

52. *Works,* IV, 130-131.

53. *The Spirit of 'Seventy-Six, the Story of the American Revolution as Told by Participants,* ed. Henry Steele Commager and Richard B. Morris, 2 vols. (Indianapolis, 1958), I, 231-233.

54. *Edmund Burke, Selected Works,* ed. W. J. Bate (New York, 1960), 111 and 113.

Notes to Chapter VII

1. *The Autobiography of Benjamin Rush: His "Travels Through Life," Together with His Commonplace Book for 1789-1813,* ed. with introd. George W. Corner (Princeton, 1948), 140-144.

2. *Works,* IX, 356-357.

3. *Adams Family Correspondence,* I, 204-205.

4. *Adams Family Correspondence,* I, 207.

5. *Diary and Autobiography,* III, 321-324.

6. *Adams Family Correspondence,* I, 215.

7. *Adams Family Correspondence,* I, 215.

8. *Diary and Autobiography,* III, 314-315.

9. *Diary and Autobiography,* III, 321.

10. *Diary and Autobiography,* III, 317-318.

11. *Adams Family Correspondence,* I, 256.

12. *Works,* I, 179.

13. *Diary and Autobiography,* III, 326.

14. *Adams Family Correspondence,* I, 410.

15. *Diary and Autobiography,* III, 386.

16. *Diary and Autobiography,* III, 335-337.

17. *Diary and Autobiography,* III, 396-397.

18. *Adams Family Correspondence,* II, 27-28.

19. *Adams Family Correspondence,* II, 30-31.

Notes to Chapter VIII

1. *Adams Family Correspondence,* I, 352-355.
2. *Adams Family Correspondence,* I, 352.
3. *Diary and Autobiography,* III, 342-344; II, 198-202, and n. 1, 201-202.
4. *Diary and Autobiography,* II, 198.
5. *Diary and Autobiography,* III, 344-350.
6. *Diary and Autobiography,* III, 358-359.
7. *Diary and Autobiography,* III, 351-354.
8. *Diary and Autobiography,* III, 353-355.
9. *Diary and Autobiography,* III, 354.
10. *Diary and Autobiography,* III, 355-356.
11. *Diary and Autobiography,* III, 356-358.
12. *Works,* I, 193-196.
13. *Adams Family Correspondence,* I, 343, and *Diary and Autobiography,* II, 226-227.
14. *Adams Family Correspondence,* I, 363.
15. *Diary and Autobiography,* III, n. 3, 331-332.
16. *Diary and Autobiography,* III, 333-334.
17. *Works,* I, 462.
18. *Works,* IV, 193-200.
19. *Works,* IV, 186.
20. *Diary and Autobiography,* III, 342.
21. *The Adams-Jefferson Letters, The Complete Correspondence Between Thomas Jefferson and Abigail and John Adams,* ed. Lester J. Cappon, 2 vols. (Chapel Hill, 1959), I, 5.
22. *Diary and Autobiography,* III, 329.
23. *Diary and Autobiography,* III, 329.
24. *Diary and Autobiography,* III, 417-423.
25. *Adams Family Correspondence,* II, 353-354.
26. *Adams Family Correspondence,* II, 370-371.
27. *Diary and Autobiography,* IV, 4.
28. *Diary and Autobiography,* IV, 6-7, and II, 269.

Notes to Chapter IX

1. *Diary and Autobiography*, II, 276-277.
2. *Diary and Autobiography*, II, 277-278.
3. *Adams Family Correspondence*, I, n. 5, 137.
4. *Diary and Autobiography*, II, 309-310, and IV, 92.
5. *Diary and Autobiography*, IV, 132-133.
6. *Diary and Autobiography*, II, 351.
7. *Diary and Autobiography*, IV, 123.
8. *Diary and Autobiography*, IV, 36-37.
9. *Diary and Autobiography*, II, 304-305.
10. *Diary and Autobiography*, II, 305.
11. *Diary and Autobiography*, II, 345.
12. *Diary and Autobiography*, II, 346-347.
13. *Diary and Autobiography*, IV, 118-119.
14. *Diary and Autobiography*, II, 347.
15. Letter to Robert R. Livingston, July 22, 1783 (Benjamin Franklin, *Writings*, ed. Albert Henry Smyth, New York and London, 1905-1907, IX, 62). Quoted in *Diary and Autobiography*, I, lxiii-lxiv.
16. *Diary and Autobiography*, IV, 107.
17. *Diary and Autobiography*, II, 353.
18. *Diary and Autobiography*, II, 362-363.
19. *Diary and Autobiography*, II, 389.

Notes to Chapter X

1. *Diary and Autobiography*, IV, 243-244.
2. *Diary and Autobiography*, IV, 245.
3. *Diary and Autobiography*, IV, 246.
4. *Diary and Autobiography*, IV, 247.
5. *Diary and Autobiography*, IV, 251-252.

6. *Diary and Autobiography,* IV, 252-253.
7. *Works,* VII, 228-230.
8. *Works,* VII, 235.
9. *Works,* VII, 243.
10. *Works,* VII, 265-312.
11. *Works,* VII, 330.
12. *Works,* VII, 396-404.
13. Reprinted in *Works,* VII, 404-406.
14. *Diary and Autobiography,* II, n. 1, 457.
15. *Works,* VII, 429.
16. *Works,* VII, 434.
17. *Works,* VII, 436-439.
18. *Works,* VII, 450-452.
19. *Works,* VII, 452, from *Correspondence in the Boston Patriot.*
20. *Diary and Autobiography,* III, 9, n. l.
21. *Diary and Autobiography,* III, 16-17, and n. 2.
22. *Diary and Autobiography,* III, 24.
23. *Diary and Autobiography,* III, 82.
24. *Works,* VII, 653.
25. *Diary and Autobiography,* III, 82.
26. *Diary and Autobiography,* III, 82.
27. *Diary and Autobiography,* III, 73.
28. *Diary and Autobiography,* III, 108.
29. *Diary and Autobiography,* III, 138.

Notes to Chapter XI

1. *Diary and Autobiography,* III, 143-144, n. 4, from the *Boston Patriot,* April 29 and May 2, 1812.
2. *Diary and Autobiography,* III, 145.
3. *Diary and Autobiography,* III, 147, and n. 1.
4. *Diary and Autobiography,* III, 147.
5. *Diary and Autobiography,* III, 148-149, and n. 1, 148-149.
6. *Diary and Autobiography,* III, 148.

7. *Diary and Autobiography*, III, 150, from the *Boston Patriot*, May 9, 13 and 16, 1812.

8. *Diary and Autobiography*, III, 150, from the *Boston Patriot*.

9. *Diary and Autobiography*, III, 150, from the *Boston Patriot*.

10. *Diary and Autobiography*, III, 150-151, from the *Boston Patriot*.

11. *Diary and Autobiography*, III, 151, from the *Boston Patriot*.

12. *Diary and Autobiography*, III, 152-153, from the *Boston Patriot*, and *Works*, VIII, 170-171.

13. *Diary and Autobiography*, III, 168, n. 1.

14. *Familiar Letters of John Adams and His Wife Abigail Adams, during the Revolution. With a Memoir of Mrs. Adams*, ed. Charles Francis Adams (New York, 1876), 409.

15. *Familiar Letters*, 411.

16. *Familiar Letters*, 413.

17. *Diary and Autobiography*, III, 157-158.

18. *Diary and Autobiography*, III, n. 1, 166-167.

19. *Diary and Autobiography*, III, 170.

20. *Diary and Autobiography*, III, 171.

21. *The Papers of Thomas Jefferson*, ed. Julian P. Boyd and others, (Princeton, 1950), TJ to Madison, Feb. 14, 1783, VI, 241.

22. *Adams-Jefferson Letters*, I, 22.

23. *Adams-Jefferson Letters*, I, 28.

24. *Works*, VIII, 255-258.

25. *Adams-Jefferson Letters*, I, 29.

26. *Adams-Jefferson Letters*, I, 31.

27. *Diary and Autobiography*, III, 184-185.

28. *Diary and Autobiography*, III, 185.

29. *Diary and Autobiography*, III, 188-189, and notes.

30. *Diary and Autobiography*, III, 183, n. 3.

31. *Diary and Autobiography*, III, 199-200.

32. *Diary and Autobiography*, III, 201, n. 1.

33. *Adams-Jefferson Letters*, I, 153.

34. For the constitution as drafted by JA and the changes made by the convention, see *Works*, IV, 219-267.

35. *Works*, IV, 216.

36. *Works*, IV, 221-224, and notes.

37. *Works*, IV, 230, and n. 1.

38. *Works*, IV, 230, and n. 2.

39. *Works*, IV, 257-259.

40. *Works*, IX, 506.

41. *Works*, IX, 509.

42. *Works*, IX, 622-623.

Notes to Chapter XII

1. *Adams-Jefferson Letters*, I, 168.

2. *Works*, IX, 623-624.

3. *Works*, I, 432.

4. Quoted in *Works*, IV, 278-279.

5. *Works*, IV, 284.

6. *Works*, IV, 381. My italics.

7. *Works*, X, 377.

8. *Works*, IV, 370.

9. *Works*, IV, 406.

10. *Works*, VI, 218.

11. *Works*, IV, 406.

12. *Works*, IV, 407.

13. *Works*, VI, 219.

14. *Works*, IV, 406-407.

15. *Works*, VI, 218.

16. *Works*, VI, 8-9.

17. *Works*, IV, 295.

18. *Works*, V, 454.

19. *Works*, V, 456-457.

20. *Works*, IV, 391-392.

21. *Works*, IV, 392.

22. *Works*, VI, 65.

23. *Works*, IV, 392-397.

24. *Works*, VI, 209.

25. *Works*, V, 488.

26. *Works,* IV, 427.
27. *Works,* IV, 385.
28. *Works,* IV, 309.
29. *Works,* IV, 359.
30. *Works,* IV, 382.
31. *Works,* IV, 587-588.
32. *Works,* VI, 68-69.
33. *Works,* VI, 64.
34. *Works,* VI, 65.
35. *Works,* VI, 60.
36. *Works,* V, 90.
37. *Works,* VI, 10.
38. *Works,* VI, 8-9.
39. *Works,* VI, 134-135.
40. *Works,* VI, 69.
41. *Works,* IV, 588.
42. *Works,* IV, 371.
43. *Works,* V, 290.
44. *Works,* IV, 444-445.
45. *Works,* VI, 208.
46. *Works,* VI, 219.
47. *Warren-Adams Letters: Being Chiefly a Correspondence Among John Adams, Samuel Adams, and James Warren (1743-1814),* 2 vols. (Boston, 1917), II, 281.
48. *Works,* VI, 220, n. 1.
49. *Adams-Jefferson Letters,* I, 174.
50. Jefferson criticized one opinion offered by Adams, the statement that the Confederation Congress was a diplomatic assembly rather than a legislative one. Adams had justified the Confederation Congress, a simple assembly, on the basis of its being "not a legislative assembly, nor a representative assembly, but only a diplomatic assembly." Because the deputies were responsible to the states, the separate states formed a check on the delegates. The amount of security of the Confederation depended not upon the Confederation Congress but upon the degree to which the governments of the states themselves were balanced. (*Works,* IV, 579-580.)

Jefferson objected to this interpretation, saying that the states had yielded part of their sovereignty to Congress, and with it some of their legislative, executive and judicial powers. "It has accordingly been the decision of our courts," he maintained, "that the Confederation is a part of the law of the land and superior in authority to the ordinary laws, because it cannot be altered by the legislature of any one state. I doubt whether they are at all a diplomatic assembly." *(Adams-Jefferson Letters,* I, 174-175.)

51. *Adams-Jefferson Letters,* I, 199.
52. *Works,* VIII, 446.
53. *Works,* IX, 553-554.
54. *Adams-Jefferson Letters,* I, 172.
55. *Adams-Jefferson Letters,* I, 176-177.
56. *New Letters of Abigail Adams, 1788-1801,* ed. with introd. Stewart Mitchell (Boston, 1947), 3.
57. *Diary and Autobiography,* III, 202, note.
58. *Adams-Jefferson Letters,* I, 178-187, *passim.*
59. *Adams-Jefferson Letters,* I, 196.
60. *Adams-Jefferson Letters,* I, 210.
61. *Adams-Jefferson Letters,* I, 212.
62. *Adams-Jefferson Letters,* I, 213-214.
63. *Adams-Jefferson Letters,* I, 210.
64. *Adams-Jefferson Letters,* I, 214-215.
65. *Works,* VIII, 472-473.
66. *Works,* VIII, 478-479.
67. *Diary and Autobiography,* III, 212, note.

Notes to Chapter XIII

1. The house contained only a paneled parlor, entry and dining room on the first floor, two bedrooms on the second floor, and three smaller rooms in the attic. When she inspected the house, Abigail, accustomed to spacious European dwellings, is said to have been close to tears that the house she remembered as one of the most luxurious in Braintree should turn out to be so modest. Immediately, she began to coax her husband to build an addition. With typical husbands' reluctance to launch into the turmoil of redoing a house, Adams did not get around to making an addition until he was President. Then Abigail got an east

entry and an elegant new parlor in which to display her French furniture, and John a fine study above the parlor.

2. *Works*, VIII, 484.

3. *Works*, IX, 556-557.

4. *Works*, IX, 557-558.

5. *The Writings of George Washington from the Original Manuscript Sources, 1745-1799*, ed. John C. Fitzpatrick, 39 vols. (Washington, D.C., 1931-1944), XXX, 174.

6. *The Papers of Alexander Hamilton*, ed. Harold C. Syrett and Jacob E. Cooke (New York, 1961), V, 225.

7. *Hamilton Papers*, V, 226.

8. *Hamilton Papers*, V, 228.

9. *Hamilton Papers*, V, 231.

10. Electors in 1789, as the Constitution specified, were chosen as their state legislature directed. In some states, such as New York, the people themselves cast ballots for their electors; in other states, such as Massachusetts, the state legislature chose the electors.

11. *Hamilton Papers*, V, 236.

12. *Hamilton Papers*, V, 247-249.

13. *Hamilton Papers*, V, 363-364.

14. *Letters of Benjamin Rush*, ed. Lyman H. Butterfield, 2 vols. (Princeton, 1951), I, 498-499.

15. *Rush Letters*, I, 501.

16. *Works*, VIII, 484.

17. *Works*, VIII, n. 1, 484-485.

18. *Washington Writings*, XXX, 219.

19. *Rush Letters*, I, 499.

20. *The Journal of William Maclay*, ed. Edgar S. Maclay, introd. Charles A. Beard (New York, 1927), 73, 114.

21. *Works*, VIII, 485-487.

22. *Maclay Journal*, 1-3.

23. *Maclay Journal*, 6-9.

24. *Maclay Journal*, 9-10, 23.

25. *Maclay Journal*, 26.

26. *Maclay Journal*, 29.

27. *Works*, VI, 433-435.

28. *Maclay Journal*, 112-114.

29. *Works*, VIII, 494.

30. *Works*, IX, 561.

31. *New Letters*, 15.

32. *Maclay Journal*, 151.

33. *Works*, IX, 563-565.

34. *Works*, VI, 221-403.

35. *Works*, VI, 227.

Notes to Chapter XIV

1. *Works*, VI, 232-233.

2. *Works*, VI, 233-234.

3. *Works*, VI, 245.

4. *Works*, VI, 234.

5. *Works*, VI, 239.

6. *Works*, VI, 246.

7. *Works*, VI, 248.

8. *Works*, VI, 267.

9. *Works*, VI, 285-286.

10. *Works*, VI, 269.

11. *Works*, VI, 249.

12. *Works*, VI, 262-263.

13. *Works*, VI, 269.

14. *Works*, VI, 270, 272.

15. *Works*, VI, 272-273.

16. *Works*, VI, 279.

17. *Works*, VI, 280-281.

18. *Works*, VI, 281.

19. *Works*, VI, 399.

20. *The Autobiography of Benjamin Rush*, 181.

21. *Rush Letters*, I, 546.

22. *Works*, IX, 565-567.

23. *Maclay Journal*, 243.

24. *Works,* IX, 568.

25. *Works,* IX, 570-571.

26. *Works,* IX, 571-572.

27. *New Letters,* 66.

28. *New Letters,* 67.

29. *The Writings of Thomas Jefferson,* ed. Albert Ellery Bergh, 18 vols. (Washington, D.C., 1907), VIII, 192-194.

30. For excerpts from "Publicola" see *The Selected Writings of John and John Quincy Adams,* ed. with introd. Adrienne Koch and William Peden (New York, 1946), 225-234.

31. *Works,* VIII, 503.

32. *Adams-Jefferson Letters,* I, 245-246.

33. *Works,* VI, 411-426.

34. *Adams-Jefferson Letters,* I, 247-250.

35. *Adams-Jefferson Letters,* I, 250-252.

36. *Hamilton Papers,* IX, 33-34.

37. *Alexander Hamilton and the Founding of the Nation,* ed. Richard B. Morris (New York, 1957), from *Gazette of the U.S.,* September 29, 1792, 528-529.

38. *The Works of Thomas Jefferson,* ed. Paul L. Ford, 12 vols. (New York, 1904), VI, 280-282.

39. Jefferson, *Works,* VI, 288-291.

40. Jefferson, *Writings,* I, 168.

41. *Rush Letters,* II, 768.

42. Authors have various opinions about the date when factions became parties.

43. *Works,* VIII, 514-515.

44. *Adams-Jefferson Letters,* I, 253.

45. *Adams-Jefferson Letters,* I, 254.

46. *Adams-Jefferson Letters,* I, 255.

Notes to Chapter XV

1. *Works,* I, 488-489.

2. *Works,* I, 483-484.

3. *Works,* I, 485.

4. *Works,* I, 486-487.

5. *Works,* I, 485.

6. *Works,* I, 495-496.

7. *Memoirs of the Administrations of Washington and John Adams, edited from the Papers of Oliver Wolcott, Secretary of the Treasury,* by George Gibbs, 2 vols. (New York, 1846), I, 408-409.

8. *Works,* I, 494-495.

9. *Works,* I, 496.

10. *Works,* I, 483.

11. *Works,* VIII, 520-522.

12. *Works,* VIII, 523, and n. 1, 524.

13. *Works,* VIII, 537.

14. *The Spur of Fame, Dialogues of John Adams and Benjamin Rush, 1805-1813,* ed. John A. Schutz and Douglass Adair (San Marino, 1966), 38-39.

15. *Adams-Jefferson Letters,* I, 262-263.

16. *Adams-Jefferson Letters,* I, 262, n. 54.

17. *Works,* IX, 284-286.

18. *Spur of Fame,* 36.

19. *Works,* VIII, 546-547.

20. Gibbs, *Memoirs,* I, 485.

21. Gibbs, *Memoirs,* I, 487, 490.

22. *Works,* IX, 156-159.

23. Gibbs, *Memoirs,* II, 52.

24. *New Letters,* 156.

25. *New Letters,* 161.

26. *Works,* IX, 186.

27. *Works,* IX, 188.

28. *Works,* IX, 223.

29. Gibbs, *Memoirs,* II, 53.

30. Gibbs, *Memoirs,* II, 50.

31. *Works,* IX, 192, 195.

32. *Works,* I, 522.

33. *Works,* IX, 119, n.1.

34. *Works,* VI, 518.

35. *Spur of Fame*, 201.

36. *Works*, IX, 14.

37. *Adams-Jefferson Letters*, II, 329.

38. *Works*, IX, 291.

39. *Works*, IX, 5.

40. *Works*, VIII, 654-657, 667-668.

41. *Works*, VIII, 644.

42. *Works*, VIII, 644-645.

43. *Works*, VIII, 648-649.

44. *Works*, VIII, 650.

45. *Works*, IX, 57-60.

46. *The Works of Alexander Hamilton*, ed. John C. Hamilton, 7 vols. (New York, 1850), VI, 269-271.

47. Gibbs, *Memoirs*, II, 51.

48. *Spur of Fame*, 36.

49. *Works*, IX, 290-291.

50. Gibbs, *Memoirs*, II, 109-110.

51. Gibbs, *Memoirs*, II, 70-71.

52. Hamilton, *Works*, VI, 380.

53. Hamilton, *Works*, VI, 384-388.

54. *Works*, VIII, 573.

55. Washington, *Writings*, XXXVI, 314.

56. *Works*, VIII, 578-579.

57. Washington, *Writings*, XXXVI, 456.

58. *Spur of Fame*, 98-99.

59. *Works*, IX, 301.

60. *Works*, IX, 300-301.

61. *Letters of John Adams, Addressed to His Wife*, ed. Charles Francis Adams, 2 vols. (Boston, 1841), II, 258-259.

62. *Works*, VIII, 612-613.

63. *Works*, VIII, 662.

64. Hamilton, *Works*, VI, 406.

65. Hamilton, *Works*, VI, 393-394.

Notes to Chapter XVI

1. *Works*, VIII, 677-684, for Murray's dispatches.
2. *Works*, VIII, 609.
3. Hamilton, *Works*, VI, 359.
4. *Works*, I, 535-536.
5. *Works*, IX, 130.
6. *Works*, VIII, 691.
7. *Works*, IX, 161-162.
8. *Works*, I, 545.
9. *Works*, VIII, 626-627.
10. Hamilton, *Works*, VI, 396-399.
11. Hamilton, *Works*, VI, 399-400.
12. *Works*, IX, 18-19.
13. *Works*, IX, 24-25.
14. *Works*, IX, 31.
15. *Works*, VIII, 629.
16. Gibbs, *Memoirs*, II, 282.
17. *Works*, IX, 51-55.
18. Hamilton, *Works*, VI, 441.
19. Hamilton, *Works*, VI, 446-447.
20. *Spur of Fame*, 225.
21. *Spur of Fame*, 113.
22. *Spur of Fame*, 48.
23. *Diary and Autobiography*, III, 434-435.
24. *Adams-Jefferson Letters*, I, 263.
25. *Adams-Jefferson Letters*, I, 264.
26. *Works*, IX, 576-577.
27. *New Letters*, 255.
28. *New Letters*, 262.
29. *Spur of Fame*, 263.
30. *Spur of Fame*, 83-84.

Notes to Chapter XVII

1. *Works*, I, 633, 639.

2. *Works*, IX, 585.

3. *Letters of Mrs. Adams, the Wife of John Adams. With an Introductory Memoir by Her Grandson, Charles Francis Adams* (Boston, 1840), 437.

4. *Works*, X, 13.

5. *Spur of Fame*, 20-21.

6. *Spur of Fame*, 197.

7. *Adams-Jefferson Letters*, I, 268-269.

8. *Adams-Jefferson Letters*, I, 270.

9. *Adams-Jefferson Letters*, I, 273-274, 281-282.

10. *Spur of Fame*, 199-200.

11. *Spur of Fame*, 200-202.

12. *Adams-Jefferson Letters*, II, 290.

13. *Adams-Jefferson Letters*, II, 600, n. 7; 601.

14. *Spur of Fame*, 108, 153.

15. *Adams-Jefferson Letters*, II, 301.

16. *Adams-Jefferson Letters*, II, 295, 502.

17. *Adams-Jefferson Letters*, II, 456.

18. *Adams-Jefferson Letters*, II, 455, 456.

19. *Adams-Jefferson Letters*, II, 523.

20. *Adams-Jefferson Letters*, II, 524.

21. *Adams-Jefferson Letters*, II, 572-573.

22. *Adams-Jefferson Letters*, II, 549, 571.

23. *Adams-Jefferson Letters*, II, 571-572.

24. *Works*, VI, 454.

25. *Adams-Jefferson Letters*, II, 456.

26. *Works*, VI, 448.

27. *Works*, VI, 450.

28. *Works*, VI, 449.

29. *Works*, VI, 453-454.

30. *Works*, VI, 451.
31. *Works*, VI, 457.
32. *Adams-Jefferson Letters*, II, 388-389.
33. *Adams-Jefferson Letters*, II, 371.
34. *Works*, VI, 451.
35. *Adams-Jefferson Letters*, II, 400-401.
36. *Adams-Jefferson Letters*, II, 400.
37. *Adams-Jefferson Letters*, II, 362, 375, 437.
38. *Adams-Jefferson Letters*, II, 361.
39. *Adams-Jefferson Letters*, II, 368, 373.
40. *Adams-Jefferson Letters*, II, 499, 509.
41. *Adams-Jefferson Letters*, II, 465.
42. *Adams-Jefferson Letters*, II, 362, 368.
43. *Adams-Jefferson Letters*, II, 461.
44. *Adams-Jefferson Letters*, II, 295, 374, 509.
45. *Works*, X, 170.
46. *Spur of Fame*, 61.
47. *Spur of Fame*, 139-140.
48. *Adams-Jefferson Letters*, II, 349, 356.
49. *Spur of Fame*, 33, 60, 152.
50. *Adams-Jefferson Letters*, II, 462-463.
51. *Adams-Jefferson Letters*, II, 339-340; *Spur of Fame*, 109.
52. *Adams-Jefferson Letters*, II, 392.
53. *Adams-Jefferson Letters*, II, 451.
54. *Adams-Jefferson Letters*, II, 455.
55. *Adams-Jefferson Letters*, II, 452-453, 455.
56. *Adams-Jefferson Letters*, II, 358.
57. *Adams-Jefferson Letters*, II, 354-355.
58. *Adams-Jefferson Letters*, II, 357-358.
59. *Spur of Fame*, 189-191.
60. *Spur of Fame*, 191.
61. *Adams-Jefferson Letters*, II, 366, 377.
62. *Adams-Jefferson Letters*, II, 529, 531.
63. *Works*, I, 632.
64. *Works*, X, 416.
65. *Adams-Jefferson Letters*, II, 530.

66. *Adams-Jefferson Letters*, II, 484.
67. *Adams-Jefferson Letters*, II, 540.
68. *Adams-Jefferson Letters*, II, 530.
69. *Adams-Jefferson Letters*, II, 579.
70. *Adams-Jefferson Letters*, II, 611.
71. *Works*, I, 634-636.

Name Index

Adams, Abigail (Mrs. William Stephens Smith, "Nabby," 1765-1813), daughter of JA, 40, 44, 45, 79; birth of, 63; death of, 390; marriage to Col. William Stephens Smith, 224; romance with Royall Tyler, 214

Adams, Abigail Smith (1744-1818), wife of JA, 8, 36, 75, 79, 85, 98, 106, 143, 144, 155, 156; abilities as letter-writer, 38; character and personality, 37, 38, 97; congratulation of husband on election, 322; correspondence with Jefferson, 370-372; death, 391; death of mother, 41; deliverance of stillborn child, 43; devotion to husband, 39; during Boston Massacre, 91, 92; faith, 41, 97; feelings on JA's election as commissioner to France, 169-170; frugality, 169; hospitality to refugees, 133-134; intellectual ability, 37, 47, 48; interest in politics, 46-48; life at Bush Hill, 300-301; loneliness during JA's absences, 39, 42, 43, 214; love of reading, 37, 47-48; marriage to JA, 37; mourning of sons's death, 364; observation of battle of Dorchester Heights, 145-146; on reconciliation during First Continental Congress, 117; patriotism, 39, 43, 97; relations with President and Mrs. Washington, 283; report of rumors to JA, 146; reunion with JA in Europe, 214-216; serious illness in 1798, 348; sorrow over Nabby's loneliness, 300; talent

as teacher of her children, 44; views on JA's election to General Court, 97; views on Shays' Rebellion, 234; visit to Netherlands, 225

Adams, Charles (1770-1800), son of JA, 40, 44; accompanies father to peace negotiations, 186; dies a drunkard, 363; joins Hamilton's law office, 271; practices law in New York, 299

Adams, Charles Francis, 339, 368

Adams, Deacon John (1691-1761), father of JA, agrees to send JA to school of Joseph Marsh, 9-10; anticipates clerical career for JA, 13; character, 7; determined to give JA a liberal education, 9; dies, 36; owns Penn's Hill farm, 7-8

Adams, Elihu (1741-1775), brother of JA, 7

Adams, Henry (ca. 1583-1646), 5

Adams, John (1735-1826), character and personality, 6, 8-9, 12-13, 17-20, 29-31, 36, 39-46, 84-86, 93-98, 102, 109-110, 138, 143, 146-147, 152-153, 157, 162, 164-165, 169-170, 173, 176-181, 265-267, 276, 299-300, 314, 350, 369, 383-386, 390; early life, 5-6, 8-22, 36-37; law career, 27-32, 63-64, 72, 86-87, 91, 93-96, 106, 169; legal education and general reading, 23-27, 151, 174-175, 237; political theory, 15-16, 20, 26-27, 33, 35, 39, 50, 53-57, 69-70, 76-77, 82-85, 88-90, 95-106, 118-119, 122-128, 146-147,

Subject Index